Damned Whiteness

Damned Whiteness

How White Christian Allies Failed the
Black Freedom Movement

· ·

DAVID F. EVANS

The University of North Carolina Press Chapel Hill

Set in Charis by Westchester Publishing Services
Manufactured in the United States of America

Library of Congress Cataloging-in-Publication Data
Names: Evans, David F., author
Title: Damned whiteness : how white Christian allies failed the
    Black freedom movement / David F. Evans.
Description: Chapel Hill : The University of North Carolina Press, [2025] |
    Includes bibliographical references and index.
Identifiers: LCCN 2025015421 | ISBN 9781469691466 cloth |
    ISBN 9781469691473 paperback | ISBN 9781469689012 epub |
    ISBN 9781469691480 pdf
Subjects: LCSH: Civil rights movements—United States—History—
    20th century | African Americans—Civil rights—History—20th
    century | Civil rights—Religious aspects—Christianity | Allyship—
    United States—History—20th century | Political activists, White—United
    States—History—20th century | BISAC: RELIGION / Christianity /
    History | HISTORY / United States / 20th Century
Classification: LCC E185.61 .E897 2025 | DDC 323.1196/0730904—dc23/
    eng/20250528
LC record available at https://lccn.loc.gov/2025015421

Cover art © Adobe Stock / Mohamed (AI generated).

For product safety concerns under the European Union's General Product
Safety Regulation (EU GPSR), please contact gpsr@mare-nostrum.co.uk
or write to the University of North Carolina Press and Mare Nostrum
Group B.V., Mauritskade 21D, 1091 GC Amsterdam, The Netherlands.

For Newnan Clarence Brown, whose memory reminds me daily that there's enough I don't know to make a whole nother universe.

Contents

Damned Whiteness

Prologue

A White Progressive Christian Problem

. . . .

While attending college, I became a student of "racial reconciliation," a white evangelical concept that assumes that Black Christians desire to build relationships with white Christians. This assumption reveals a skin-deep analysis of American racial divisions—divisions that stem from long histories of colonial domination, white supremacist theology, and political discrimination, which were often validated by Christian leaders. After a decade of participating in workshops that promoted Christian fellowship between Black and white churches, reading books on multicultural communities, and facilitating workshops that promoted racial reconciliation, I learned that the predominantly white Christian communities who made it a cornerstone of their response to racial injustices failed to take seriously the history and assumptions that segregated Black and white Christians in the first place.

Prior to any personal encounters with evangelical Christians, I was, like others in my Black community, more concerned with being racially profiled by the police or being attacked by white supremacists than I was with working toward racial harmony. By the time I graduated college and shared evangelical concerns for healing racial divisions, I understood that segregation was so endemic to American Christianity that a solution would require an entirely new paradigm. After graduate school, I began to see that if there was any possibility for Christian unity in America, white evangelicals would need to join in solidarity with Black Christians and support their quest for racial justice and Black liberation.

In 2005, I received the opportunity to share my views when organizers of an Emerging Church panel at Princeton Theological Seminary invited me to discuss the possibility of what Brian McClaren called *A New Kind of Christianity*.[1] Many of the Christians active in the development of the emerging church movement—also known as the emergent church—were white pastors who no longer wanted to be associated with evangelicalism. I was curious about the emerging church because its advocates seemed to be moving away from the mean-spirited litmus tests of fundamentalist religion toward something more ancient and authentic than trendy seeker-friendly gimmicks popularized in megachurches. I also thought that "emergent" meant that whatever this new movement was to become, it was yet to be defined and open to creative configuration. If that was true, then I thought that I might find like-minded Christians who were open not only to moving away from white evangelicalism but also to moving toward Black liberation.

So I accepted the invitation to speak at the conference with the intention of challenging the paternalistic gaze of white evangelicalism with Black perspectives. Whereas white evangelicals saw racial reconciliation as a tool that took for granted that white Christianity was the only "true religion" and therefore the location to which Black Christians needed to relocate, my new "oppositional gaze" (to borrow a term from bell hooks) engendered questions of the emerging movement that they were not prepared to answer, namely, "Why was the movement so white?"[2]

At the conference, I sharply pointed out the dominance of white male intellectuals leading this new effort, the movement's lack of attention to Black perspectives, and the absence of Latin American Pentecostal influences, where churches were emerging in epic numbers. I charged the group to slow down, even to stop planning for the future, until they had contributions from Christians that might truly represent emerging church communities around the world that were demonstrating signs of great growth. I closed my comments by warning them that if they did not include people with very different experiences than the white men currently represented in their movement, they would simply re-create the church they were attempting to run from and be trapped in a new church building decorated with what the scriptures referred to as "whitewashed walls."

My comments on their lack of attention to Black perspectives and insights from Latin America in the emerging movement were met with frustration and defensiveness. I had been in close conversation with an author who was a mentor to many in the group and who championed the need for a neo-evangelicalism. After sharing my plan to present a race-conscious critique of the emerging church movement, he offered his belief that my fellow panelists would be receptive to it. So when one of the white co-panelists rejoined that he was puzzled by my comments and his body language gave away his discomfort, I was caught off guard. The white emerging church panelist shared that his organization included a Black woman on their leadership team and that they were very much open to adding people like me to their movement. To demonstrate his passion for welcoming me, he said,

"David, I'd love to be your friend and have you come to my house and sleep on my couch."

What I did not know then, but I know now, was that the white panelist and I were caught up in a pattern of parallel organizing between white progressive movements and Black freedom movements that was decades old. The white practitioner wanted to be viewed as an ally who welcomed diversity and cared about racial unity, whereas I wanted a church that preached racial justice and advocated for Black liberation. Our opposition to racial oppression appeared to be the same; however, our movements resembled the parallel play of schoolchildren—that is, we worked and moved parallel to each other, in the same direction but not together. Of course, I was not playing with words, and the panelist was angered at my insinuation that he was. As a result of the failures of white progressives to comprehend critiques like mine, Black freedom fighters have learned to look upon white ally movements with skepticism because too few of their actions support the claims that they make.

It was white allies' failure to support the Black freedom movement that gave freedom fighters reason to be skeptical of their moderate, liberal, and radical programs. The failure of white progressives to advocate for Black freedom in solidarity with freedom fighters is the focus of *Damned Whiteness*. In the pages that follow, I claim that this failure is due to the reality that white progressive visions are often disconnected from the actions, the ideas, and the communities of Black activists, so that while the two groups can appear to be moving in the same direction against racial injustice, they are more accurately moving toward different goals. Thus, white progressives and Black freedom fighters hold opposing philosophies and competing methods for combating anti-Black oppression. This pattern continues, and it will continue as long as the practices that animate it remain hidden. Until they are exposed, we should expect to find ourselves working in racially segregated communities that are parallel or coexisting but rarely, if ever, in solidarity.

Introduction

Fractures in Fellowship

. . . .

My primary concern is not with saving white America;
I am concerned with liberating Black America.

—Floyd McKissick, *Three-Fifths of a Man*

The effectiveness of white allies in movements for Black freedom are both understudied and misrepresented. Studies that center white allies tend to focus on their intentions. Due to the lack of principled scrutiny of the impacts of those intentions, white ally scholarship misrepresents the role and significance of allies whose histories are riddled with tensions between their white initiatives and Black liberation struggles. These narratives tell stories that represent well-intentioned allies as essential agents in Black-led social movements, despite Black freedom fighters frequently testifying to more complicated experiences with interracial coalition building. Such realities came into focus during the Black freedom era, especially as Black radicals—Christian and otherwise—syncretized their political, economic, and civic dreams with communism, mass demonstrations, and Black Power.

On a nationally televised special edition of *Meet the Press* that NBC aired on August 21, 1966, Floyd McKissick, Black Power advocate and the national director of the Congress of Racial Equality (CORE), named "self-determination" as the key factor for Black people to control "the direction and the pace in which they will become total citizens in this society." That statement summarized CORE's philosophy of Black Power, which it had adopted earlier that summer. The adoption of Black Power, which McKissick spearheaded, made the summer of 1966 a turning point in the distinguished history of one of the oldest civil rights organizations in the Black freedom movement.[1]

With CORE's adoption of Black Power came a new policy that redefined nonviolence so that it included self-defense. As McKissick said in one exchange, "Self-defense and nonviolence are not incompatible."[2] In response, many of CORE's white members withdrew their membership while decrying the organization's new Black Power direction as racist and antiwhite.

CORE, undeterred by the white flight from their association, stayed the course. Its leadership, like others in Black freedom organizations, had become impatient with accommodating white allies who often seemed more passionate for dogmatic approaches to interracial leadership and principled nonviolence than they were for urgently securing freedom for Black people. Viewed through the lens of Black freedom history, the failures of white allies to prioritize Black liberation over abstract philosophies fractured their coalitions with Black freedom fighters, especially when allies misinterpreted Black movements, undermined Black leadership, tokenized Black presence, or required Black folks to assimilate to radical white communities for acceptance.

When a journalist asked McKissick if he was disturbed by fractures in relationships between white allies and CORE, McKissick answered, "Of course we would like to have everyone love us if at all possible and of course we hate to lose friends."[3] The journalist's question, however, did not concern random white friends of CORE. The fracture between allies and freedom fighters at CORE reached the press through a telegram from Lillian Smith, in which she declared her resignation from CORE's Advisory Committee. Smith, the renowned author of *Killers of the Dream*, also denounced CORE's Black Power leadership in a scathing attack on McKissick. Using language that she had formerly reserved for Southern white supremacists, she protested, "Now we have new killers of the dream."[4]

As a member of CORE for two decades, Smith was among the most respected of white allies in the civil rights movement. Martin Luther King Jr., whom she counted as a friend, spoke highly of her in his "Letter from Birmingham Jail" and "The Drum Major Instinct." In 1960, Smith spoke to a mostly Black-attended Student Nonviolent Coordinating Committee (SNCC) gathering, where she chastised Southern politicians for "still trying to buy a future for the South, and for our country, with currency that is worthless: with ideas that have no validity, opinions that are not based on fact, values that are not human and Earth-size."[5] Moreover, she had earned her strong reputation during the Montgomery bus boycott, when she encouraged the Montgomery Improvement Association to be extremists and celebrated them for avoiding moderation, declaring that "the right way is not a moderate way."[6]

In other words, Smith was not like the white moderates who King referred to as a "great stumbling block" in Birmingham. Her departure from CORE could not be dismissed that easily. Quoting from her telegram, one member of the press asked McKissick to explain why Smith believed that

"CORE has been infiltrated by adventurers, nihilists, black nationalists and plain old-fashioned haters who have finally taken over."[7] After initially responding with bewilderment, he offered an interpretation that redirected the accusation back to Smith: "It is possibly because she has not been attending the meetings of the organization and has not met its Board of Directors and its chapter members."[8] McKissick had received the telegram more than a month before he appeared on television. It is likely that he understood but disagreed with Smith's public missive. In the time that he had to prepare for questions concerning Smith, who was battling cancer but was able to communicate from her hospital bed, he carefully voiced his regret for "Miss Smith's" departure from the Advisory Committee. He also verbalized appreciation for her "notable contributions to the organization." Leaning forward as he addressed her characterization of CORE's membership and leaders, McKissick continued, "I don't think that her interpretations, or the way she defines people in CORE would be a correct one in any sense." Then, seemingly girding himself with the spirit of the Black Power movement—a movement that refused to be deterred by white anxieties over the direction, methods, or tone of Black demands for self-determination—he concluded that when "people get disturbed by a change in policy, [it] simply means that we will have to move the organization alone, without those people, if those people decide not to go with us."[9]

The public nature of Smith's conflict with CORE made for one of the more dramatic moments in the history of relationships between white allies and Black freedom fighters, but it was hardly novel. James Farmer, CORE's only director prior to McKissick, led CORE at a time when it identified as a color-blind organization, open to people of any race who wanted to further its goals for racial equality. As early as 1963, Black nationalists criticized it as a "white-led organization with a black front."[10] Faced with the conviction that he would need to step down someday, Farmer thought, "It could not be a black organization, but it had to be black-led."[11] After learning of Farmer's plans to permit only a Black leader to direct CORE after he resigned, a small interracial contingent of the organization's National Action Council called him "a racist, a black nationalist, a Garveyite, a Black Muslim" and questioned his commitment to CORE's color-blind philosophy.[12] Resistance to the concept of excluding white allies from leading one of the most powerful organizations for Black liberation landed as a direct criticism of the color-blind coalition that many CORE members hoped to build.

It took almost three years for Farmer to find the right Black leader to succeed him. When Farmer floated McKissick's name as his replacement in

1965, it was clear that he had chosen wisely. One member of the nominations committee said, "I think we all know who Floyd McKissick is. We don't need a nominating speech for him. I move that attorney Floyd McKissick be elected national chairman by acclamation." According to Farmer, "The motion was seconded and overwhelmingly passed by voice vote."[13] McKissick was well-known among CORE members as an attorney who had represented civil rights workers after they were arrested at demonstrations. The success of his leadership was obvious in that he also organized multiple CORE chapters among North Carolinians. As evidenced by his nomination of McKissick, Farmer welcomed CORE's turn toward Black Power, but he also noted that the growing acceptance of Black Power marked the death of civil rights movement principles. "Sharing the tomb with nonviolence was the interracialism that had been the trademark of the movement," Farmer reflected in his autobiographical history of the civil rights movement. The signs were clear to him: "SNCC, under Stokely Carmichael, had put whites out. CORE, under Floyd McKissick, had not done that, but the black power rhetoric had made them uncomfortable, and they were rapidly drifting away." SNCC's and CORE's movements away from interracial organizing to Black Power did not happen overnight, but the election of Stokely Carmichael over John Lewis in SNCC and McKissick's appointment to replace Farmer all but guaranteed that organizations that concerned themselves with America's racial configuration would need to renegotiate their position to one another.[14]

Lillian Smith would have understood that her renegotiated relationship to CORE did not need to be public. As a longtime member of CORE's Advisory Committee, Smith advised others that organizing involved "much more than what happens in public places."[15] Publicly withdrawing her association dramatized her decision and sealed it in history as her last public act before she died. Smith's battle with cancer undoubtedly kept her from attending meetings and contributed to her ignorance of the internal pressures and decisions CORE faced. However, in her public telegram, she did not appeal to any of these concerns or seek explanations. Just as she had publicly lambasted Black people who questioned nonviolence in her 1964 essay "The Day It Happens," Smith left no room for compromise with violence in the summer of 1966. While she believed that massive resistance to racial integration was responsible for making Black Power more appealing, Smith made no excuses for Black nationalists, whom she accused of intruding on the movement and seducing young people by pretending to be nonviolent. Her analysis of Black nationalists, like Nation of Islam spokesperson

Malcolm X, was that they embraced a superficial nonviolence. Although they rarely initiated physical attacks against their enemies, Smith suggested that they were not willing to make "the inner sacrifices and spiritual decisions" of those who ruled out self-defense.[16] Her public excoriation of CORE, SNCC, and Black nationalist leaders put to rest any chance that there would be a reconciliation between her and McKissick.

Though the press should have been criticized for showing little interest in reporting the Black Power movement on its own terms, media questions about Smith's breakup with CORE rightly implied that something larger was brewing between Black freedom organizations and white allies, no matter the position on Black Power. Just as Smith's telegram spoke to the discomfort that was growing among white allies, McKissick's indifference to her concerns represented the increasing impatience that Black leaders felt toward white allies. The conflict between white ally discomfort and Black freedom fighter impatience typified the fractured relationship between the two groups.

It is this fracturing of alliances between white allies and Black freedom fighters from 1933 to 1969 that is the subject of *Damned Whiteness*. The central question of this book asks, What was it about the anti-segregationist work of white allies that caused Black freedom fighters to dismiss their concerns, avoid their organizations, or move on without them? I find this question particularly poignant when I consider that allies chose paths that put them at odds with other white people and put their lives at risk each time they publicly confronted racial segregation. It was white allies' willingness to risk life, limb, livelihood, and reputation, sometimes outside their relationships with Black activists, that inspired me to investigate rather than theorize why they were out of step with Black movements.[17] My research relies on close attention to archival material, because some white allies could not be dismissed easily with theories suggesting that they accommodated calls for Black equality or joined the struggle for Black civil rights only when it suited their material interests. Black freedom fighters possessed different visions from their white counterparts, who were bound by commitments to ideological purity to pacifism and limited by their inexperience with Black freedom traditions. These limitations led them to misinterpret the goals of freedom fighters' anti-segregation speeches and mass demonstrations as pleas for interracial fellowship rather than demands for Black freedom. From this view, breakdowns in coalition building owed more to the plausibility structures that allies' white social position allowed for than what a hidden self-interest might suggest. Historical evidence reveals that Black Americans showed varying levels of interest in associating with white allies but believed less in the viability of interracial coalitions over time. This was especially evident as Black freedom organizations insisted on Black leadership or other methods that white allies failed to find consistent with their visions of interracial fellowship.

This book argues that investigating the missions of white Christian allies in the context of Black freedom movements reveals that freedom fighters and allies organized parallel movements that appeared to move in the same direction but aspired toward different visions and adopted conflicting methods of reaching them. Allies envisioned interracial relationships that appealed to diversity, but they often tokenized Black participation. Allies also established programs that claimed to support Black people who suffered from oppressive work environments and unjust economic systems, but they created charitable programs that inadequately analyzed systems of wealth and poverty in America. Allies also championed fellowships of racial reconciliation but required Black people to assimilate to predominantly white spaces to achieve full inclusion. It was with these methods, which purposed to reduce enmity between Black and white Americans, that freedom fighters grew frustrated, and these frustrations provoked them to fracture their fellowship with white allies. These fractured relationships reveal that ally methods fell short of joining in solidarity with Black leaders in their fight for the freedom that they defined as communal self-determinism, economic self-sufficiency, and political power. In short, their visions did not align; and over time, their methods proved to be incompatible.

This study shows that freedom fighters' quest for Black liberation sometimes inspired innovative mixtures of communist philosophies with Christian beliefs, struggles for American civil rights with Indian independence strategies, urban rebellions with New Testament interpretations, and Black nationalism with electoral politics. It also shows that those innovations were sometimes indecipherable to allies, who were so committed to ideological purity that they did not comprehend that such creativity was possible. The needs of Black communities influenced the direction of Black leaders, which made for diverse leadership styles, varied freedom philosophies, and sometimes conflicting political strategies. Freedom fighters were no monolith, famously disagreeing with one another. Still, they admonished their communities to keep their eyes on the prize of freedom, which led them to adopt methods that shifted as they determined the most effective strategies for any given moment.

Black activists tended to understand that effective methods involved access to economic resources, leading them to express interest in economic empowerment, whereas many mid-nineteenth-century white activist communities advocated for anti-capitalism, which they equated with voluntary poverty. Mandatory economic asceticism in these communities often discouraged Black members from pursuing full participation. The cost of downward mobility was not the same for Black and white associates. Even in their voluntary poverty, allies typically maintained access to wealthy networks that kept their organizations in positions of charity and made it easier for white members to live with fewer resources than Black members, who were forced into economic instability by segregationist policies in housing and employment. Access to well-endowed networks also allowed white allies to bypass Black freedom fighter initiatives. With these connections, allies' self-sufficiency seldom inspired them to reflect on the fact that their strategies opposed to racial discrimination, urban poverty, and anti-Black animosity were devoid of partnerships with Black organizations who were already engaged in liberating themselves. But their connections to wealth meant that they did not need Black partnerships to implement their plans. Moreover, from the perspective of their charitable organizations, it was easy to surmise that potential Black partners were in no position to offer material resources that white allies did not already have.

Instead of partnering with Black organizations, predominantly white ally organizations insisted on interracialism—an antecedent to the racial reconciliation movement that evangelicals would adopt later in the century—which viewed anti-segregationist activism as valid only if it included white participation. Beyond participation, interracialists often insisted on white leadership. In most cases, the founders of these groups established their programs without any recognition of existing Black efforts. Thus, white allies assumed that it was their role to help Black people by creating communities that addressed issues they assumed oppressed people were unequipped to handle. The paternalism that accompanied these assumptions was eventually enough to convince Black folks to avoid white allies altogether.

White allyship is nothing new to the United States of America, nor was it new in the mid-twentieth century. Allies have voiced displeasure for slavery and segregation since the early republic. However, ally histories are hardly popular, and to the extent that Americans are aware of them, their narratives lack sufficient nuance concerning the effectiveness of allies in movements for Black freedom. The histories of white allies generally neglect to ask the following questions: What relationship, if any, did white allies have to Black freedom fighters? How did Black activists perceive white ally organizing? What might explain the skepticism Black activists had toward white allies? And how effective was white ally advocacy? *Damned Whiteness: How White Christian Allies Failed the Black Freedom Movement* is my attempt to answer those questions with histories of three of the most celebrated white Christian allies of the Black freedom era: Clarence Jordan, Dorothy Day, and Ralph Templin.

Freedom Fighters and Allies

The allyship of Jordan, Day, and Templin is significant to Black freedom history because they exemplify the practices of white Christian allies. Each of these allies either created or led movements that launched them into similar trajectories with Black freedom organizations that opposed racial segregation, but because the visions of these movements were disconnected from the Black communities they aimed to help, they failed to meet them on the path for liberation. That is, while Black organizations traveled on the long road toward Black freedom, fighting for the right of Black people to determine their own destiny, allies took a trail that stopped short of freedom and settled, instead, for interracialism—which proposed that interracial relationships should provide the primary mission and vision for eradicating racial enmity. The limited missions of these white allies thwarted the possibility of seeing their visions come to completion, because Black freedom fighters, even when they shared the same church or organizational fellowship with white allies, tended to unloose the ties of interracial friendship when they felt they had to choose between freedom for Black communities or fellowship with white associates. In turn, white fellows denounced the separation of their former Black associates as counterproductive because, in their view, any successful challenge to racial inequality had to emerge from interracial fellowship.

Allies were not alone in celebrating the possibility of interracial fellowship. Some freedom fighters, particularly civil rights leaders, also believed that "the creation of a society where men will live as brothers" was the end they aimed to reach. This was the vision of the Beloved Community, as articulated by Martin Luther King Jr., the meaning of which he described in his "I Have a Dream" speech. He proclaimed from the steps of the Lincoln Memorial, "I have a dream that one day on the red hills of Georgia, the sons of former slaves and the sons of former slave owners will be able to sit down together at the table of brotherhood."[18] For King, that day existed sometime in a future made possible through the struggle for civil rights.

For Black and white Americans to arrive at a day when they would sit together in fellowship, King taught that they needed to abolish anti-Black discrimination as expressed in the official laws of the nation and in the policies and procedures of its institutions and systems. He believed that Black Americans had a central role in that effort. "As we move in this transition from the old age into the new," King explained, "we will have to rise up in protest."[19] Protest meant confrontational forgiveness, or the loving strength to rebuke the racial inequalities in white American systems, institutions, and individual behaviors. His dream carried within it the faith that if people co-labored to confront white supremacist laws, institutions, and systems, then reconciliation was possible. "With this faith," he continued, "we will be able to work together, to pray together, to struggle together, to go to jail together, to stand up for freedom together, knowing that we will be free one day."[20] Reconciliation, then, required putting faith into action by working against the systems and institutions that restricted Black self-determination. Without work, there could not be freedom. For King, the process was clear: "One day," after struggle produced freedom, then people divided by racial segregation would be able to find togetherness. There could be no shortcut.

Other freedom fighters agreed that there could be no shortcut to beloved community. The freedom struggle required confronting white supremacist systems that were sustained and protected by powerful state and national officials. These freedom fighters understood what Frederick Douglass had proclaimed when their ancestors struggled to break the chains of enslavement in the previous century: "This struggle may be a moral one, or it may be a physical one, and it may be both moral and physical, but it must be a struggle." Douglass assumed that "power concedes nothing without a demand."[21] And just as he believed that the demand could be made through either moral suasion or self-defense, the freedom fighters of the twentieth century debated which methods were best to win freedom—nonviolence, self-defense, education, farming, moral suasion, mass demonstrations, respectability politics, elections, artistic creativity, institution building, boycotts, protests, or coalition building. In other words, by referring to civil rights workers and Black Power advocates collectively as freedom fighters, I do not mean that they were always of one accord in anything other than their pursuit of something they each called "freedom." Their rules for fighting varied, as did their methods. They understood that whatever method they chose would require confrontations that could cost them everything.

On the other side of the color line, white Christian allies often ignored the need to adopt institutional or systemic reform methods that might have allowed for the interracial fellowship that they envisioned. Their interracial organizations generally avoided conflict with existing institutions, churches, neighborhoods, local laws, and federal policies so that they could pursue utopian visions of Christian community without publicly challenging racial rules or regulations. White allies did not often agree with King's confrontational interpretation of Christian forgiveness, which required the strength to confront enemies with loving rebuke and thereby present them opportunities to confess their complicity with anti-Black oppression and make reparations. Instead, they shortened the path to racial reconciliation by engaging in programs that maintained power differences between themselves and the objects of their charity. They used theology to avoid addressing the realities of socioeconomic inequality, so that they could cast a Christian vision that portrayed all people as equal.

White Christian allies agreed that Jim Crow denied the goodness of the gospel. Ongoing racial hostilities between the races was evidence of that, especially in churches. With that knowledge, they surmised that the best way to proclaim the power of the gospel was to bring the races together, without animosity toward white society, apart from legal or constitutional reform, and in the safety of white Christian communalism, where they could practice in private what was illegal in public. Therein, their Christianity could be free of the blemish of racial violence and enmity. They carved out this shortened path to their vision of alternative communal living in houses and on farms. Yet their leadership styles and one-size-fits-all programs provided no mechanisms for Black people to pursue their own destiny within or outside these spaces.

Catholic, Southern Baptist, and Methodist Church Peacemakers

There is speculation that King had in mind one of these white alternative communities when he mentioned Georgian children in his "I Have a Dream" speech. That community, Koinonia, is one of the subjects of this book. Koinonia was able to capture the dreams of many who longed to see an end to the problem of racial segregation in America. A major issue that arose between these groups was how to diagnose precisely what that problem constituted. For Black people, the problem was a continuation of the bondage that their ancestors had suffered during enslavement and the ongoing bondage to oppression that they had to endure during Jim Crow. Oppression morphed in form, but the resulting exploitation of Black bodies was the same. In contrast, allies often named the problem as racial hatred or racial division, which made the race problem a matter of the heart and interpersonal relationships. These diagnoses are key to how these groups imagined solving the racial crisis: If the problem was bondage, then freedom was the solution. However, if the problem was division and enmity, then friendship was the best hope.

Koinonia provided a setting where the radical allyship of Day, Jordan, and Templin revealed how white Christians, who courageously risked their lives with the intention of making friends with Black people, failed to strategize against the barriers that made interracial relationships so difficult in the first place. Their efforts were parcels in the legacy of white Christian allies' attempts to end racial animosity through moral suasion, abolitionism in the antebellum period, social uplift in the Reconstruction era, interracialism through the Jim Crow era, racial reconciliation programs during the post–Cold War era, and racial healing workshops in the new millennium. The public advocacy of the three allies profiled in this book spans forty years, from the Jim Crow era through civil rights. The allies met, or were acquainted with, the most well-known social activists of their day—both Black and white. And they established or worked with the most renowned social organizations of their time, which were predominantly white: the Catholic Worker, the Fellowship of Reconciliation, Koinonia, Peacemakers, and the School of Living. As such, these three allies were revered by their white peers. Though they lived in different states, belonged to different denominations, and addressed racial oppression with different skill sets, they modeled behavior for white people who desired to make a positive impact in race relations. It is instructive that these three allies developed relationships with one another, operated in the same networks, and shared similar values while representing different denominational affiliations and regional environments. Such differences provided distinct opportunities for their racial formation, yet they arrived at very similar conclusions regarding the problems of racial segregation. In other words, Day, Jordan, and Templin demonstrate importantly distinct social locations but still have enough in common to provide a narrative that reveals common assumptions and positions of white allies. These commonalities consistently demonstrated patterns that frustrated Black activists in their pursuits of freedom.

These patterns brought Day, Jordan, and Templin together in the 1950s, when they rallied around Koinonia Farm to demonstrate their rejection of racial segregation in the United States. As was the reality with many of their white peers in the Fellowship of Reconciliation and its A. J. Muste–led arm, the Peacemakers, they believed that Koinonia's interracial experiment was the Christian cause that allies should support to further interracialism. Interracialism allowed white religious leaders to reject racial segregation on the grounds that it did not represent a true Christian vision of community. It also led them to reject efforts by monolithically Black groups, even when Black leaders initiated actions for the purpose of advancing the rights of Black citizens as equals. White allies insisted that opposition to racial division needed to operate out of interracial fellowships.

Among Catholic fellowships, renewed interest has put Dorothy Day's interracial activities into the spotlight as twenty-first-century members of the Catholic Worker movement wrestle with her legacy of opposition to racial prejudice. The 2017 Midwest Catholic Worker Faith and Resistance Gathering produced a statement, "Lament. Repent. Repair. An Open Letter on Racism to the Catholic Worker Movement," that named failures of the Catholic Worker movement to adequately address racism.[22] The public letter provoked some to ask, "Is the Catholic Worker racist?" which became the title of an article in July 2023.[23] The question is of utmost importance, especially for Catholics adjudicating Day's candidacy for sainthood, and of no less importance to millions of Protestants who view Day as an inspiration.[24]

By all accounts, Day is the most well-known of American Catholics. She and her mentor, Peter Maurin, cofounded the Catholic Worker community with its newspaper, hospitality houses, and farming projects. When Day died in 1980, newspapers all over the world celebrated her practice of Catholic social principles. She is the subject of numerous biographies and documentaries, including *Revolution of the Heart: The Dorothy Day Story*, which aired in 2020.[25] As such, her life continues to inspire people who are interested in challenging the oppressive economic social conditions of American life.

As an innovator of programs for people suffering from poverty, Clarence Jordan shared Day's critique of the oppressive effects of capitalism. That is why his name is sometimes mentioned alongside that of President Jimmy Carter for dreaming up Habitat for Humanity. But most often his fame is associated with establishing an interracial Christian community near Carter's home, in Americus, Georgia. As the founder of Koinonia Farm and author of the *Cotton Patch Gospels* translation of the New Testament, Jordan became a hero to evangelicals who opposed racially divided churches. Evangelical and evangelical-adjacent Christians have gathered at symposiums twice in the last decade to celebrate Jordan's legacy, the most recent being in 2018 where they hosted the likes of Shane Claiborne and Rev. Dr. William Barber as keynote speakers. Beyond formal meetings, Koinonia Farm remains an active destination for evangelical pilgrims to this day. Jordan's popularity continues to grow through performances of a play that was inspired by his *Cotton Patch Gospels*. For allies who are convinced by appeals to work for racial reconciliation, Jordan resembles something like a prophet.[26]

It is easy to see why Jordan and Day have become important role models for Christian educators who want white students to understand that they too can oppose racial discrimination. It was rare for white people in Catholic and Southern Baptist denominations to oppose racial injustices publicly in the way that Jordan and Day did. Their actions demonstrate that it may be possible for others. Dorothy Day implied as much when she famously implored people inspired by her work to not set her apart as special. "Don't call me a saint. I don't want to be dismissed that easily," she reportedly said.[27] Historian David Southern stopped just short of excoriating the entire white labor movement for generally showing indifference and hostility toward racial change when he noted that white Catholics were largely indifferent to racism. But he excluded her from that judgment when he added, "Dorothy Day, a radical journalist and reformer, and her Catholic Worker notwithstanding."[28] Her story of transition from the socialist movement to Catholicism, loss of significant relationships for her faith, and even failed social experiments is not a typical hagiographical account; it reads very human. Perhaps that is what makes her impact so extraordinary.

Clarence Jordan's extraordinary reputation among evangelicals, and the scholars who study them, is a consequence of his opposition to Jim Crow segregation. There is good reason to study the attention Jordan gave to racial division. He was a leader among his white ally peers for speaking against it and forcing institutions to face the immorality of their anti-Black positions. He brought scrutiny upon himself by making his opposition to Jim Crow segregation and anti-Black violence known, and he made himself a target by standing up to the Ku Klux Klan in Georgia using his Southern charm and masculine bravado. Such anti-segregationist deeds almost cost him his life. Because of this, Frederick Downing, the most recent of his biographers, wrote in 2017 that he should be thought of in the same light as Martin Luther King Jr. and Mohandas Gandhi.[29]

I am dubious of such comparisons. By what standard should we compare Jordan to King or Gandhi? If the standard is simply a contrast from the segregationist Christianity of Jordan's white Southern peers, then we can agree that he shared disdain for violence and racial division with the two international leaders. That, however, is where the comparisons end. By contrast, the accomplishments of King and Gandhi were precipitated by very different assessments of the problems with violence and racial division. Their analyses of racial apartheid that followed led them to confront their nations with mass demonstrations and legal challenges. King led a movement to expand the rights of American citizens, which resulted in federal policy changes and contributed to a new generation of civil rights and Black Power activists. Gandhi lent his leadership to a successful struggle for Indian independence that also influenced the nonviolent strategies of American freedom fighters. Not only did Jordan oppose King's mass demonstrations, but he also championed an alternative God movement, which he saw as the corrective to King's appeals to federal lawmakers. His philosophy of nonresistance conflicted with King's and Gandhi's philosophy of nonviolence in that nonresistance encouraged avoiding conflict with evildoers. Thus, while Jordan intended to create an interracial fellowship that would bear witness to God's movement for Black and white Christians in the South, his views alienated the project from freedom fighters when they launched a movement to secure voting rights or combat racial segregation in the public schools, even those where his children attended.

As a self-proclaimed abolitionist, Ralph Templin's relationship to capitalism, nonviolence, and eventually freedom fighters was different. Furthermore, his contributions to white ally history are lesser known than Day's and Jordan's but no less important. During his lifetime, his peers, both Black and white, respected him as an important ally in the fight to end racial animosity—so much so that Day and Jordan regularly corresponded with him and invited him to speak to their communities. He cofounded an ashram in Harlem with Jay Holmes, where freedom fighters the likes of James Farmer, Pauli Murray, and Bayard Rustin congregated. Rustin's mentor, A. J. Muste, frequently called on Templin to lead initiatives for his organization as well. In the late 1960s, Templin made headlines as a white preacher who advocated for Black Power.[30] He is known among Methodists as the first white minister to be received as an elder in the all-Black Central Jurisdiction. In addition, he has the distinction of being the first tenured faculty member of a historically Black college in Ohio, Central State College. And yet he has been largely forgotten, save for a few footnotes in histories of Christian radicals.[31]

It was Templin's angst and conversion to Black Power that inspired the title of this book. In a 1961 poem, Templin named "damned whiteness" as a "frightening disease" that seeped into his soul. He wrote longingly "to have some color—some humanity—some solidarity" that could cure him of "the white problem of the world."[32] This longing was the result of his reflection on fifteen years of work in India as a leader whose sole credential for leadership was membership in the white race. His insights were strengthened by his time in the Central Jurisdiction and at Central State College. It was due to these experiences that Templin adopted Black Power as the only cure for the problem of whiteness and traveled the United States preaching Black Power to white people. His journey of relationship building and vexation over his white privilege interrupts what would be an otherwise straightforward narrative of well-intentioned white allies getting in their own way.

I first became aware of the connections between these three allies while combing through the papers of Ralph Templin, which are housed in the United Methodist Archives and History Center at Drew University. Templin, a Methodist missionary who was expelled from India in 1940 by a Methodist bishop due to his opposition to the British occupation of India, returned to the United States with insightful critiques of US imperialism. Most of what is written about Templin can only be found accompanying lists of pacifist Christians from the 1950s and 1960s. His work as a public intellectual who transcended the interracialist teachings of his white contemporaries and adopted Black Power philosophy to combat the pervasive white supremacist structures of US society, politics, and religion sets him apart from his white peers. His solidarity with Black leaders around the nation offers a departure from the ally strategies of Day and Jordan, whose interracialism never produced the interracial communities they envisioned.

The correspondence from Jordan and Day among Templin's papers reveals their respect for his knowledge of pacifism, homesteading, and facilitation. However, their awareness of the anatomy of racism in the United States reads as individualist and lacking input from the people who were most directly affected by anti-Black oppression—Black Americans. While Templin's journey toward Black freedom advocacy was evident in the trajectory of his publishing record and tenure at Central State College, I was surprised to find very little in the lives of Jordan and Day to parallel the maturation of Templin on these matters. Templin struggled for decades with what he called the "white prerogative," which allowed him to assume leadership positions in arenas in which he had no experience.[33] He felt implicated in the culturally destructive practices of white imperialism in a way that his white peers did not confess.

This discovery provoked me to ask how Jordan and Day could both engage in conversations concerning race relations and found organizations that stated opposition to racial segregation yet demonstrate little knowledge or engagement with Black perspectives in their work. *Damned Whiteness* shows how white allies were often unfamiliar with nuanced Black critiques of American life because they had few intimate relationships with Black people. And it narrates how white allies, when confronted with Black perspectives that challenged their deeply held assumptions about economics, religion, and politics, failed to adapt.

It was white allies' failure to adapt to the Black freedom movement that gave freedom fighters reason to be skeptical of them. Through my research, it becomes apparent that the failure of white allies to adapt to Black freedom was due to the ambitious visions of allies who were so disconnected from Black actions, Black ideas, and Black freedom communities that they were strangely positioned in opposition to them. While the two groups appeared to be moving against racial injustice, they strategized for different goals: allies envisioned interracial fellowship that required racial amicability and communal uniformity, while freedom fighters envisioned freedom from anti-Black oppression. As a result, allies and freedom fighters held conflicting philosophies and competing methods for combating racial segregation.

The idea that those who wish to pursue racial justice need to study white allies has become a fundamental principle of antiracism education. Beverly Tatum, who was one of the first to suggest this pedagogical strategy, lamented that antiracist white role models were too often invisible to students because they were understudied.[34] Almost thirty years later, Jennifer Harvey echoed Tatum's advice in her groundbreaking book, *Raising White Kids*, when she wrote, "Offering white youth a meaningful place to stand means sharing with them models of white people."[35] Unlike Tatum, Harvey did not provide a list of allies in her lesson, because in the decades that followed Tatum's charge, scholarship on allies had grown to such a degree that resources on the topic were widely available.

One such resource, *Refusing Racism* by Cynthia Stokes Brown, presents four white allies whose antiracist activities were generally omitted from popular historical texts on race history. Brown aims to "show, in detail, how some of those considered white were able to join unequivocably [*sic*] in the fight for the liberation of those considered other 'races,' as well as for their own freedom from racism."[36] In Brown's zeal to share the determination of allies' refusal to participate in racism, she gives scant attention to the absence of their relationships with Black people or conflicts with Black leaders. *Damned Whiteness* investigates these oversights because they hold potential for understanding why ally zeal for racial harmony did not result in strong interracial coalitions.

Another white ally text, Drick Boyd's *White Allies in the Struggle for Racial Justice*, builds on Brown's research by introducing twelve "role models of antiracist white identity and action."[37] Boyd divides the chapters between white abolitionists who participated in the Underground Railroad and anti-segregationists from the civil rights era. Again, the relational conflicts that white allies had with Black freedom fighters is not a feature of his text. Boyd notes that at times, strains in relationships between allies and Black freedom fighters caused them to "cut ties," but he does not reflect much on what caused those fractures. In *Damned Whiteness*, I investigate these moments of strain between white allies and Black freedom fighters because they reveal obstacles that white allies failed to overcome when working to end segregation. As important as it is to narrate stories of transformation from white racist to white ally, I think it is also important to analyze the difficult moments Black freedom fighters experienced with white allies. In so doing, we might understand why the stated anti-segregationist intentions of allies did not always produce the impacts that they desired.

As a Black history professor who teaches intercultural studies in a predominantly white progressive Christian university, I am convinced that studies like Brown's and Boyd's are essential for students and professors who endeavor to oppose the exploitative and extractive systems of white domination. I am also convinced that knowledge of the anti-segregationist intentions of white allies is not enough; we need to study the impact of white ally actions as well. In this way, *Damned Whiteness* shares with Anthea Butler's *White Evangelical Racism* a critical investigation of the anti-Black racism inherent to white Christianity in America.[38] A major difference in my project is that *Damned Whiteness* focuses on white progressive evangelical religion, white liberal Protestantism, and white radical Catholicism to show the unexpected ways that even white Christians who oppose overt anti-Black animus can operate out of paradigms that assume whiteness as normative.

The cast of characters in *Damned Whiteness* share networks with the subjects of Patricia Appelbaum's *Kingdom to Commune* and take cues from Monica M. White's *Freedom Farmers*, which further demonstrates the racially parallel activism that signified the period. White allies in this book overlap with pacifist movements and organizations that emerged in mid-twentieth-century America with designs to build agrarian communal alternatives to the violent capitalist society in which they lived. If we consider both Appelbaum's important recognition of white Protestants' "agricultural resistance" movement and the Black agricultural activist activities found in White's study, we begin to see that there were possibilities for incredible interracial coalitions. Yet white communes never achieved anything close to the interracial communities that some envisioned, and in most cases, Black farmers were too busy fighting the unjust systems of sharecropping with their own farming cooperative initiatives to concern themselves with making agricultural cooperatives with white people. Though allies criticized Jim Crow laws in the South, racial discrimination in the North, and nationwide anti-Black violence, Black farmers' concerns for physical survival rarely became features in white allies' "agronomic" strategies.

The failure of white Protestant agrarian pacifists to adequately take up the most pressing concerns of Black Americans is just one example of how white allies talked about the value of interracial community but walked away from initiatives that Black communities organized around. Karen Johnson's *One in Christ* and Ansley Quiros's *God with Us* provide helpful histories that add to our knowledge of the practical and theological efforts Christian people made to overcome the racial obstacles that threatened to make Christian appeals to unity and harmony sound insincere. Not only do these important resources make the theme of interracial activism central to their narratives, but they also engage with historical people that I investigate in this book.

Johnson's well-researched and important excavation of the interracial activity that fueled Catholic support for the civil rights movement in the racially segregated city of Chicago details the personal dedication of Catholics who committed themselves to "interracial justice." Aided by the experiences of Arthur Falls, she names the triumphs as well as the tensions that made interracialism seem a miraculous feat in a city that reflected white society's anti-Black animus and American Catholicism's racially bound parish limitations. While there is no doubt that the heart commitments Catholics made to work across racial lines inspired them to participate in a movement that threatened both their connections to other white people and their safety, it is also true that the lasting effects of their participation show no signs that Black Catholics—or Black Americans more broadly—came to view Catholicism as a particularly hospitable site where Black people might be empowered to organize for freedom. Nor did white participation in interracial Catholicism prepare white Catholics to support demands for freedom as Black leaders grew more militant after 1963. To the contrary, the evidence suggests that by the late 1960s, Black Catholics grew disillusioned with the philosophy of interracialism because its adherents were generally skeptical of predominantly Black organizations, especially if their leadership made Black freedom the primary goal.[39]

Quiros also explores civil rights activism, but her narrative takes place in the Southern city of Americus, Georgia, among Protestants. In *God with Us*, Quiros insightfully names the struggle for civil rights as not only a racial conflict over whether or not Black Americans should have the same rights as white citizens but also a theological contest over Christian orthodoxy. Beginning with Clarence Jordan and his Koinonia community as Christians who claim that true Christian fellowship should be interracial, Quiros weaves the story of interracial fellowship through the text to demonstrate the challenge it posed to segregationist Christianity. This approach invites readers to take seriously the words, ideas, and intentions of interracialists like Jordan and the Koinonians and pits their views squarely against the beliefs of white Christian segregationists. Koinonian orthodoxy suggests that the integrity of a Christian community that claims to have good news to share with Black people is questionable if that community also proclaims that God condones anti-Black oppression. They insist that the Christian message is only good news if it is good news for every race.[40]

By focusing on the intentions of interracialists, however, this approach obscures the unequal consequences of the warring theological approaches. Segregationist theology had the power of their denomination, state laws, and the Supreme Court. Therefore, their views were dominant and enforced. As Quiros narrates, deviation from segregationist practices came with material consequences: jail, expulsion from school, police brutality, and verbal assault, among other punitive outcomes. The products of interracial theology, spiritual satisfaction, and moral uprightness were far less tangible and did nothing to rid Black Southerners of the violence of Jim Crow segregation. Nor did the good intentions of interracialists improve the number of interracial families in their fellowship or directly reform the Americus region.

Johnson and Quiros recognize in their respective texts the dissatisfaction that Black leaders felt toward interracial communities and philosophies. The thrusts of their texts, however, assume a virtue in attempting to build interracial fellowships. From the perspectives of Black freedom fighters, who enjoyed aspects of these communities and acknowledged the risks that allies took to stand against their white peers, virtues beyond good intentions are difficult to find. In this way, *Damned Whiteness* is a complementary addition to the work of these texts in that it gives necessary attention to explaining why white Christian allies failed to create strategies that produced the results they intended. This book explains that the key to understanding how allies failed to effectively challenge racial injustice is by privileging the voices and actions of Black freedom fighters over the congratulatory words of white interracialists. It is through Black narratives that we learn how white mission strategies required Black folks to assimilate to white spaces. And we see how white organizations romanticized relationships at the expense of confrontational strategies that had the potential to empower Black Americans to find liberation on their own terms.

Methods

Black interpretive lenses pair well with viewing history from the perspectives of those whose power to effectively change their environment is limited by oppressive forces. My method of recontextualizing the histories of white radical Christian pacifists in the era of Black freedom movements reverses the gaze from interpreting American history with perspectives of white progress narratives to recognizing Black history as a more comprehensive interpretive lens. Black history allows historians to interpret more data, especially because if Black thinkers were to thrive in the American context, they were required to understand it through the perspectives of both oppressed peoples and those who oppressed them.

In the *Souls of Black Folk*, W. E. B. Du Bois described a white gaze that was so pervasive that even Black people looked through it to survive a society that catered to the whims of white people. Du Bois's perspective on white society emerged from his Black oppositional analysis, especially as he wrote in *Black Reconstruction in America*. Other Black thinkers offered their own perspectives on whiteness in the decades that followed. *Damned Whiteness* joins that tradition by taking cues from the gaze of Black theorists, such as Du Bois, Ralph Ellison, James Baldwin, Toni Morrison, and bell hooks. They reversed the gaze to consider what we might explain better if we took seriously the initiatives of those most directly affected by racial, religious, national, and gender oppression to provide a comprehensive view of American society. In this case, by looking at the racial activism of self-proclaimed white peacemakers from the context of the Black freedom era, historical evidence demonstrates that their practice of exclusively white leadership, focus on fellowship over freedom, and commitment to models of white charity to Black communities instead of solidarity with them hindered their vision to create communities that practiced racial equality. In this vein, a less visible but consistent argument I will make is that histories that celebrate white progressives for opposing racial segregation distort the problematic legacies of allies who conflicted with and, at times, undermined Black freedom movements. Such histories teach those who consume them to value the intentions of white progressives over the impact of their actions, to value charity to racially oppressed people over solidarity with them, and to value white charity toward Black communities over solidarity with Black movements for freedom.[41]

Damned Whiteness narrates pivotal moments in the Black freedom era (for this project, 1930–69) to contextualize the actions of white allies. This periodization serves two purposes. First, it builds on the periodization work that historians of Black Power have done to aid our understanding of the continuities between the civil rights and Black Power movements. Through the development of historiographical analyses that demonstrate the continuities among people, events, and the philosophies of civil rights workers and Black power activists, we learn that movements we once thought were wholly distinct, or even rivals, overlap and inform one another in significant ways. Classically speaking, these movements have yielded their own periods, with beginning and end dates for each. But as seen in the brief story of CORE that I narrated at the beginning of this introduction, civil rights and Black Power histories overlap, intertwine, and are co-constituting. CORE's turn to Black Power illustrates that attempts to neatly separate Black Power from civil rights obscures this reality.

This Black freedom paradigm allows historians to account for both the antecedents of the standard civil rights era and their shared histories with the emergence of Black Power. Peniel Joseph's important excavations of Black Power histories render the dichotomous reading of civil rights versus Black Power untenable, especially when one considers the relationships between the National Association for the Advancement of Colored People (NAACP), the Southern Christian Leadership Conference (SCLC), SNCC, and CORE. Dichotomous narratives of Stokely Carmichael as a civil rights leader or a Black Power advocate, not both, make it very difficult if not impossible to interpret his life. And histories of Robert Williams, Ella Baker, James Farmer, Floyd McKissick, and Fannie Lou Hamer similarly make a farse out of histories that clearly distinguish civil rights from Black Power.[42]

Second, this periodization provides nomenclature for the shared liberative work of the civil rights and Black Power movements. While it is essential that we accurately represent points of disagreement between civil rights activists and Black Power advocates, which were significant, it is just as important to note that they fought for a common prize—freedom. Black freedom fighters engaged in intense debates, which at times led to unfair criticisms and even name-calling. These issues were usually announced in Black spaces. When they reached white audiences, they were used to pit leaders against one another. It would be a mistake to assume that squabbles between freedom fighters began with the emergence of the Black Power movement—they did not. Male civil rights leaders famously needed mediators like Ella Baker to convince them to work together. And contrary to popular thinking, Black Power leaders typically took great care not to speak against other Black leaders when in the presence of the white press.

Historians of Black Power have not been alone in revising the demarcations between the eras in Black political history. Over the last twenty years, historians who specialize in civil rights have explored the antecedents to mass demonstrations and institutional Black politics and argued for a long civil rights era. Jaquelyn Dowd Hall's 2005 essay on the "long civil rights movement" still speaks to the problems involved in periodizing the era solely through the lens of legal decisions and importantly points out the pervasiveness of racial hierarchy throughout the structures of the American project—economic, political, and religious.[43] Recently, Gary Dorrien delineated three phases of the civil rights movement to make the case that a longer period helps us understand that ignorance of religious antecedents to the classic era of civil rights has led historians to overlook a Black social gospel that existed parallel to white social gospels. Dorrien's schema dates back a few decades further than most, but it is not far from the recent work of Sarah Azaransky, Karen Johnson, and Ansley Quiros, which all benefit from breaking free from the confines of classical civil rights histories that begin with *Brown v. Board of Education* and end with the Fair Housing Act. This legal history is insufficient in other ways as well. It hardly considers the processes necessary to tell the histories of those cases, not to mention their outcomes, which are still in question. Certainly, the civil rights era constitutes more than a series of Supreme Court decisions and legislative victories against discrimination. In addition to recognizing the ways that racial segregation influenced legal realities, a long civil rights periodization recognizes the implications of Jim Crow in shaping the regions where those policies were binding beyond the South. By now, anyone who writes on civil rights history can tell you why the career of Jim Crow was familiar to most people living in Northern cities too.[44]

Taking these issues into account, I refer to the period of this study, 1930–69, as the "Black freedom era." I refer to the Black leaders who initiated liberative programs in institutional politics, behavioral politics, cultural politics, party politics, and movement politics as "freedom fighters." At times, the biographies of the historical actors date back before 1930 and their contributions extend beyond 1969. Still, narratives need starting points from which to begin and summaries that bring story lines together. While this narrative sometimes reaches back to the nineteenth century to explain important antecedents to twentieth-century freedom movements, the focus of this text is on the work initiated by Black agents who organized to abolish all forms of anti-Black oppression and white Christian allies who dared to position themselves in opposition to the racial segregation that began in the 1930s and continued through the 1960s. Thus, any deviation from those parameters will be brief and serve only to illuminate the traditions that contributed to the contexts in which they worked.

Whiteness

White Christian allies' agronomic interracialism presented a significant challenge to capitalist industrial norms during the Black freedom era, which explains why segregationists were so hostile toward them. Their political position made them what historian Noel Ignatiev called "race traitors."[45] They resisted racial whiteness when they refused to arrange their communities according to Jim Crow politics or align themselves with capitalist hierarchies. However, allies also undertheorized the extent to which the structures of capitalism, being imperialist in nature, were necessarily racially exploitative and environmentally extractive. That is, because whiteness is a political position that places white elites at the apex of capitalism and is made possible through European imperialism, its effectiveness depends on the exploitation of colonized workers and the extraction of colonized resources. Allies tended to view racial exploitation as an evil that was separate from the poverty of white workers or the environmentally destructive practices of industrialization. When they rejected pejorative terms for racial minorities or criticized segregationist policies, they could do so without recognizing that it was upon these racial logics that capitalists justified worker exploitation and environmental extraction. Ruth Wilson Gilmore's explanation, that "capitalism requires inequality and racism enshrines it," clarifies what was missing in ally analyses.[46] In failing to recognize the relationship between anti-Black exploitation and environmental extraction, allies offered a different kind of whiteness rather than a wholesale rejection of it. In other words, despite their attempts to provide alternatives to racial segregation, their interracialist communities reproduced aspects of whiteness, but in the forms of voluntary poverty, farming, and interracialism.[47]

While the academic study of whiteness, as a discipline, is relatively new (dating back to the 1990s), questions concerning white society and the institutions it produced have been under the scrutiny of Black intellectuals—and other people oppressed by American racial hierarchies—since at least 1829, when David Walker published his *Appeal to the Coloured Citizens of the World*. In this way, whiteness is a historically observable political phenomenon, in which white officials vested with state, or equivalent power, consolidated economic and political benefits for European colonial settlers. To pass on these goods, they negotiated the terms of inclusion in that economic and political context based on the needs of the wealthy landowners who were empowered by the violent force that legitimized their wealth.[48]

In its earliest stages, whiteness was not defined explicitly, which contributed to the ability of those who benefited from it to exploit the rumor that every person had equal opportunity—through hard work, dedication, education, and even luck—to earn a wage great enough to gain economic self-sufficiency for themselves and their immediate family. In truth, as Toni Morrison writes, it was the undesirable characteristics of not-white people, rather than the white Protestant work ethic, that marked the first boundaries of white identity formation. Europeans looked upon the lands and people that they colonized, defining those "others" by what English, French, and Spanish Christians were not supposed to be: savage, heathen, superstitious, magical, demonic, or subhuman.[49]

Thus, the construction of whiteness must be understood in relationship to its antithesis, what it is not supposed to be. The "not-me," as Toni Morrison calls it, is reflexive in that the nonwhite antithesis of the white protagonist is an imaginative tool that connotes what the white character should not be.[50] Because American authors tend to leave whiteness undefined, Morrison recommends that to understand it, we must investigate "the ways in which a nonwhite, Africanlike (or Africanist) presence or persona was constructed in the United States, and the imaginative uses this fabricated presence served."[51] From Mary Rowlandson's puritan captivity narrative to Mark Twain's enslaved character Jim, the denigration of the African presence in the white literary imagination became essential to constructing the ideology of "white supremacy," and it also served as a justification for Western imperialism. Through the "not-me" process, the ideology of white supremacy presented the white race as the standard against which all races should be imagined. "The subject of the dream is the dreamer," Morrison writes.[52] Similarly, Ralph Ellison suggests in his novel *Invisible Man* that the vision of those who have internalized the fiction of white superiority reflexively see themselves when looking upon their supposed inferiors.

These negative constructions of whiteness developed in domains that Colin Kidd refers to as "race-as-biology," "race-as-ethnicity," and "race-as-class or -caste"—and I add race-as-religion.[53] The process of negotiating what, or more importantly who, constituted the white race in the Americas was long and costly. As James Baldwin put it, "No one was white before he or she came here. It took generations, and a vast amount of coercion, before this became a white country."[54] Thus whiteness is, in addition to being an economic and political position, a contextually dependent social, political, and economic tool that is best understood by studying two things: first, its antithesis Black presence (actual, implied, and imagined), and second, how it is performed and rewarded. In this study, I investigate the missions, visions, stated intentions, actions, and impacts of white allies in contrast to the missions, visions, stated intentions, actions, and impacts of Black freedom fighters to, in the words of Hazel Carby, "make visible what is rendered invisible when viewed as the normative state of existence."[55]

As an invisible social position, the racially informed behaviors and beliefs that white allies held toward the Black objects of their mission—and themselves—were largely hidden. They were often oblivious to the decades, ideas, institutions, and strategies that animated Black resistance. Moreover, allies engaged in very little critical reflection on white society and their complicity with it. While they were treated as traitors to whiteness by other white people when they refused to perform anti-Black exclusion, discrimination, or denigration, they were still trapped in behaviors and beliefs that assumed Black Americans lacked knowledge, skills, and experiences that only white people could provide. Thus, they burdened themselves with the self-appointed responsibility of rescuing oppressed Black people from a racial context that they did not understand. Even as so-called race traitors, they performed a type of whiteness that they passed on to their white associates, which left them ill-equipped to face the racially discriminatory policies and practices that plagued their predominantly white institutions long after the founders were gone.

To narrate how this happened, *Damned Whiteness* relies heavily on archived materials from the Ralph Templin Collection, part of the United

Methodist Archives and History Center housed at Drew University. The collection includes copies of the *Peacemaker*, the *Catholic Worker*, and the *Koinonia Farm Newsletter*. University of Georgia Special Collections Libraries gave me access to the internal letters of Koinonia Farm through its Clarence L. Jordan Papers. Along with those sources, I used Dorothy Day's published books and letters—which are mostly accessible to the public through edited volumes and the online *Catholic Worker* archives. Day was a prolific writer who penned an autobiography and published her thoughts on her community in the *Catholic Worker*.[56] Jordan's works are also publicly available in the form of sermons and his translation of the Bible.[57] Along with the published works of Jordan, Tracy K'Meyer, author of *Interracialism and Christian Community in the Postwar South*, provided me with access to the interviews she conducted in Koinonia.[58] In addition to Templin's archive, which includes many unpublished letters, manuscripts, and lecture outlines, he published a book titled *Democracy and Nonviolence*, which provides important insights into the development of his thoughts on the need to address race as US citizens attempted to expand democracy for all. Finally, I obtained materials from the Swarthmore College Peace Collection that describe the mission of the Harlem Ashram and the vision of its allies.[59]

Allies are the subject of *Damned Whiteness*, but the intellectual and activist work of freedom fighters provides the context through which I will interpret them. Thus, primary sources from Black radical newspapers—*The Crisis*, *The Messenger*, and *The Chicago Defender*—are crucial to understanding Black perspectives on allies' work. Commentary expressed in the writings of Black activists such as Ella Baker, James Farmer, Bayard Rustin, W. E. B. Du Bois, Arthur Falls, Thomas Wyatt Turner, Vincent Harding, Booker T. Whatley, Black Americus residents, Stokely Carmichael, Albert Cleage, Martin Luther King Jr., and others inform my interpretations of the effectiveness of ally goals. The missions and visions of Black Freedom organizations—the Montgomery Improvement Association, the SCLC, CORE, the Brotherhood of Sleeping Car Porters (BSCP), the NAACP, the Tuskegee Institute Experiment Station, and Black churches are also significant touchpoints from which to answer the questions that frame this project.

Taken together, these resources describe how allies' promotion of Christian communal living, agrarian economics, and the primacy of principled pacifism rendered racial injustice a secondary problem. They addressed racial injustice through charity paradigms that they believed would assimilate Black people into the community. Even though Black radicals regularly wrestled with the complexity of the color line, which led them to conclude that the problems of class and capitalism required alternative solutions to achieve liberty and democracy, allies believed that racial injustice was mostly an obstacle to improving race relations, not a threat to the economic or political well-being of their interracial dreams.

Chapter Outline

The book is divided into seven chapters. The first chapter, "Parallel Politics," uses the history of the Black-led Prayer Pilgrimage for Freedom as a lens through which to introduce the three main subjects and their movements: Clarence Jordan's Koinonia Farm, Dorothy Day's Catholic Worker movement, and Ralph Templin's leadership at the School of Living. These three white allies' work coalesced around a drama that unfolded at Koinonia Farm when news of white segregationists, who were upset by the interracial efforts of Jordan, terrorized his farm with drive-by shootings and dynamite bombings in 1957. The chapter argues that while freedom fighters organized their first march on Washington, white allies promoted agrarian cooperative communities that resulted in "white flight" from newly Black-populated urban communities, creating racially bifurcated parallel movements. The allies were inspired by a renewed "back-to-the-land" movement in the 1940s, which took them far from the new neighborhoods that Black people created in the Great Migration and hindered them from working in close proximity to Black freedom movements. Though their rural communities in Ohio, New York, and Georgia were distant from one another, their participation in the Peacemakers group—founded by A. J. Muste, the most well-known white Christian pacifist of his generation—provided a shared community from which members could rally around Koinonia. Yet Peacemakers' focus on pacifism and agronomic movements left allies philosophically ill equipped to mount a significant challenge to the ideology of white supremacy. Their regional and philosophical distance from Black communities hindered even the few Black Peacemakers among them, who established the CORE, from gaining much support for their freedom efforts.

To explain why white allies were committed to challenging segregation and fostering interracial fellowship, chapter 2, "Diversity," investigates Dorothy Day's decision to include the NAACP's reports on the 1930s Mississippi Delta camps in the first edition of her *Catholic Worker* newspaper. Instead of submitting to the opinion of her mentor, Peter Maurin, Day followed the lessons she learned from socialists like Eugene Debs, who decried racial oppression but offered no strategies to oppose it. Day published the first edition of the paper on May Day to promote the idea that communism was not the only option for Black laborers and to suggest that laborers of all races were welcome in the mystical body of Christ. However, I argue that this invitation offered little more than token reprinting of stories that first appeared in the NAACP's *The Crisis*. Day reprinted the news stories to suggest that Catholics cared about the plight of Black people, but the racial diversity represented by those stories was not accompanied with strategies to end Black exploitation. Moreover, Day's class-over-race view thwarted her ability to adopt the racial-Marxist analyses of the NAACP and communists, who competed over who could best provide legal defense for Black laborers in the Mississippi Delta and Scottsboro, Alabama. Day did not adopt their analyses in part because she was content to use the stories of Black people in the *Catholic Worker* as anticommunist propaganda. Rather than transforming the Catholic Worker movement into a multiracial coalition, in which Black contributions were welcome to transform white Catholic assumptions about the virtues of interracialism, the stories offered symbolic representations of diversity that were not present in her community. Thus, these Black labor stories provide insight into the role Day held open for Blacks to play in her movement; that is, the implied and real presence of Blacks in the newspaper amounted to token representations. These stories accurately portrayed the horrors of Jim Crow segregation, but they implied that the only solution to segregation was conversion to Catholicism.

Dorothy Day was not alone in her token inclusion of Blacks in American Catholicism. Chapter 3, "Charity," reveals that white Catholic priests' dissolution of Thomas Wyatt Turner's Federated Colored Catholics foreshadowed the interracial work of Dorothy Day's Catholic Worker Hospitality Houses. That is, Day undermined a Black initiative within her Catholic Worker movement when she rejected the economic education initiative of Arthur Falls in Chicago's first Catholic Worker house. I argue that Day tokenized Arthur Falls, using him and his ideas to increase Black representation in the Catholic Worker movement and to enhance the potential for a larger voluntary poverty community. Instead of wrestling with Falls's analysis that Black Chicagoans needed economic education as much as Catholic catechism, Day undermined his Chicago Catholic Worker house to bolster her charity program. In her mystical body of Christ view, racism was an ecclesial issue that would cease when workers embraced Catholicism and voluntary poverty. From this position, she supported the white Catholic interracial efforts of priests who worked against Black organizing in favor of efforts that celebrated white oversight. Her anticommunist position assumed that economic inequality was the only source of injustice, and racial injustice, as opposed to being constitutive of capitalism, was but one of many negative consequences. To the contrary, Black freedom fighters—including Ella Baker, the first woman director of the NAACP, whose office was only a few blocks from Day's, and A. Philip Randolph, the founder of the BSCP—believed that capitalism was one significant component of white violence that pervaded the United States. They believed that a socialist critique of capitalism that did not recognize the fundamental anti-Blackness of the American economy would be impotent in addressing the power of white supremacist philosophy and systems that thwarted Black freedom.

The failure of white allies to adequately understand the power of white supremacist systems is also evident in Clarence Jordan's work at Koinonia Farm. In chapter 4, "Relationships," I introduce the stories of Black sharecroppers near Americus, Georgia, to provide necessary sociohistorical context for Jordan's work at Koinonia. Specifically, the chapter begins with the story of Rosa Lee Ingram, who was entangled in a legal battle after she killed her white neighbor in self-defense. Her story demonstrates the main argument of the chapter, that Jordan's white saviorism was predicated on his failure to understand the capabilities of skilled Black Americus farmers and church leaders to fight for themselves. Considering this context, the chapter compares Jordan's two purposes for founding Koinonia in 1942—to teach Black farmers about agriculture and to teach Black preachers about religion—to the history of Black farming and Black activist organizing in the region. By doing so, I show that in addition to the International Labor Defense, the NAACP, and the Black churches that organized on Ingram's behalf, she and her children represented generations of Black families who struggled against anti-Black violence on Georgian soil for centuries. In truth, Jordan had very little to teach his new Black neighbors about religious activity, of which they were innovators. And as one who confessed that he knew very little about farming—what he knew he learned by watching neighboring farms—he had even less to teach them about working the land. Black farmers had years of experience with the red Georgian soil. Jordan, on the other hand, who knew only agricultural theory, assumed that even his ignorance was enough to establish a community that could educate Black farmers and preachers.

Chapter 5, "Reconciliation," reveals that Jordan's *Cotton Patch Gospels* prized Christian fellowship over civic engagement and led to his anti–civil rights movement doctrine that he called "the God movement." By portraying Jesus and his disciples as Southern white men in his version of the New Testament, Jordan's God movement informed his posture toward Black farmers and preachers. This theological concept became his bulwark against developing a Christology that could conceive of a stained-glass Black Jesus like the one that replaced the window that white Georgians bombed at the 16th Street Baptist Church in Birmingham, Alabama. This contrast provides a lens through which to interpret the theological ideas that informed Jordan's vision for Koinonia—that of a racially reconciled community of Black and white farmers living together in harmony. I show that a tradition of portraying Jesus as Black in the American context offered an alternative to Jordan's white Christological imagination. Jordan's white Jesus encouraged an interpretation of the Christian gospel that centered white Protestants as God's chosen people and invited Black outsiders to assimilate to white Anglo-Saxon Protestantism in order to be reconciled to God and one another. His reconciling strategy was also informed by the white Christian pacifism of mid-twentieth-century Protestantism. It was a philosophy that required its adherents to not resist evil. This helps explain why in Jordan's only face-to-face engagement with Martin Luther King Jr., he rebuked the public demonstrations of the civil rights movement. Jordan's commitment to nonresistance and his failure to analyze the power dynamics at work in the New Testament left the Koinonian community, beyond providing sanctuary, unable to consistently support Black freedom fighters as they protested racial injustices in Americus. Consequently, when the Americus movement began, Jordan preached against it.

In chapter 6, "The White Problem," I highlight the international spirit of activism that had reached Harlem through its Black renaissance. Black activists like Pauli Murray, James Farmer, and Bayard Rustin experimented with Gandhian nonviolent methods that permeated the culture. Black culture in 1940s Harlem showed fascination for international politics, which expanded Harlemites' understanding of how nonviolence could be used to further the cause for freedom. So, when Ralph Templin arrived from his missionary experience in India, he and his partner Jay Holmes entered a Harlem context that needed no introduction to the Indian independence movement. Nevertheless, they founded an ashram through which they taught Gandhian nonviolence to combat antisemitism and anti-Black discrimination. Their ashram attempted to combine faith in Christ with Gandhi's satyagraha philosophy, which they believed provided the necessary international education that Black Harlemites needed. But unlike the allies

I have mentioned to this point, Templin's disdain for imperialism, which he developed in India, left him unsettled in American pacifist groups. The tensions he experienced therein eventually provoked him to question if it was possible for white people to overcome white supremacist practices in their white domestic and international projects.

Templin's answer presented itself when young Black freedom fighters and Black church leaders claimed Black Power as the successor to the nonviolent mass demonstrations of the civil rights movement. Though Templin was a major actor in the nonviolent movements, his commitment to resisting evil allowed him to adopt views that his white peers, with their insistence on nonresistance, interracialism, and charity, rarely considered. Chapter 7, "Black Power," demonstrates that though Templin, who coined the phrase "damned whiteness," expressed discomfort with the part he played in colonizing forms of white Protestant missions and pacifist organizations, he felt confined to those white movements until he claimed Black Power as the remedy for the problem of white supremacy in America. Templin found writing and homesteading inadequate ways to bridge his two worlds—white Americanism and the colonized people who opposed it. He experienced a paralyzing impotence to effectively participate in reforming society, naming whiteness as the prison that kept him from joining with freedom fighters in their mission to abolish evil. This changed when he realized that Black Power could liberate him from the prison of whiteness. Abandoning white spaces to join in solidarity with Black institutions provided the context for Ralph Templin's adoption of the Black Power philosophy as the best antithesis to the forces of domination that were at the heart of the white problem. Black Power, then, became the organizing principle that aligned his belief with that of W. E. B. Du Bois: that the color line, not war or capitalism, was the greatest problem of the twentieth century. Consequently, Templin joined in solidarity with the Black Power movement's quest to gain Black freedom.

Part I   **Making Movements**

. . . .

1 Parallel Politics

. . . .

> We call for a liberalism from the North which will be thoroughly
> committed to the ideal of racial justice and will not be deterred by
> the propaganda and subtle words of those who say: "Slow up for
> a while; you're pushing too fast."
> —Martin Luther King Jr., "Give Us the Ballot"

"I been 'buked, Lord, and I been scorned," Mahalia Jackson sang from the steps of the Lincoln Memorial at the beginning of the Prayer Pilgrimage for Freedom on May 17, 1957.[1] The church-like event was a monumental testament to the aims of the movement for Black freedom. It marked three years since the 1954 *Brown v. Board of Education* decision ruled that Jim Crow segregation was unconstitutional. The Prayer Pilgrimage for Freedom was the first of many protests where people gathered at the nation's capital to advance the cause of civil rights for African Americans in the United States. The gathering featured speakers from the Southern Christian Leadership Conference (SCLC), the Brotherhood of Sleeping Car Porters (BSCP), and the National Association for the Advancement of Colored People (NAACP). The spirit of the movement was reflected in the mottoes that each organization had chosen for their membership: the SCLC adopted the declaration "Not one hair of one head of one person should be harmed," the BSCP rallied its members to "Fight or Be Slaves," and the NAACP called on its associates to "Fight for Freedom."[2]

That freedom fighters gathered in the spirit of a centuries-long struggle against slavery, three years after the *Brown* decision, testifies to the reality that while *Brown* declared the unconstitutionality of segregation, it did not free Black people sufficiently to move throughout the nation with the confidence that they would receive the full protections of citizenship in equal proportion to white Americans. It was apparent to them that freedom required more than racial integration; freedom required the power of social movements to make economic upward mobility, civil rights, and racial justice available to Black people by abolishing Jim Crow and establishing new policies.

In this chapter, I contrast movements aimed at challenging racial segregation that were organized by Black freedom fighters from those that were organized by white Christian allies. Freedom fighters who organized the first march on Washington—the Prayer Pilgrimage for Freedom—faced the challenge of convincing the white press that their freedom goals were not synonymous with integration. While freedom fighters broadcast their message to the nation in cities like Washington, white allies fled from cities to organize farming communes in the rural North. In these rural spaces, white allies experimented with alternative economies and convinced one another that these newly constructed white spaces could host Christian fellowship that they called "interracialism." Their newfound commitment to interracialism, a concept that promoted friendship between Black and white Christians, was meant to prove the efficacy of Christian fellowship. Instead, interracialism became a barrier between the few Black members of their movements, who pressed them to prioritize Christian kinship over cooperation with institutions that practiced racial oppression, and white allies, who debated the validity of using practices that involved coercion and polluted the purity of their pacifism—even if the coercive methods in question were not physical.

In the middle years of the Black freedom era (1930–57), white allies criticized racial oppression with their words and moved to create white spaces where they might practice interracial fellowship. Meanwhile, freedom fighters developed movements that promoted freedom from white violence. Pointing out that these affinity groups moved in different directions even though they often used similar rhetoric is important because it demonstrates the inconsistencies of word, deed, mission, and vision in many white radical movements. In efforts to teach that white allies contributed to Black freedom movements, historians have implied that allies' invitations to Black people modeled anti-segregationist behavior. In their interpretation, these gestures offered sharp contrasts to the exclusionary practices of segregationists and inspired other white Christians to do the same. Invitations like these, however, did not consider the limited access Black people had to white rural spaces, the unique dangers that crossing the color line presented to Black folks, or the possibility that gaining white friendships was not the primary reason that freedom fighters welcomed white activists to join their efforts. If we look closely at white Christian ally movements, we see that their purchases of land, focus on alternative economics, and limited views of pacifism did more than place them in distant proximity from the Black people they desired as fellows; these efforts demonstrated that white ally strategies for interracialism were out of step with movements for Black freedom.

The Prayer Pilgrimage coincided with Black migrations out of southern countrysides to Northern cities and Midwestern towns, and into national headlines. The Great Migration transformed Black experiences in American history beginning in the early twentieth century. Historian Milton Sernett explains that we must also recognize the importance of the mid-twentieth-century migrations when he writes that "the magnitude of the exodus from the South during the years from 1940 to 1960 was larger than that of the World War I era." The Great Migration that began in the 1910s transformed the demographics of US cities from the District of Columbia to St. Louis, from Chicago to Detroit, from Indianapolis to New York City. As a result of these ongoing migrations, 1957 marked the first year that Washington, D.C., became a majority Black population.[3]

The migrations of Black Southerners to cities coincided with a movement of white pacifists, who left Northern cities to create white agricultural spaces for anti-capitalist organizing. One group, the Southern Agrarians, who followed "general" back-to-the-land philosophies, rejected commercialized farming in favor of what they called "backward" methods and believed that their radical return to homesteading would lead the United States to a utopian democratic future. Dona Brown writes that this movement found new life in "the 1940s and 1950s by small groups of pacifists and other marginalized dissidents."[4] Some of these dissidents were progressive Christians, Catholics and Protestants, who publicly opposed racial segregation. Christians who coupled farming with inviting Black people to cross the color line into white spaces also inspired other white people into an exodus from cities so that they could explore agricultural economics, pacifist political agendas, and interracial fellowship in nonindustrial locations. Though it does not appear that they were exiting city life to escape Black people, the fact that they were fleeing the city while Black people were entering would have consequences for the racial composition of their communes.[5]

By initiating a "white flight" from cities—where the presence of potential Black neighbors grew—to rural farms, these white allies thwarted their own efforts toward building interracial community. Too often, the distance between white allies' rural farms and new Black urban communities put integration, as anything more than an abstract idea, out of reach. From those white spaces they championed a Christian orthodoxy that called for interracial fellowship. For their plan to work, Black people needed to assimilate into their white communities, which only happened under rare circumstances where geographical distance was not an issue. So when news of a farm led by Clarence Jordan, a white Southern Baptist who advocated interracial fellowship, reached progressive Northern white networks, they rallied to support it. Koinonia Farm's proximity to Southern Black communities and experiences with white terrorist attacks convinced Northern allies of the righteousness of Koinonia's cause and the potential for interracial fellowship to become a reality.

It was white racial violence that Blacks in the Great Migration fled when they moved to Northern cities. It was also white violence, not solely segregation, that Black freedom fighters made the focus of their protests. They understood that integration had inflamed the anti-Black passions of white Southerners, which inspired an uptick of white cruelty. It was not that most Black freedom fighters advocated for continued racial segregation, though some did because they feared integration would lead to a loss of leadership opportunities and development of the Black culture. Rather, freedom fighters prioritized their right as US citizens to live free from the threat of white violence and considered it a prerequisite to the kind of interracial fellowship white allies envisioned.[6]

Black activists rarely heard nor heeded the call for interracial fellowship for at least two reasons: in addition to lacking physical proximity to these Northern rural farms, they prioritized advancing the cause for freedom in their new urban neighborhoods over building relationships with white people in predominantly white communities. Even Black leaders who made integration a centerpiece of their advocacy lived to lament the costs involved. Benjamin Mays, who spent much of his career advocating for an end to segregated churches, looked back over decades of integration efforts and cautioned an audience that "desegregation may render a disservice to the nation if it means a one-way traffic, always moving from black to white and never from white to black."[7] His insight explained how freedom fighters sometimes received invitations from white allies to assimilate to white culture as devaluing Black culture. Another Black church leader, James Lawson, who lent significant theological wisdom to the civil rights movement, explained his rebuke of segregation theologically: "The Christian favors the breaking down of racial barriers because the redeemed community of which he is already a citizen recognizes no barriers dividing humanity." He warned that even the rejection of those boundaries did not necessitate interracialism: "The kingdom is far more than the immediate need for integration."[8] Leaders like Mays and Lawson suggested that integration was no guarantee of the redeemed community for which freedom fighters longed unless it involved dismantling racially discriminatory structures.

While Black migrants in the North became city dwellers, where neighborhood and county lines distanced them from white allies, African Americans who remained in the South were familiar with segregation of a different kind. Southern segregation created a culture in which Black and white people came into regular contact with one another. Thus, when Clarence Jordan established his farm for interracial fellowship in Americus, Georgia, his Black neighbors knew that Southern segregation required that they adhere to social customs that would keep them from provoking white retribution. Jim Crow rules dictated that Black laborers dance delicately along the color line in a way that never suggested they were peers with white people but instead demonstrated that they were performing for them. This awkward manner for Black people to navigate white spaces dated back to the earliest days of chattel slavery, when enslaved Africans worked in intimate spaces with white enslavers who routinely used abusive tactics to remind them that white people did not consider Black people their social equals. Jordan's Black neighbors, who sometimes worked for Koinonia, understood these social arrangements and actively avoided situations that would give the appearance that they planned to challenge racially hierarchical norms.

Jim Crow segregation established policies and processes to reinforce power distances between Black and white people because the work of Black domestic workers brought them into intimate spaces—like white Southern homes. W. E. B. Du Bois's description of how this intimacy emerged is instructive: "Before and directly after the [Civil] war, when all the best of the Negroes were domestic servants in the best of the white families, there were bonds of intimacy, affection, and sometimes blood relationship, between the races."[9] Du Bois did not romanticize these bonds in the way that defenders of the Lost Cause myth did. Rather, he understood that these bonds were regulated by Southern cultural taboos, mores, and laws. Black folks who agreed with Du Bois, that the color line was the great problem of the twentieth century, also understood that even if Jordan's interracial experiment took great courage, interracial intimacy was as much a feature of segregation as was anti-Black violence. They feared no amount of farming or Christian fellowship would change that.

The planners of the Prayer Pilgrimage made evident that their Black freedom efforts represented another leg in the long journey out of American slavery. In his "Give Us the Ballot" speech, Martin Luther King Jr., president of the SCLC, beseeched all in his hearing to "work passionately and unrelentingly for the goal of freedom." He explained that freedom results not in a society "where black men are superior and other men are inferior and vice versa, but a society in which all men will live together as brothers and respect the dignity and worth of human personality."[10] A. Philip Randolph, the founder of the BSCP, proclaimed that the gathering testified to "our renewal of faith in and consecration to the sacred cause of a rebirth of freedom and human dignity."[11] The assertion that freedom would result from respecting the dignity and worth of each human was the organizing principle that allowed Black leaders from different regions and associations to work together to promote the event.

The message of the Prayer Pilgrimage required both movement and strategy to disseminate. The march itself was a strategy employed by Randolph, who first threatened a similar action during a civil rights standoff with President Roosevelt in the 1940s. The threat convinced Roosevelt to acquiesce to Randolph's demand for greater racial equality in US military ranks. Admittedly, the idea of a march proved to be a formidable threat to presidential administrations, but because Randolph never organized the event, its full potential had yet to be realized. The Prayer Pilgrimage tested the potential of a national gathering to inspire Black folks to join together in protest and also provided data on the efficacy of a march to adequately communicate to media outlets what Black freedom fighters wanted from lawmakers.[12]

Ella Baker, who was the director of the New York chapter of the NAACP and instrumental in establishing the SCLC and the Student Nonviolent Coordinating Committee (SNCC), knew firsthand how difficult it was to communicate effectively through the media. In her work against school segregation, she expressed frustration that the news reports on her activism focused solely on integration rather than the lack of quality resources to aid Black educators and students. "The headlines especially are designed," she wrote to a friend, "to give the impression that the only thing with which we are concerned is integration rather than the fact that integration is desirable because where there is separation, even in New York, the schools are too often inadequate."[13]

This was one component of the argument that Thurgood Marshall, the NAACP's lead attorney, used to win a series of court cases against Jim Crow laws. He pointed out that "with education, this Court has made segregation and inequality equivalent concepts." Following the Supreme Court's logic, Thurman argued, "If segregation thus necessarily imports inequality, it makes no great difference whether we say that the Negro is wronged because he is segregated, or that he is wronged because he received unequal treatment."[14] The problem with segregation was that it guaranteed inequality. Equality and desegregation were necessary steps toward freedom. He made these connections clearer before a gathering of the NAACP in Virginia a few years later: "We demand freedom and we will take nothing less." He explained further, "As long as there is segregation, we are not free and we are not progressing."[15] Marshall's analysis of segregation interpreted it as a threat to democracy, equality, and freedom. But media ignored the nuances of Marshall's argument. Instead, white presses focused on the Supreme Court's decision to address Jim Crow segregation by mandating racial integration in public schools. Marshall had indeed made the case, using a moral argument from a Howard law student named Pauli Murray, that segregation was a moral problem that harmed the dignity of Black children, but this was a new angle that represented a departure from the prevailing view that equated segregation with inequality. Nevertheless, integration as the remedy for segregation, rather than equality, became a theme for white Americans whether they fought against segregation or welcomed it. As a result, it took deliberate efforts and messaging to ensure that the media accurately represented Black freedom as the purpose for the Prayer Pilgrimage in the headlines.[16]

The media's incomplete portrayal was due, in part, to the fact that neither freedom nor equality were the focus of the *Brown* decision. Rather than condemning inequality, Chief Justice Warren, who wrote the decision, was convinced by the argument that segregation caused Black children to suffer psychologically from their lack of contact with white children. Warren went beyond Murray's argument, however, when he claimed that lack of access to resources and funding was no longer an issue because the Black and white schools "involved have been equalized, or are being equalized, with respect to buildings, curricula, qualifications and salaries of teachers, and other 'tangible' factors." Segregation, then, was a problem, according to Warren, because separating Black students "from others of similar age and qualifications solely because of their race generates a feeling of inferiority as to their status in the community that may affect their hearts and minds in a way unlikely ever to be undone."[17]

In addition to psychological harms, Marshall had also argued that segregation was synonymous with inequality in tangible ways, such that if those tangible inequalities were remedied, then Black students could expect the same benefits from education as white students. He concluded that the only justification for ongoing segregation was that the white government endorsed "an inherent determination that the people who were formerly in slavery, regardless of anything else, shall be kept as near that stage as is possible."[18] It was plain to him that segregation was an extension of the institution of American slavery. Segregation was a problem because inequality guaranteed that Black people would never experience full freedom. Integration represented a challenge to racial segregation, but it did not directly address the tangible inequalities that kept Black people from experiencing social, economic, and geographical freedom. Still, many white people who celebrated the Warren decision adopted the view that integration, rather than equal protections of citizenship rights, was the solution.

The court's explanation of integration taught that Black children needed the presence of white children to succeed, which suggested that like civil rights activist marches, integration required movement. The immediate call to desegregate schools led to efforts to bus Black and white students to formerly segregated schools. White parents and white city governments sometimes responded to the movement of Black students to white schools by closing them and establishing private, generally Christian "segregation academies," where they could guarantee that white schoolchildren would not fraternize with Black schoolchildren. One might surmise that the "massive resistance" of white parents to desegregation meant that Black freedom activists were in favor of integration, but Black people's responses to desegregation were more complicated than that.[19]

Black leaders accepted integration as only one potential step in their march for freedom. At times, Black leaders—from nationalists to religious spokespeople—criticized integration for the negative effects it would have on Black communities. From the nineteenth century through the mid-twentieth century, leaders like Martin Delaney and Marcus Garvey advocated for the Black nationalist virtues of self-sufficiency and personal responsibility to overcome the negative effects of white nationalism. They understood that Black institutions held space for Black leadership in a way that white society would not allow for, especially in a racially integrated society where whites maintained disproportionate social and political power. Following the *Brown* decision, white Southerners put their power to resist the social and political mobility of Black people on violent display.

Challenging white resistance to Black freedom was one of the chief purposes for which Baker and the other leaders moved on Washington, DC. Prior to the 1950s, white Southern violence against Blacks was more urgent than school desegregation. Police brutality, voting restrictions, unfair labor practices, and inadequate funds for Black schools inspired Black activists to organize across a wide spectrum of religious and political orientations. *Brown* did nothing to end the terror of white Southern violence against Black citizens. To the contrary, the Supreme Court decision inspired a white Southern backlash against Black people and integrationist policies. White politicians voiced threats following the decision, including this statement by Harry Flood Byrd: "If we can organize the Southern States for massive resistance to this order I think that, in time, the rest of the country will realize that racial integration is not going to be accepted in the South."[20] Many white Southerners endorsed Byrd's threat by resisting the integration decision and defending their white supremacist project.

"Massive resistance" to integration metastasized into a violent Southern movement. Two years before the *Brown* decision, F. D. Patterson—the president of Tuskegee Institute—reported that 1952 was the first year without any lynching of Black people since lynching data was recorded. White vigilante violence that persisted between 1949 and 1952 was the result of opposition to Black residents who "attempted to move into what were considered white neighborhoods."[21] John Bell Williams memorialized white opposition to the threat of integrated neighborhoods when he referred to the day the courts decided the *Brown* decision, May 17, 1954, as Black Monday. On that day, Bell inspired the creation of the White Citizens' Council, a movement in which white neighborhoods organized against integration. By December 1954, there were 253 chapters of White Citizens' Councils in seven states, all with dues-paying members.[22] The following year, a group of white men lynched Emmett Till, a fourteen-year-old Black boy from Chicago who, while visiting family in Money, Mississippi, was accused of making a flirtatious comment to a white woman.[23]

When Mamie Till Mobley held an open-casket funeral for her mutilated son, more than 50,000 people attended. Her public comments against white violence helped grow membership in the NAACP and support for the Black freedom movement. With increased attention from the public funeral, the mass media gave more credibility to the idea that freedom for Black people meant that they should be able to move throughout the nation without fear of violence. But the focus on freedom was not without problematic associations. Due in part to the fact that communists had worked to support Black labor and provide legal representation for Black people since the 1930s, and because it served segregationists to discredit Black activism, the press also associated Black freedom activism with communism.[24]

There were other reasons to question the Prayer Pilgrimage's association with communism. In the "Call to a Prayer Pilgrimage for Freedom,"

Randolph, King, and Wilkins claimed that the immorality and injustice of segregation had grave economic consequences for Black citizens. They claimed that "privately organized groups," motivated by "massive resistance," created the conditions for economic inequality through anti-Black intimidation and violence. The collaborators reported that these white groups "exerted economic pressure upon Negro citizens who have simply asked [for] obedience to the Supreme Court."[25] Economic pressure had successfully disrupted the ability of African Americans to gain adequate wages to sustain their families. The leaders protested that Black men and women were "fired from their jobs. Merchants have been refused credit and goods. Farmers have been denied loans."[26] Their rhetoric suggested that social equality for Black people required economic equality that the government should have guaranteed.

Randolph's statement on the day of the pilgrimage recommended that the federal government grant economic equality to Black workers who suffered in states that resisted the Supreme Court ruling. He encouraged those workers by predicting that white supremacy would not be eternal: "Its death will come as a result of the emergence of the dynamic impulse for freedom surging in the hearts of Negroes." He encouraged the pilgrims that "the march of industrialization, urbanization, [and] labor union organization" made the end to racism a near inevitability. To make this a reality, he argued, the government had to act using the "extension of education and the modernization of government through the spread of the ballot."[27]

Randolph led the fight to spread the message of freedom for workers for more than twenty years. So when he explained how the efforts of the NAACP and other Black freedom organizations would "create and build a new South, free for white and black masses to pursue a life of dignity and decency," he was speaking as someone who had personally given his energy to win fair labor practices.[28] His union organizing earned him a reputation of having communist sympathies, which he publicly rebuked. Had he not publicly opposed communism, his work as a labor organizer would have seemed very similar to Communist Party politics among Southern Black farmers and other Black freedom fighters. Indeed, freedom fighters from W. E. B. Du Bois to Bayard Rustin appreciated the philosophies of the Communist Party so much so that they became members at different points in their life. Despite his position as a labor leader, Randolph vocally opposed communism.

Organizers of the Prayer Pilgrimage believed that to legitimize the gathering, they needed to emphasize that they were not part of a godless communist plot. Theirs was a new movement that used the religious rituals of prayer and pilgrimage to signal that their gathering was explicitly Christian. Organizers also made the message of the pilgrimage conspicuously patriotic when they announced that the demonstration was open to "all who love justice and dignity and liberty, who love their country."[29] They used their Christianity to protect themselves from accusations that they were anti-American. And by gathering at the nation's capital, they placed themselves in a position to demand that the government guarantee the movement's right to assemble and the right to freedom from white violence.

Flight from the City

Most white Christian allies did not collaborate enough with the Black freedom movement in their anti-segregationist efforts to comprehend how vital the use of white terrorist violence was in maintaining the Southern racial hierarchy, but they learned. In 1957, while freedom fighters prayed and pilgrimaged for freedom, white Christian allies Dorothy Day, founder of the Catholic Worker movement, and Ralph Templin, board member of the Peacemaker movement, rallied behind Clarence Jordan's vision of interracial fellowship at Koinonia Farm. Jordan's interracial experiment represented the type of opportunity that white "back-to-the-land" allies did not have in the Northern rural spaces, where they romanticized agrarian life and resisted certain aspects of capitalism. While living in New York City, Day and Templin sought out and found rural spaces that they transformed into communities for experimentation with alternative economies. However, when Day turned her attention away from Manhattan and Templin did likewise from Harlem to go back to the land in Staten Island, upstate New York, and Pennsylvania, they also limited possibilities for interracial community building with Black folks who did not typically live in those locations. Their geographic movements onto rural farmlands did not consider the racial limitations of these new white spaces because economic concerns and antiwar initiatives overshadowed their objections to racial segregation. To be sure, Day and Templin still supported charity efforts for impoverished people in cities, many of whom were Black. However, their lack of association with Black people in their agricultural initiatives divided their attention between economically sustainable alternatives to capitalism and racial injustices that neither Day nor Templin interpreted as essential to their anti-capitalist experiments.[30]

Day's and Templin's decisions to pursue agricultural economics reveal one pattern that emerged for white Christian allies: they regularly created predominantly white spaces wherein they assumed that their participants had access to white social and economic privileges. These white spaces took on many forms, but as Patricia Appelbaum writes, "One such social structure was the pacifist cooperative, which was most often a farm."[31] The farming communities that Day and Templin envisioned relied on networks of economic privilege that many Black folks did not have. These decisions impeded prospects for building strong relationships with Black folks who fought to free their communities from poverty, among other things. Black communities could not easily opt out of poverty, which made Day's idea of building relationships on a principle of voluntary poverty a nonstarter for many. And because Northern cities did not provide great opportunities for Black folks to purchase land, Templin's homestead education at the School of Living lacked feasibility for Black transplants. In this way, white Christian farming cooperatives virtually precluded the possibility of advancing Black freedom, because by initiating white rural programs, they diminished the possibility of building solidarity with freedom fighters. For their part, Black activists proposed agricultural ideas that could sustain Black communities, but they practiced those ideas in Black spaces—Black colleges and Southern farms. Even Clarence Jordan's farm in Georgia, located in a community with a substantial Black farming population, followed this pattern of creating white space for white sojourners to practice charity, through which they pursued their interracial vision. When Blacks worked at Koinonia, Jordan made no plans with those farmers to combat anti-Black laws or the poverty sharecroppers and tenant farmers faced under Jim Crow.

Eradicating poverty through communal farming was the dream of Dorothy Day and her mentor, Peter Maurin. Maurin's vision of "agronomic universities" captivated Day from the early days of the Catholic Worker movement, ever since Maurin envisioned agricultural autonomy as an important component of alleviating the social ills created by capitalism. Maurin proposed the concept in the spring of 1935, soon after he and Day purchased their first "farming commune" on Staten Island. The property was so small that they jokingly referred to it as a "garden commune."[32]

Day and Maurin knew next to nothing about farming, and Day admitted to being too eager to engage in "proper study or planning."[33] She wanted land that placed scholars and workers in community together, with a goal of both honoring the worker and providing space to consider scholarship that advocated for Maurin's central lesson: "Voluntary poverty is essential.

To live poor, to start poor, to make beginnings even with meager means at hand, this is to get the 'green revolution' under way."[34]

Back-to-the-landers proposed the green revolution as the alternative to the environmental and human degradations caused by the industrial revolution. By Day's own account, their farming commune was caught up in the spirit of "Back to the Land!" In 1935, Catholic Workers perused New Jersey for plots larger than the one-acre farming garden in Staten Island until they finally settled on a farm in Easton, Pennsylvania. A familiar eagerness ruled their purchase; they did not do enough research on the property. Though they had not secured the $1,250 asking price for the property, their network of financial contributors helped them produce a down payment. Soon after they began to farm, they discovered that the stream that they had thought was part of their purchased property belonged to their neighbors. The only water to which they had access was what they could collect in rain barrels. Even with the water limitations, however, they could now respond adequately to the question, "How could we write about farming communes unless we had one?"[35] With the property they had secured and water from storage cisterns that caught rain from the barn and house, they could practice voluntary poverty in the back-to-the-land spirit.

Day's farming commune was not unique in requiring participants to submit to voluntary poverty. A crucial component of many such communal experiments involved forfeiting possessions or at least questioning whether building a social economy on financial capital benefited the working class. As the director of the School of Living in Suffern, New York, from 1941 to 1945, Ralph Templin taught, "The farm community involves the 'economic means,' . . . where man [sic] produces, individually or cooperatively, with his own hands" as opposed to the "appropriation of wealth produced by others."[36] Templin, following the idealism of Ralph Borsodi, proposed an alternative economy to capitalist competition, which left many laborers destitute. Without access to land or the ability to sustain their lives by their own hands, laborers were vulnerable to the conditions that gave rise to war, which he and other peacemakers wanted to avoid.

Templin and other back-to-the-land movement advocates celebrated backward economic mobility. Like the white Christian radicals previously mentioned, Templin had networks reaching benefactors on the other side of the Atlantic Ocean, mainline and evangelical denominational support, and donors nationwide. While the prospect of living with less individual resources presented risks, their access to property and social capital increased because of their green revolution advocacy and charity models for solving poverty. These networks shared privileges that racial segregation did not afford to African Americans. So even if they invited Black people to join their movement through membership and mentoring, they failed to comprehend that Black people, who began with less financial safeguards, risked suffering greater impoverishment by agreeing to forgo private property in favor of communal living.

Black freedom fighters represented communities that without government support seldom experienced the privilege of social structures that could support land purchases and offer the type of economic gifts that the Catholic Worker community used to purchase their farm. That is not to say that Black communities were destitute. The fact that groups like the NAACP, the SCLC, and the BSCP could organize the Prayer Pilgrimage is evidence of the social power generated by these communities. Black freedom movements used that power to march against violent opposition that was too often supported or ignored by state and federal law enforcement. Thus, even while they empowered each other, they could not take for granted basic civil and human rights due to Jim Crow segregation, which limited their access to economic resources that might have allowed them to pursue land for experimental farming efforts.

White allies like Templin worked out his philosophy of "total pacifism" on land provided by his employer, Ralph Borsodi. The School of Living, as understood by its board, was meant to spread "decentralist thought and action developing as a national movement with members as the nuclei of the decentralist way of life in their own communities."[37] Borsodi founded the School of Living in 1934 in response to what he called "the quest of comfort in a civilization evidently intolerably uncomfortable."[38] Borsodi described these uncomfortable conditions in detail in his book *This Ugly Civilization.* His critique of the poor conditions brought on by industrialization in both the city and the country flowed consistently through his work. The book explained the problems with industrialization and provided an alternative response to rebuilding the American state after the economic collapse of 1929. The School of Living used Borsodi's ideas to teach that modern societies need not succumb to the poor conditions but rather flee the crowded ways of city life.[39]

Borsodi's follow-up text, *Flight from the City,* displayed the positive outgrowth of his thinking by describing a "way of life" that Templin put into practice at the School of Living. In the book, Borsodi deplored the ways that industrialization made life difficult for both city and country dwellers, but he maintained that city conditions were endemically problematic and therefore incompatible with his homesteading vision. The proof, according to Borsodi, was that "millions of urban families are considering the possibility of flight from the city to the country."[40] The School of Living was the perfect setting for Templin to combine his own belief with Borsodi's idea that every man should "oppose ceaselessly, with his love, the violence within society which only periodically breaks out with war."[41]

The two homesteading advocates taught that "decentralization" was the key to ending the waste and exploitation associated with the industrial state. Templin referred to decentralization, that independent family-led homesteads should be the cornerstone of the back-to-the-land movement, as Borsodi's "big idea." Borsodi shared with *Christian Century* readers that this idea exposed the lies of industrialization: that mass production was more efficient than human work, that America needs coal and iron, and that interdependence with social institutions is the key to civilization. "The modern world," Borsodi wailed, "thinks in terms of giant farms, of industrializing all agriculture, and of moving people from the country to madhouses like New York."[42] He stated that though Americans were indoctrinated with the notion that bigger is better, all mass production, commercialization, and urbanization inevitably leads to war.

Templin was persuaded that abandoning city life for a new agricultural environment was essential to the antiwar movement. And though he was not alone in seeing a connection between war and agriculture, not everyone who made this connection believed it was necessary to move out of cities. White feminist social worker Jane Addams argued as early as 1922 that "peace and bread had become inseparably connected."[43] Her secular Hull House movement encouraged settlements in cities to aid those who were negatively affected by urbanization, industrialization, and immigration with the education, aesthetics, and food that Borsodi and Templin complained were missing.[44]

Instead of working in cities to build a radical movement that would aid African Americans and immigrants to overcome poverty and food insecurity, Templin encouraged fellow white progressives to look at the roots of war and flee the city to establish farm colonies, where they could take the soil as a radical alternative to militarism. Building on Borsodi's big idea, Templin argued, "Decentralized agriculture is one method of opposing centralized, intrenched privilege with its violence." Templin noted in the early 1940s that the farm community held significant "potential to set an example of creative production" for other pacifists to follow. He was a true believer in the notion that the farm involved the "economic means" to "[replace] violence with creative, cooperative love."[45]

Templin's belief in cooperative love was rooted in the decentralist value that the most important group in the world was the nuclear family. Decentralism also taught that industrialization destabilized that family and enslaved its members to capitalism. The School of Living's "Declaration of Principles for Decentralists," a statement against World War II, declared that nationalist governments forced families, who should be independent, to choose between a free and an enslaved state, and declared that freedom would only happen through a green revolution. In this paradigm, slavery was possible in both capitalism and socialism because their systems of ownership and control of property were centralized in a government. Government control of property guaranteed that the goods produced would serve the militaristic state. Centralization, then, was the opposite of the decentralized family groups, who had no desire for war and benefited only from their free associations with one another and the shared resources they produced on small-scale homesteads. Through this hands-in-the-soil approach, Templin believed the first and primary goal of the pacifist movement would be to "meet the needs of all God's children."[46]

However, Templin's experiments with the School of Living did not place him in close enough proximity to Black children to necessitate that he address their needs. His use of freedom and slavery metaphors at the School of Living did not refer to Black struggles in any way. Neither Templin's nor Borsodi's writings demonstrate any effort to invite their white colleagues to support descendants of enslaved Africans in their freedom movements, which were directly tied to the abolitionist tradition of fighting chattel slavery in the nineteenth century. Instead, what Templin called "the freedom tradition" referred to European groups escaping "the tyranny of church or state."[47] The decentralists' essays spoke of British tyranny and figurative notions of oppression due to unfair taxation. Like their white American revolutionary ancestors, they neglected to consider the differences between their cause and the struggle for Black freedom from federally mandated enslavement. As someone who was savvy in his correspondence with allies with whom he disagreed, it is possible that Templin omitted associating anti-Black oppression with the School of Living's project because Borsodi did not share his abolitionist values. It is just as likely that as the green movement rejected urbanization, Templin moved farther away from Black influences that might have encouraged him to make those connections.

Unlike Templin and Borsodi, Day never succumbed to the most extreme aspects of city antipathy. She maintained a headquarters for the Catholic Worker in New York City while pursuing Catholic Worker farms to complement them. Still, the Catholic Worker community did not make Black freedom a central component of its work either. While the *Catholic Worker* regularly published stories of the Black freedom struggle, often reprinted from the NAACP, those stories did not inform the farms in Staten Island, Pennsylvania, or upstate New York. Thus, Day's association with the back-to-the-land movement, like Templin's, was devoid of considering how Black activists addressed the loss of farm ownership and the capitalist exploitation of their bodies.

Clarence Jordan's initiative explicitly identified teaching Black farmers about agriculture as one of two emphases for Koinonia; the other was to support Black preachers. As previously stated, Day and Templin showed compassion for Black struggles against segregation, but this was mostly in the form of charity or abstract opposition to the American version of racial apartheid. Thus, Koinonia Farm presented a unique opportunity for Day and Templin to further their movements toward agricultural economies while challenging racial segregation—something they failed to do in their efforts to promote white homesteads.

Jordan was rare among white Southern Baptist preachers, as most of them were not known for their anti-segregationist activism. To Northern white agricultural pacifists who developed communities from which to support one another and the peace movement, Jordan was something like a folk hero. His jovial personality and bold opposition to Southern segregationist culture certainly buttressed that sentiment. Jordan's Southern context included a large population of Black sharecroppers and tenant farmers, of which neither the Catholic Worker farming commune nor the School of Living could boast. The possibility of racially integrated work, together with a preacher that boldly advocated for it, made Koinonia an exemplary organization for Day and Templin to support. Its context also made Koinonia a target for white supremacist violence.[48]

That Koinonia was in danger made Day's and Templin's charitable support for Jordan's farm more pressing and dramatic. Periodic newsletters provided supporters with updates of life on the farm. In a March 1957 newsletter, Jordan called on Koinonia's supporters to persevere in donating to his vision for Christian interracial fellowship because violence aimed at people and property threatened its survival.[49] Given this news, financial donations were not enough for Day. She was moved by Jordan's urgent and unrelenting reports that described the terror that Koinonians suffered from their white neighbors.

In April, one month before the Prayer Pilgrimage, Day took Jordan's call for support a step further than donations and traveled to the farm during Holy Week. During this visit, Day experienced the terror of challenging the color line in the South. "Last night I was shot at for the first time in my life," she shared with *Catholic Worker* readers. "I was shaken of course," Day recalled, "both from the fright and the cold air night." "Shaken" should not be confused with surprised. Everyone who supported Koinonia was aware of the white terrorism Koinonians faced for challenging Jim Crow norms. Reflecting on her stay in Americus, Day wrote that she had been aware of "dynamiting, machine gunning, isolated shots from high powered rifles," and a "long continuing economic boycott" against Koinonia prior to her visit. Many people were.[50]

Will Campbell, a white Baptist preacher, was also visiting Koinonia the same week as Day. He recalled that "firings always came on Thursday nights." When Campbell met Day, Jordan introduced her to him by saying, "This is Dorothy Day. Y'all have probably heard of her. She's from off up north. She stands her watch like the rest of us."[51] On the day she arrived, members of the community informed her that they had heard gunfire and found that five hogs had been shot the night before. White neighbors had also burned one house to the ground. The Koinonians did not passively receive these attacks. According to Day, they kept two watches, "one from eight until twelve, and the next from twelve until after three." Women and men took turns on the watch, though women most often participated in the early watch because it was viewed as the less taxing of the two. The watch was not devoid of danger, as it also consisted of sitting in a car and watching the cars that passed to see if they would stop to cut the fences or set fire to buildings.[52]

Day and her companion, Elizabeth Morgan, had been keeping the longer watch on Friday night when they were shaken by gunshots. Day read her breviary and Morgan played hymns on her accordion to pass the time. The Koinonians informed Day that Friday nights were notoriously "bad nights" because a lot of traffic passed the farm. Apparently believing that the farm's opponents would be reluctant to attack if they saw white Koinonians, the watchers had grown accustomed to exiting the car so that passersby could see that people were present. "But this time," Day recalled, "at one thirty, we were sitting in the first and second seats of a station wagon, under a floodlight, under a huge oak tree, and a car slowed up as it passed and peppered the car with shot." Though they "were too startled to duck," to their good fortune no one was hurt.[53]

Ralph Templin's support of Koinonia involved far less danger. He, like most supporters, paid a subscription to receive the farm's produce. He had visited the farm in 1956 but did not report any frightening personal experiences. Templin made a positive impression on the community. He engaged in regular correspondence with Clarence and his spouse, Florence Jordan. The Jordans remembered his visit fondly as a "happy weekend."[54] As an organizer of the *Peacemakers* newsletter, Templin regularly reported on or read about the farm. Due to his vocal support, the community reached out to him in hopes that he would return to the farm and offer hands-on support.

Wally Nelson, one of the few Black activists to ever live on the farm, represented the community's request in a letter he sent to Templin dated March 27, 1957—just a few weeks before Day arrived. Nelson and his partner, Juanita Morrow, were highly respected for their lifelong commitment to progressive activism and belief in Koinonia's mission. They volunteered to live at Koinonia to support the community's interracial efforts and to help them purchase supplies during the region's boycott. As a fellow member of the Peacemakers, Nelson knew of Templin's influence in the group. Aware of his networks and that his outsider status would enable him to also subvert the boycott secretly, Nelson informed Templin of the trouble he witnessed on the farm. He explained that the previous night, "Two shot gun blasts were fired into one of the farm's houses."[55] It is likely that the attack especially alarmed Nelson because Pop Wilson, a Black day laborer, and his partner lived at the house. This was not within the main cluster of houses in which white members of the Koinonia project lived. Instead, it was located approximately one mile away, where Wilson was thought to be far from the danger posed by interracial living. According to Nelson, "The racists have been trying to run him off the place." While the shooting at Wilson's house was most alarming, Nelson added, "In addition to the shooting[,] the hog field fence was cut four times. To say the least[,] business is picking up."[56] Thus, Nelson welcomed any aid that Templin could offer.

Koinonia's network was considerable. The Peacemakers' support gave the farm access to a wide array of Christian radicals, some of whom came to understand Koinonia's difficulties to a greater extent than Nelson and Morrow could in the three months they stayed there. To that end, Nelson recommended that Templin consult with their fellow friend, Elizabeth Morgan. Morgan had been at the farm longer than Nelson and would often keep watch at the gates of the farm in the evening. As such, she was fully informed of the latest events. Though Templin did not make another visit to the farm after the uptick in violence, he continued to support Jordan's work with financial donations and back-to-the-land advocacy. Three weeks after Nelson sent his letter to Templin, it was Morgan who sat in the car with Day, playing her accordion, when attackers shot at them. She was but one of many connections that Day and Templin shared.

Jordan, Day, and Templin were active members of the largest Christian pacifist group in the United States, the Fellowship of Reconciliation (FOR), which had a similar philosophy on racial segregation as the three white allies. The FOR was a multidenominational organization at the center of Christian pacifism in the United States since 1915. According to Leilah Danielson, "Though the FOR favored socialism, many of its members opposed strikes, viewing their coercive character as a form of violence." Their aversion to coercive practices would prove to be a significant hindrance to actualizing their rhetorical and philosophical opposition to segregation. That was because the predominantly white fellowship used their skepticism of coercion to avoid fully supporting Black initiatives against segregation. The white Christian allies featured the concepts of fellowship and race relations as organizing principles to address racial segregation, which amounted to little beyond rhetoric. By contextualizing segregation as a relational problem, they assessed the problem with Jim Crow segregation as a lack of interracial relationships and proposed activities that would move people to transgress racial boundaries that few of them crossed.[57]

US clergy founded FOR USA in 1915, a year after the International Fellowship of Reconciliation formed, to address issues unique to the US context. The terms "fellowship" and "reconciliation" doubly emphasized FOR's mission: "to end enmity between people, one to another, and to end the enmity between humans and God."[58] Reconciliation as understood by FOR referred to unity as a method for action against the forces of violence. When members created the US chapter, they believed, as W. E. B. Du Bois famously stated in 1903, that "the problem of the color line" was one of the central issues of American life and a small number of members of FOR organized to face it.[59] The word "reconciliation" in the organization's name did not refer specifically to race but more generally to the problems of war that separated people. Most members valued reconciliation in the manner Richard Roberts, a Quaker member, explained as "the convergence of two great movements of God to man and of man to God."[60] To the extent that the predominately white membership of the FOR addressed racial discrimination, they preferred a predictable pattern of prioritizing race relations, or getting along, over racial justice that aimed to end white supremacy in America.

The creation of the Congress of Racial Equality (CORE) is indicative of the manner FOR engaged with, or failed to engage with, racial justice. In 1942, James Farmer, Homer Jack, Bernice Fisher, and George Houser conceived a plan to give "birth to a revolution in race relations with a technique new to America that would change the face of this nation."[61] The plan was inspired by actions they undertook in Chicago. Farmer had led an action against a skating rink, aptly named White City, that refused to welcome Black skaters. He instructed a group of white co-conspirators to purchase tickets to White City and give them to Black members of the group. The action created circumstances that forced the skating rink to give account for why they denied entry to Black patrons. The staff explained that to enter White City, skaters needed to show membership cards that identified them as members of the private club that they claimed hosted the skate party. When Farmer pressed them to name the private club or prove that everyone inside the building had a membership card, it was evident that they could not because the white co-conspirators in Farmer's action had been permitted entry. It later occurred to Farmer that if they had been prepared, his group could have pursued legal action.

According to Farmer, the non-resistant purists of the FOR National Council considered "legal action to be *violent* because it did not seek to be loving, and because it relied upon police action for its enforcement, and police action is based ultimately on violence." Farmer, like many Black freedom fighters, was interested in strategies that would end racial discrimination through nonviolent means, but he was no purist. He argued, "Nonviolence and legal action must be twin weapons—either one being used when it seems to be most applicable, with each bolstering the other." Using this philosophy, Farmer "swore out warrants for the arrest of three persons at White City Roller Skating Rink: the manager, the ticket seller, and the ticket taker." Then he called an emergency meeting and raised enough cash to post bail for the three segregationists. As he put it, "The bailees were astonished." His use of nonviolent actions sought to shame and astonish. Most important to Farmer, they were effective.[62]

FOR had scheduled Farmer, one of the few Black members, to address an agenda item listed as "The Brotherhood Mobilization Plan." He proposed, "The FOR, because of its thorough-going commitment to nonviolence and brotherhood, take the lead in setting up a vehicle through which that non-cooperation with evil can be forged into a national movement." Debate ensued among the forty pacifists around whether his race relations methods constituted acts of persuasion or coercion and would cause conflict. Farmer won the debate by reminding the group of the theologian Gregory Vlastos's words: "He who preaches love in a society based upon injustice can purchase immunity from conflict only at the price of hypocrisy!"[63]

Though the group recognized the need for a group to address racism, instead of taking the lead in this race relations pursuit, FOR members passed responsibility on to Farmer to start an organization in Chicago as he saw fit. This organization became the Congress of Racial Equality. To say that FOR helped launch CORE in 1942 is technically true, given that Farmer was a member. It is also clear from the deliberations that most white members were not in favor of sponsoring an organization focused on race relations. Farmer's relationships went beyond FOR, which meant that he could establish the initiative without them. Since the idea was made public at FOR and the members blessed it, CORE became an entity through which white affiliates of FOR could claim that they had a part in promoting interracial fellowship, and when it was convenient to do so, they did.

Day, Templin, and Jordan showed interest in interracial fellowship prior to the creation of CORE, and their interests morphed into professional actions. FOR provided them with a network of like-minded white allies, plus a few Black ones. Thus, their associations with FOR ran deep. Day joined FOR in 1927 and remained a lifelong member. Jordan met Martin England, the cofounder of Koinonia, at a FOR meeting in 1941. Under the leadership of A. J. Muste, Christian radicals left FOR to establish the Peacemakers, which was dedicated to "holy Disobedience against the war-making and conscripting state." Muste invited Templin to organize the *Peacemakers* newsletter, which gave Templin a leadership platform to publish articles and to develop his vast network in the 1940s, which included Day and Jordan.[64]

As diverse as the Peacemakers' network was in denominational affiliation, it was not in racial, economic, or nonviolent philosophy. They were the inheritors of white social gospel ubiquity among Christian American progressives. Their unanimity on these matters produced a new stage in what Rayford Logan called "the astigmatism" of the social gospel.[65] White allies did not ignore race as their white social gospel forebears did. Rather, these midcentury social Christians managed to verbally advocate for an end to racial segregation while having little to no relationship with Black people. Whether Catholic, Baptist, or Methodist, white members routinely preferred to support white spaces, experiment with downwardly mobile economic strategies, and preach purist pacifist actions that failed to consider Black freedom perspectives. Their failures were likely one consequence of the racial segregation they critiqued; that is, even in their scorn for racial segregation, they often self-segregated into white spaces that they created to combat so-called economic slavery. Their main foe was capitalism, not racial injustice. Meanwhile, the descendants of chattel slavery, African Americans—some of whom were also social gospel practitioners—moved into urban spaces like the nation's capital to call for an end to racial violence and discrimination. Unlike their white counterparts, they demanded that politicians make the legal changes necessary for all races to pursue freedom by guaranteeing voting rights and equal opportunities for jobs.[66]

Allies failed to support Black pursuits of freedom because they often tokenized Black perspectives to give the appearance that their movements welcomed all people. Black participants were essential to Jordan's work at Koinonia, but they never achieved a level of decision-making authority to become true partners in the organization. Aware of the worldwide reputation of racial discrimination that sullied the reputation of Christianity in India, Templin started an ashram in Harlem to aid Black Americans in the struggle against racial oppression, but he did not stay long enough to see it through. Day's *Catholic Worker* used reports on Black struggles against racial exploitation to further her campaign to condemn communism and demonstrate that Christian socialism was the best alternative to capitalism. By the time Day visited Koinonia Farm, she had been engaged in this type of work for almost a quarter century. From the moment she established the *Catholic Worker* newspaper in 1933, she made notable efforts to portray it as a paper for all people—despite the internal opposition she received challenging that idea. Due, however, to her lack of structural racial analysis, she managed to manufacture a message that was more clearly anticommunist than pro-Black freedom.

Part II **For All People**

. . . .

2 Diversity

. . . .

> [The] black proletariat is not part of the white proletariat. Black
> and white work together in many cases and influence each other's
> wages. They have similar complaints against capitalists, save that
> the grievances of the Negro worker are more fundamental and
> indefensible, ranging as they do, since the day of Karl Marx,
> from chattel slavery, to the worst paid, sweated, mobbed and
> cheated labor in any civilized land.
>
> —W. E. B. Du Bois, "Marxism and the Negro Problem"

James Gooden relaxed on his porch in Greenville, Mississippi, after work-ing a long shift at the Mississippi Delta levee on July 7, 1927. He was one of thousands of Black men who were forced to rebuild the levees after the worst flood in US history destroyed the Army Corps of Engineers "levee-only plan." The great flood took over 1,000 lives and caused hundreds of millions of dollars in damage. The waters that flooded the region for months began receding in June, which encouraged Black and white residents of Greenville to celebrate together at an event sponsored by the Red Cross. Greenville's racial politics were unusual in Mississippi. Leroy Percy, a power-ful businessman and political figure, had successfully led a campaign to condemn the Ku Klux Klan five years earlier, keeping them out of the county. So when two white police officers, James Mosely and Pat Simmons, yelled an order for Gooden to enter their truck and work a shift at the levees, there was no reason for him to think his refusal to return that day would turn deadly. To Gooden's surprise, Officer Mosely pursued him into his home and once more commanded him to get in the vehicle while reaching for his gun. Gooden defiantly responded, "White man. Don't pull no gun on me!" To Gooden's misfortune, and the sorrow of many Greenville residents, Mosely shot him. Gooden died at the hospital. Mosely was arrested to de-escalate the racial fears of 4,000 white residents who thought the 10,000 Black resi-dents would riot, but he faced no further punishment. He was never even indicted.[1]

Similar stories from the levee camps became commonplace in Black presses throughout the nation and were tragically all too common for Black laborers who were forced to work inhumane hours under threat of physical violence. Due to the investigative work of the NAACP and the stories published in *The Crisis*, along with other Black press coverage, the issues that plagued Black delta residents gained attention even in some white publications. The inaugural issue of Dorothy Day's *Catholic Worker*, May 1, 1933, put the story "Negro Labor on Levees Exploited by U.S. War Dept." on the front page.[2] The story was not researched by the paper's staff but based on information that it republished from NAACP reports.

Whereas Black presses often concluded their reports with action items for their readers, much of *The Catholic Worker*'s coverage of Black exploitation revealed that Day's primary goal in publishing these stories was to attract Black laborers by showing them that the Catholic Church was racially diverse. She established the paper to combat communism, which was growing among Black workers. Out of her awareness that Black people were attracted to the Communist Party (CP), she used her paper to advertise the church as an alternative.

Day was not indifferent to racial prejudice. To the contrary, inclusion of stories that advocated for better treatment of Black laborers demonstrate her disdain for racial injustice. They also reveal that this disdain was somewhat superficially purposed to portray the Catholic Worker community as being hospitable to racial diversity. But the use of racially diverse stories that simply reported on Black issues exposed her lack of capacity to theorize capitalism's dependence on the exploitation of Black people in the American context. Day's inability to see the co-constitution of race and class in America was likely the result of her early experiences in socialist communities that acknowledged racial oppression but chose to organize only for general labor rights. In contrast to the Black radical presses from which she republished these stories, a close look at *The Catholic Worker*'s coverage of Black exploitation—especially in the Mississippi Delta levee camps and the Scottsboro Boys case—reveals that the paper actually tokenized Black experiences. Rather than take seriously the Black radical analysis of racial exploitation, *The Catholic Worker*'s coverage was largely a ploy to compete with the Communist Party rather than a way to join in solidarity with Black presses to strategize for Black freedom.

Lincoln Rice, author of *Healing the Racial Divide*, writes that Day's racial views were a product of her "racial liberalism, which describes a mind-set that does not tolerate 'overt bigotry,' but leaves institutional or structural forms of racism largely unaddressed."[3] This is a helpful starting place for contextualizing Day's understanding of what Du Bois calls "the problem of the color line."[4] To interpret her views further, I think it is necessary to recognize that Day's racial analysis emerged from the radical wing of white politics. That is, Day was interested in institutional and structural revolution, but her interpretation of Catholic social principles led her to believe ending racial discrimination was an ecclesial concern that depended on the masses converting to an anti-capitalist Catholicism. As we will see in the first issue of *The Catholic Worker*, this ecclesial perspective influenced her discussion of the problems of capitalism for Black people, but it did not recognize the ways in which class in America was built upon the scaffold of racial hierarchies. In other words, it accounted for white control of the means of production but *not* for the relegation of Black folks—and other minoritized races—to the labor class. Day's philosophy constituted a race-blind radicalism in the tradition of Eugene Debs and other socialists who did not make the shift, as did the CP in the 1920s, to attacking anti-Black oppression as central to the war against capitalist inequality.

Given that Black radicals and communists increasingly viewed race as a necessary obstacle to overcome for their revolutionary struggle, it may seem important, as Benjamin Peters recommends, to interpret Day's racial views through the lens of "racial capitalism"—the term made popular by Cedric Robinson that suggests that race and class are mutually constituting.[5] Certainly, the concept of racial capitalism enables us to more accurately interpret Day's understanding of race, but not in the way that Peters supposes. While the term itself was not available to Day, the ideas that undergirded this term predate Cedric Robinson's *Black Marxism* and can be found in Black radical interpretations of Marx in the earliest years of the Black freedom era. Simply put, Day's analysis of race and class did not share the same conclusions as the Black radicals we will discuss in this chapter. The more the freedom fighters wrestled with capitalism, the more they reworked Marxism to upend white supremacist economics. Day, on the other hand, actively campaigned against Marxism.

There can be little doubt that Debsian socialism continued to influence Day, but she consciously replaced her socialist allegiances, intellectually and personally, with a radical Catholicism that she used as an ecclesial alternative to CP politics. Make no mistake, Day shared with Black radicals an absolute disgust for anti-Black oppression, and she even risked her life while opposing racial violence in Americus, Georgia. That said, the articles that Day republished from *The Crisis* omitted Black radical interpretations of

Marx. Instead, her commentary on racial inequalities, while condemning anti-Black injustices, offered no explanation for why Black laborers were consistently exploited with greater violence than their white counterparts or why white unions refused to include Black labor. Nor did she offer any insight into the attraction Blacks felt for Marxism.

Day's failure to consistently report Black stories after the Great Depression or to confront racial injustices after 1957 demonstrated the paradox of her opposition to anti-Black oppression. On the one hand, she despised individual and state acts of racial discrimination; on the other, her focus solely on racial animus toward Black laborers, and not on the systemic conditions that sustained it, left her with little to say about the freedom struggle that continued after her visit to Americus. Furthermore, her trip to the predominantly white farm at Koinonia did not connect her to Black peers with whom she could have conversed over the ways Black radicals were remaking Marxism. Thus, after nearly a quarter century of highlighting news stories that condemned racial discrimination, Day failed to develop an analysis of racial exploitation that could explain why Black Americans were attracted to Marxism. The fact was that from the mid-1920s to the mid-1940s, Blacks found communists instrumental in their freedom struggle. Ironically, the same reports of labor exploitation at the Mississippi Delta levee camps and legal discrimination of the Scottsboro Boys that Day used to discredit communists contained all the data necessary to understand why Black American interest in Marxism grew. However, Day's ideological opposition to communism precluded her from making the connections necessary to accept that communism presented Black Americans with strategies for freedom that her evangelistic efforts did not. The interventions of the International Labor Defense (ILD) after the Mississippi Delta flood demonstrate this reality.

Mississippi Delta Levee Camps

The delta levee camps, which inspired blues artist Gene Campbell to sing in protest, "A levee camp man ain't got but two legs you know, but he puts in the same hours that a mule do on four," became the site for numerous investigations and news reports. One investigator, Helen Boardman, cursed the camps, saying conditions there were "worse than slavery." Boardman's condemnation of the camps provoked Roy Wilkins and George S. Schuyler to infiltrate the emergency shelters while posing as laborers. Wilkins labeled the work of Black laborers at the Mississippi levee construction camps "virtual slavery" because the camp management required twelve-to-fourteen-hour shifts seven days a week—rain, heat, sleet, or snow.[6]

"In some counties," Wilkins criticized the hypocrisy of the Bible belt culture, "it is that good old-fashioned religion which sees nothing wrong in working the hearts out of God's children and robbing them for six days a week, but insists the seventh day must be for rest and worship—to say nothing of counting profits and figuring out the exploitation of the next six days." This oppressive religion, with its feigned relief for Black labor under the guise of recognizing a Sabbath rest, did not differ much from the Christianity of the colonies, which persuaded Southern planters that proselytizing thousands of enslaved Africans would make them more manageable. The little profits that levee workers earned were nullified by commissary prices that required workers to assume debts that charged upwards of 25 percent interest. "These white folks don't do us right. . . . We works too hard and too long for the little money we gets," one laborer complained. Even clothed in the virtues of Christianity, levee camp work constituted something analogous to slavery.[7]

The 1927 flood destroyed almost 100,000 homes and displaced more than 636,000 people in Arkansas, Louisiana, and Mississippi. The flood "was the most significant event in America following the end of World War I," according to Richard Mizelle, author of *Backwater Blues*.[8] Over 75 percent of the people who became refugees in Mississippi were Black sharecroppers and tenant farmers. However, the Red Cross and Herbert Hoover—the secretary of commerce and chair of the Mississippi River Flood Committee—deliberately withheld information on the terrible abuses that Black people suffered at the levees. By doing so, they made it easier to collect donations for the rebuilding effort and hoped to boost Hoover's record on the flood, which he used to bolster his run for the presidency.[9]

The combination of the flood and the hazardous working conditions stirred an anonymous reader of *The Chicago Defender* to write a letter to Ida B. Wells that confirmed her reports of the Mississippi Delta as "the gridiron of hell."[10] Black men were separated from their families and forced to provide disaster labor after white refugees were relocated to safety. White people were housed in higher ground facilities and provided food, clothing, and health care. The Red Cross prohibited Black women from collecting relief unless they had a man in their family working the levees, details that had to be certified by a white man.

Not everyone who worked the levees had a home to return to after their shift. Black laborers were kept under the watchful eyes of white overseers who overworked them to the point of exhaustion. To ensure that the planters retained their labor after the flood work was complete, the Red Cross used soldiers who monitored entry to and exit from the camps. No unauthorized people were allowed into Black camps, nor were Black laborers allowed to leave unless the Red Cross approved of their destination. Officials mandated that Black laborers wear tags displaying the planter for whom they worked before the flood. White planters and the Red Cross relied fully on Black labor for repair of the levees and future cultivation of the land. For their labor, Black men were supposed to receive a dollar per day. That money was rarely paid. Meanwhile, Black laborers and their families accrued massive debts due to withheld pay and the high prices of goods in the commissaries.[11]

The Crisis

White presses like *The New York Times* reported on the flood, but their stories conveyed fantasies of "hard-working refugees, benevolent Red Cross leaders, and renewed kinship between the South and the North."[12] If not for the Black press, the plight of laborers at the camps would be largely unknown outside the region. Thanks to the NAACP's *The Crisis* magazine, news of the injustices spread. Unfortunately, conditions at the camps had not changed in five years since the flood, despite Black requests and American Federation of Labor petitions made to Herbert Hoover, who was four years into his presidency, to intervene. Instead of putting an end to abusive management, Hoover limited the scope of responsibility in the region by absolving the Red Cross of any wrongdoing: "The national agencies have no responsibility for the economic system which exists in the South or for matters which have taken place in previous years."[13]

Stories of racial injustices at the levees filled Black newspapers across the nation. National white presses reflected Jim Crow attitudes as much as any institution with gross misrepresentation of the facts or with no coverage at all. As such, it was imperative that Black communities establish their own publications to guarantee that their stories and values would be represented in ink. It was this reality that inspired W. E. B. Du Bois to establish *The Crisis* as counterpropaganda to white news outlets that seldom mentioned Black people. What white media reported about Black concerns could too often be described as disinformation and justification for anti-Black violence. Generally, when Black people made the pages of white newspapers, they were portrayed in the worst light as vagrants, violent criminals, or victims in need of white saviors. Black editors understood that if public opinion was to ever look favorably on African American life, even if only among other Black people, then they would need alternative sources of information than white presses were willing to offer. The injustices Blacks suffered at the levee camps became feature stories in *The Crisis*. Indeed, the Wilkins and Schuyler investigation led to a crucial report titled "Mississippi Slavery in 1933."[14]

As one of the vanguards of Black journalism, Day's use of *The Crisis* was a savvy way to gather stories from a radical Black source whose headquarters was not far from that of *The Catholic Worker*. *The Crisis* office, located at 69 Fifth Avenue in New York City, was the NAACP's first official publication. Du Bois founded the magazine in 1910, one year after the Niagara movement established the NAACP. The publication included visual art, photographs, plays, poems, and other print pieces that represented Black life, but Du Bois emphasized that it would first be a vehicle for issues that affect Black people. Second, *The Crisis* valued the opinions of people concerned with the race problem. Unlike white editors, Du Bois made his bias and agenda explicit: "Its editorial page will stand for the rights of men, irrespective of color or race, for the highest ideals of American democracy, and for reasonable but earnest and persistent attempts to gain these rights and realize these ideals."[15] This stand for rights that were denied by anti-Black laws did not mean that the magazine would lack journalistic integrity. To the contrary, by stating very clearly its commitment to truth and a race-informed perspective, it held honesty in the highest regard. Du Bois's ultimate purpose was to counter the inadequate coverage of African American life and interests in the white press with a publication that would be "a record of the Darker Races." In all of this, he implored readers to "remember that we have one chief cause—the emancipation of the Negro."[16]

The Crisis was the most popular of several Black radical New York City news sources that provided powerful critiques of economic, social, and political life in America, but as an arm of the NAACP, it was not the most radical.[17] Du Bois, as editor, agreed with a frequent criticism that *The Crisis* was not revolutionary. Chandler Owens, editor of *The Messenger*, disagreed. From his perspective, Du Bois's views too narrowly defined revolution as violent. Dismissing the criticism, Owens suggested that Du Bois's sympathies for Marxist social change made him as much of a revolutionary as other Black editors, even if they disagreed on how anti-capitalist change should come about.[18] Instead of violence, Du Bois advocated reform for the people of color in the world and rejected white radicals who did not include the plight of Black labor in world economic philosophies. He argued, "There is no sense in a peace program which takes no account of the world-wide economic war upon colored peoples."[19]

The Voice, The Challenge, The Messenger, The Negro World, The Crusader, and *The Emancipator* were each among the radically orientated Black presses that opposed white exploitation of Black labor and Jim Crow injustices. These news sources demonstrated the importance of the Black press, namely that Black subject matter and Black perspectives were crucial to the Black freedom movement. The media outlets openly campaigned against white lynch mobs, especially challenging the failure of white presses, white Christians, and white officials to address the plague of lynching. In response, James Weldon Johnson, the esteemed activist and diplomat, explained, "The utterances of these publications drew the notice of the Federal Government, and under the caption 'Radicalism and Sedition among the Negroes as Reflected in their Publications' they were cited in a Department of Justice report made by Attorney General Palmer in 1919." In *Black Manhattan,* Johnson wrote, "The radicalism of these publications ranged from left centre to extreme left; at the extreme it was submerged in what might be called racialism." The notoriety of *The Crisis,* which Johnson viewed as representative of the threat that the Black press represented to state and federal institutions, garnered a visit from the Department of Justice. Johnson believed that Du Bois's response to one of the Department of Justice's questions during that encounter, "What are you fighting for?" best encapsulated the significance of the Black press: "We are fighting for enforcement of the Constitution of the United States."[20]

These news sources held back no criticisms of white society. According to Johnson's research, *The Challenge* was the most radical of the presses. Provoked by the Red Summer of 1919, the editor of *The Challenge,* William Bridges, blamed the US government for the ongoing lynching epidemic across the country. That summer, twenty-six cities witnessed ordinary white people join mobs that lynched over eighty Black people and destroyed Black-owned property. Bridges demanded "that full responsibility for lynching be placed where it properly belongs—on the American Government." He argued, "Each and all of these are component parts simply of the organism of the United States subject to its laws and not above them."[21] From his position, nothing was gained by isolating responsibility with either the mobs who practiced lynching or the state governments that permitted it. In a 1927 *Negro World* op-ed, Ernest Mair called out "The Hypocrisy of White Liberalism," whose socialism shortsightedly criticized capitalists for living luxuriously while others starve. "If you think they are talking about the Negro, then you have another guess coming," Mair cautioned his readers.[22] He summed up the feeling among his peers, "They tell you that they see no reason why they should single the Negro out for favor when there are so many of their own race in need in which I concur, and by the same sign I will have none of them or their works."[23] Just as the white press spoke from the perspectives and concerns of the white middle class, Black presses made no apologies for centering the concerns of their race.

The Catholic Worker

By the time Day created a newspaper for the Catholic Worker movement, she had already gained considerable experience in print media. During college, she wrote articles for the school paper inspired by her participation in socialist gatherings. Soon after, she joined the staff at *The Masses* and continued with its successor, *The Liberator*, under Max Eastman. Day was not a story chaser; rather, her journalism was tied to knowledge she gained from socialist-leaning circles, where she learned the philosophies of SP leader Eugene Debs, among others. Socialist advocacy against capitalist exploitation of laborers was central to her reporting. Upon joining the Catholic Church, Day found components of socialist antagonism to religion untenable. Unlike Protestant social gospelers, who had found ways to integrate socialism into Christian practice, Day viewed socialism as inherently atheist.

From the first issue of *The Catholic Worker*, Day wanted readers to know two things: that it was an alternative to the communist *Daily Worker* newspaper, and that she published it for laborers of all races. "*The Catholic Worker*, as the name implied, was directed to the worker, but we used the word in its broadest sense . . . we thought primarily of the poor, the dispossessed, the exploited," she wrote in her autobiography.[24] Perhaps no group in America was as exploited as levee camp laborers. Day explained, "In the first issue of the paper we dealt with Negro labor on the levees in the South, exploited as cheap labor by the War Department."[25] Day purposed to make the paper racially diverse, with stories about Black labor by Black authors, and thereby draw Black workers whose interests in communism had intensified as the CP fought for their right to living wages and humane working conditions.

By naming her paper *The Catholic Worker* and issuing it on May Day, she placed her movement in direct competition to the CP. From the very beginning, Day made clear that "the purpose of the paper is to combat

communism and atheism by showing the social program of the Church."
In her campaign against communism, she believed that the newspaper was
"taking away from them one of the weapons communists have been using against the Church, namely, the charge that it is allied with capitalism
and an enemy of the worker." Throughout her crusade against communism,
Day was able to maintain friendly relationships with Marxists in Greenwich Village, who chided her on her Catholic beliefs. In an editorial for *The
Daily Worker*, her communist friend Mike Gold criticized the Catholic
Worker movement as "a Trojan horse for the Vatican in the progressive
movement, a stalking horse, window-dressing."[26]

Day was not pleased with Gold's characterization, but there was merit
to his claim that the movement endeavored to infiltrate communist gatherings and gain converts to Catholicism. Communism posed a problem for
Day's desire to attract Black laborers, because by 1933 the party's popularity had grown significantly among Black communities. "Our idea is to have
Negro artists and writers get out the paper," she explained in a letter. "So
that," she continued, "by the time we have reached two hundred thousand
circulation and are well established, the fact will be well established in the
minds of Catholic America (and Communist America too) that the paper is
not a paper for black or white but for the Catholic Worker—all Catholic
Workers."[27]

Under the suggestion of Arthur Falls, a Black Catholic from Chicago, Day
changed the masthead in the third issue to reflect her intent for racial diversity. "The paper is for the Negro and white," she said. "On the masthead
there is a white worker on one side and a Negro worker on the other, and in
addition to handling the problems of the Negro race, we want to have Negro writers for our paper, writing not only on race problems but on social
justice in general." For the first decade, *The Catholic Worker* consistently
printed stories of national concern to Black Americans. In total, the paper
published forty-five stories that directly opposed anti-Black discrimination,
making those themes the third most in the paper. Nearly half of the stories,
twenty, were printed in the first three years. Interestingly, the highest number of articles opposing anti-Black discrimination appeared in the first
year; none appeared after 1966.[28]

The frequency of the race stories caused conflict within the movement.
On the day the first proofs returned, Peter Maurin, Day's mentor and movement cofounder, appeared less than pleased with the subject matter. Stories
describing "exploitation of Negroes in the South, and the plight of sharecroppers; child labor in our own neighborhood; some recent evictions; a lo-

cal strike over wages and hours; [and] pleas for better home relief" did not reflect Maurin's intent. He was a Catholic layperson with a deep passion for personalism, voluntary poverty, hospitality houses, and agronomic communities. He believed that individuals ought to be the initiators of changes in society. Those individuals would experience the most freedom to transform society by unbinding themselves from capitalism. This freedom was made possible through the mystical body of Christ, where they could experience the spiritual equality and community of Catholicism. The Catholic community could then extend charity to less favored fellows in Houses of Hospitality, which Day and Maurin saw as the essential arms of their movement. As a vehicle to share those messages, Maurin supported the concept of a paper. But he objected to publishing stories that were not directly related to those issues, stating that race concerns were a distraction.[29]

Day "was pleased" that the stories clearly reflected her desire to build a racially diverse community. In her mind, that was their collective goal. After a few days, Maurin verbalized his "great sadness" over features that included Black concerns in the paper. "It's a paper for everyone. And everyone's paper is no one's paper," he lamented. After voicing his disapproval, Maurin retreated to upstate New York for a significant time. Day was disheartened, but she pressed on.[30]

Maurin's displeasure did not thwart Day's designs for the paper to attract laborers from all racial groups. It was not the first time that she had directly opposed a friend who dismissed her hatred of racial prejudice. During her time with *The Masses*, Claude McKay, her Black colleague at the socialist paper, recalled that when an editor would casually use the word "nigger" to refer to Blacks, a few white writers would "feel embarrassed, but do nothing." Day, on the other hand, "would rise and threaten to slap the face of the offender" if they used the word again. Her pacifism was well known, but her indignation concerning overt racism superseded it. Upon joining Catholicism, she brought her indignation at racial prejudice with her. She believed that there was no place for racial animus in the mystical body of Christ. *The Catholic Worker* provided another space for her to express her refusal to acquiesce to racial discrimination. Her membership in the church and career as a journalist further motivated her to confront unjust treatment of racially minoritized people. Her work on the levee camps story, then, was consistent with her longtime personal commitment to racial kindness.

Growing up around her father, Day learned of racial animus firsthand. She once described him as a journalist and a typical Southerner who shared typical segregationist attitudes about Blacks. In a later interview, Day named her father as a racist from Tennessee. She recalled that he used the word "nigger" casually, like when he said, "Of course nothing is so cute as a little nigger baby." Comparing Black babies to mules, he taught her that "baby mules and baby niggers are the cutest things on God's earth."[31] His use of racial slurs was not solely a type of infantilization. In her autobiography, Day said she was aware of her father's distrust of immigrants and social-ists. Despite this, she believed him to be a good man. In her opinion, nei-ther his anti-Black nor his xenophobic views disqualified him from the human family. Therefore, she was required to love him. Day asked rhetori-cally, "Who are we to go ahead in righteous indignation condemn?"[32] She had learned, no matter the repugnancy of her family members' racial atti-tudes, how to retain relationships with them. Judging from the stories in *The Catholic Worker*, retaining relationships included naming the transgres-sions of even her most respected authority figures. From her home life to her stint with *The Masses, The Liberator*, and finally *The Catholic Worker*, she put her confrontational tolerance for overt racial hostility to the test.

On May 1, 1933, Day brought the paper to a May Day celebration to share with communists. Whereas, Maurin had qualms with the newspaper's race coverage, the May Day radicals who gathered in New York City's Union Square were most troubled by *The Catholic Worker*'s religious appeals. The gathering exemplified the efforts that the CP, the Industrial Workers of the World (IWW), and the editors at *The Liberator* had put into fighting the ex-ploitation of Black workers. Day complained that despite their openness to Black people, they still had no intellectual space for Catholicism. Amid the leftist speeches and literature, *The Catholic Worker* sold very few copies that day. Day's literature championing radical Catholic religion littered Union Square but did not find its way into many hands. However, May Day was just the beginning. The paper grew in circulation, from 2,500 copies in the first issue to 55,000 over ten years. At its height, May 1938, the paper was distributing 190,000 copies.[33]

The Catholic Worker was late to the coverage of the levee camps, but it provided opportunities for its readers to catch up quickly through its reprint-ing of NAACP reports. In the first two paragraphs of the article "Negro Labor on Levees Exploited by U.S. War Dept.," it summarized Roy Wilkins's report, mostly to communicate that since 1932, the state had been made aware of the issues and done nothing to remedy the problems. According to Wilkins, two private investigations had revealed that Black people work-ing on the levees labored seven days a week for upwards of sixteen hours a day without overtime. In addition to the injustices associated with the commissary overcharging laborers, the story mentioned that "men have been beaten and kicked by brutal foremen."[34]

The feature explained that when Wilkins and Schuyler traveled to the region in 1932, they encountered first- and secondhand stories like the one's detailed in other sources. Word of their investigation traveled around the city after they shared their report at Abyssinian Baptist Church in Harlem. *The Crisis* staff wanted the public to understand that everything the Black press communicated about the situation in Mississippi was accurate—even though the camps were worse than anything anyone could describe in print. Most importantly, Wilkins and Schuyler were the best people to share it because they had insider knowledge of the situation. Who could refute them? They experienced the camps firsthand.[35]

Wilkins worked a camp in Greenville, and Schuyler worked a camp in Vicksburg. The camp at Greenville operated closer to residential populations. Such camps were typically nonresidential, which required workers to either live at home and commute or reside temporarily at boardinghouses. The conditions of the camps were unsanitary and rife with disease. Being separated from Schuyler, Wilkins likened his mission to that of being "a spy deep within enemy lines."[36] He learned of the treachery of War Department officials after they were confronted with Boardman's report. Unsurprisingly, perhaps, the officials were more upset about the NAACP investigations than the inhumane treatment of the laborers.[37]

In his 1933 article for *The Crisis*, Wilkins made three propositions: first, to "secure a senate investigation which will officially record the existence of levee slavery"; second, to "get the levee construction placed within the provisions of the eight-hour law"; and third, to "secure the prevailing rate of wage scale for levee workers."[38] Wilkins's main point was that Hoover and his War Department disregarded the first two reports and made no efforts to follow up with them. Yet Wilkins persisted in his agitations until Hoover appointed a new commission. The president had appointed a group of Black commissioners in 1927, but few people trusted that they would be able to act freely given their federal allegiance. Furthermore, the recommendations they made were not the kind that the government wanted to address. After numerous complaints, Hoover appointed new commissioners in 1928—three Black and one white, two Republicans (which most Black voters supported as the party of Lincoln and Douglass) and two conservatives—but this new commission also lacked the support of the people. In truth, more than support, it needed resources. The commission never got off the ground, and there was likely little intention for it to actually conduct any research. It was appointed shortly before the presidential election, which meant that most political resources and attention were given to campaigning. According to the NAACP report, "Immediately after the election it was found that there were no funds available."[39]

The details Wilkins and Schuyler provided in January at Abyssinian Baptist Church became the material they used for the reports they sent to the White House and printed in *The Crisis* in April. Day reprinted only segments of their reports. In what would become a pattern in *The Catholic Worker*, the editors highlighted the shortcomings of radical groups that represented competition to Day's goal to win communists over to Catholicism. For instance, during his investigation, Wilkins discovered that Holt Ross and Thomas Carroll of the American Federation of Labor (AFL) had also engaged in an unofficial investigation. However, the AFL fired Ross, presumably because the president of the organization disapproved. The NAACP, particularly Du Bois, regularly criticized the AFL for clandestinely creating barriers for Black laborers to join their unions while publicly stating that Black laborers were not interested in joining them. Du Bois saw such claims as outright lies. Day seized this opportunity to casually ridicule the AFL by including Wilkins's criticism, which was the longest paragraph in the paper's reprint of the story. Though there was no commentary in the paper's first story about the delta levee situation, an editorial attack on the AFL was an attempt to signal to workers that *The Catholic Worker* cared about the welfare of Black people more than the AFL did.

It was uncommon for a white newspaper to put Black stories on its front page and to cover other stories that criticized white abuses throughout the same issue. In this way, *The Catholic Worker* was no common paper. Day's desire to win Black laborers required the paper to feature stories pertinent to Black experiences. But while the newspaper explicitly criticized the officials at the levee camps, its inclusion of *Crisis* reports was of secondary importance to its primary agenda: competing with the Communist Party for the loyalties of Black laborers. The Catholic Worker movement valued increased Black fellowship, not Black freedom. This agenda becomes clearer in *The Catholic Worker*'s coverage of another national story about racial injustice in that same issue: the Scottsboro Boys case.

Known popularly as "the Scottsboro Boys," the nine young Black men involved in the case were neither all boys, nor were they from Scottsboro. These nine young men—some adults, some children—had found themselves in legal trouble with a white mob while on their way to Chattanooga, Tennessee, in pursuit of employment.

Economic depression in the 1930s caused many folks, Black and white, to seek employment far from their homes. The Scottsboro case, along with the CP's rise in popularity, was a direct result of the Jim Crow conditions of the Great Depression and set the stage for one of the most infamous court cases in US history. The Depression was a notoriously difficult time for most Americans, but it was devastating for the Black population. By 1932, the urban unemployment rate for Black Americans, at over 50 percent, was twice that of white unemployment. Still, both groups were desperate for work, which often inspired able-bodied laborers to jump train cars in the hope that new locations could provide better opportunities.[40]

On March 25, 1931, a group of Black youths got into an altercation with a group of young white jumpers on the Southern Railroad freight run from Chattanooga to Memphis. After being dispelled by the Black youths from the train, the group of white youths alerted an official at the nearby depot that they had been assaulted by a Black gang. That official reported the white jumpers' version of events to authorities at Paint Rock, Alabama. The county sheriff proceeded to deputize every gun-owning white man in Paint Rock. When the train reached the town, the white mob accosted the nine Black young people. In a twist, two white women emerged from the train and, out of fear that they would be arrested for illegally crossing state lines to engage in sex work, accused the nine Black youths of rape—a conviction punishable by death in Alabama. Eight of the nine were sentenced to death in Scottsboro the next day. The Scottsboro Boys, "together or separately, endured 16 trials, two United States Court reversals, as many as four series of death sentences, and prison terms ranging from 6 to nearly 17 years."[41]

The page 2 story of the May Day issue—"Communists, Despite Noise, Are Not Only Defenders of Scottsboro Case"—announced the competition Day had initiated with communists. The article began, "Nowadays the streets of New York are lively with the shouted slogans of Communist Negroes who are parading, holding meetings of protest against the decision in the Scottsboro case." In naming the political persuasion of the protesters, Day set up the article to be primarily about something other than "one of the nine Negro boys who have been in jail for the last two years" having been "condemned to death once more." Instead, the story made Day's competition with communists the focal point. "Communists have a flair for getting hold of an outstanding case of injustice," she wrote, "and making of it a cause célèbre and a means of publicizing their propaganda and making converts." Out of outrage that newspapers, like *The New York Times*, had given communists too much attention, Day highlighted the NAACP's recent attempts to represent the nine young men. The article claimed that the ILD—the communist legal advocacy group—was simply using the controversy to inflate the reputation of the Communist Party. To reinforce this idea, the article concluded with a dig at the communist press, claiming it had nothing to say about the "Negroes who are doing work along the Mississippi."[42]

Black Marxism

Day offered no explanation as to why Blacks were attracted to the CP in New York, only displeasure. Details may have provided important context for the increasing Black membership in the party during the Scottsboro trial; in fact, New York was not the only state where Blacks were persuaded by the communist message. Robin D. G. Kelley writes, "Communists were all over the South, from Chattanooga, Tennessee, to Oxford, Mississippi, influencing communities and individuals in ways we have yet to understand, making history we have yet to know."[43] Black sharecroppers, tenant farmers, church members, and caretakers found outlets in communist organizing for opposing Jim Crow practices and gender proscriptions. According to Kelley, "The Party and its various auxiliaries served as vehicles for black working-class opposition on a variety of different levels ranging from anti-racist activities to intraracial class conflict." As such, it might have been illuminating for Day to investigate the aspects of communism that drew Black laborers to its ideas, rather than to assume that they had no agency and were merely manipulated by communist propaganda. Black laborers were not passive in their decision to participate in the party. To the contrary, their participation inspired innovations that made local communist chapters appealing to Black folks in ways that *The Catholic Worker* failed to convey.[44]

In the previous decade, the CP had made major changes to its platform, which opened possibilities for Black innovations. In 1919, the Communist Party of the United States of America established itself as a new home for disaffected members of the Socialist Party (SP) who demanded revolution. At that point, neither the SP nor the early CP voiced much concern for the plight of Black laborers. Largely composed of recent immigrants to the United States, socialist and communist groups neglected issues in Black life. It was not that they never voiced outrage over racial discrimination, but rather that they did not believe it could be solved by addressing race. They taught that all discrimination, even when it was obviously racial, was a by-product of class issues, which they defined as solely economic. Though most left-wing socialists at the time opposed racism, they tolerated "openly racist" members. Capitalism was their enemy, and their analysis of capitalism did not understand racial exploitation to be a necessary component of it. Therefore, they were in no position to adequately address anti-Black exploitation.

Eugene Debs, a founding member of the SP and its five-time presidential candidate, once described Black history, through its narration of the exploitative practices of white society, as "a history of crime without parallel." He opposed racial discrimination, but he reduced it to a class problem. "The real issue," he argued, "is not social equality, but economic freedom." Debs advocated a color-blind position. He instructed members of his party to say "'The class struggle is colorless.' The capitalists, white, black and other shades, are on one side and the workers, white, black, and all other colors, on the other."[45] Marxists began to reject that advice in 1919, when Vladimir Lenin issued a worldwide purpose for communists to defend workers of every race in every region. He singled out Black Americans as those in need of communist revolution. At the 1924 American Communist Conference, the opening address placed racial equality as the CP's primary goal. By 1928, many of the speakers at the national assembly were Black, and in 1932, the CP ran a Black vice presidential candidate, James Ford, on its presidential ticket. It was clear that the party was ready to take down Jim Crow.[46]

Black presses took notice. *The Crisis* published a manifesto from the CP's executive committee that made demands consistent with the NAACP's campaigns: a federal law against lynching, political and social equality, abolition of all Jim Crow laws, abolition of laws that disenfranchise, abolition of laws that prohibit Black children from attending public schools and universities, abolition of all laws forbidding intermarriage, abolition of the convict lease system and the chain gang, removal of restrictions from trade unions, and equal opportunity for equal pay for equal work for Black and white workers. This was a remarkable change from the behavior Du Bois had witnessed in related labor organizations, where they routinely prohibited Black workers from membership. While recognizing the shift, Du Bois criticized pro-union voices for neglecting to offer effective strategies for Black equality. This new communist position was far superior to that of the SP, which kept Blacks out of the AFL, and even to that of the Brotherhood of Sleeping Car Porters, which supported the Democrat presidential candidate solely because he was in favor of prohibition.[47]

Du Bois's editorials in *The Crisis* routinely pointed to the problems represented in political organizations that thwarted the progress of Black people. He criticized the white supremacist attitudes and actions of Southern Democrats, whom he referred to as "lynchocrats." He also recommended Marx's *Capital* as one of the greatest books ever written, but he did not trust socialists because they ignored racial discrimination in their gatherings when it was advantageous to add numbers to their white unions. The new positions from the CP were in step with his own, but communism was far from mainstream at the time. In addition to the challenge communism represented to capitalism in America, the party's vocal solidarity with Black workers incited hostility from white governmental and nongovernmental institutions alike. Black communities, however, were intrigued.[48]

Day's understanding of racial discrimination mirrored that of Debs. She had learned of Debs through a newspaper she read during college. While there, she joined the Socialist Worker's Party at the age of sixteen and continued to surround herself with socialists through young adulthood. In 1916, she became a writer for a socialist paper, *The Call*, through which she interviewed Leon Trotsky and heard from Emma Goldman, anarchists, radicals, and members of the IWW. A year later, she joined *The Masses* under the leadership of Max Eastman, the Greenwich village radical journalist. In these circles, in which Debs was viewed as a hero, color-blind approaches to racial animosity prevailed. Thus, as a budding Marxist, Day's views on race remained unchanged. After she joined the Catholic Church in 1927, her major criticism of the party concerned her understanding of communism's animosity toward religion. As a college student, one of her professors had convinced her to adopt the Marxist argument that religion was "the opiate of the masses," which she obviously rejected when she converted. However, the atheism of her Greenwich Village Marxist friends and colleagues reinforced this idea. Consequently, Day concluded that communism was godless. This view left Day with little intellectual curiosity for discovering what may have attracted so many Black laborers to it.

Kelley's study of Black communists in Alabama demonstrates that Black Christians—like the Black communist who escorted a *Daily Worker* reporter, Joseph North, to Chambers County, Alabama—studied communism alongside Christianity. North noted that the Black communist was an African Methodist Episcopal elder who read his Christian Bible nightly. In addition, he could quote extensively from "the Book of Daniel and the Book of Job . . . and he's been studying the Stalin book on the Nation question."[49] And he was not alone. Other Black Christian farmers in Alabama believed that communism offered solutions to their struggles to improve working conditions in the South. Instead of interpreting communism as conflicting with their

Christianity, they integrated communist teachings with their reading of biblical sources.

That said, Black farmers' syncretistic practices were due just as much to their own persistence as to the party's outreach. As of 1930, the party had "all but ignored the black belt during their first year in Birmingham."[50] In 1931, however, Black farmers responded to the exhortation of Birmingham communist leaders to follow the example of Arkansas sharecroppers who organized with unemployed townspeople to demand poverty relief. The *Southern Worker* received increased requests for full information on ending food insecurity and details on the CP.[51] This curiosity did not require that Birminghamians leave their religion behind. The 1931 Black cohort of new members in the Birmingham CP were all active church members, some of whom sang in gospel quartets. The CP appeared to have strategies to improve the quality of the lives of Black laborers, and they were eager to act on them. As the legal arm of the CP, the ILD offered Black farmers power in the courts that they had not yet experienced. The Communist Party, unlike the Socialist Party and the Catholic Worker movement, was more than talk. Their work with the Scottsboro case proved that they would fight for every demand they published in the 1928 manifesto.

White Salvation

Instead of being encouraged by the thought of Black communist Christians, Day viewed the communist presence as an intrusion to Black churches. In an article titled "Communists Seek Entry to Negro Churches," she complained about the attention communists gave to churches in Scottsboro as a tactic to propagandize Black Christians. She was disturbed that the ILD's efforts caused "Negro ministers to throw their church doors wide open to Communist speakers" and continued to press her program to reject communist expansion into Southern life.[52] Noting that Leon Trotsky believed that Black laborers were more likely than the larger group of white workers to lead the proletariat struggle for equality, she admired the tenacity of the communist efforts. Day saw and knew firsthand the strides that communists were making among Black communities, in both the North and the South. Her friend and colleague Claude McKay represented the growth of the CP among Black New Yorkers. Through her anticommunist hermeneutic, she interpreted these advances as threats to the welfare of Black people. For this reason, she issued a command to the Catholic Church that it must consider imitating the communists' efforts to win over Black workers. Justice and love were important, but Day also believed that it was of greater import to save Black workers from the communist efforts in Scottsboro.

The NAACP advocated for the Scottsboro Boys in *The Crisis*, but its reluctance to provide legal defense opened the door for the CP to represent them. When the NAACP finally decided to get involved with the legal defense, it was too late. The ILD seized the opportunity to represent the young men as soon as they learned of the case, and with their years of practice, they prepared them for the events to come. The ILD, which provided free legal representation to victims of labor disputes, lynchings, the KKK, and numerous forms of anti-Black discrimination, was formed by the Communist Party in 1926. The Scottsboro case was different in that it had the potential to be the highest profile case of them all. The communist attorneys marketed and strategized a historic defense for the Scottsboro Boys that would capture the attention of the nation. As a result of their efforts, the Scottsboro case established two important legal precedents—that defendants had a right to trial by a jury of their racial peers, and that defendants had a right to adequate legal defense. The NAACP accused the ILD of using the publicity to bolster its reputation, which was probably true. It was also likely that the NAACP recognized the ILD's intentions because it also wanted to benefit from the publicity once it had determined the innocence of the accused.[53]

The high-profile case provided publicity for everyone involved. Day, too, used the case to bolster the profile of the Catholic Worker. She did not perform her own investigations or research into the case; rather, she echoed the opinions of the NAACP through its reports in *The Crisis*. Her own anticommunist leanings convinced her to side with the NAACP in its dispute with the communists and subsequently to trust the reports coming from *The Crisis*. Based on her reading of *The Crisis*, Day reported that the ILD was unjustly commandeering the legal defense for the Scottsboro Boys and ineptly taking their futures into its organization. But the ILD hired competent attorneys, like the ACLU's Clarence Darrow of Scopes trial fame, and swayed national opinion toward the accused. Due to the party's Black membership, neither was it offering charity to a group to which it had no relation. The failure of Day to recognize that the feud between the NAACP and the ILD in the 1930s could have been construed as an intra-Marxist debate as much as an intra-racial fight—or simply a conflict between political organizations who shared the same wing of radical struggle—shows a lack of appreciation for the attraction Black people, including Du Bois, had to communism. The NAACP's competition with the ILD made it appear anticommunist, even though Du Bois's views on socialism, the Communist Party, and radicalism in general were more complicated than outright dismissal. Black freedom fighters, like Du Bois, were not looking for anyone to save them; they were creating new conditions that would prove Leon Trotsky right—that a radical coalition of Black workers, church folk, and writers would lead the United States out of economic slavery into a Marxist future of freedom.

In a May 1933 article in *The Crisis* titled "Marxism and the Negro Problem," Du Bois recommended that Marx's *Capital* was one of four books that everyone needed to read, along with the Bible, Immanuel Kant's *Critique of Pure Reason*, and Charles Darwin's *On the Origin of Species*.[54] Du Bois, a Sunday school teacher and lifelong Episcopalian, would, in the twilight of his life, come to see communism as the fulfillment of Christian ideals in political life. He concluded that Marx's thesis in his *Communist Manifesto*—that the "whole history of mankind . . . has been a history of class struggles"—was a "living and insistent truth."[55] Du Bois had integrated Marx's historical analysis decades prior in his articulation of race history in America in a number of projects: "Die Negerfrage in den Vereinigten Staaten (The Negro Question in the United States" (1906), "The Economics of Negro Emancipation" (1911), and "L'Ouvrier Negre en Amerique" (The Negro worker in America," 1911).[56] Even as early as 1897, Du Bois pointed to the essential connection between race and class as an all-encompassing history of "the races," which Americans minimized because of their allegiance to "the laissez-faire philosophy of Adam Smith."[57] In the decades that followed, Du Bois argued that in the United States, class was replaced by making color into a caste.[58] As the editor of *The Crisis*, Du Bois also published articles in which authors equated the words of Jesus with those of Lenin, and on one occasion made Du Bois himself part of a triumvirate of pro-labor intellectuals alongside Marx and Lenin.[59]

As the NAACP's founder, Du Bois's perspective on Marxism was the most prominent. Furthermore, like Du Bois, the NAACP was not of one opinion as it concerned communism. Du Bois voted for the party's presidential candidate in 1928, but mostly because he believed that "neither Hoover (the Republican) nor Smith (the Democrat) wanted the Negro vote and both publicly insulted us."[60] He advocated for Black people to use their vote opportunistically, by which he meant that they should vote for candidates that offered the best quality of life for Black people, whatever their party. Du Bois offered praise to the CP in the late 1920s for their recruitment of Black voters, as opposed to the Republicans or Democrats. He had never witnessed either of the two parties put together a recruitment strategy as strong as the CP's.

Despite his praise of Marxist ideas, he did not join either the SP or the CP. As he understood it, socialism was too silent on Black labor to move white people to oppose anti-Black discrimination, and white people were too committed to exploiting Black labor to listen to the communist push for Black freedom.[61] In addition, the NAACP's indecision in deciding to represent the Scottsboro Boys, coupled with the swift actions of the ILD, put the organization in competition with the communists, which Du Bois took personally. Nevertheless, some NAACP staff commended the ILD's efforts. The front page of the April 24, 1931, edition of *The Daily Worker*, for example, displayed a letter written on NAACP letterhead from William Pickens, field secretary of the NAACP, in which he wrote of the Scottsboro case, "This is one occasion for every Negro who has intelligence enough to read, to send aid to you [*The Daily Worker*] and to I.L.D."[62] In other words, *The Crisis*'s relationship to Marxist-influenced activity was complicated.

The Crisis's coverage of the Scottsboro case was rife with attacks on the CP over the perceived insults the NAACP experienced during the conflict. The NAACP's frustration with the party had everything to do with the ILD stealing the limelight and very little to do with philosophical disagreements. As the world would see in two years, when Du Bois published *Black Reconstruction*, freedom fighters employed thorough analyses of the capitalist problem that put Black labor at the center. "Indeed," Du Bois wrote, "the plight of the white working class throughout the world today is directly traceable to Negro slavery in America, on which modern commerce and industry was founded, and which persisted to threaten free labor until it was partially overthrown in 1863."[63] He argued that any remedy for the problem would need to consider that race was not an accidental by-product of the issues facing white workers but rather the source.

Whatever struggles Du Bois had articulating the relationship between capitalism and anti-Black exploitation in the 1920s, it was absent by the early 1930s. He anticipated Cedric Robinson's concept of "racial capitalism" when he argued, "The resulting color caste founded and retained by capitalism was adopted, forwarded and approved by white labor, and resulted in subordination of colored labor to white profits the world over." Herein he surmised that capitalism and race were inextricably linked, but the result only benefited white economic elites, regardless of white labor support. White labor's support of white elites unknowingly committed them to their own demise. He continued, "Thus the majority of the world's laborers, by the insistence of white labor, became the basis of a system of industry which ruined democracy and showed its perfect fruit in World War and Depression."[64]

Based on what we have seen in Black radical engagement with Marxist theory, Day's analysis of the conflict between the NAACP and communists was overly simplistic. Day used the NAACP's polemics to convince her readers that it was possible to be "Radical but Not Communist," as one of *The Catholic Worker* headlines read. Black radicals not only proved that it was plausible to be Black and communist but also proved that it was possible to be communist and Christian. Radicals like Du Bois also learned that the "black proletariat is not part of the white proletariat." This was borne out by white radicals who minimized anti-Blackness in the labor struggle. Day, in her tokenizing Debsian approach, exemplified Du Bois's critique. Her suggestions insufficiently comprehended how the particular experience of Black labor had led freedom fighters to different conclusions that neither entirely embraced nor rejected the CP.[65]

In a short article in the same issue of *The Catholic Worker*, Day included a warning from Black historian Rayford W. Logan to the 24th annual congress of the NAACP that "a new radicalism among American Negroes, stimulated by the migration northward from the South, the World War, and the depression, is spreading steadily."[66] But it was not a radicalism stimulated by the Great Migration; the new Black radicalism was the result of thorough academic study, private conversations, and public debates in Black radical presses. Through *The Catholic Worker*, Day intimated that she could stop the spread of communism. Though siding with the NAACP in its conflict with the CP became a primary tactic that allowed Day to portray *The Catholic Worker* as an ally to the NAACP, she failed to accurately represent the spirit of the NAACP's radicalism, because that was not her goal.

Day's anticommunist goals and the allyship she portrayed with the NAACP proved largely ineffective among Black workers. It did not help that her friend circles were mostly composed of Greenwich Village white radicals. Even when she networked beyond those circles, she failed to recognize the appeal of communism for Black workers. Thus, opportunities to influence them were few. There were, however, two significant exceptions to her attempts to make *The Catholic Worker* a paper for all races: First, Chicago physician Arthur Falls embraced the paper as an opportunity to educate Black Catholics about the pitfalls of capitalism and the social teachings of the Catholic Church; and second, Claude McKay—her longtime communist friend—credited Day for his conversion to Catholicism after spending time at Catherine de Hueck's Friendship House in Harlem in 1944.[67]

These two men were easily the most notable of the Black converts to Day's movement. McKay, a prominent author whose poetry and short stories helped define the Harlem Renaissance, shocked his Greenwich Village community when he converted. It was a dramatic turn because he left the Communist Party and experienced a religious transformation that seemed out of character to his past associates. Despite her distaste for the term, he credited Day's "Catholic Communism" for spurring his conversion.[68]

Day's other close Black associate, Arthur Falls, did not require her goading. His participation in the Catholic Worker movement was more of a lateral move than a conversion. Falls was a lifelong Catholic who shared Day's concerns about the oppressive forces of capitalism for Black people. In the first edition of *The Catholic Worker*, he saw common cause with Day. His vision for the paper paralleled Day's. He, too, wanted the paper to be for all people. That was why he recommended that she change the masthead from two white workers to one Black and one white—an idea to which Day eagerly assented. Yet soon thereafter, the elation over their masthead collaboration waned. Day allowed Falls to start a Catholic Worker meeting in Chicago, but he took it in an economic direction of embourgeoisement rather than voluntary poverty. Falls's desire for economic uplift put him at odds with Day, and her disappointment with Falls's efforts sharpened her commitment to the reductive class analysis of her white radical Catholicism.

3 Charity

· ·

> It would seem that the time is ripe for the development of a Catholic
> Worker group in this city to further stimulate not only the interest in
> race-relations but also in all other social and economic problems with
> which Christian groups must concern themselves and about which, it is
> reported, our Catholic people show an appalling lack of knowledge.
>
> —Arthur Falls, "Chicago Letter," 1936

The NAACP's *The Crisis* had its proverbial fingers on the pulse of more than
Marxist debates in Black communities. In 1933, it noted that a Black
organization, the Federated Colored Catholics (FCC), was under siege by
white Jesuits who plotted "to make the white priest instead of the black lay-
man the real head of the organization." The circumstances were so familiar to *The Crisis*'s editor, W. E. B. Du Bois, that he mocked the priests'
motivations with a parody that other Black leaders who worked with white
allies would recognize: "Don't segregate yourselves!" he pilloried the priests.
"Let's all get together, whites and blacks, and let the wise whites lead you!"[1]
With this caricature, Du Bois voiced the feelings of many Black freedom
fighters in the FCC, whose faith in the power of white allyship to further
the cause for Black liberation was in short supply.

The former president of the FCC, Thomas Wyatt Turner, founded the
organization because he believed that Black Catholics needed to draw their
white peers' attention to the degradations they suffered in Catholic institutions. He surmised that if the group was able to gather stories of Black Catholic experiences from around the nation, then they would prove that racial
discrimination was "too flagrant and positive a wrong to be tolerated for a
moment by the Church after its attention has been sufficiently called to it."[2]
With this intention, the organization became a powerful voice for Black
Catholics when its leaders called for increased ordination of Black priests,
admission of Black students into Catholic schools, and the unity of all Catholics in 1924. According to Marilyn Nickels, the FCC's demand for more
Black clergy was an indictment against the Josephite Fathers and Brothers.
The Josephites were charged with ministering to Black people after the Civil

War. However, their "failure to admit Black candidates to their seminary" exposed the pervasiveness of anti-Black discrimination even among Catholic leadership who intended to give special attention to Black Catholics.[3]

The FCC's demand for white officials to admit Black students to Catholic schools was also a direct rebuke of Catholic University's conformity to Jim Crow Catholicism, which had not been a factor when Turner attended the institution twenty-three years earlier. As bothered as he was by Catholic University's new policy, the issue went beyond his alma mater. Turner was deeply committed to the Catholic Church and believed that Catholic education was essential to keeping Black youth connected to the tradition. Without educational connections, he believed it would be impossible for them to share unity with their worldwide Catholic kin. It was important to Turner that Black Catholics were empowered to gather their own evidence for their faith and use their own voices to champion their concerns for their church. Turner and his associates explained, "We do not feel that adequate opinion of [the] needs and necessities of the Negro can be received from anyone except the Negro himself."[4]

Priests saw Turner's attempt to organize Black voices as a problem. In 1932, two priests, Father John LaFarge and Father William Markoe, removed Turner from leadership and briefly changed the name of the FCC to the National Catholic Federation for the Promotion of Better Race Relations (NCFPBRR), which changed to the Congress for Interracial Federation (CIF) two years later. This change in nomenclature was one step toward securing LaFarge's vision for an interracial fellowship led by white clergy and putting an end to the lay-led Black federation that Turner built. Furthermore, the takeover allowed Markoe to assume sole leadership of the FCC's journal, *The Chronicle*, which LaFarge renamed the *Interracial Review*.[5]

The *Interracial Review* quickly became a force in defining Catholic solutions for racial segregation in the church and the nation, which directly influenced Dorothy Day after Arthur Falls, the Black physician from Chicago, introduced it to her in 1934. A year later, the *Interracial Review* listed Day and Falls as board members of the new federation. By that time, Markoe had released the journal to LaFarge because the Jesuit council threatened to censor it. Under LaFarge's editorial oversight, the journal espoused the philosophy he called "interracialism," which "shunned all mass organization, boycotts, pickets, and demonstrations."[6] In 1936, Day gave LaFarge a regular column in *The Catholic Worker*, where he made pitches to potential subscribers. It is unclear what Day knew of the interracial leadership controversy that had ensued over the three years prior to her involvement, but between her acquaintance with Falls and the national gossip surrounding the white Jesuits' takeover, it was likely she had some awareness of the events that had transpired. Nevertheless, her new Black acquaintance's optimism about white leadership was likely enough to quell any of Day's concerns.

Day met Falls during a time when he believed in the power of white clergy to strengthen Black membership in Catholicism. Falls participated in the FCC during Turner's presidency in the 1920s, but unlike Turner, he initially welcomed the possibility that LaFarge's and Markoe's status would enhance the federation's influence. Falls's optimism for the NCFPBRR's interracial philosophy coincided with his excitement for Day's radical Catholicism. Thus, he became an enthusiastic supporter of *The Catholic Worker* upon reading it in 1933. Shortly thereafter, he wrote a letter to Day in which he suggested that she replace one of the two white laborers on the masthead with a Black one. She enthusiastically agreed.

Day and Falls subsequently developed a relationship that inspired the creation of a Catholic Worker community in Chicago. However, Falls's vision for the community in Chicago was quite different from Day's. She wanted to expand the House of Hospitality movement. Falls organized an intellectual house where he led discussions about raising the financial status of Black Americans. In short, he encouraged Black embourgeoisement, which would render charity unnecessary.

In my analysis of these models, charity and interracialism relied on assumptions that Black people needed white leadership to thrive in the Catholic Church. This chapter will show that Falls sought solidarity with white Christian kin that would result in economic empowerment rather than charity. He understood that charity paradigms did not promote economic freedom. Instead, they kept Black people perpetually dependent on powerful white people, who gained little more than moral standing from joining in solidarity with poor Black people. The clash in paradigms—charity versus solidarity—eventually fractured the relationship between Day and Falls, especially after she undermined his Black Catholic Worker activities in Chicago.

The subversive actions of white Catholic leaders, in both the FCC and the Catholic Worker movement, expose a trend whereby white Catholics undermined Black-led movements for decades. The propensity of white leaders to hinder Black movements—in the Church and otherwise—also impeded their own interracial efforts. Furthermore, while some white Catholics valued integration with Black Catholics because it demonstrated the power of Catholicism to overcome racial division, they disagreed on which methods were most effective. White Catholics generally barred Black people from enjoying the full fruits of Catholic fellowship. Those white Catholics who wanted racial barriers lifted tended to support charity models of ministry like the Josephite Fathers and Brothers or Dorothy Day's Catholic Worker Houses of Hospitality.

Black leaders of the FCC, on the other hand, largely rejected charity programs for those who were not facing immediate crises. Instead, they created organizations that urged white people to reimagine the doctrine of charity by sharing the blessings of Christian equality, not by supposing that Black people existed in a perpetual state of material poverty. Nor did they desire white Catholics to believe that Black people lacked the ability to make decisions or the capacity to lead initiatives, which would require charity. The white charity model was built on the notion that white people should be benefactors for Black people who would never transcend impoverishment. Looking at the Catholic Worker movement through the history of Black Catholic organizing reveals that neither the philosophies of interracialism nor charity were effective in making it the movement for all people that Day insisted on. Most importantly, they were ineffective strategies for liberating Black Catholics from the racial control of Jim Crowism within the church and beyond.

A Legacy of Black Catholic Resistance

The story of the FCC—and the white priests who dismantled it—reminds us that most Black Catholics did not seek white saviors. Black Catholics had a history of organizing to empower themselves through reforming the church. That is, before Dorothy Day devised her strategy for reaching out to Black laborers, Black Catholics had established orders, circulated publications, and developed church leaders so that the church might live up to its creed of unity. But these efforts were often undermined in the process. Remarkably, Black Catholics held on to their faith that despite its anti-Black animosity, the church could sustain them in body and spirit.[7]

A brief survey of Black Catholic history demonstrates that faithfulness was a consistent attribute of Black Catholicism. Records of Black baptisms and marriage dating back to colonial America show that Catholicism provided spiritual sustenance for Black families who escaped the Anglican Carolinas and chased freedom into Catholic Florida colonies. Later in the antebellum period, the Oblate Sisters of Providence established a religious society challenging white Catholic racial myths that denied Black women the attributes of virtue that white women received. Black men overcame racial stereotypes by gaining membership into the American clergy—like Father John Tolton, the first Black priest in 1886, and John Randolph Uncles, John Henry Dorsey, and John J. Plantevigne through the Josephite seminary. And a generation before Turner and Falls, Daniel Rudd's newspaper and his movement of Black congresses proved that Black Catholics could make changes in post-Reconstruction Catholicism.[8]

Rudd's *American Catholic Tribune* (the *Tribune*) set the stage for the FCC and predated *The Catholic Worker*'s appeals to Catholic social teaching and calls for racial justice. Coincidentally, Rudd died in 1933, the same year that Day put *The Catholic Worker* into circulation. Rudd began publishing the *Tribune*, the first Black Catholic newspaper, in 1886. Continuing until 1897, the paper was a testament to the work Black Catholics undertook to make their witness visible in the church. Rudd was more than a publisher and journalist; before his death, he created a movement for racial change that transformed the trajectory of Black Catholic organizing. In 1897, Rudd called together Black Catholics to participate in the Colored Catholic Congress, almost thirty years before Turner convened the first meeting of the FCC. His organizing vision was so influential that white Catholics imitated his congress structure too. In this way, Rudd's activism anticipated the most important social movements in the church at the turn of the century. As such, his congresses provide important context for the interracial conflicts between Turner and LaFarge and between Falls and Day.[9]

According to Catholic historian Cyprian Davis, the first congress gathering demonstrated two things. First, it indicated that an "active, devoted, articulate, and proud" Black Catholic community existed.[10] Second, it showed that members of the Black Catholic community could be trained for clerical leadership. Rudd had originally called for a gathering like this in the May 1888 edition of the *Tribune* with an article titled "Congress of Colored Catholics."[11] The congresses, he reasoned, were comparable to Catholic immigrant conferences that met to discuss issues pertinent to their communities. Rudd aspired to bring together Black Catholics from across the United States to learn of the resources they possessed to contribute to improving their status in the church. Through such a gathering, Rudd believed that the Catholic Church could erase the color line. He was also convinced that heretical parish boundaries existed between, and within, Catholic structures that could thwart his plan.

Rudd thought that Jim Crowed parish boundaries resulted from white priests' toleration for anti-Black discrimination. He believed that they were heretical because they fractured the unity of the body of Christ. Instead of distancing himself from the church, however, he offered a theological perspective that was representative of many Black Catholics who remained dedicated to a community that inadequately recognized their gifts. Through the *Tribune*, Rudd presented perspectives of underappreciated Black people who loved the church but who also faced anti-Black discrimination. Anti-Black barriers barred them from opportunities to enjoy the Christian unity that was central to Catholic teaching. To reform American Catholicism, Rudd appealed to the witness of Catholics in Africa, where the pope encouraged Black Catholics to obtain clerical positions that guaranteed their full participation in true Catholic orthopraxy.

Aimed at Africa and Asia, Pope Pius XI's 1926 encyclical discouraged missionaries from viewing the objects of their activities as "members of an inferior race."[12] Consequently, African and Asian Catholics benefited from a rise in Indigenous clergy. Rudd appealed to this teaching in the American Catholic Church context. However, he found that a distant notion of Catholic universality on other continents was no substitute for Catholic unity in the United States. Catholicism's failure to promote Black clergy inspired him to publicly protest the hypocrisies in church life through the *Tribune* and to organize meetings at which Black Catholics could demand that their white Christian kin change their ways.

White clergy also attended the congresses, but they opposed Rudd. At the fifth congress, for example, Father John Slattery, a representative of the Josephites and therefore viewed as an expert on Black Catholics, preached that Catholicism was the best religion for Black Americans because the "holiness and sanctification" of Methodist camp meetings and revivals led to too much "whirl and excitement."[13] His sermon took a sharp turn when he implored the Colored Catholic Congress to quell their activism by embracing two virtues: patience and silence. His admonition for Blacks to wait silently was a gradualist position that had charmed white moderates since the antebellum period and exasperated Black activists, who had waited too long for their voices to be heard.

The congress met only a few times, and the *Tribune* barely lasted eleven years. Though Rudd's projects did not last as long as he would have liked, Davis suggests that "the black lay Catholic congresses were not a failure."[14] Rudd's appeal to Catholic unity energized Black Catholics to unite against their second-class church status and inspired them to seek empowerment for Black Americans. Rudd's message was not limited to reforming Catholicism, for he hoped it would have positive consequences for the nation. In his original "Congress of Colored Catholics" article, he explained that there was a "tendency on the part of some people to ignore the Negro as a man and citizen in the United States," but with a united course of action he persuaded present and future Black Catholics that they could transform both church and state.[15]

With unity at the heart of his work, Rudd's newspaper and congresses set the stage for Turner's FCC. Like Rudd, Turner understood that Jim Crow Catholicism threatened any hope for the American church to achieve the singular ecclesial vision of the mystical body of Christ. Lack of unity was at the heart of Black Catholics' struggle with the church. They were disheartened by the discrimination they experienced from congregations who were unwelcoming, by white ethnic priests who discouraged them from living in their neighborhoods, by schools that refused them admission, and by an episcopacy that would not ordain them. Their frustrations arose from the dissonance between Catholic ecclesiology established on the doctrine that Christians shared one baptism and one communion, and practices in local parishes that contradicted that theological conviction through racial discrimination.[16]

Regardless of the hypocrisies they experienced, Black Catholics strived to practice the unity in Christ. It was a doctrine handed down from the fourth century that, according to Albert Raboteau, enabled twentieth-century theologians to explain how "individual priests might be bigots," but "the sacraments worked *ex opere operato*, independent of the disposition of the priest." He explained that Black Catholics held the contradictions paradoxically: "The mass and popular devotion linked black Catholics to the timeless, cosmopolitan church of Rome, which was one, holy, apostolic, and catholic. And yet, the tension remained."[17] Something akin to Du Bois's double consciousness manifested in Black Catholic membership. They were Black and Catholic, "born with a veil and gifted with second-sight in this American world," and therefore they "knew all too painfully that race did matter in the church in America."[18]

Interracialism and the Federated Colored Catholics

Just as Rudd had organized talented Black Catholics to make strategic changes in Catholic fellowship, Turner's organization made space for them to further the work of Catholic unity. Therein, they held the Catholic Church to the claims of its ideals and called for church leaders to cease proclaiming unity while simultaneously raising barriers to Black participation. Turner's experience of such hypocrisies motivated him to create the FCC.

The organization began as a fifteen-member group in 1918 that moved to action when they learned that Black soldiers did not receive the same services from the Catholic Church as did their white counterparts during World War I. A year later, they criticized the Josephites—the missional order created as an outreach to African Americans—for not allowing Black Catholics to study in their white seminary. Following these actions, the FCC announced four goals: union among all Catholics, eradication of racial obstacles, equal status of Black Catholics, and cooperation with episcopal leadership to promote the welfare of all Catholics.[19]

Turner argued that only a Black-led organization could accomplish these goals. His opposition cleverly used interracialist rhetoric to rebut him. In a letter to his attorney, Turner explained that because the FCC was initially created as an avenue for Black Catholics to address concerns unique to their race, detractors accused them of discriminating against whites. He argued that there was a vast difference between the de jure and the de facto Jim Crow segregation enforced by white American institutions and the Black-led structure of the FCC. Anyone familiar with the FCC knew that white people were welcome to participate—Markoe had done so for years. From Turner's perspective, the priests' accusation misleadingly equated racial-justice-minded rejections of segregation with objections to Black-led organizations empowering disenfranchised members of the church. Without acknowledging the imbalances in decision-making power—episcopal power, economic power, or social power—of the predominantly white church membership and clergy, Turner's opposition used the rhetoric of interracialism to claim that racially monolithic gatherings discouraged Christian unity. From this perspective, the only legitimate way to lift Black people above their inferior status in the racial hierarchy was through methods that included white leadership. But Turner refused to equate Black-initiated caucuses that empowered their collective agency with Jim Crow–inspired segregation that used white episcopal power to isolate Black groups from one another and silence their dissent. With this power analysis, Turner asserted that a Black-led FCC was necessary because "it is the only organization in the Church which will ultimately succeed in breaking down Jim-Crowism, and certainly it is the only vehicle through which the Negro Catholics have had a chance for free expression on the questions of policy in the Church."[20]

An organization that existed to speak to Black Catholic concerns was essential to a people that claimed only 2 percent of church membership.[21] The dearth of Black Catholic leaders meant that there were few official ways to voice concerns about the pervasiveness of racial discrimination in American Catholicism. In the South, where the majority of Black Catholics lived, the church "was essentially a Jim Crow church, with parishes, schools, church societies, and even Catholic Universities usually segregated."[22] The vast majority of Southern bishops refused to support Black clergy or orders in the region. Not to be outdone, Northern parishes were typically embroiled in turf battles between established white Americans and new European immigrants who were restricted to neighborhoods that protected notions of white purity and high property values. Priests in these neighborhoods encouraged their members to purchase houses that would create stronger bonds between their ethnic kinship and their parish. Following the lead of their priests, Irish neighborhoods attempted to protect Irish congregations from Italian immigrants, Italian parishes attempted to bar Polish immigrants, and European immigrant communities discouraged Black people from living among them.

The instructions of white clergy, not immigrant obedience, represented the greatest obstacles to Black Catholic freedom in the Jim Crow era. Priests disrupted the attempts of Black Christians to enjoy the full blessings of their churches. Jay Dolan explains that among clergy, "boss rule was not so commonplace or real in the nineteenth century, but by the twentieth century it had become the accepted norm."[23] It was in this spirit that LaFarge and Markoe opposed Turner's composition of the FCC. LaFarge outlined his interracialist argument in a white paper addressing the validity of the organization. Using his knowledge of church procedure, he argued that because the FCC was a federation, it had to be approved by the episcopacy, an approval that could only be made official by putting clergy in advisory roles. Moreover, he posited that Black and white representatives were required in the federation to offer evidence that it encouraged unity. LaFarge reasoned that "a possible change of name (Catholic Interracial Federation) should be seriously considered."[24] Through establishing themselves as proper institutional authority, the priests executed a takeover of the FCC and its journal, ousting Turner from leadership in a closed-door meeting.

With Turner gone, the FCC, an organization that began as an idea for empowering Black Catholics, briefly became the NCFPBRR, and finally emerged as the CIF. The CIF was led by two white priests who acknowledged the efficacy of Black affinity groups but failed to see any value in Black-led

Catholic movements. The changes in the names of the organization and the journal were more than cosmetic. LaFarge and Markoe transformed the federation's purpose from increasing Black agency to increasing white comfort in Black initiatives. LaFarge strangely admitted that even though collaboration with white people had its advantages, "the Negro will find in certain instances that it is more practical and profitable to have his own fraternal organization, or his own church society."[25] He even named a few organizations in which that was the case. However, LaFarge denied that possibility to the former FCC. The CIF required an interracial fellowship of cooperation, trust, and faith in the motives of its white members. LaFarge prohibited Black members from questioning the goodwill or motives of white participants. They were ordered, instead, to give them the benefit of the doubt. Apart from the members who remained and adapted themselves to LaFarge's vision of the mystical body of Christ, nothing of Turner's FCC remained. "Instead of raising a cadre of black leaders," concludes historian David Southern, "the Catholic interracial movement actually helped create a vacuum of black leadership in the church."[26]

When Day joined the CIF, those who opposed the new configuration were gone. Falls and other Black members of the former FCC remained, but Turner had no role in the new organization. (Turner rejoined the FCC when a small number of supporters reconstituted it and appointed him as president. The FCC continued to meet in that capacity until 1952, but with no publication to amplify their voices, the reconstituted FCC gained very little momentum.) A great concern for Falls and those who had put their faith in ousting Turner was that the new white leaders of the CIF, LaFarge and Markoe, were conspicuously aloof from the organization. By 1935, they had completely moved on from it. The Jesuits sent Markoe to Minneapolis, where he had no affiliation with Turner or LaFarge. Meanwhile, LaFarge continued his interracial crusade through what he identified as a "more effective organization," the Catholic Interracial Council of New York (CIC).[27] Without a robust philosophy of the racial politics in America that went beyond the color-blind class analysis that Day gained in college and in her associations with her Greenwich village circle of atheists, it was LaFarge's CIC that informed her on the philosophy of Christian interracialism.

The events that led to the demise of the FCC are instructive to a general trend in the Catholic interracial movement and what transpired in Day's work with Falls in Chicago. The words of white leaders often contradicted their actions. LaFarge worked out this dissonance through the *Interracial Review*, in which he declared his intention to improve Black people. He also centered his belief in the importance for "white friends of the Negro to re-member that Negroes as a body, have a vast fund of experience," but he de-nied Black Catholics the power to challenge white concepts of fellowship or to implement Black ideas.[28]

Interracialism amplified the voices and participation of white people in racial harmony programs, but it weakened Black ideas and efforts to im-prove Black people's status in church and society. The impact of the white clergy's takeover of the FCC and subjugation of Turner led to an entirely new organization. Without Black colleagues, LaFarge made himself the sole administrator of the CIC. In that role, he instructed white people to respect the expertise of Black people, but he denied that expertise in his own prac-tice. After a thirty-year career in interracial ministry, LaFarge confessed to be the true expert on racial healing. He explained, "Although the Negro is the victim of discrimination, he does not necessarily know the answer or the cure."[29] Southern argues that by ousting Turner, transforming the mag-azine, and preaching interracialism, "LaFarge was more successful at im-proving the church's image than in changing the church's behavior."[30] LaFarge's interracialism influenced Catholics, white and Black, for decades. Day and Falls were among his disciples, and each hoped that interracial-ism would benefit their cause.

Houses of Hospitality

As we see from this history, by the time Day thought her newspaper could be used to evangelize Black laborers, the church already had an antagonis-tic relationship with Black Catholics. The Catholic Worker movement did not share the racial animosity of some Catholic clergy and institutions, but the concept of racial animus inadequately describes the depth of the barri-ers Black people faced in the Catholic Church during the Black freedom era. To be Black and Catholic required a parishioner to hold to the universality of Christian kinship in theory while struggling against anti-Black discrimi-nation in practice. For Rudd, the absence of Black leadership in the church motivated him to organize Black affinity groups that would force the church to recognize their presence and hear their calls for reform. For Turner, the conflict between theory and practice inspired him to transform the church by organizing Black Catholics against the racial contradictions that re-stricted their opportunities for Christian fellowship. Falls surmised that to organize against apparent contradictions between orthodoxy and ortho-praxy, he needed to align himself with white clergy who had the power to make institutional changes. Day did not recognize any contradictions. Rather, she idealized the Catholic fellowship as a possible site to convert Black people without warning them about the paucity of Black clergy or the general state of Jim Crow Catholicism that freedom fighters struggled against daily.

Day's failure to represent the church in its fullness may be due to her belief in the mystical body of Christ, which is composed of the members of the church with Christ as their head. She believed that conversion to Catholicism would overcome any societal divisions that kept members from spiritual union with God and one another. This view was precisely what Black Catholics struggled to actualize. In contrast, Falls referred to the distance between the doctrinal ideal and the lived reality of Blacks as "the mythical body." Black sensitivities to the contradictions between church teaching and church practice comport well with Falls's mythical body critique. Lincoln R. Rice points out that it was due to Falls's high view of the mystical body of Christ, of which he believed that all races were part, that he fought for full integration. Falls believed that the mystical body should grant equal access for all races to the blessings of unity with Christ and one another throughout American Catholic life. The mythical body, by contrast, excluded Blacks from aspects of church fellowship, especially in higher education and the clergy.[31]

Day's belief in the promise of the mystical body made starting a hospitality house an urgent matter. How else could the Catholic Worker prove that all people could share in the unity of a Christian economy if her pro-labor movement did not embody that in practice? "We need Houses of Hospitality to show what idealism looks like when it is practiced," Maurin agreed.[32] On another occasion he told Day, "We need houses of hospitality to give to the rich an opportunity to serve the poor."[33] Maurin taught that the heart of a truly Christian economy was charity and voluntary poverty. His emphasis on charity was essential to his and Day's understanding of the structure of Christian fellowship. The church took seriously Paul's lesson to the Corinthians on the importance of faith, hope, and charity—the latter being the virtue that "binds everything together in perfect harmony."[34] Charity was, as expressed in the church's catechism, both "to all commanded" and a duty "towards all without exception."[35] This requirement for charity was met by the Catholic Worker movement through a hierarchical economy that required poverty so that others could practice charitable giving.

Maurin believed that money was important insofar as it was exchanged for goods or services and between the rich and the poor, but not when the rich invested it in markets. It needed to change hands so that it could serve its purpose. Poor people were important to his philosophy because they used money as he thought it was intended: to purchase goods. Contrarily, using money for investment was a capitalist strategy that, in his understanding, only benefited the wealthy. Investments discouraged businesses from focusing on products that served society and ultimately increased unemployment. From his view, such business practices were detrimental to the quality of life for impoverished people. Maurin's perspective on voluntary poverty celebrated the have-nots in ways that challenged American culture's myth of the American dream. Rags to riches novels like F. Scott Fitzgerald's *The Great Gatsby*, along with the biographies of Andrew Carnegie, Edward Bok, and Jacob Riis, taught that America was the land of opportunity, where upward mobility was not only possible but also the goal of a progressive society.[36] Maurin lamented, "Poverty and charity are no longer looked up to, they are looked down upon. The poor have ceased to accept poverty and the rich have ceased to practice charity. When the poor are satisfied to be poor, the rich become charitable toward the poor."[37] By enshrining poverty in virtue, Catholic Worker Houses of Hospitality represented a countermovement to the progressive era ideal of upward mobility.

"Our first house of hospitality," Day explained, "came into being very shortly after *The Catholic Worker* did—while we were working on the second issue, in fact—in the barbershop we had taken below our Fifteenth Street apartment." It had a garden where Day had fond memories of visitors and members of the community walking and talking with one another. She boasted that professors and college students engaged in discussions on the most pressing issues of their time. Day was proud of the voices that offered their expertise to the community. "We had a workers' school of our own at the office that first winter," she explained. "The best was none too good for the poor, we thought, so we had such priests as Father LaFarge, S.J., Father Joseph McSorley, and Father Paul Hanly Furfey of Catholic University, not to mention such distinguished visitors as Jacques Maritain and Hilaire Belloc."[38] Maurin said the school's objective was to search for the common good. They held ecumenical meetings with talks on liturgy, worship, and scripture. Day's descriptions were idyllic. To her, there was only one flaw: the space became too small to host every person who was attracted to the Fifteenth Street location.

In 1935, they began renting apartments and rooms to house men and women separately. The community grew very large. At one point, Day reported that they occupied "thirty-eight rooms and two stores."[39] She used a *Catholic Worker* report of an early morning breadline, at which they served one hundred gallons of coffee to hungry people, to describe typical house activities and growth of the movement. Later that year, they moved to Greenwich Village on Charles Street, where they started a maternity guild. The space was bigger than the Fifteenth Street office, but Day knew immediately that it was not a place that would sustain them indefinitely. So she began searching for a more suitable location.

In 1936, Day learned of a space on Mott Street that was available for rent. It was large enough to provide what they needed; however, upon seeing the location, she was appalled that it was being rented in such a dilapidated condition. Day was discouraged, but consistent with her strong personality, she was not deterred. She learned that the widows in charge of the building had established an organization called the House of Calvary that ministered to poor cancer patients. She told the widows about her charitable work for the poor and asked if they would make the space available for free. Not only did they consent, but they prepared the space for occupancy. They painted, fire-proofed the walls, and built fire escapes. They even offered to pay the property taxes, which Day accepted with gratitude because her community could not afford it. "The Catholic Worker was a movement," she explained, not "an accredited charitable organization."[40] The House of Hospitality remained at 115 Mott Street for the next fourteen years.

Catholic Worker Hospitality Houses, like the newspaper, boasted of racially diverse practices. On a few occasions, Day wrote of Black people who participated in the house communities. She pointed out the "Negro" and provided a few details about the individual to emphasize her value for the full inclusion of all people—no matter their racial background, church membership, or political affiliation. It came as a surprise to some that despite her anticommunist crusade, she was still able to fraternize with communists in Greenwich Village and welcome leftist-leaning folks into the Catholic Worker community. If those folks remained with the community long enough, they would understand that Day's mission began with communists in mind. She specifically wanted laborers sympathetic to communism to partake in breadlines, coffee distribution, and workers' school lectures to demonstrate that Catholic social teachings were more profoundly transformative than any Marxist-sympathizing organization. Falls, too, was surprised to learn how willingly Day took cues from communist strategies. This inclusion was nothing new for Day. Her perspective on pacifism required such radical hospitality. And she stretched that requirement far enough to tenderly host white people whose racial bigotry made the Catholic Worker community unwelcoming to potential Black participants.

Mr. Breen, a seventy-year-old unhoused man who became a member of the Catholic Worker community in the 1930s, was one of these white people. Day gave Breen, a former newspaper professional, responsibility for acknowledging letters from readers. She soon learned this was a mistake. After he sent an unprofessional letter to a subscriber, Day apologized by offering a detailed description of her feelings about Breen to the offended party: "He is our cross, specially sent by God, so we treasure him." She continued, "[His] greatest affliction was having to share the hospitality of the city with Negroes." Apparently, his behavior toward Blacks was so overtly hostile that Day believed he had been physically beaten by a group of Black men who had suffered from one of his verbal assaults when they shared shelter space with him in another part of the city. His frequent use of pejorative language for immigrant groups was well known in the Mott Street house. Day reported that he regularly referred to people with degrading terms like "dagos," "dinges," and "kikes."[41] Yet she provided lodging for him anyway.[42]

Day's reflections on Breen, even with the full transparency of his most repugnant traits, reads sentimental and loving, as though the trouble he caused in the community was a minor nuisance but also endearing. The letters she wrote to him when she was away speak to the fondness she had for him. To tend to his illness from afar, she addressed Breen, "you poor dear," then encouraged him to seek help from her colleagues to gather any "pills, laundry, paper, cigarettes, etc." that he needed.[43] Day praised his growth: "Your wants are so few, you so seldom complain—you are getting to resemble Peter [Maurin] in your detachment in regard to material goods."[44] Perhaps his unpredictable receptivity to her kindness encouraged her that he was maturing. He responded with gratitude to Day: "Your glimpses into my mind on personal responsibility a few days ago remade me and I have, thank you, ceased to hate people as I was wont to."[45]

These transformations, as encouraging as they must have been, were temporary. Stanley Vishnewski, a seventeen-year-old Lithuanian immigrant who remained with the community for the rest of his life, referred to the Mott Street location as a "house of hostility" due to Breen's overbearing presence. Day, too, was a recipient of Breen's vitriol. Once, after seeing her fraternizing with a Black man, he called her a "nigger lover." Day's recollection of that moment connoted a tenderness that she did not confess to when she reflected on receiving the insult as an "expression of hate and contempt" at Koinonia.[46] She expressed disgust for that word, enough to threaten her friends with violence if they used it. Yet instead of protecting others from Breen's verbal attacks, Day wrote that his mischief gave the Mott Street community opportunities to practice pacifism.[47]

A Black member of the community, Mr. Rose, found no redeeming qualities in Breen's degrading words or hostile behavior. Day recalled that Rose, who in her opinion was not interested in "racial justice," opposed Breen's racial bigotry immediately upon making his acquaintance. He learned that Breen disliked the idea of interracial romance, so Rose repeatedly flaunted his knowledge of white women's attractions to him. According to Day, Rose sat at her desk when she was away, with his feet up, telling racially provocative stories to Breen. Perhaps Rose was no public freedom fighter, but her description of his behavior suggests that Rose was at least mildly annoyed by Breen's overt racial insults and attempted to fight back in his own goading way.[48]

Reflecting thirty years later, Day expressed no remorse for the hostile environment that Rose endured. She only offered a vague confession: "Sometimes we did feel sad, indeed, when our houses seemed to be filled more with hate and angry words than with the love we were seeking." The tone of her letters concerning Breen, both to him and about him, as well as her reflections on her relationship with him, read as fond memorials with amusing antidotes rather than regretful reflections on missed opportunities she may have made to curb his behavior. The hostile environment that she allowed may have been tolerable for her, but it created challenges to the racially diverse environment she aspired to create. Despite Rose's visible frustrations and remarks from other community members, Day mentioned no deliberations on procedures or any rules that could have made the environment less hostile for immigrants or Black visitors. Moreover, her conspicuous affections for Breen could have communicated that white Catholic Workers in the house shared his prejudices. For every Black person, like Rose, that frequented the Mott Street house, we will never know how many avoided it because Day made no prohibitions against Breen's hostilities.

Breen's bigotry was not restricted to words. He had a habit of reading newspapers and then discarding them on the floor when he had read enough. On one occasion, he dropped a match onto a pile of those newspapers, but he had failed to put it out after lighting his cigarette. Mr. Freeman, a former rabbi who had recently converted to Catholicism, noticed that the match ignited a fire. Freeman intervened by putting out the flame, but Breen was not interested in being saved by a Jew, even if he was now Catholic. "All the while the old man kept beating him off with his cane," Day explained, "and calling him a "g—d—Jew. But Mr. Freeman saved him anyway."[49]

The cane became symbolic of Breen's presence. He needed the cane to walk, but he also used the cane to threaten other members of the community. On his death bed, he offered it to Day. She narrated the last moments of his life when she and others from the community gathered around him: "Mr. Breen looked up at us and said, 'I have only one possession left in the world—my cane. I want you to have it. Take it—take it and wrap it around the necks of some of those bastards around here.'" Day imparted a sense of holiness to the moment, describing his expression as a "beatific smile." She added, "In his weak voice he whispered, 'God has been good to me.' And smiling, he died." Breen was a unique member of the community, but Day found his story representative of hundreds of people with housing insecurity whom she refused to turn away and whose presence had a profound impact on the Mott Street house.[50]

Word about the care unhoused people received from Mott Street traveled and popularized the hospitality house movement with social service agencies. According to Day, "The Travelers Aid, the city hospitals, the police, social workers, psychiatrists, doctors, priests, lawyers—all kinds of people called on hospitality houses for help in sheltering the homeless." The houses fulfilled a social need in the city; therefore, it was important to her that Catholic Worker volunteers made the breadlines and workers' schools major features of their houses of hospitality nationwide. She thought that this consistency would aid many cities and keep charity at the heart of the movement. Day cautioned that no one should expect every hospitality house to conduct itself in the manner Mott Street did. "No two houses of hospitality have ever been alike," she wrote years later. "The house directors have differed widely in personality and in their approach to their work; though poverty's problems may seem the same everywhere, poverty's conditions within each community have varied."[51]

Chicago *Catholic Worker*

Day's words were certainly true of the Falls-led house in Chicago, which proved to be a stark contrast to the daily activities on Mott Street, particularly in the methods it employed to address poverty and racism. That was due, in part, to Day's charity paradigm, which was the sole tool she used to address both issues. Nothing about the daily practices of the Catholic Worker community offered a remedy to the anti-Black exploitation that Day opposed. Neither her socialist experiences nor her interracialism did much to equip her to address anti-Black labor abuses beyond calling on laborers to find a home beyond capitalism; in her case, that meant converting to Catholicism. Falls also promoted Catholicism, but he did so through study groups on economic empowerment and racial justice.

For Black people who demanded racial justice, even those who were cradle Catholics, the church in America was rarely a friend. Falls, for example, believed that "many of our local Catholic institutions" were influenced by "the Jim Crow policy." He lamented that the word "Catholic" was known among many laypeople, especially youth, as a symbol of injustice because of the church's discriminatory practices against Black Chicagoans. Remembering his childhood, Falls said, "On Saturdays, when we went to confession, whites had their confessions heard first. We had to keep going to the back of the line. Each parish had its way of telling you that you didn't belong." Falls recalled decades later, "Until the appearance of the Catholic Worker my colleagues and I often considered the Catholic Church to be on the side of the enemy on race issues."[52] At an FCC meeting, he and his colleagues once debated "whether or not there was such a thing as a decent white man."[53] Through the newly established CIF, Falls sought to reform the church by ridding it of its inimical associations with racial injustice and bringing it to the side of Black freedom, but the turmoil surrounding the organization created insurmountable obstacles to that goal. Though he was hopeful about the new priests' leadership, the interracial work proved unable to bring together his economic concerns with his racial critique.[54]

Having grown up with white priests in interracial Catholic neighborhoods and churches, Falls believed that the movement for Black freedom would have greater opportunity for success if white clergy led the cause. The headline in an article he wrote on the priests' new direction for the federation communicated as much: "Chicago Catholics Flay Prejudice." He would eventually regret that interpretation. As historian Karen Johnson explains, "By 1935 Falls had given up hope that he could work effectively under priests' influence."[55] He lamented that the clergy used their power to undercut Black ideas and agency. The clergy's refusal to incorporate Black creativity meant that Day had joined what Black Catholics interpreted as a weak and ineffectual federation. Thus, her affiliation as a board member, rather than strengthening her ability to join with Blacks in their quest for freedom, reinforced the idea that Black and white people simply needed more opportunities for fellowship rather than a specific strategy to combat racial capitalism.

Without Black leadership, the CIF's white clergy muted the voices of Black members, especially when their suggestions made the white leaders uncomfortable. Ultimately, the takeover rendered the organization little more than a tool to satisfy white desires for interracial fellowship, but it did not offer a robust analysis of racial discrimination in Catholic institutions. Moreover, the leadership that replaced Turner gave little direction. LaFarge was absent from three of the first four yearly conferences. This meant that Falls had given his allegiance to a philosophy of interracialism that was absent of leadership and offered integration as the only solution to racial inequality. The new president gave lip service to ending racial prejudice in the church, but he provided no specific plan for carrying it out beyond requiring Black and white Catholics to work together. In short, the CIF gave Catholics the appearance that their church was free of racial hostility, but by dismissing the most damning concerns of Black Catholics, it undermined their efforts to truly address it. For this reason, continued association with the CIF became anathema for Falls.

Similarly, *Catholic Worker* newspaper headlines gave Falls the impression that he had found an organization that was motivated to integrate class and race concerns. Within two years of his discovering the paper, Falls had a column and designs to develop a local movement in Chicago, which eventually led to the establishment of a Catholic Worker house. True to Day's description of the diversity between the houses of hospitality, Falls's unique personality, approach, and analysis of poverty defined the movement in Chicago. He guided the Chicago Catholic Worker house to educate participants in economics and racial equality with a new program. He divided the house participants into four sections: labor, co-operatives, church, and school. Each section was instructed to apply "Christian doctrine to social and economic problems."[56] From their particular focus, he assigned sections to lead one Sunday forum each month.

The Sunday forum provided space for in-depth discussion on a variety of topics that were important to the group. For example, the co-operative section invited a board member from Hyde Park Federal Credit Union to inform the group of the potential for parishes to develop similar financial institutions. On another Sunday, the labor section called on college students to learn more about labor organizing to prepare them for life after graduation. Falls hoped each section would "carry out an active program in its particular field, spreading not only the sale of the paper, but also the phi-losophy of the Catholic Worker group."[57]

Falls shared his views on the development of the Chicago Catholic Worker community in a new *Catholic Worker* column, the Chicago Letter. His first post, December 1, 1935, opened with an analysis of the final negotiations of the violent milk strikes that Wisconsin workers had initiated two years prior.[58] Falls noted that though the milk companies had negotiated for better prices, the farmers did not receive a fair share of the profits. Next, he cele-brated a group of Chicago Theological Seminary students who organized a co-operative dining club and the potential of co-operative associations to ful-fill the promise of democracy and Christian community. As he saw it, those in the co-operative movement, with their power-sharing practices between white and Black members, latitudinarian decision-making structures, and overall racial inclusivity, showed the way to positive interracial interaction that rejected exploitation in all its forms. Falls summarized the promise of these associations by arguing that Black communities suffered because they had little economic power to transform their social situation. He believed that when given the chance to organize, Black communities could prove that they had great purchasing power. There was a logic to Falls's reports on the milk labor strikes, seminary student co-operatives, and Black capital. They were not disparate issues but rather important subjects of interest that Falls believed could liberate Black Chicagoans from racial oppression.[59]

It became apparent in Falls's first report that the Chicago Catholic Worker was not simply a second site of the New York Catholic Worker. Its emphases on investments and strikes challenged assumptions that Day and Maurin took for granted. From their perspective, the heart of the Catholic Worker movement was voluntary poverty. Day agreed completely with Maurin that voluntary poverty and charity worked hand in glove. The two also agreed that communism was atheist and Catholicism was the only hope for the ex-ploited American labor class. However, they were not as aligned on the ef-ficacy of strikes or on the attention that the newspaper should give to anti-Black discrimination. Day was more open to labor organizing and strikes than Maurin was. Prone to maxims, he often said, "Strikes don't strike me." Nevertheless, the New York Catholic Worker supported labor organizing. Day published news of the strikes in the paper, and she led work-ers to participate directly in a brewery strike. She justified the actions to Maurin by saying, "Their work was a work of mercy because they gave drink to the thirsty!"[60] Similarly, it was Day's passion for courting Black laborers that was responsible for the newspaper's attention to capitalists' exploitation of Black workers. Maurin was not indifferent to Black suffering, but he did not approve of pointing out the peculiarity of it, because it distracted from his concerns for personalism, voluntary poverty, and charity.

In contrast, the Chicago Catholic Worker community had no such divisions in leadership. Ed Marciniak, a white leader in Catholic social action who became a leading advocate for Black people, joined Falls in the basement of St. Patrick's Church in late June 1936 to organize the Chicago Catholic Worker movement. Dozens of others joined them. The first meeting gave the impression that conflicts that plagued the New York community would soon befall the Chicago community. Some people attended because they were Catholics; others attended to share their communist vision for the future. Those who understood the Catholic Worker were likely held together by their commitment to ending poverty. The first meeting was peculiarly large in size and lacked the focus that would be typical of future meetings, which were never larger than fifty people. With the smaller group, they were able to decide on a mission and vision. Their deliberations aligned with Falls's designs for Chicago. Consequently, unlike the often two-minded realities of decision-making and philosophies that colored the New York community, Falls's single-minded vision for the economic uplift of Black citizens defined the emerging Chicago movement.[61]

Without internal opposition in Chicago, the community had no need to use time or energy creating justifications for the work ahead. Being of one mind, they sought a location that would be attractive to people on the street and be able to host intellectual discussions. If the location had a library, they imagined that they could study communism, race relations, and "the application of Christian doctrine to social and economic problems."[62] Their search for a home ended November 26, 1936, when they moved into 1841 West Taylor St. The Near West Side neighborhood emerged because city residents relocated there after the Great Fire of 1871. Between 1880 and 1920, neighborhoods to the west of downtown took shape and grew in unique character. The Taylor Street house was only a few blocks from a number of large Catholic parishes. One of these was St. Mel's, which would claim to be the largest Catholic church in the world just one decade later. A neighborhood to the northwest, sometimes pejoratively called "Deutschland" because of class comparisons to Germans, was known for large populations of Russian Jews. Visitors to the neighborhood southwest of the Taylor house observed it to be a "pretty tight Italian community."[63] A small number of Black Chicagoans who had not settled in Bronzeville, Chicago's southside neighborhood, rounded out the population of the region.

Being a part of the small enclave of Black people on the west side set Falls apart from most others who lived in predominantly Black neighborhoods, but his west-side affiliation was not the only thing that distinguished him. Falls came from a long line of Black Catholics in New Orleans, some of whom had become priests and nuns. In Chicago, Falls lived on a side of town that was known for its majority white, although ethnically diverse, residents. Moreover, his profession as a physician boosted his status in the community. As a white-collar professional, he made white colleagues aware that he would not allow them to relegate him "into the stereotype subservient Negro to which most whites were accustomed at the time."[64] His white contemporaries experienced him as "remarkably sophisticated, almost patronizing to his inferiors."[65] Falls did not apologize for his outward expressions of dignity and composure. Rather, he used his experiences, heritage, education, and wealth to envision the Catholic Worker community as a tool to provide similar opportunities to other Blacks.

Falls had no interest in charity, whether giving or receiving. Thus, it was no surprise to those who knew him that he did not find soup lines, breadlines, or hot coffee distribution empowering endeavors. Instead, he found value in teaching people who suffered from poverty to escape the need for charity. Falls's attention to self-reliance fell in line with the Black philosophies of notable leaders such as Booker T. Washington and Marcus Garvey. To this end, the Taylor house "replaced the characteristic soup-line with an information center which contained suggestions for utilizing meager resources to their fullest extent."[66] The community also coordinated a credit union. Through this initiative, struggling families could secure low-interest loans and save money with greater frequency. The project lasted until 1948, when it failed because its loose lending strategy routinely practiced granting loans to people who could not repay them.[67] Yet the community did not rely solely on the credit union. Falls also encouraged consumer cooperatives, through which groups could make purchases that would otherwise be difficult for one person to make. Falls hoped that these attempts at building solidarity among people in the community would make the charity model increasingly less necessary.

Antiracial Activism

In addition to correspondence related to the newspaper, Day and Falls' acquaintance grew through in-person collaborations. Day and Maurin's visit to Chicago in 1936 was Falls's inspiration to elevate varied interest in the

Catholic Worker movement from reading newspapers and sending donations to developing an organized community. Falls believed that their visit had also inspired students in the area to protest "the barring of Negros from Catholic schools." As a result, he seized the opportunity to organize a group "not only to further interest in race relations, but in all other social and economic problems with which our Catholic people show an appalling lack of knowledge."[68] Educating people on Catholic social doctrine and economics primarily meant that Falls was challenging the influence of local priests' racial prejudices.

Falls visited Day in New York, and Day visited him in Chicago. They even attended national Catholic gatherings together in the name of the Catholic Worker. These in-person experiences were important to the expansion of the movement's reach in the Midwest. Despite his misgivings about the racial empowerment focus of Falls's work, Maurin also visited Falls. His doubts about racial justice activism did not seem to deter him or affect the movement. Instead, it was Day who was displeased with Falls's Chicago program. It was the implementation of his upwardly mobile economic philosophy that ultimately led to a rift in Day's enthusiasm about the movement's direction in Chicago.

The differences in direction were not apparent at the outset of Falls's collaboration with Day. Like his interracial work with the CIF, Falls and Day were energized by their new relationship at first. Their views on communism and the economy were different, but they seemed not to notice the extent to which they differed. For example, Taylor Street welcomed people like Joe Diggles, who identified as both a devout Catholic and a card-carrying communist. He seemed flamboyantly interested in making sure that both his Catholic workers and his communist comrades knew that the two identities could co-exist. Unfortunately for Diggles, his dual membership did not continue indefinitely. The Communist Party expelled him for supporting the "wrong side" of a labor dispute during World War II.[69] Falls never voiced a problem with Diggles's participation at Taylor Street. In contrast, Day appreciated aspects of communism, but that appreciation ended where Catholic community began.

The mere mention of Marxism at a 1937 Christian meeting in Chicago was enough to provoke Day to express her strong condemnation of any possible compatibility between communism and Christianity. The meeting on fascism and religion at the University of Chicago became an occasion for her to engage in an impromptu debate with Harry F. Ward, the white self-proclaimed Christian Marxist from Union Theological Seminary. Ward was a founder of the Methodist Federation for Social Service and the main author of the Social Creed of the Churches. No one was aware that Day or Falls had planned to attend the meeting, but upon recognizing Day in the audience, they asked her to share a word.[70]

According to a *Catholic Worker* article, Day challenged Ward's Christian-Marxist identity. She "quoted from the encyclical on the Church and State in Italy to show the condemnation of Fascism and quoted from the new Soviet Constitution" to show that Christianity and communism were incompatible. She declared that by her analysis of communist literature, there were no circumstances under which a communist group would "allow freedom of religious worship and freedom of anti-religious propaganda." She prognosticated that a communist regime would condemn children "to an education which was atheistic." In contrast, she argued, "[The Catholic Worker] would advocate an 'unpopular front.'" She advocated Maurin's position that such a coalition would allow for the "possibility of united action between the agnostic, who recognized The Common Good, the Jew who recognized God the Father, the Protestant, who believed in the Incarnation, and the Catholic, who believed in the Mystical body, which includes all."[71] In short, she denied that Ward was a Christian at all, because Marxism precluded the possibility of believing in the divinity of Christ.

Ward represented a tradition that Day did not understand. The language of his Protestant Christian socialism signaled to her that he was at heart an atheist. Ward's Christian Marxism was rooted in a social gospel movement that began in the late nineteenth century. Championed by theologians like Walter Rauschenbusch, ministers like Josiah Strong, and lay people like W. E. B. Du Bois, as well as women deaconesses who administered domestic aid to new immigrants, the social gospel was a Protestant attempt to apply the tools of social science to Christian reform in America. At the turn of the century, white Christian socialist programs redirected the energies once used to participate in the uplift of formerly enslaved Black people to convert Catholic immigrants to Protestantism, while Black Christian socialists developed holistic ministries that aimed to address the needs of Black neighborhoods, where people attempted to gain footing in industrialized America.

In Chicago, the white fundamentalist evangelist D. L. Moody criticized social gospelers for placing too much importance on hunger and shelter. But Protestant reformers like African Episcopal Church minister Reverdy Ransom recognized the imperative to attend to the physical needs of Black communities through church buildings that had kitchens, gymnasiums, and large auditoriums where people could gather to meet one another's physical needs. In this way, the Christian socialist movement was the Protestant version of the Catholic Worker movement, a parish-based ministry that attended to the physical and spiritual needs of a neighborhood without the knee-jerk dismissal of Marxist language. And like the Catholic Worker movement, social gospel movements recognized the concept of corporate sin that manifested in systems such as capitalism. White social gospelers also shared with Catholic workers a myopic attention to white labor issues that called for an end to capitalist exploitation. In other words, white social gospelers duplicitously campaigned for a republic with rights for labor, sharply condemning the economic exploitation of white workers, but had no strategies for ending anti-Black exploitation. It was this lack of strategy for dismantling the structures that gave power to the color line that the movements shared, excepting that the Catholic Worker movement, following Day's lead, more consistently condemned anti-Black violence than white Protestant socialists did.[72]

Ward was among the variety of Christian Marxists who challenged their white peers on the problems of racial inequality and, as such, had a lot in common with Day. He was not afraid to confront white audiences with the need for more empathy toward Black people, even when their labor unions viewed them as strikebreakers. Just as Day opposed anti-Black violence consistently through her life, as early as 1907 Ward used the example of a lynch mob in a sermon to remind his white congregation that affluent members of the church and society who appeared to be good people could be malformed by greed. His analysis was a direct result of his opposition to capitalism. "The capitalist economy," he argued, "operates on the basis of functional inequality. . . . It keeps the Jew, the Negro, woman, most of the children of the low income group in a subordinate position."[73] With all that they had in common, Ward could have been an interesting conversation partner for Day, but she was not as open to different expressions of communism as Falls seemed to be.[74]

On another trip to Chicago, Day's disappointment with Falls's vision became apparent. John Cogley, a founding member of the community and head of Falls's liturgical committee, wrote in his autobiography that Falls's vision for the Chicago movement did not comport with "Dorothy Day's idea of how the Catholic Worker should be running in the nation's second largest city." The focus on education, library books, and academic speakers led Cogley to conclude that "we were running a kind of conference center with religious overtones." While the community could boast, through Day's

Catholic Worker, that it attracted the attention of important voices—from Thomist scholars and naturalist sociologists to Benedictine philosophers and Detroit autoworkers—these debates were central to the Chicago group in a manner that overshadowed the charity work that Day had in mind.[75]

Day did not make her disappointment known to the broader Catholic Worker community, but both Cogley and Falls intuited her disapproval. Perhaps it was evident in the headline of the article in which she reported on her trip, which read, "More Houses of Hospitality Are Needed." In the article, written from a Chicago Inter-Student Action office, she thanked John Bowers and Falls for their care—Bowers had secured her lodging, and Falls had performed an operation on an abscess in Day's throat. Interestingly, she said very little about the Taylor Street house, only that "the important work of caring for children and families continues" there. Instead, she wrote glowingly of new plans "for opening a House of Hospitality near Hull House to feed the hungry and shelter a few of the harborless." She may have attempted to quell any suspicion that this meant the end of the Taylor Street house by stating that the work there would continue. She also mentioned that there was a rift in the Chicago group, such that Cogley had formed a separate group two years ago.[76]

Years later, Falls told an interviewer, "Dorothy never really agreed with my concept of the Catholic Worker." But, he maintained, "I thought it was the more realistic approach." Cogley felt that "there was really nothing wrong with the program and people did remain interested," but he was certain that "a bit of conventional social work among children and numerous committees among the group" did not coincide with "Dorothy Day's idea of how the Catholic Worker should be running in the nation's second largest city."[77]

Cogley's respect for Falls's status and demeanor may have compelled him to support the Taylor Street vision. His disagreements with Falls's approach, however, surfaced when Day tasked him with opening a hospitality house that was consistent with her vision. Before leaving Chicago for her return trip to New York, she asked him to accompany her to the bus station, where she quietly offered him a set of keys to a house in a poor Black neighborhood on Wabash Avenue. She told him that the house could supplement the charity work of a nearby Catholic parish. Cogley said it was the happiest moment of his life at the time. "At last," he celebrated, "we were behaving as we were supposed to, we were finally in the true Catholic Worker movement. It was great to be young and feel alive and be participating in something so vital."[78]

Almost as quietly as the Wabash Avenue house opened, Falls's association with the national Catholic Worker movement dissipated without much sound. Cogley and others from Chicago took over the Chicago Letter column in *The Catholic Worker*. John Bowers had directed the Taylor Street house since the year after Falls founded it. By the summer of 1937, *The Catholic Worker* had mentioned his name only in passing—on one occasion his name was embedded among a list of judges for an interracial hearing at Fordham University. Cogley, Hellen Ferrell, and Dorothy Day took turns through 1938 and 1939 reporting on the work at Wabash Avenue and Taylor Street in the Chicago Letter column. Although Falls was not the lead organizer at Taylor Street or a contributor to the national newspaper, his involvement in the Chicago work did not noticeably decrease until 1942.

Absent of Falls's direction, the Catholic Worker in Chicago was never the same. Cogley's Wabash house appeared to be unnecessary in the St. Elizabeth neighborhood, where the local priest needed no help from a house of charity. Father Drescher was already actively involved in social justice work when Cogley arrived. Over the course of the year, it became clear to Cogley that it was necessary to close the Wabash house in the summer of 1938. The Taylor house, known as Holy Rood House, mostly served children and families as a safe place for young people to gather and receive after-school resources, tutoring, and childcare. Some aspects of Falls's influence persisted, especially in the organizational structure of committees.

Though his work with Catholic Worker waned, Arthur Falls did not cease to raise his voice for Black liberation. He continued to challenge the heretical practice of Jim Crow Catholicism that he referred to as the "mythical body of Christ," and he called on the church to live out its creed as the mystical body. In his personal life, he integrated a wealthy white neighborhood where simply living at home was a daily proclamation of his belief in the rights of Black citizens to have equal access to every opportunity that white people took for granted. In 1961, he and nine other physicians brought a lawsuit against a network that represented 75 percent of white hospitals in the Chicago area because Black doctors were being barred from practicing medicine. Though it never went to trial, the suit convinced those hospitals to hire over 100 Black physicians.[79]

Dorothy Day, on the other hand, was never more vocal about racial segregation than she was in the 1930s and was never closer to Black causes than she was when she worked with Falls. Her commitment to charity meant that downtrodden Black people who visited hospitality houses would always be served food and have a place to stay. But the frequency of articles that opposed racism declined in the next few decades—that is, until a small interracial farm project gained national attention in Americus, Georgia, for being targeted by white supremacists. The persecution the Koinonians suffered moved Day to lend her support to the community and its fiery white founder, New Testament scholar and preacher Clarence Jordan. Her visit to the farm in 1957 left her with an enduring impression of the terrors of racial animus, but it did little to change her methods for addressing racial inequality with more than the personal charity white Christians could find in their hearts and homes to offer.

Part III **Freedom or Fellowship**

· ·

4 Relationships

· ·

> There are some people who will look at you and say, "It is the
> demonstrations that cause violence." They say, "It's extremism that
> cause violence." I'm here to ask you a question today, "Would you
> condemn Jesus Christ because he believed in the will of God so
> much that he was willing to die for it?" This is extremism. . . . What
> will it take for this community to realize that all we want is an
> opportunity to participate in the government of this city. We wish to
> make it emphatically clear that we are not here to destroy the image of
> Americus, Georgia. We simply want to be free. We're not here to see
> the people here killed day in and day out. We just want to be free.
> —Benjamin Clarke, "Speech in Americus," July 5, 1965

In the late 1940s, Black churches across the nation rallied behind Black
Georgian congregations to "Save the Ingrams." Rosa Lee Ingram and her
sons were jailed for defending themselves against a white sharecropper who
carried a rifle to their doorstep in Schley County, about fifteen miles north
of Americus. The communist newspaper *The Daily Worker* informed its readers that the legal battle involving the middle-aged Black sharecropper and
her sons "may be the new Scottsboro."[1] The Ingrams' plight became a high-
profile legal saga that tested the integrity of Southern courts and the ability of Black freedom fighters, along with their comrades, to use their
resources to free the family from Jim Crow justice.

In 1947, the Schley County prosecutor put Ingram on trial for the murder of a white sharecropper named John Ethron Stratford. Stratford lived
adjacent to Ingram and worked for the same landowner. Ingram's family
testified that Stratford was upset because Rosa Lee refused his sexual advances, claiming that he attacked her out of frustration. While defending
herself against Stratford, Ingram and two of her children killed him. Schley County police arrested Ingram and three of her twelve children for murder. According to the testimony of Ingram and her boys, who were kept in
separate jails and were the only eyewitnesses, just two of them had defended
their mother in the confrontation.[2] John Stratford's spouse, Irene, alleged,

to the contrary, that her husband had lost his patience with Ingram's animals eating his crops. According to her testimony, John said he planned to use the rifle simply to kill Ingram's livestock. To this end, he took his rifle, walked over to Ingram's home, and confronted her. Shortly thereafter, the Ingrams killed him.

The all-white twelve-man jury found Ingram and her three accused sons guilty of murder, and the judge sentenced them to death. In another hearing, the judge commuted their sentence to life in prison and released the youngest of the boys. After twelve years, a parole board released them because Black churches had solicited national Black organizations, the legal defense of attorneys in nearby Americus, NAACP legal counsel, the Women's Committee for Equal Justice (created on behalf of the Ingrams), the Black press, and communist news sources to intervene.[3]

While the Ingram case inspired Black Christians around Americus to organize, a nearby predominantly white community formed to demonstrate the interracial possibilities of the kingdom of God through charity programs for Black farmers and preachers. The leader and cofounder of Koinonia Farm, Clarence Jordan, described its purpose through a pamphlet that declared that it was "devoted to the proclamation of Jesus Christ and the application of his teachings."[4] The objects of Koinonia's proclamation and application, as described in the pamphlet, were "those who suffer and are oppressed; who are bound by ignorance and sin; and who are desperately searching for a way in the wilderness." Jordan clarified later in the pamphlet that those suffering, oppressed, ignorant, sinful, and desperate people were Black Southerners. By representing them in this way, Jordan hoped to make their need for white Christian charity apparent. He made it his mission to combat his judgment of Black Georgians' "ignorance of sin" with Christian education. Through the farm, he also endeavored to provide those he identified as "desperately searching" with white friends. In drawing their Black neighbors into charity programs, the white missionaries hoped their "demonstration plot" would show that interracial Christian relationships could overcome racial segregation.[5]

The interventions of Black churches against Jim Crow justice in the legal proceedings of the Ingram case provides important context for the Koinonian community's mission: "to undertake to train Negro preachers in religion and agriculture."[6] The assumptions behind Koinonia's mission were twofold. First, Jordan assumed that he was qualified to train the Black citizens of Americus in religion and agriculture. Second, the missionaries assumed that Black preachers and farmers needed their help. Neither assumption was informed by the religious needs or agricultural experiences of Black people in Southwestern Georgia. The Ingram case demonstrated that Black churches had constructed religious communities that actively advanced justice and civil rights in Sumter County prior to Koinonia's involvement in Americus. Also, Koinonians, who were new to the region, were not nearly as experienced with farming the red Georgian soil as Black farmers whose ancestors were forced into agricultural labor as enslaved people.[7]

Jordan admitted to lacking the farming skills necessary to offer training to the Black farmers. So he and his partner, Martin England, planned to learn how to farm in the first few years of the venture. His admission of ignorance did not stem from any comparison to the knowledge of Black farmers who had been farming the land for generations as enslaved people and sharecroppers. Jordan simply had zero experience. Equipped with white hubris, he assumed that the average Southern Black community needed whatever amount of farming knowledge he would learn in his first few years. Having only a general concept about what Black people faced in the South, Jordan decided that his "agricultural missionary enterprise" needed time "to gain much needed practical experience and afford opportunity for studying the needs of the people." Nevertheless, he was confident that whatever those needs were, he and his fellow white partners would be able to understand and meet them. Despite his admission of ignorance, Jordan laid out a program that included training in practical farming methods, religious education, and cultural development—even before he had secured a location.[8]

Jordan was not alone in his concern for Black sharecroppers. Black freedom fighters and white allies both understood that the needs of sharecroppers, who toiled under impossible obstacles created by unjust landowners, were great. Jordan aimed to teach agricultural knowledge that would free Black sharecroppers from the inequities of the sharecropping system. He shared a view held by Black Christians like Booker T. Washington and W. E. B. Du Bois that agricultural activism was essential to liberating sharecroppers from the clutches of Jim Crow. Moreover, like Washington and Du Bois, whose public disagreements over the best methods to pursue Black freedom obscured the fact that they shared some of the same strategies, Jordan believed that he knew best what Black people needed to overcome racial animus in the South. Unlike the two Black leaders, however, Jordan—having never experienced slavery, sharecropping, or Black community—offered help as an outsider. From this outsider perspective, he surmised that Black Southerners would benefit from his charity—a belief that led him to assume a position of decision-making power to determine what the Black residents of Sumter County needed while ignoring the knowledge and self-determination already present in the region.

This chapter uses the Black freedom traditions of Americus and nearby communities as the context in which Clarence Jordan practiced interracialism at Koinonia. Using this context as a lens reveals that Koinonia Farm's demonstration for interracial Christian fellowship failed to fully support Black Georgians' quests for justice and freedom. Koinonia's twin goals of educating Black farmers and training Black preachers to demonstrate that interracial fellowship was possible in the kingdom of God disregarded Black struggles against white supremacy. Black citizens organized for the right to maintain unity in their families, the right to equal protection under the law, the right to earn a living wage—in short, the right to self-determination. In celebrating Jordan's interracial vision, histories of Koinonia have minimized his lack of partnerships with Black communities in their quest for civil rights even though he made building interracial relationships a primary goal. His reliance on interpersonal relationships rather than building solidarity through multi-racial coalitions demonstrated Jordan's refusal to confront anti-Black policies, laws, structures, or systems beyond the farm. Furthermore, his failure to integrate the knowledge and practices of Black communities hindered Koinonia's self-proclaimed mission to produce an interracial fellowship that witnessed to "the Kingdom of God and its righteousness." Because Jordan did not learn from the Black community's social justice tradition in the Americus region, Koinonia's interracial program became a hazard for Black citizens, which caused them to participate with caution, if they participated at all. The disparate missions and visions of Black civil rights activists and white interracialist Christians, who both opposed Jim Crow segregation, never integrated. Koinonia, then, functioned as more of a Christian symbol of resistance to Jim Crow segregation than a potent constituent in the march for freedom. As such, it committed to interpersonal relationships and left the work of organizing the legal and economic strategies to overcome racial inequality to Black Americus.

Fighting for the Ingrams

Rosa Lee Ingram's status as a sharecropper from Schley County made her Black family vulnerable to poverty and a white supremacist criminal justice system. In Southern locations like Americus and surrounding Sumter County, African Americans maintained their relationship to farmland by raising livestock and growing crops through sharecropping—a system whereby white landowners exploited Black farmers' labor, leaving them economically dependent on the landlord. As a person accused of murder, Ingram's situation was unique, but many Black Americans identified with the circumstances that led to her arrest and conviction. Across the country, Black laborers farmed land and worked in factories not their own, while being confronted daily with violent threats from white men who challenged their attempts at upward mobility.

Ingram's story is particularly important for Americus because it was the first time that a generation of Black preachers and organizers participated in a large-scale freedom movement in the context of the sharecropping system. Black churches in the region organized with the Georgia Defense Committee, the National Association for the Advancement of Colored People (NAACP) (both national and local chapters), and the Civil Rights Congress to advocate for the Ingrams. They believed the mother and her children were wrongly convicted and unjustly sentenced to execution. The fact that these churches and organizations quickly mobilized Rosa Lee's mother to lift her family's story to national prominence further demonstrates the strength of Black networks to organize and build capacity to fight for racial justice.

Some news outlets compared the Ingram legal trial to the Scottsboro Boys case because of the lack of evidence against the Ingrams, the swiftness of the trial, and the extreme sentencing of the court. The *Pittsburgh Courier* selected the case as its number one news story for 1948. The communist *Daily Worker* also frequently featured the story in its pages. The Communist Party–affiliated Civil Rights Congress—the successor to the National Federation for Constitutional Liberties and the International Labor Defense—initiated a marketing campaign on the Ingrams' behalf. Local churches in Americus and the Georgia Defense Committee raised funds for the Ingrams' defense. A defense team composed first of Americus attorneys but later only NAACP attorneys represented the family in court.[9]

The activism surrounding the Ingram case was possible because Black institutions in the area lent their support to it. These institutions dated back to 1866, when Black Baptists founded the first independent congregation in the region. Black churches and dozens of Black preachers had contributed their unique styles and cadences to the Americus community since the Civil War, almost eighty years prior to Jordan's arrival. The first independent Black church, Bethesda Baptist, was established one year after the end of the Civil War. The congregation that founded the church emerged from First Baptist Church after the Black population grew to out-number the white membership. Another congregation, Campbell Chapel AME Church, was created in 1869 when a small group of formerly enslaved Methodists desired to worship independently from the white Methodists. In the years that followed, the number of Black churches grew from these two congregations to more than five Baptist and four African Methodist churches. By 1940, Americus was home to more than a dozen Black churches. This network of churches constituted the religious context that Koinonia entered, in which Black people had significant traditions of religious fellowship, community support, and Christian resistance to the horrors of Jim Crow.[10]

In addition to the support of churches, Black Christians organized resistance through the NAACP and the Communist Party. The NAACP had been present in Sumter County since 1945, when John B. Dorsey established the chapter. The work of the local NAACP was crucial to sustaining the Ingram family. Because the NAACP provided legal representation, the Communist Party focused more on winning the public relations contest in the court of public opinion. Beyond legal defense, the local NAACP collected funds to support the Ingrams' physical needs. Dorsey informed the national NAACP's Roy Wilkins, who would later become the organization's director, that the Ingrams had received twenty-dollar donations of weekly grocery allowance and hundreds of items of clothing to support the cause. In addition to providing aid for the Ingrams, their Black network created an important experience of resistance that demonstrated its ability to affect the destinies of Black Southerners before white organizations, like Koinonia, offered their charity.[11]

Koinonia Farm was established in 1942, four years before the "Save the Ingrams" campaign, but Jordan and his community were not among the organizations that joined in solidarity. Instead, Clarence and Florence Jordan and Martin and Mabel England devoted those early years to their new experiment. They worked to make Koinonia an example of Christian fellowship that would demonstrate God's opposition to Jim Crow segregation. A fundraising pamphlet described the farm as "an Agricultural Missionary Enterprise."[12] Jordan envisioned using the enterprise as religious training for the Black people in the South and community service for white visitors and members. His hope of providing aid to the suffering, oppressed, ignorant, sinful, and lost positioned Koinonia as a Christian charity and one example of what his interpretation of community could look like in action. This effort would involve wholehearted commitment to his understanding of a "loving fellowship where there is neither Jew nor Greek, Barbarian or

Scythian, Baptist nor Methodist, Korean, Russian, bond nor free, but Christ is all and in all."[13] It was a vision that relied on minimizing racial differences in favor of promoting a shared Christian identity.

The color-blind approach at Koinonia represented an alternative (Jordan was careful not to mistake it with a utopia) for white Christians who opposed the racial animosity that plagued American race relations. Despite their domestic and cultural programs, Koinonians claimed the responsibility to end racial division rather than to confront the racially discriminatory institutions, policies, and practices of the United States. These fellowship goals left Koinonia impotent to do much more than to provide opportunities for white people to befriend Black people, to offer their resources as charity, and to teach their vision of Christian interracialism.[14]

Jordan's academic and practical experiences were essential to creating the vision for Koinonia. Jordan had earned a PhD in New Testament from Southern Baptist Theological Seminary. Equipped with expertise he gained from graduate school, he taught New Testament at Simmons University, a secondary educational institution for Black students. It was while teaching students there that he engaged in one of his earliest actions against institutional segregation. In 1938, white students from Southern Baptist Theological Seminary asked him to bring Black students from Simmons for a Bible study. When the administration objected to having Black students eat in the dining hall, Jordan and his white students confronted the university president. The drama of this conflict resolved when the president allowed the Black and white students to fellowship in the dining room with Clarence and Florence Jordan.[15]

To demonstrate a permanent program at Koinonia, Jordan and England agreed on a four-part mission for the farm: First, it would seek "to relate, through a ministry to both individuals and community, the entire life of the people to Jesus Christ and his teachings." Second, it would endeavor "*to train Negro preachers in religion and agriculture.*" Third, in order to provide a missionary setting, the farm would "provide an opportunity for Christian students to serve a period of apprenticeship in developing community life on the teachings and principles of Jesus." Finally, influenced by the green movement, the community would seek "to conserve the soil, which we believe to be God's holy earth."[16] Based on these four parts, the farm identified first as a ministry. Beyond farming, the plan was for Koinonia to be a training ground for Black preachers and farmers. Jordan's role as a New Testament professor provided him with the confidence he needed to teach Black preachers. His undergraduate degree in agriculture from the University of

Georgia assured him that he could also train Black farmers in agricultural science. Through these training emphases, Jordan envisioned that Koinonia would become an interracial community that exemplified his Southern Baptist eschatological vision on earth.

For Jordan and England, as well as for many white radical Christians who would hear of Koinonia in the years to come, the mission and vision challenged racial segregation far beyond Americus. Koinonia was to become a demonstration plot that indicated what was possible in Southern culture. In the early stages of their brainstorming, they pursued properties in Alabama because they thought it was "fairly typical of the entire South."[17] Jordan's brother, however, suggested an old run-down farm that he had found in Georgia, which was still close to the Alabama line. Neither Jordan nor England had any prior knowledge of Americus, but because they found the ratio of Black to white citizens representative of the whole South, they agreed to begin their experiment there.

Jordan's memory of the early years in Americus speak to the obstacles he and his partner faced as farmers. Neither he nor England had farmed before. While speaking to an audience in Cincinnati, Ohio, in 1956, he recalled thinking that his agriculture degree had prepared him "to answer all problems related to agriculture."[18] However, he confessed that he was not prepared to address the actual problems of farming. His degree was concerned more with the economics of farming rather than the cultivation of plant crops and livestock.

England and Jordan identified themselves as agricultural missionaries, which Jordan explained with his signature whimsy: "So every morning our missionary activity consisted of getting up on the top story and seeing what our neighbors were doing." After some time observing the farmers around them, he recalled, they would do "the same things. If they were plowing, we plowed. If they were planting, we planted." They continued like this for "a year or two," becoming what he called those "kind of agricultural missionaries, absorbing all that we could from our environment." His account of how they learned to farm climaxed with his interaction with a mule. "I had learned in college how to farm scientifically. Unfortunately, the mule that we had hadn't had the same course that I had. He didn't know anything about scientific farming!"[19] Neighbor farmers laughed with him at his ignorance, but nothing in those early days spurred him to reconsider his plan.

The partners' inexperience was common among white radicals. Carl Landes, a participant in the 1942 Conference of Pacifist Farming at Ralph Templin's School of Living, comedically quipped, "Too many pacifists say,

'I want to start a Farm Community,' and wonder why they can't begin next week by buying a 100 acre farm; though they may not know on what end of the cow to sit down and milk."[20] Even rural life was foreign to some members of the foundational group. Florence Jordan admitted that she had never lived outside the big city before they moved to Americus.[21] Despite their ignorance, Jordan was confident that they knew enough to teach the Black people in the region how to farm the soil that they and their ancestors had farmed for generations as enslaved people and sharecroppers.

Black Farming

Black farming in Americus was rooted in the history of American slavery. After the Civil War, many Black citizens who had learned to farm the land as enslaved people became sharecroppers who lived and worked a landlord's property in exchange for keeping a small portion of their harvest. Opponents of the sharecropping system understood that little had changed for Black laborers after emancipation.[22] Few people explained the problem with sharecropping more concisely than Frederick Douglass when he said, "The black man does the work and the white man gets the money."[23] This became the common experience of Black people in Sumter County. A biographer of President Jimmy Carter, who was the region's most famous son, explained that well into the 1940s "the familiar silhouette of the Black sharecropper and his mules plowing the red Georgia earth against a blue Georgia sky still dominated the real landscape of the Flint River region."[24]

The familiar image of the Black sharecropper in Sumter County reinforced Jordan's view that it was a place where his agricultural ideas would be helpful to Black farmers throughout the South. Interestingly, his desire to increase the agricultural production of Black farms was like those of Black leaders who developed strategies to increase production and liberate sharecroppers from their economic bondage to the sharecropping system. Du Bois, for instance, suggested that agricultural expertise was the first step in creating "economic solidarity" within Black communities: "By letting Negro farmers feed Negro artisans and Negro technicians guide Negro home industries, and Negro thinkers plan this integration of cooperation, while Negro artists dramatize and beautify the struggle, economic independence can be achieved."[25] Similarly, Booker T. Washington, founder of Tuskegee Institute, believed that "if a negro farmer in the cotton belt can feed himself and his family[,] he is bound to become a respectable member of society; for in order to do it he must own, not rent, his house and his mules."[26] Du Bois and Washington understood that too many Black farmers worked land owned by white people. Because of this, these farmers would struggle to yield the level of agricultural production necessary to secure a place in society from which they could assert their rights as equal citizens to their wealthy white landlords.

Black leaders not only theorized about agriculture as a step toward freedom but also provided access to the agricultural practices that could make freedom possible. Washington did as much for his students at Tuskegee as he did for their communities back home when he established conferences and cooperatives to educate them in crop production. Many of the farmers from those communities were invited to the first Negro Farmers' Conference in 1892 to hear Booker T. Washington expound "on the virtues of land ownership, crop diversification, and Christian morality." These annual conferences resolved to acquire enough land to free Black farmers from the tenant system and to encourage them in their religious piety. The influence of these conferences expanded well beyond Tuskegee. By 1909, ninety-three local conferences had been established, most of them in Alabama but also two in Georgia.[27]

It is unclear to what extent the influence of the Negro Farmers' Conference reached Sumter County. We do know, however, that the influence of Tuskegee's work was expansive. Tuskegee Institute became a home base for Black US Department of Agriculture (USDA) agents. Through the institute, Washington connected the USDA to Tuskegee alumni, who were crucial in increasing Black farmers' access to the USDA's Cooperative Farm Demonstration Service in the Black Belt. Tuskegee's partnership with the USDA was just one way that Washington's institute gained federal resources that benefited Black farmers.[28]

The 1887 Hatch Act made it possible for states to disseminate funds to land grant institutions, which were often colleges. Unlike Alabama's two Black training schools—Tuskegee Institute and Huntsville Normal College— most Black colleges founded in the Southern states were not established until 1890. Consequently, those grants, which amounted to upwards of $15,000, went exclusively to white institutions, as did the land grants of 1862, made possible by the first Morrill Act. The second Morrill Act (1890), by increasing funding for land-grant institutions and including a provision for the establishment of Black land-grant colleges, changed that. The seventeen colleges established through funding from the second Morrill Act came to be known as "the 1890 colleges." In Georgia, this resulted in the creation of Savannah State College. Yet funding for land-grant institutions hardly provided benefits for schools like Savannah State. Instead, state allocators favored granting monies to white schools that had already benefited from the land-grant acts of 1862 and 1887.[29]

The exclusion of Black schools from this funding, either because they were not eligible or because state legislatures blatantly discriminated against them, left leaders of Huntsville Normal School and Washington's Tuskegee to compete for a small amount of funds made available to Black colleges at the turn of the century. Huntsville won the 1890 grant, but due to Washington's political prowess in the latter part of the decade, the institute secured an 1896 grant. With this financial support, Washington was able to begin the Tuskegee Institute Experiment Station. Word of its conference work spread through experiment station agents and instructional bulletins.[30]

As director of Tuskegee Institute Experiment Station, George Washington Carver began producing a series of instructional bulletins in 1898 for tenant farmers who struggled to grow a crop that would yield a profit. Tuskegee's experiment station provided information on research from its field experiments and detailed instructions on a wide array of crops: acorns, sweet potatoes, cotton, cow peas, small grain, wild plum, corn, ornamental trees, and shrubs. The bulletins were comprehensive in their attention to scientific information that farmers needed to understand. Between 1898 and 1943, the institute published forty-four bulletins, many of which included recipes, the uses of clay for dyes, advice on dairying, and even guides for raising livestock. Because Carver was popularly known as "the Peanut Man" for his 105 uses of the peanut and testimony defending the peanut industry at the House Ways and Means Committee in 1921, his promotion of the peanut has overshadowed his campaign to use agriculture as a tool to liberate Black tenant farmers from bondage to crippling capitalist practices. Carver's "chief aim was to keep every operation within reach of the poorest tenant farmer occupying the poorest possible soil—worthy of consideration from an agricultural point of view." Along with this goal, he endeavored "to further illustrate that the productive power of all such soils can be increased from year to year until the maximum of fertility is reached." His efforts to expand the reach of Tuskegee's scientific agricultural education beyond Macon County, Alabama, should be traced, in addition to the Farmers' Conferences, to his instructional bulletins, which provided hundreds of Black farmers with research they could use to increase their profits.[31]

Carver was not alone in his recognition that capitalism posed debilitating problems for Black farmers. Du Bois also recognized the exploitative perils of capitalism and championed the potential of cooperatives to liberate Black people from the sharecropping system. According to Monica White, "Du Bois insisted that in order for agriculture to be pursued as a liberator strategy, it must be done collectively."[32] He was confident that "if leading the way as intelligent cooperating consumers, we rid ourselves of the ideas of a price system and become pioneer servants of the common good, we can enter the new city as men and not mules."[33] It was no small thing that Du Bois, Washington, and Carver shared the belief that agricultural innovations were essential to lifting the status of Black people, even if they disagreed on how far it could take them.

Had Ingram owned her land, it may have kept her from the awful circumstances that created her legal crisis. That is, the Ingrams' case was a direct result of sharecropping, which made her and her children vulnerable to daily confrontations with white men who had no legal reason to respect the spaces where sharecroppers worked. The Ingrams garnered the empathy of Black America because their housing situation and livelihood were far from unique. Black Americans knew firsthand the injustice of the sharecropping system, which offered no protections from the entitlements of white landowners and their white neighbors. What they needed more than training was land, which would provide them with the freedom to determine who could enter their property and at what prices they could sell their own crops, and free them from the unfair wages and overpriced rent that kept them indebted to white landowners.

Agricultural land in the United States has been a site for both resisting white supremacy and perpetuating anti-Black oppression from the first days that enslavers forced Africans to work it. Nineteenth-century freedom fighter Sojourner Truth, unlike her male counterparts who generally wanted to escape the South, encouraged Black people to procure land that would benefit them and their progeny. Out of this sensibility, a tradition of Black women emerged and inspired farmers like Fannie Lou Hamer to encourage other Black people to make use of the land for agriculture. They also believed that the land could be used to organize for freedom and against white supremacy because they understood the significance of property ownership in the American context.[34]

Unfortunately, due to the racial injustices of the sharecropping system—the Farmers Home Administration and the USDA, lack of institutional support, anti-Black commercial lending practices, and tax structures geared toward benefiting large farm operations—few Black folks were able to heed calls to own land. This was especially true beginning in 1920, when Black farming faced systematic decreases in the number of Black farmers and Black-owned farms. At that point, Black farmers represented 14 percent of the farms in America, peaking at 925,710. By 1940, that number had fallen to 681,790, a 23 percent decline. Truth, Hamer, Washington, Carver, and Du Bois understood that the loss of this land had grave consequences for the economic future of Black Americans.

Koinonia and the Movement

Though Jordan and England seemed to understand the unfairness of the sharecropping system, their dream of interracial Christian community did not directly address the imbalance of power that was built into the system of white ownership and Black tenancy. Instead, Koinonia focused on interracial relationships. Ironically, their lack of attention to the power imbalances in society mirrored the power imbalances in their interracial fellowships. Charity requires such imbalances; for one party to give to another, the other entity must be in need. Targeting impoverished Black families ensured that the Jordans and the Englands would have recipients for their charity and a Black community to help them accomplish their interracial vision. Whether or not they intended to sustain a charity paradigm, Jordan's and England's lack of power analysis offered them no way to address it. With power imbalances implied in all aspects of their community, they invited Black people to join the community. Few took them up on it, and those who did found that there were requirements of group membership that were unappealing or impractical given the anti-Black threats that awaited them in the surrounding community.

The capabilities of Koinonia's methods for achieving its interracial vision would be tested in the wake of the *Brown* decision. Koinonia had done little to directly confront the institutional policies of Jim Crow until 1956. That year, Jordan represented two Black students who sought admission to the University of Georgia business school. One way that the University of Georgia resisted desegregation and remained an institution that only graduated white people was through a policy that admitted only those students who had an endorsement from an alumnus. Since only white people had graduated from the university, there was little chance that alumni would endorse a prospective Black student. Clarence Jordan, however, endorsed two Black students, Thelma B. Boone and Edward J. Clemons. The action made headlines and drew the ire of local and state officials. From that point onward, Koinonia faced the retribution of white segregationists. White people from as far as Albany boycotted the farm. Local white residents dynamited farm stands, engaged in drive-by shootings, and destroyed farm property.[35]

What the Ingrams and other Black residents of Sumter and nearby Schley County knew firsthand about the Georgian justice system—that it prohibited movements and institutions that promoted Black self-determination and self-protection—Koinonia was learning anew. Of course, the Koinonians were aware of the hostility that white Georgians held toward people who promoted racial equality, but they had yet to face physical retribution on account of those views. Black communities in and around Americus, on the other hand, were no strangers to the violence of Southwest Georgia. Their bodies, especially when found outside the places Southern tradition had designated for them, were always under threat. The history of Jim Crow segregation was proof that the justice system would be of little help to Black people who wanted laws to protect them from white lynch mobs, nor could they be confident in law enforcement to control violent white vigilantes.

Two stories of white violence lived in infamy in the region. In 1913, John M. Collum, a white educator, responded to an article in which Booker T. Washington asserted that lynchings were declining in the South. Collum informed Washington that a white mob had lynched a Black man named Will Redding in Americus. Three white preachers—J. B. Lawrence, J. W. Stokes, and R. L. Bivins—attempted to intervene, but vacated the situation when they were physically removed from it. One of the preachers, Bivins, returned to the scene to plead with the crowd to refrain from burning the body, but someone in the crowd threatened, "If you do not leave we will burn you too."[36] A decade later, in a blatant display of white power, Police Chief John T. Bragg rallied 200 Ku Klux Klansmen on horseback for a parade. The alignment of law enforcement and white supremacist vigilantes riding together on horseback celebrated the terrors of lynching and reminded Black residents of the constant threat of anti-Black violence.

The violent response to Jordan's attempt to integrate his alma mater over forty years later, then, was part of a Sumter County tradition that continued when Koinonia Farm suffered a series of attacks. That was the year Dorothy Day and Elizabeth Morgan came under fire while sitting night watch over the community. The *Atlanta Journal-Constitution* shared photographs of the rubble that followed with a caption: "Koinonia's roadside market after explosion and fire."[37] The caption also shared the conclusion of a grand jury that found no one guilty of a crime: "Grand jury says farm profited from violence." Koinonia was on the receiving end of Southern justice that Blacks had come to expect. The experiment on the farm both frightened and emboldened Black people. Even if the Koinonians were not entirely successful, the farm demonstrated two realities: *Brown* emboldened people to work together across the color line, and many of them were no longer as afraid of the Klan.[38]

News of Koinonia's stand caught the attention of Martin Luther King Jr. In 1957, Jordan contacted King to request his help with an insurance plan that might cover costs related to the damages caused by segregationists. In reply, King shared the name of his insurance company and extended heartfelt words of encouragement. He told Jordan that he was aware of Koinonia and had been praying for them ever since he first heard of their plight. Given the challenges that King had faced since the Montgomery Bus Boycott, he could identify with the conflicting feelings of distress and conviction that Jordan and the community must have felt because of the attacks. "I hope," King wrote compassionately, "that you will gain consolation from the fact that in your struggle for freedom and a true Christian community you have cosmic companionship."[39] He closed the letter with a prayer he would repeat many times for those who shared his desire to end the nation's racial nightmare: "God grant that this tragic midnight of man's inhumanity to man will soon pass and the bright daybreak of freedom and brotherhood will come into being."[40]

This correspondence was not the last time that King and Jordan interacted. The next year (1958), King invited Jordan to preach at the Dexter Avenue Baptist Church's spring lecture series. Jordan's messages on the church and the kingdom were well received. The interactions between King and Jordan created goodwill between the Koinonians and civil rights leaders, so much so that the farm became a place for workers to stay and retreat when they moved their activities to Americus. In 1963, as the Americus movement was getting underway, Koinonia served as a haven where Student Nonviolent Coordinating Committee (SNCC) leaders could do their work.[41]

Numerous Black leaders recognized Koinonia as a safe space for SNCC activists when they came to town. Prior to his time organizing the Americus movement, Charles Sherrod, a young Black veteran of SNCC, had led protests in Richmond and Petersburg, Virginia; McComb, Mississippi; and Albany, Georgia. He expressed gratitude that Koinonia provided him with a peaceful refuge to rest and even prepare for mass demonstrations. On two occasions, Koinonians welcomed Sherrod's army of SNCC workers: once in 1962, when Koinonia hosted a SNCC retreat for the Albany movement, and then in the summer of 1963, as the Americus movement trained activists.

Sherrod also found a conversation partner in Jordan. Indeed, many volunteers, who dedicated their lives to expanding the embrace of democracy through voting registrations and faced danger when they participated in demonstrations, viewed Koinonia as an essential foundation for their work in Sumter County.[42]

Koinonia was not the only place at which SNCC workers gathered for mass meetings, organizing, or for general hospitality. Mabel Barnum, "the mother" of the Americus movement, and her husband John hosted SNCC workers, including Stokely Carmichael and John Lewis, at their funeral home—the oldest Black business in town. Local churches like Allen Chapel, where the president of the Americus movement, Joseph R. Campbell, ministered, and Bethesda Baptist, where Robert L. Freeman served as pastor, more regularly hosted civil rights workers because of their direct involvement. From their perspective, Koinonia's role in the organizing efforts early in the Americus movement was just as essential as any other.[43]

SNCC became aware of the unjust racial conditions in Americus when King and others were arrested during the Albany movement and placed in the Sumter County jail. Civil rights activists had noted the conditions of the city and judged it to be a suitable place to organize a movement. For a year, SNCC organizers met with Americus residents to train them in mass actions. Black Americus residents were frustrated from years spent in racially segregated neighborhoods with under-resourced schools, dilapidated playgrounds, unmaintained ballparks, under-serviced swimming pools, and substandard health care, which symbolically proclaimed to the public that Black people were inferior to whites. Inequality was the intentional outcome of segregation, and the Supreme Court decision to integrate schools did not change that. There were no Black judges, no Black jurors, no Black attorneys, no Black doctors, and no Black police officers in Americus. Black anger over the publicly denigrating circumstances in which they lived found outlets in civil rights actions. While many Black residents did not participate in the Americus movement out of fear of Sheriff Chappell, who King said was "the meanest man on earth," those who did, testified to the worst treatment.[44]

Under the instruction of SNCC organizers, youths, teens, and adults staged marches, which usually began at churches. The marchers stopped at segregated venues, like the movie theater or the courthouse, to defy segregation laws. Expecting to be confronted, participants in the Americus movement refused to disperse when asked. Police officers responded to demonstrators, young and old, with billy clubs, fire hose blasts, and arrests.

Americus movement participants were trained to respond to police aggression using nonviolent methods, like those practiced in the civil rights actions that preceded it. Civil rights action was not new to Sumter County residents. Families like the Barnums and a few Koinonians had traveled to support efforts in Montgomery and Albany years before the civil rights movement came to them. The Americus movement provided Sumter County freedom fighters with ways to use their experiences to serve their own community. Demonstrations like kneel-ins, in which Black demonstrators sought to worship in white congregations, forced unwelcoming white worshippers to justify rejecting prayer warriors from the sanctuary. Similarly, when freedom fighters prayed or publicly sang freedom songs while marching together in the streets or in front of the courthouse, any intervention by law enforcement put their cruelty on display. Through mass demonstrations, marches, prayers, and song, the Americus movement demonstrated the passions that had been stirred among Black people of all ages in Southwestern Georgia, who were willing to risk their lives for freedom.[45]

After Albany, the Southern Christian Leadership Conference (SCLC) and SNCC were increasingly open to allowing young people to put themselves in harm's way for the cause, and in Americus, youths were eager to fight for a future where they could walk the streets with dignity. While their parents may have agreed with the ends, they did not always agree with the means. For this reason, many Black parents forbade their children from participating in the Americus movement. These fears were well founded. One group of teenage girls planned to protest at the movie theater in 1963 but were thwarted before their plan came together. They reported that as they approached the theater, paddy wagons arrived. The police rounded them up, and then placed the dozens of girls in an outdated military prison.[46]

The conditions of the Leesburg Stockade—a facility not used since the Civil War—were inhumane. According to reports and personal testimony, children as young as ten years old were given little food—and it was often inedible. Water was scarce, available only through the dripping shower. There was no toilet, so the girls decided to hide their feces in one of the old bug-infested mattresses that their jailers threw into the concrete slab room where they were being detained. Some of the girls lived in these conditions for months. Adding to their horror, the police would occasionally put snakes in their cells and threaten them with execution. Black parents who forbade their children from attending mass meetings knew of the inhumane treatment that was possible at the hands of Americus police officers. They understood that no matter how noble their acts of nonviolent resistance, no one who participated in these mass actions could be assured of their physical safety.[47]

Clarence Jordan also forbade his daughter from participating in the Americus movement, but he did so out of principle, not fear. Jan, his daughter, recalled, "Koinonia never took part in any demonstrations."[48] As I have noted, individuals from Koinonia participated, but not as representatives of the farm. Some children who grew up at Koinonia listening to sermons on interracial fellowship and watching the adults stand up to segregationists seized opportunities to join their friends from school in mass meetings, singing, and registering people to vote. However, Jan explained that her father believed that participation was wrong. "Jannie, I can go out and kill Sheriff Chappell," he said, "but what I'd be doing wouldn't be right."[49] Jordan allowed his daughter to make her own decision, but he informed her that if she chose to march and she got arrested in the process, "I won't get you out."[50] She would need to stay in jail or contact someone else. Based on his Christian conviction of nonresistance, Jordan believed that marching was wrong, and he could not support it. Nonresistance required Christians to receive unprovoked evil as redemptive violence, but Jordan's "God movement" theology did not permit them to provoke it. Koinonia, then, was a sanctuary for organizers who needed the peace and tranquility of the farm, even though SNCC and SCLC workers' strategies were not entirely compatible with the Koinonian community—especially its unofficial leader, Clarence Jordan. Over time, Koinonia's Jordan-inspired sectarian posture placed tensions on the possibilities of deepening relationships between the groups.[51]

This was essentially the issue that led Jordan and King to fall out of favor with each other. The two men maintained a fondness for each other's early contributions to combating segregation, but they did not grow significantly acquainted after Jordan spoke at the Dexter Avenue Baptist lecture series.[52] That changed in December 1961, when Vincent Harding convened a meeting with King and Jordan in Albany, Georgia, at Jordan's request. According to Harding's memory of the conversation that ensued, "Clarence quickly moved to the direct concern that he had."[53] He advised King to stop marching, boycotting, and making public demonstrations, because he believed those actions repaid evil with evil. Koinonia had been on the other side of boycotts from people who disagreed with them, and based on this experience, Jordan suggested that boycotts were not loving actions. King politely disagreed and Jordan rejected King's perspective, marking the end of their interactions. As we have seen, Jordan allowed SNCC workers to congregate and even organize on the farm until 1963. Undoubtedly, he shared his contrarian views on mass demonstrations with freedom fighters like Sherrod. By 1965, Jordan had preached and penned numerous arguments against the civil rights movement, calling for a "God movement" instead.[54]

Interracial Fellowship

The tensions between civil rights organizing and Koinonian nonresistance expose a significant contradiction at Koinonia: The farm identified itself as an interracial experiment, but interracial interactions on the farm rarely left the property or reached the depth Jordan hoped for. Not only was there a notable difference between most Black freedom fighters in the Americus movement and white allies at Koinonia, but few African Americans ever lived there. The few Black families who came to live on the farm because they believed in the interracial vision—like Sue and Rufus Angry, Eddie and Mildred Johnson, and Wally and Juanita Nelson—did not stay very long. In fact, while Jordan lived, no Black person became a full member of the farm after the white Koinonians created the process for full membership in 1951. Before that transition, Black and white people on the farm shared the same benefits of life together. Full membership, however, required working through a few steps that culminated in signing a document with commitments to the mission and vision of Koinonia as an intentional community. The document represented two virtues that were very important to Jordan: "unconditional commitment" to the "Kingdom of God," and submission to "the body of Christ on earth," as represented by members of the community.[55]

At one meeting, Conrad Browne, a conscientious objector with experience in communal living at the Civilian Public Service camps during World War II, insightfully challenged the power dynamics involved in the new arrangement when he asked, "Are we trying to bring people into Koinonia and our patterns rather than reach them through their own experience?" Jordan's response revealed his belief that living on the farm, for Black or white people, came with obligations to the farm. They were offering housing and fellowship that their Black friends would not find elsewhere. "We shouldn't be encouraging people to think we can help them with living arrangements if they aren't going to come into the Koinonia relationship," he retorted. Despite their interest in Christian living and their disdain for racial segregation, the Black individuals and families who lived on, or adjacent to, the farm did not feel that total surrender to Koinonia was necessary.

"I don't think you have to live in community to be a Christian," Sue Angry explained. For her, it was "an experience you get from being in community that enhanced what [she] already [had]."[56] Moreover, the demands of membership included total reliance on the community for financial resources and expectations that free time would be spent together. When members were not together, they were expected to neglect their quest to overcome generational poverty as well as the freedom that would come with economic stability.

Instead of becoming members, Black neighbors participated on the farm as laborers. They appreciated their ability to receive equal pay on the farm, but the quality of their interactions did not always amount to the type of relationships that either party desired. Koinonians employed several Black laborers and paid them at the same rate as their white peers, which was virtually unheard of in the region. Some of these folks earned a wage and lived elsewhere. Others stayed on the property during the week but lived in the surrounding region on weekends. A smaller few lived at Koinonia or across the road from the farm in a row of tenant houses. Since many of these workers were young county sharecroppers, they celebrated receiving decent pay. As the farm became embroiled in controversy, most of these workers stopped coming. There was not much work or money for them once the shooting and bombing began. Those who stayed worked the farm in defiance of local customs, but defiance fell short of fellowship.

Black folks in Americus had ambivalent views about Koinonia. On the one hand, the farm represented a white Christian alternative to the Jim Crow churches in town. Its charitable outreach to Black Georgians in the region was creative. The cow library, for example, lent dairy cows to families in the community. When a cow no longer produced milk, the patron could bring it back and check out a new one, free of charge. Koinonia also hosted an interracial Sunday school. Perhaps the actions that attracted more Blacks from the community than any other were the farm's employment practices. All these initiatives were created by the predominantly white Koinonian community without any consultation with their Black neighbors. As a result, the Sumter County library patrons, Americus Sunday school students, and day laborers were perpetual visitors who attended activities created for them but without significant opinions, advice, ideas, or input from them.[57]

Reverend Robert L. Freeman, pastor of Bethesda Baptist since 1946, had a different relationship to the farm than most visitors. Freeman met Jordan during the Americus movement. His daughter, Robertina Freeman, was among the first three Black students to integrate Americus High School in 1965. Their courageous act inspired eighty-five other students to apply for transfer the following year, but intimidation tactics by school officials dissuaded them. Freeman and one of her peers, Alex Brown, were charged with fornication. They were fifteen years old and sentenced to detainment until they were eighteen and twenty-one, respectively. SNCC leaders saw the action for what it was: a warning to parents and students that anyone who planned to force integration would be met with maximum retribution. Jordan saw it as an injustice in which he could intervene. When she was detained, Jordan helped Freeman negotiate his daughter's release with the understanding that she would attend a reform school in California. From that point on, Freeman had a special relationship with the farm. He spoke there, and they reserved fresh produce for his family.[58]

The impact of Koinonia's charity was mixed. Invitations for Black workers to congregate with white people at tables of fellowship, for instance, largely failed. The laborers feared that segregationist whites would target Black people who visibly broke the color line. The threat of law enforcement interventions also cast an ominous energy over the farm. Sumter County sheriff Fred Chappell warned that anyone involved with Koinonia "would get hurt." Given the history of intimidation by government officials and vigilantes, many folks heeded the warning. Black folks who moved to the farm from the county expressed that their family members feared they would suffer severe repercussions. Still, some day laborers participated with full knowledge of the danger. They received decent pay from the farm, and it gave them the opportunity to defy the degrading culture.[59]

Dorothy Day only stayed for a short time, but it was long enough to note the different experiences of terror felt by white and Black people on the farm. Koinonians kept two watches each night: late evening and early morning. Trespassers had cut fences a dozen times, destroying property and causing the farm to lose livestock. Bullet holes decorated signs and windows on the property. Day reported in her weekly column that "dynamiting, machine gunning, [and] isolated shots from high powered rifles" were common harassment strategies for enemies of the predominantly white community.[60] She noted that she was shaken by the mortal threats in a way the white Koinonians were not. "It is hard for these white southerners to really believe that anything can happen to them," she observed. "The danger to their bodies," Day explained, "seems remote. In spite of the shootings."[61] From her perspective, nothing shook their resolve more than the boycotts—not the shootings, the fires, or the dynamite. The economic hardship brought on by white neighbors who refused to conduct business with the farm engendered fears of foreclosure. Without steady income and regular damage to the farm, white Koinonians anxieties rose over their inability to secure insurance that would cover the property and its machines when it was damaged. Their concerns for safety were not equal to their financial fears or to the physical fears that Blacks faced.[62]

Jordan claimed otherwise. In the early days of the farm, Klansmen used intimidation to try to scare Jordan and England away. Jordan liked to tell audiences about one such occasion when members of the Klan heard that he had dinners with a Black day laborer who was indebted to a white farmer in the region. Two men approached the farm and introduced themselves as representatives of the Ku Klux Klan who were looking for a man named Clarence Jordan. Jordan narrated that they wasted no time before they announced, "We're here to tell you that we don't allow the sun to set on anybody who eats with niggers."[63] He responded with a handshake and a grin, "I'm a Baptist preacher and I just graduated from the Southern Baptist Seminary. I've heard about people who had power of the sun, but I never hoped I'd meet one!"[64] Jordan made certain to let his audiences know that he was scared, but as a Christian, he believed it was more important to be obedient. In his estimation, not only was "God blind to externalities . . . We knew white men could disappear just like black men."[65] Still, the likelihood that a white minister would suffer the same fate as the thousands of lynched Black people in the South or suffer the injustices of the Ingrams or the Scottsboro Boys was not great. Jordan proudly reported that the encounter with the Klansmen ended with laughter and swapping stories late into the evening—a nearly inconceivable conclusion for a Black farmer in the same position.

Thus, a major issue that undermined white Koinonians' efforts to build interracial relationships was that they underestimated the risks that Black participants took each time they engaged with the farm. Most Black people steered clear of Koinonia. The white Koinonians eventually came to understand that the differences were significant. Most of the shootings seemed to be indiscriminately aimed into the air, at buildings, cars, or hogs. No human beings were killed as a result of the drive-by shootings.

On one series of nights, white terrorists targeted Black residents and neighbors with burning crosses. The home of the Wilsons, a Black family who worked at the farm, was shot at and became a location for a cross burning shortly after. On another evening, Alma Jackson's parents, who did not live on the farm, were also terrorized by a burning cross in their yard. White supremacists raised two more crosses that evening. Law enforcement was of no avail, and the incidents led some of the Black folks to cease their participation with the farm.[66]

Wally and Juanita Nelson, who were members of the Fellowship of Reconciliation, represented a different role for Black folks at the farm. They had no need of it beyond the symbolic inspiration that it offered to their white Protestant peers. The Nelsons were well known for their activism and leadership in major radical Christian pacifist organizations. They were founding members of the Peacemakers and were present at the beginnings of the Congress of Racial Equality. Moreover, each had their own résumé of activist experiences that made them major assets to Koinonia for the few months they lived there. Wally had been a conscientious objector during World War II and was one of the first "freedom riders." Juanita had participated in the first wave of sit-ins while a student at Howard.[67]

Answering the call of the Koinonia community to have their presence during its greatest time of need in 1956, the Nelsons chose to take the fearless spirit that they had cultivated in their decades of activism to the farm. During the boycott, the Koinonians needed to travel outside the local region to gather feed, fertilizer, seeds, and basic household goods because their white opponents recognized their faces. Day, for instance, traveled with Florence Jordan to Albany to purchase supplies when she stayed at the farm. The Koinonians had made it clear that "being a Yankee, an outsider, a Negro, and an agitator all rolled into one, you would be quite loathsome" and would face danger from their white enemies.[68] However, as fresh faces, the Nelsons could purchase basic items at local stores without anyone questioning their affiliations. They also served the community as two more adults who could watch over the farm at night.

When planning their watch, they refused to concede to fear. White Koinonians eventually recognized that Black people were in more danger than Jordan had assumed, so they arranged for white members to take the latest watch. But the Nelsons insisted that they also take a turn; to do less would be to let the segregationist Christians win. Juanita admitted that they were embarrassed one night when lights from an oncoming car and its accompanying backfire provoked them to duck—their faith required that they confront evil, not duck from it. Their witness heartened the community.[69]

Beyond their ability to make purchases for the farm or to stand watch at night, the couple's presence allowed for the project to continue its experiment in interracialism. The combination of white terrorist violence, the requirement for communal commitment, and the inability of Koinonia to continue to support laborers during the boycott led to an exodus of Black people from the property. Thus, the Nelsons served an essential service by being there for those months when members seriously contemplated whether the community could continue. Without relationships with Black participants, Koinonia could not complete its mission.

The few Black participants who remained at Koinonia were committed to many aspects of the project, but without full membership in the community, they did not participate in major decisions, like who could join and which individuals would be dismissed. In 1956, the power of the full members would affect the relationship of Eddie and Mildred Johnson, who had moved to the farm seeking membership. Eddie was one of the few people who lived at Koinonia and traveled to Montgomery soon after the Montgomery Bus Boycott began. He expressed his devotion to the community in a letter he labeled, "A Letter of Clarification and Justification on the Status of Edward Johnson's Noviceship." The tone of the letter communicated Johnson's great distress about tensions that threatened his ongoing participation in the community. Johnson wanted to attend college. He denied the charges of some full members who felt that he was using Koinonia to "further [his] own ends."[70] Johnson admitted to having the desire to better himself, but he pleaded with the full members to understand that he was also committed to Koinonia. With the power to vote him out, his fate as a novice was in the full members' hands.

It was likely that Johnson had entered the three-step process of membership that began with a declaration of desire to become a member. Still, there seemed to be some debate about the legitimacy of his novitiate status in the first place. "I know that in reality I am not a novice," he admitted, "but theoretically, I am."[71] As a novice, Johnson would have entered a status that could result in provisional membership. Novices committed to a long interview process. As they adjusted to life in the community, members observed their fitness for the community. After Koinonia changed its membership standards, each participant had to decide whether or not to seek full membership. If accepted to full membership, Johnson would have more responsibilities and decision-making power in the community. Until then, he was under the authority of the white membership, who made all the decisions on the farm.[72]

The white full members did not intend to communicate any significant difference between visitors, novices, provisional members, or full members. They emphasized within and without the community that they practiced equality. For example, when a caravan of white neighbors came to Koinonia looking for "the leader," members who met them at the gate informed them that they did not have one. Yet the impact of their membership structure and Jordan's charismatic personality suggested otherwise; unequal power dynamics within the community were undeniable.

Tracy K'Meyer writes that "the Koinonians' effort to strengthen their inner community led them to define membership in a way that alienated African Americans, setting up a barrier between whites and blacks and creating separate categories for them at the farm."[73] Another Black resident, Sue Angry, noted in an interview decades later that there was a group of full members that she was not a part of who made most of the decisions. The Angry family arrived at Koinonia from Sumter County in 1954, after Eddie Johnson and Norman Long recruited them, but they did not stay long. She and her husband, Rufus, had concerns that the white membership did not understand. Since there were no Black residents in the decision-making body, they felt that it was unlikely that they would be added to it. Angry did not feel that white full members were particularly "authoritarian" or "more in control."[74] She understood that they made important decisions concerning the status of the experiment that sometimes kept them up all night. Still, they decided important matters like membership processes, whether members could hold on to personal insurance, and what constituted true communitarianism.

Reconfiguring Relationships

Evidence suggests that while the predominantly white membership at Koinonia intended for the interracial experiment to operate out of a spirit of racial equality, their policies and decision-making processes betrayed their intentions. Instead, they re-created a racial hierarchy wherein white Koinonians decided who could stay and which candidates for membership could not. The land itself became a site of contest over not the equality of Black Georgians but whether it would become a sanctuary for assimilation. The ideology associated with membership required members to trust in the common purse for their economic vitality, which offered no security if they left to join the outside world. Beyond inspiring folks with a vision, that world remained unchanged by the interracialist program at the farm. For Black freedom fighters and Koinonia's Black neighbors, inspiration did not satisfy their need to abolish Jim Crow and live free from the daily humiliations of segregation, nor did it weaken the threats of violent retribution from white supremacists who interpreted any suggestion of

Black equality as an endorsement of the civil rights movement, even if Jordan taught otherwise.

After a quarter century in Americus, Jordan realized that the mission and vision of Koinonia Farm had little to offer a Black Southern context that cultivated a civil rights movement and welcomed Black empowerment. In recognition that the charity model could not create the vision for which he longed, he and his team changed the name to Koinonia Partners in 1968. A pamphlet from that year proclaimed, "What the poor need is not charity but capital, not case-workers but co-workers. And what the rich need is a wise, honorable and just way of divesting themselves of their overabundance."[75] This transition was the beginning of what would become Habitat for Humanity, a nonprofit organization that built affordable homes for impoverished people. Interestingly, this turn to partnerships included a former IBM executive and about fifteen other men who convinced Jordan that this course of action held the greatest potential for Koinonia to effectively serve the needs of Black people in the future. It remained to be seen if Koinonia could make the transition from charity to solidarity, from making programs for Black folks to building a mission and vision with them. For as much as Koinonia had changed, Jordan's biblical interpretation remained a central instructive tool his partners used to build that future. They may have insisted that Jordan was not their leader, but it was his theological imagination and biblical hermeneutics that animated their determination to continue with the work. That imagination held the key to explaining why Jordan's organization never integrated with Black-led movements for freedom.

5 Reconciliation

. . . .

> To Stokely and the young men in SNCC, I would just say briefly that
> the Christian religion you are rejecting, that you are so opposed to,
> is a slave Christianity that has no roots in the teachings of the Black
> Messiah. You could be ordained in this Church as civil rights workers
> if we could somehow do away with the distinctions which exist in
> people's minds between what's religious and what's not religious. To
> ordain civil rights workers for civil rights work would declare that the
> Christian Church believes that this is what Christianity is all about,
> that individuals who give their lives in the struggle for human freedom
> are Christian and that the movement is not only Christian, but that the
> Movement is the Church.
>
> —Albert Cleage Jr., *The Black Messiah*

Pearl Reed Cleage admonished her son to reject his New Testament professor's portrayal of Jesus. She told him that the professor was wrong "because Jesus was Black." It was this lesson from his mother that inspired the founder of the Shrine of the Black Madonna, Albert Cleage, to teach Christians to embrace a Black Messiah and reject the notion of a white Christ. Cleage believed that such a move was essential for Black people to break free from the bondage of white oppression and embrace their full dignity as persons created in the divine image. "Black people cannot build dignity on their knees worshipping a white Christ," he preached. Yet Cleage found that when he and other Black preachers and theologians insisted on recognizing God as Black, white Christians ridiculed them.[1]

Cleage desired for Black people to be counted among the self-respecting communities of the world, celebrating the unique contributions of Black politics and Black religion. To his dismay, however, pictures of white Jesus decorated many Black churches and homes. By the 1960s, Werner Sallman's painting of Jesus in white face had become the most popular image of Jesus in America.[2] This reality provided great fodder for other Black nationalists. Cleage's colleague Malcolm X often campaigned against American

Christianity by presenting it as a white religion: "Brothers and sisters, the white man has brainwashed us black people to fasten our gaze upon a blond-haired blue-eyed Jesus!"[3] Though a Muslim, Cleage welcomed Malcolm's voice whenever possible because the two shared a Black nationalist vision that he believed would be the realization of his mother's Black Messiah.

By the time Albert Cleage completed his book, *The Black Messiah*, in 1968, he had constructed a Black Christology that fully endorsed Black freedom fighters—student civil rights workers and Black Power advocates—in their pursuit of national equality. Due to his promotion of Black Christian nationalism, he advocated ordaining them as ministers. As he saw it, a Christianity that embraced freedom fighters was essential to Black nationalism because the church was the center of Black life in America. At the same time, he believed that Black Christians who internalized self-hatred when they worshipped the god of their oppressors were hindrances to the realization of the Black nation, and they needed to repent. But if they confessed with their mouth the beauty of the Black Madonna and believed in their heart in the power of the Black child in her arms, then they would find pride in building a Black nation.[4]

More than an aesthetic to adore, Cleage taught that the literal Blackness of Jesus's phenotypical features, as well as his revolutionary actions, supplied ethics to be followed. He believed that this revolutionary ethic of Jesus was a judgment on American churches. Thus, Cleage's ministry celebrated movements that fought for Black freedom as Christian and dismissed churches as false that did not. "The Black Messiah Jesus," he taught, "did not build a Church, but a movement." The movement, he explained, "is the Christian Church in the 20th Century and . . . the Christian Church cannot truly be the church until it also becomes the Movement."[5]

In a sermon dedicated to Stokely Carmichael, the president of the Student Nonviolent Coordinating Committee (SNCC), Cleage said that true Christians were more "like today's young black prophets," who, like Jesus, "rejected the institutionalization of religion."[6] Cleage believed that the young people of SNCC were revolutionaries whose activism represented the will of God. The Black Messiah "rejected the Church deliberately because," he declared, "it's wrong, it's hypocritical, and it's opposed to the will of God." He reasoned that if Jesus "rejected the morality of his time and rejected the Church of his time," then these young people, even in rejecting Christianity, were the true Christians. Their demands were the will of God. "And," he added, "almost everything you have heard about Christianity is essentially a lie."[7]

Cleage's unabashed call to ordain civil rights activists of SNCC for acting on the "will of God" could not have been more different from Clarence Jordan's repudiation of their methods as too "political." It is surprising, then, how much Cleage's Black nationalist position shared with Jordan's interracial sectarianism, especially in the way both ministers cast biblical characters in the drama of America's racial context. They each viewed the New Testament narrative as instructive of the role that Americans should take in the nation's racial drama. For them, the failure of churches to properly address racial segregation determined their true relationship to God's mission. That said, Cleage's Black Messiah represented a stark contrast from the white Jesus of Jordan's *Cotton Patch Gospel*. Whereas Cleage embraced the civil rights movement as the "will of God," Jordan's decision to recast white Jesus in the Southern context led him to place civil rights workers in opposition to the "God movement." And though the white Southern Baptist church members who were cast as disciples in Jordan's cultural translation of the New Testament were narrative tools, not historical claims, his *Cotton Patch Gospel* informed the strategies that Koinonia mounted against segregation.

In this chapter, I compare Cleage's *Black Messiah* to the white Jesus Jordan constructed in his *Cotton Patch Gospel*. In so doing, I will show that the application of Cleage's Black imagination to Christian scriptures celebrated the revolutionary impulses of freedom fighters, while Jordan's white reimagining of the New Testament encouraged allies to privilege racial reconciliation over revolutionary action. In other words, Black and white hermeneutics produced conflicting visions of Christian community in America. Black hermeneutics centered Black liberation, and white hermeneutics centered assimilation to white Protestantism. By analyzing these visions, I argue that Black and white Christians who opposed Jim Crow, who similarly took their cues from scripture, who made Christology an important point of reflection, and who risked their lives to do so had drastically different understandings of Christian community.

Cleage's Christological approach in *Black Messiah* has been largely dismissed by theologians as too reliant on racial literalism and by integrationists as anti-white, while the Jesus of Jordan's *Cotton Patch Gospel* has been overlooked as a racial figure altogether.[8] Ansley Quiros's important research on competing racial orthodoxies between Christians in Jim Crow Americus offers a keen analysis of white Southerners' racial purity narratives, especially as they pertain to Jesus. Informed by J. Kameron Carter's incisive critique of supersessionist interpretations that imagine Jesus as racially white, Quiros writes, "This Christology did not subvert racism; it buttressed it." She helpfully names the power of white Southern Christology when she writes, "Jesus was at the top, the whitest of the white (he was God, after all), followed by white Americans, with Southerners imagining themselves at the peak, since they were the ones preserving America's racial stock and the fundamentals of Christianity."[9] Quiros does not name Jordan as a participant in making white Southern Christology, but his white Jesus warrants no less consideration than his fellow white Southern Baptists. He, too, is a Southerner who reimagines Jesus as one of his own and, in so doing, reinforces the notion that salvation is made available through a white Christ. The difference, which is significant, is that Jordan's white Jesus abolishes racial segregation. Jesus, then, as the racially pure, whitest of white, savior in Jordan's framework offers Black people salvation through reconciling themselves to a white Christ, who is represented by white Christians in white Baptist congregations.

Having too quickly dismissed Black and white Christologies as represented by Cleage and Jordan, scholars have neglected to consider the significance of centering Black hermeneutics in Black freedom movements and the impact of white hermeneutics in white allyship. In Cleage's and Jordan's cases, the production of racial myths that erased the Jewish context of the Bible inspired communities to organize against racial segregation. As we have seen in previous chapters, Black and white visions led to parallel movements that often opposed one another. Furthermore, replacing the Jewish Jesus with a Black Messiah in Cleage's theology and a white Southern Baptist in Jordan's translation had profound effects on the two men's interpretation of the American context and the choices they made to engage with it—or, for Jordan, disengage from it.[10]

For Cleage, Jesus's blackness placed Black people, and their struggle against racial injustice, at the center of the biblical narrative. His afro-styled, kinky-haired Black Messiah testified to the dignity that was inherent to Black life. Cleage preached, "Black is beautiful!"[11] This beauty led Cleage to consider all of life against one maxim: "If anything gives a black man a sense of pride and dignity, it is good. If it destroys his pride and dignity, it is bad."[12] Centering Black beauty in Christianity affirmed the worth of adults and children who lived in a predominantly white nation that looked paternalistically at them as inferior.

The Black Madonna and child did more than affirm the beauty of Black people. In Cleage's ministry, it became the doctrine upon which Christians should be inspired to act. Cleage's Black Christian National movement reconstructed the meaning of ecclesiology, orthodoxy, and orthopraxy. Cleage viewed the true Black Church as the Black nation. Correct belief required a transformation of the mind from seeking the approval of white people to fighting "to be free by any means necessary." None of this was possible without first acknowledging that Jesus was Black. For if Jesus was Black, and Black people were created in God's image, then Cleage reasoned that Black was beautiful, the Christian church was a Black nation, and Black Christians should be revolutionaries who followed God in overturning the racial injustices of the American government—including its systems and institutions. As Cleage put it, "This is the task of the church because God created us in his own image and as children of God we must walk with pride and dignity."[13]

There was nothing figurative about Cleage's claims. His teachings were unique in this way. Most theologians in the Black Jesus tradition were reluctant to claim that God was literally Black. In addition to his mother, Cleage was inspired by Garvey's African Orthodox Church, with its "black hierarchy, including a Black God, a Black Jesus, a Black Madonna, and Black angels." Garvey used this Black aesthetic to offer the United Negro Improvement Association (UNIA) a spiritual identity that affirmed Black beauty. While Jesus's blackness was important, it was symbolically important. Garvey suggested that God was no color at all. In contrast, Cleage referred to Jesus as the "historic Black Messiah" to emphasize that Jesus's historical context in the biblical narrative was congruous to the context of Black Americans in twentieth century. The Black Messiah, then, was based in geographic, social, and racial realities that could not be reconciled to a white vision of Christianity—a vision in which white people were the protagonists of a tradition that began in a predominantly white world.[14]

Alternatively, Jordan changed the setting of the New Testament from first-century Palestine to twentieth-century America. His task, as he described it in "A Note on *The Cotton Patch Gospel*" was to share God's word with his "humble" companions "on a farm in southwest Georgia." To apply the scriptures to his contemporary context, to recognize the ways the scriptures speak to "problems of this region," he replaced "Jew and Gentile" identities with "white man and Negro."[15] The choice to racialize the text in this way centered the white race as God's people. The Israelites, the Jews, the disciples, Paul, and the other authors of the New Testament became white Angle-Saxon Protestants. Black people became gentiles who were invited into fellowship with the white nation. And Jesus became the model for all people to become true "white" men—whether white or Black.[16] The choice was strained in several ways. First, some twentieth-century Jews lived in the American South and were hated by white supremacists as much as Blacks and Catholics were. Second, Jordan acknowledged that Jews despised the hegemony of Roman imperial power, but in his New Testament he made Jews representatives of the Roman Empire.

Jordan made no attempt to align the New Testament with the Southern context's power relations in first-century Rome. If he had, then he would have needed to account for the culpability of white Protestant hegemony in legitimizing the racial hierarchy as well as religious violence against Catholic and Jewish immigrants. Such an analysis would have necessitated accounting for the negligence of state officers to protect Black people and non-Protestant immigrants in their support for white segregationists. Moreover, after the 1954 *Brown* decision, Jordan would have needed to account for state and local government assistance to white Protestants in defying the federal mandate to integrate public spaces. These circumstances may have led him to conclude that white people, not Jews, more accurately represented the Roman Empire. A power analysis might have enabled him to view the courts and federal officials as resources against segregation, but his theology of nonresistance prohibited him from advocating such action. Jordan was not concerned with power dynamics; he translated the New Testament to convince white Christians to condemn racial segregation in order to elevate his understanding of the God movement.

The assimilationist implications of the text were lost on many who read his translation, likely because it also overtly condemns racial segregation. In his commentary on Ephesians, Jordan writes, "Any church or any person who erects these barriers of race or external differences is guilty of the worst kind of heresy and should no longer consider himself a member of God's family."[17] Yet in making the decision to racialize Jesus and other Jews as white, his New Testament compels the reader to accept white Southern tradition as the proxy for Judaism and the foundation upon which Christianity is built. Consequently, Black people who were "outside" white Southern tradition could only come "inside" through a white Jesus who grafted them into the white Southern Christian community.

Unlike Cleage, Jordan did not argue for a literal reading of his racial or regional translation choices, but he did aim to transform the ecclesiology, orthodoxy, and orthopraxy of Christianity in America. Quiros points out that "Koinonia Farm, white Southern Protestants, and the black churches of Americus represented distinct groups with particular theologies and competing claims to Christian orthodoxy and to the Christian view of race."[18]

Jordan distinguished his theology by spiritualizing segregation and by proposing that only through a sole concern for the God movement could Christians become allies with the divine to end it. His community was not a church building; rather, it was a demonstration plot on farmland where Christians could practice interracial fellowship. Jordan's orthodoxy required racial equality, but his failure to recognize the power differences between white and Black Americans in his strategies led him to believe this equality could be achieved by ignoring the systems and structures of the world beyond his Christian community.

Cleage could do no such thing. In his reflections on Black life, it was clear that the struggle against white supremacy was not restricted to city streets, courthouses, police departments, or auto factories—it pervaded all aspects of American society from the supreme court to the sanctuary. Oppressive forces of white domination threatened to hold Black people in bondage to poverty, housing insecurity, isolation, and self-hatred. In Detroit, Michigan, where Cleage led the Shrine of the Black Madonna congregation, Christian communities could not afford to be refuges from the world that advocated for an otherworldly future of prosperity, nor could they form a separate space where Black people could escape into a spiritual fellowship, because history demonstrated that even Black churches faced physical threats of state-supported white violence.

Cleage believed that Black churches had compromised their position as institutions for Black empowerment. Pastors of Black congregations in Detroit had positioned themselves to partner with exploitative white bosses and spiritualized social and political inequalities in America. Reverend Cleage surmised that Christian communities had to see themselves as revolutionary outposts of a Black nation whose purpose was to transform the world. Their Christian members had to become revolutionaries like Jesus, who "pitted himself against the power structure which was holding his people in bondage."[19]

From the perspective of Black Jesus traditions, Jordan's apolitical white Jesus only broke down barriers of animosity between individuals. Even if a white Christ could elevate their Christian identity above their racial status, he was impotent to do more than create brief opportunities for interracial work or communal meals in a society dominated by white systems. White Jesus could not lift the pride and dignity of a Black nation. Cleage's revolutionary Black Messiah, on the other hand, provided Black Christians with a divine model who promised to overcome systems of white supremacy.

A Black Jesus Tradition

That Black people worshipped a white Jesus increasingly became a concern of Black preachers and theologians across Black freedom movements. Black freedom activists were keenly aware of the symbols and structures that hindered them from exercising their rights as citizens of the United States and as members of Christian congregations. Symbols of white Jesus were ubiquitous in churches, homes, and public spaces. Despite this, some Black Christians had developed a Black Jesus tradition that spanned more than one hundred years, beginning at least in 1829, when David Walker suggested that Black and white Christians worshipped two different Gods, "The God of the Blacks" and "The oppressor's God."[20] In the decades that ensued, followers of the Black God mused that the God of the Exodus identified with the colonial oppression they endured in the Americas, and with God on their side, they voiced their skepticism of white sermons, white interpretations of scripture, and white theology.

In 1898, Bishop Henry McNeal Turner taught his African Methodist Episcopal denomination that God must be Black because there can be no "hope for a race of people who do not believe that they look like God." Turner, also a former Georgia state representative, whose theological views were well known, scoffed when white opponents called him demented for suggesting that he and God were the same race. "Every race of people since time began," he rebutted, "who have attempted to describe their God by words, or by paintings, or by carvings, or by any other form or figure have conveyed the idea that the God who made them and shaped their destinies was symbolized in themselves." Then he asked rhetorically, "And why should not the Negro believe that he resembles God as much as other people?"[21]

Instead, through enslavement and indoctrination, Black Christians learned that they must worship a white deity. Turner warned his Christian kin, "Demented though we be, whenever we reach the conclusion that God or even that Jesus Christ, while in the flesh, was a white man, we shall hang our gospel trumpet upon the willow and cease to preach." For Turner, preaching, ministry, worship, and any other association with Christianity was undesirable if it meant denying the beauty and strength of the descendants of Africans. He concluded, "We had rather be an atheist and believe in no God or a pantheist and believe that all nature is God than to believe in the personality of a God and not believe that He is Negro."[22]

During the New Negro movement of the 1920s, UNIA founder Marcus Garvey claimed that it was important to the humanity of Black people to affirm their theological perspectives: "It is human to see everything through one's own spectacles." He suggested, like Turner, that it was natural for other races to have an idea of God that looked like them. It was not that God had a race. He claimed that "our God has no color." Still, for a race to have a positive view of itself, its members needed a positive perspective through which to look upon the world. For Garvey, that perspective became the land of Ethiopia, the cradle of Black civilization. Garvey described how he harmonized this view with a trinitarian Christology: "We Negroes believe in the God of Ethiopia, the everlasting God—God the Father, God the Son and God the Holy Ghost, the One God of all ages."[23]

Much of Black Christology was a response to the insistence from white Christians that Christ was white. For many Black people who openly expressed tenuous relationships to Christianity, the white Jesus was a loathsome point of departure. This was true for James Baldwin, the 1960s author and social critic who expressed longing for the energy of ancient Christianity to return to the world with "the hope of liberation." Since the rise of Western nation-states, however, Baldwin believed that the transformational potential of the desert religion had been subjugated under white supremacist "details and symbols" that were "deliberately constructed to make [Black people] believe what white people say about [them]."[24] In the Pentecostal Christian world, in which he was formed, he learned that God was white.

One doctrine of the Nation of Islam that appealed to Baldwin was its teaching that "God is black." It charged that "all black men belong to Islam; they have been chosen. And Islam shall rule the world." Baldwin had encountered theological claims that God took sides before. "The dream, the sentiment is old," he remembered; "only the color is new." He found beauty in dreaming of divine blackness and sympathized with many other Black Americans who converted. "And it is this dream, this sweet possibility," he explained, "that thousands of oppressed black men and women in this country now carry away with them after the Muslim minister has spoken, through the dark, noisome ghetto streets, into the hovels where so many have perished." The payoff of this dream, however, was not simply that they could carry God into Black neighborhoods; it was rather the new possibility that since "the white God has not delivered them; perhaps the Black God will."[25] Ultimately, even with the optimism it inspired, Baldwin could not accept the new allegiance of God to only Black America. Bound by an ethic of radical love for all humanity, he resolved, "If the concept of God has any validity or any use, it can only be to make us larger, freer, and more loving. If God cannot do this, then it is time we got rid of Him."[26]

Freedom fighters pursued the concept of a Black God that might empower Black people to love themselves better for decades. For Turner and Garvey, the color of God was a symbolic affirmation that Black people were created in the divine image and therefore God loved them and would bring about a just end to their struggle. Garvey explicitly stated that God was a spirit and colorless. In the face of white propaganda that used theology to preach a doctrine of white racial superiority, however, Garvey recognized the efficacy of Black people meditating upon the idea that God could be Black. Turner's justification for his Black theology was similar in that he found the suggestion that God could be Black a credible source for Black empowerment.

The Messiah in Motown

Empowered by the Black Jesus tradition Cleage developed the idea of a Black God more thoroughly than any Christian theologian before him. Practically speaking, his application of divine Blackness in his preaching and aesthetic had a lot in common with the Nation of Islam, but due to his Christianity, it owed mostly to Garvey. Cleage's Black Christian aesthetic lent cosmic significance to the Great Migration, which by the 1960s had produced a Black community that made up 40 percent of the total population in Detroit. He reconstructed Christian liturgies to heal Black residents of the oppressive actions of Detroit's white institutions. Ultimately, the Detroit context inspired Cleage to organize political opposition to white supremacy in the name of the revolutionary Black Messiah, who taught that it was God's will to oppose white power.

Cleage's theology was a product of the presence and experiences of Black people in Detroit. Black people who had relocated to Detroit were like other migrants who had moved to the North in search of industrial work and freedom from the control of racial segregation. Upon their arrival to the North, they found a strange Jim Crow that was not enshrined in law but in custom. To their dismay, the Black arrivals in Detroit faced housing, employment, education, and law enforcement discrimination from the 1910s onward. Having been raised in Detroit, Cleage also experienced discrimination at each of these levels.

Like other Northern cities, Detroit neighborhoods were segregated by racial designations—middle-class white residents on one side of the tracks, and struggling white ethnic and Black residents (sometimes divided by street lines) on the other. City services, though officially available to all races, routinely failed to attend to the needs of the city's Black residents. Cleage's father, Albert Cleage Sr., was a physician whose frustration over the failure of hospitals to provide medical assistance to Black people led him to join a group of other Black physicians to found Dunbar Hospital in 1918—the first Black hospital in Detroit. Some Black residents denounced Dunbar, believing it was a plot to further expand segregation in the city. The Cleage family's unusually prominent status through Cleage Sr.'s occupation and his appointment by the mayor, Charles Boyles, to city physician caused other Black people to distrust them. The distrust that many Blacks held against the family was felt by the Cleage children too. It was so pronounced that Cleage Jr. and his sister recalled that their classmates ridiculed them and even barred them from joining school activities. Such experiences remained in Cleage Jr.'s memory throughout his life.[27]

When Cleage left the city to pursue a college education and eventually join the Christian clergy, Detroit became a racial tinderbox that burst into a violent uprising in 1943—the first of a series of racial conflicts that continued for decades. Most Black Detroiters were not able to secure the kind of housing that the Cleages had with their home on the west-side neighborhood of Tireman because few Black laborers found the industrial jobs that they had hoped for when they journeyed north. The Ford Motor Company—the largest employer in the city, led by the anti-unionist Henry Ford—employed only those Black men who received recommendations from a small group of Black clergy. Other industries followed suit. As a result, their employment was often a replacement for white United Auto Workers strikers, who came to resent the role that Black workers represented in making the strikes less effective. The confluence of white resentment and low Black employment created housing insecurity for many Black families.

As US factories transitioned to support the war effort in the 1940s, Charles F. Palmer—coordinator of defense housing for the National Defense Office for Emergency Management—was tasked with providing housing for new defense laborers in industrial cities. In Detroit, which included a Black population that had grown from 6,000 to 120,000, representing 8 percent of the population in 1910 and nearly 35 percent in 1940, Palmer estimated that the war effort would create 84,000 new jobs. In 1941, he called for "1,000 government financed homes, and 10,000 privately built homes"—of which 200 would be set aside for Black workers.[28] Vested with Federal Housing Administration (FHA) funds, the Detroit Housing Commission (DHC) built the temporary housing close to an already existing middle-class community intermixed with Black and Polish residents. According to historian Angela Dillard, "Both the FHA and DHC had an explicit policy against 'any attempt to change the racial pattern of any area in Detroit' since such an action 'will result in violent opposition to the housing program.'"[29] Officials reasoned that this location would not upset white residents who typically resented the thought of living next door to Black people. They were wrong. The proponents of the Sojourner Truth housing development, named for the Black abolitionist and women's rights activist, miscalculated the feelings of the nearby Polish community.

According to Rev. Charles A. Hill—a Black social gospel minister and leftist political leader—the Polish residents of Conant Gardens mistakenly believed that Sojourner Truth was a Polish name and assumed that the new housing was for them. When they learned of the city's plans to house more Black people there, they protested first with words and then with violence. A Polish Catholic priest, Father Constantine Dzink, fomented Polish resentment through the organization of a white citizens commission, the Seven Mile–Fenlon Improvement Association, that villainized Black and Jewish alliances as dangers to both the property values and the safety of white girls. Initially, their complaints successfully convinced the DHC and the FHA to designate the Sojourner Truth homes to white people.

In the summer of 1942, Hill became chair of the Sojourner Truth Citizens Committee (STCC), initially an all-Black committee, and gathered its members on the Sojourner Truth grounds, where they demanded that the city return the development to Black people. Over time, the committee built interracial coalitions with white leftists, white liberals, Jews, and other Black organizations. The groups shared information, supported the effort financially, and met regularly to strategize. They also sent delegations to influence officials who had the power to meet their demands. Hill was a featured speaker at the mass demonstrations and rallies, where he appealed to shared national and even world interests. On one occasion, Hill reminded Poles and his coalition that they shared a common World War II enemy when he preached, "Hitler hates both of us."[30]

As a result of STCC's efforts, the DHC relented and returned to the original plan. But white residents were not pleased with the decision, and a violent clash ensued. As the first Black family attempted to move in, a mob designed to consist of mostly white women and children was present to meet them with pickets signs and weapons. Supporters of the Black family lined the other side of the street, prepared to see to it that they were able to safely make residence. One hundred and fifty white police officers watched the parties hurl angry remarks at one another, only intervening after rocks were thrown and knives were drawn. To quell the violence, the Detroit Police Department arrested 220 people; 109 of them were held for trial—only 3 of whom were white.[31]

It was clear to many that the police had targeted Black people at the move-in. As was the design of those who planned for white protesters, the police department claimed that they were protecting the white women and children. Their failure to protect the would-be residents meant that the Black family was unable to move in that day. But that was not the end of the story. Two months later, accompanied by police and the Michigan Home Guard, fourteen Black families finally moved into their homes. This time, only one incident was reported: a mob of angry white people threw a stone at a Black man's car.[32]

The incident at the Sojourner Truth homes revealed biases and foreshadowed racial conflicts that plagued the city for years to come. Many Black Detroiters viewed the police as antagonists who could not be trusted to protect their interests; local officials blamed radical groups like communists for stirring animosities between groups; Black leaders believed the power of clandestine white organizations like the KKK had motivated white citizens and city officials; and the federal government blamed labor organizations for upsetting workers. All these suspicions raised in 1942 fueled the first of a series of uprisings that represented Black Detroit's discontent.

Only a year later, discontented Black and resentful white Detroiters clashed in devastating fashion. On June 20, 1943, the city exploded with violence, leaving 34 people dead, 675 injured, and nearly 2,000 jailed. Local Black frustrations were fueled by lack of housing, struggles to find stable employment, and discrimination that they faced at restaurants, at schools, and in public recreational spaces. These ongoing racial aggressions contradicted the World War II messages sent to Detroit, where motor companies were supposed to employ more residents when factories were converted to make war materials. Such innovations were supposed to encourage US Americans of all races to find common cause in their war efforts. In 1941, President Franklin Delano Roosevelt encouraged the nation's citizens to join the fight for four freedoms: the freedom of speech, the freedom of worship, the freedom from want, and the freedom from fear. The failure of Detroit officials to pursue these freedoms for Black residents engendered rage throughout a population already devastated by the Depression. They did not need to cross the Atlantic to fight for freedom. The "Double V" campaign of the National Association for the Advancement of Colored People (NAACP) pointed out that in cities across America, Black people were fighting for victory on two fronts—at home and abroad.[33]

Black Christian Nationalism

Though the war abroad ended, the fight for freedom in America continued through the 1950s. Tensions caused by segregation in housing were conspicuous in neighborhood schools, where de facto Jim Crow segregation kept Black children out of white schools. Following the 1954 *Brown* decision, the NAACP urged city officials to end neighborhood school districting in favor of busing students to schools where they could experience racial integration. However, city school board officials were under no mandate to desegregate schools, because neighborhood districting was not explicitly racial in language. Black leaders understood these crafty maneuvers, whereby white officials used restrictive covenants to keep Black people out of neighborhoods so that racially segregated city schools could remain. This was the Detroit climate that Cleage reentered after years of schooling and experience in church ministry.

Shortly after his return, Cleage inserted himself into Detroit's political environment. It would not have been apparent from his short stint at a white United Church of Christ congregation in Massachusetts or in an interracial experiment in California (where he served as an interim co-pastor before Howard Thurman's arrival) that Cleage would become a major participant in Detroit politics, but in the years that followed, that is precisely what happened.

In 1963, Cleage was appointed to the board of directors of the Detroit Commission on Human Rights. That summer, he and the other members of the commission arranged for Martin Luther King Jr. to lead the Walk to Freedom.[34] Estimates of 100,000 to 200,000 people marched down Woodward Avenue, Detroit's main street, and King gave a version of what would become known as the "I Have a Dream" speech at Cobo Hall. King, the leader of the Southern Christian Leadership Conference (SCLC), recognized the racial tensions particular to Detroit when he proclaimed "that one day right here in Detroit, Negroes will be able to buy a house or rent a house anywhere that their money will carry them and they will be able to get a job."[35]

Cleage's emerging Black nationalism led him to criticize the event for including white officials. He believed that Black folks did not need their actions legitimized by white leaders or values. At the heart of this critique was his belief that Black integrationists insisted on including white people in the event because they were under the influence of "Uncle Tomism"—a term he used to accused Blacks of being committed to "individualism and identification with their oppressor."[36] The term itself was pejorative in Black circles. Historically it referred to an Africanist character from Harriet Beecher Stowe's *Uncle Tom's Cabin*. Patricia Turner explains that although Stowe's protest novel depicted Tom as a "proactive Christian warrior," later portrayals of Uncle Tom, on stage and in film, depict him as a docile old Black Christian who deferred to his white enslavers and betrayed fellow Black people.[37] Due to these popular portrayals of the character, Black folks used the term to express their disapproval of Black complicity with the racial status quo. Cleage adopted this usage and referred to betrayals of the Black race as "Tomming"—a self-serving attempt to please white people. In his theology, Uncle Tomism was the outcome of enslavement and was the root of the corrupted nature of Black humanity.[38] To purify themselves, they needed to repent. So he created a liturgy for just that purpose.[39]

Cleage's doctrine of Uncle Tomism emerged from his Black biblical hermeneutic. Through this method, he reinterpreted the Exodus narrative and Jesus's ministry to explain how the nation of Israel and the disciples created new communities. In his biblical imagination, Rome was a white oppressor that had caused the collapse of God's chosen people's unity and purpose: "Each person plotted only for his own individual advancement. Each individual was willing to sell out the Nation for personal gain."[40] Cleage wanted his congregation to understand that as individuals they could not stand against an empire, be it Rome or America. "The white oppressor, Rome," he warned them, "took advantage of this situation by pitting one individual against another, preventing the unity of the Black Nation, Israel."[41] The lessons for Black people were unmistakable. In America, federal officials and local governments were responsible for dividing Black people into individuals who sought their own fortune by appealing to white Americans. From his perspective, white Americans—whether they were poor, exploited, liberal, or radical—were united against Black people. With that understanding, Cleage believed that Black institutions that aligned themselves with the white power structure were guilty of the worst forms of Tomism.

In Cleage's opinion, no institutions of Black society were more guilty of Tomism than the NAACP and the Black Church. In 1963, the Detroit NAACP opposed the Walk to Freedom and regularly insisted on allowing white officials to set the pace of city reforms. While Cleage did not agree with King's integrationist vision, he credited King for giving Black Americans an occasion to envision what it must have felt like to see Jesus enter Jerusalem, even claiming that King's march was more triumphant. "In a sense," Cleage explained, "the kind of nationalistic demonstration Jesus had when he entered Jerusalem was what we had walking down Woodward Avenue. Instead of Jesus, we had Dr. Martin Luther King." He continued, "When you marched down Woodward Avenue, you thought Dr. King was the leader who was going to build a Black Nation and give us deliverance."[42]

Cleage did not reserve his criticisms solely for the local chapter of the NAACP; he also criticized its leader, Roy Wilkins. Wilkins, the organization's executive director, was a vocal opponent of Black militancy, which Cleage found hypocritical. From Cleage's perspective, the NAACP's victory over school segregation was the first violent blow to racial segregation. Wilkins's leadership of the NAACP, however, was marked by his opposition to direct action and boycotts. Standing on the foundation of the NAACP's monumental victory over school segregation, Wilkins insisted that "legal victories rooted in the law formed the basis on which other methods could proceed."[43] In his opinion, the victories represented by marches, bus boycotts, and sit-ins were due to the unique circumstances of place and population where they were won. His insistence on legal appeals as the foundation for other actions made the NAACP slow to respond to calls for immediate social transformation and necessitated that white officials dictate the pace of racial justice.

As Cleage saw it, Black churches were no better than the NAACP. He found their visions for interracial churches weak and ineffectual because they appealed to white desires.[44] Integrationists' loyalties to white people meant that their gospel did not attend enough to the everyday experiences of Black people. Cleage concluded that "the Negro church has prospered poorly in the North because it has been unable to relate the gospel of Jesus Christ meaningfully to the everyday problems of an underprivileged people in urban industrial communities."[45] Instead of supporting the revolution for Black freedom, Cleage accused Black churches of being the "one force that will be against you from beginning to end."[46] Some of his frustration emerged from his clergy peers' opposition to his 1963 "No Taxation for Discrimination" campaign, which derided a millage to increase funding for the segregated school system. Neither did it help that they failed to support his brother's campaign for Wayne County prosecutor a year later. He complained, "Anytime an independent black man decides to run for political office, who will work night and day to defeat him? Black preachers."[47]

That said, Cleage's most consistent criticism of Black churches concerned their lack of a Black theology strong enough to support Black freedom fighters. "The Black Church has failed miserably to relate itself to the seething ghetto rebellions," he observed, "and therefore has practically cut itself off from vast segments of the black community." In his opinion, the "Black" in "Black Church" was cosmetic: "The Northern Church has been black on the outside only, borrowing its theology, its orientation and its social ideology largely from the white Church and the white power structure." Cleage characterized the pie-in-the-sky theology of many American Christian churches as indicative of most Black churches in Detroit: "They tell us that the things on earth are unimportant." It enraged him that apolitical preaching from metaphysically minded pastors had convinced "black congregations of thousands that we don't have to worry because God is going to take care of everything."[48] Such otherworldly spiritualities devalued the earthly needs of future citizens of his Black Christian nation.

How could they fight for a better life, he challenged his colleagues, when their religious leaders taught them "that the problems of life are not their problems to deal with and solve?" A passive Christianity that led them to ignore racial discrimination today by focusing on the salvation of their individual souls someday in the future struck Cleage as unbiblical. "Everything in the Old Testament upon which Jesus built his teachings, talks in terms of a Nation," he proclaimed, "not in terms of an individual seeking individual salvation." Instead, Cleage envisioned a Black nation that was endorsed by God. In this nation, members traded their individual goals for a community through which they could determine their own destiny on earth as it is in heaven.[49]

Cleage rejected any soteriology that allowed the political or social status quo to remain. His gospel was explicitly revolutionary. He sided with an emerging consensus among freedom fighters, like King, who dismissed notions that the Motor City needed to put the brakes on racial reform, especially when he declared, "The motor's now cranked up and we're moving up the highway of freedom toward the city of equality."[50] He agreed with Malcolm X, whose "Message to the Grassroots" speech in Detroit argued that white inclusion in civil rights activism allowed white people to stop any designs for Black revolution.[51] By the mid-1960s, similar sentiments could be found among large segments of Black America that demanded Black Power and self-determination. This was true for Black students in the National

Student Association, Black teachers in the American Federation for Teachers, and the Black Caucus of the National Conference for New Politics, which included representatives of the Fellowship of Reconciliation.

Ongoing housing discrimination, poorly funded Black schools, and police brutality in Detroit motivated Cleage to embrace a Black militancy that demanded immediate Black control of Black communities. The need for control was no more evident than when police murdered Cynthia Scott in the Twelfth Street neighborhood of Cleage's Central United Church of Christ. According to police, at 5:00 A.M. on July 5, 1963, Scott, a convicted felon, pulled a knife on two officers. One of the officers then shot her three times before she fell face down on the sidewalk. "Saint Cynthia," as she was known, was a Black sex worker who had been arrested by police many times on questionable charges. On this early morning, eyewitnesses who saw the incident claimed that the officer killed her without any justification. Cleage, James Boggs, and others organized rallies demanding that the officers face accountability for their actions. As Black residents had come to expect, the officer who shot Scott was exonerated by the Detroit Police Department and the Wayne County Prosecutor's Office following a very brief investigation. Decades of police violence toward unarmed Black Detroiters increased insecurities in Black neighborhoods—especially in Cleage's, where four years later another incident with the police inspired a Black rebellion.[52]

At 3:45 A.M. on July 23, 1967, the Detroit police raided the United Community League for Civic Action on Twelfth Street, a local hangout. Police raids at this location were commonplace. The establishment was one of many well-known "pig blinds" and therefore prone to police harassment. Pig blinds were known in the community for serving alcohol, but because the city did not often authorize liquor licenses to Black businesses, they did so illegally. On this occasion, a dozen officers arrested eighty-two Black customers, an unusually high number for a location that often saw only half as many. Perhaps that can explain why an unusually large crowd of around 200 neighbors gathered to watch. Agitators attempted to incite the crowd and yelled threats at the officers. Then, while the officers carried their detainees away, the crowd began throwing bottles at police cars. These were the first moments of what would become the largest uprising in the history of the city at that time. Once again, Cleage's Twelfth Street church neighborhood was the epicenter of an altercation between the police and Black Detroiters. This time, federal military was deployed to stop it.[53]

The confluence of discontent, struggle, discouragement, and rage led some provocateurs to instigate fights across the city and to spread rumors that white people had thrown a Black woman and child into the river at Belle Isle Park. White Detroiters responded with rumors that Black men had assaulted white women. This time, forty-three people were killed— three-quarters of them Black. Over 1,000 people were injured, and the police arrested around 3,800 in the uprising. Fifty million dollars of damage to buildings in the city further exacerbated the housing crisis. Around 5,000 people were rendered homeless because of the conflict, most of whom were Black.[54]

Cleage's analysis of the conflict and proximity to its epicenter drew media outlets to him. He interpreted journalists' interest in his work as attempts to characterize the uprisings as representing only the views of a few unhinged individuals, but Cleage linked the Detroit situation to "rebellions" across the nation, from Watts to Harlem, wherein Black people found common outrage against unequal treatment. "They are doing that all over the country," he complained about the media reports, "because they can't face the simple fact that all of us black people are tired of the way white folks have been treating us. That's all there is to it. We are tired of it everywhere and we are not going to stand it any longer."[55] Cleage preferred the term "rebellions" to the media's "riots." He also believed the term "uprisings" carried with it political aspirations that could lead to "revolutionary struggle designed to change the world and to establish us in our rightful position," whereas the language of riot only connoted a small group of unorganized discontented people. Just as the Black Messiah followed God's will for revolution in the New Testament, Cleage preached during the Detroit uprisings that "we must have faith that we are doing the will of God who created us in his own image."[56]

This was the heart of Cleage's Black Christology: Jesus was a Black political revolutionary. In his interpretation of the biblical drama, the accusations Rome "brought against Jesus were political charges against a revolutionary who was leading a nation into conflict against an oppressor." Jesus was not crucified in this framework because this was the only satisfaction God could make for saving souls. According to Cleage, "It was necessary that he be crucified because he taught revolution. He brought together a fragmented Black Nation and he pitted it against the power of Rome."[57] Furthermore, because "Jesus was a revolutionary black leader, a Zealot, seeking to lead a Black Nation to freedom," the central task of the Black Church was to "carefully define the nature of the revolution."[58]

In Cleage's view, revolution did not require violence. At the Shrine of the Black Madonna, he preached political action. He explained, "We have got to try political action because that is an alternative to violence. We have got to use picket lines, boycotts, all the things that offer the possibility of power without the necessity of violence."[59] This view of political revolution influenced national figures like James Cone and young Black political activists who heard him preach on college campuses and in churches nationwide. They found in Cleage's church a powerful source of support in their shared dedication "to one purpose, freedom for black people."[60]

A Southern Imagination

Detroit was also an important place for Clarence Jordan to imagine the implications of the New Testament in the context of America's racially segregated society. In 1963, white Detroiters of the American Baptist Convention invited him to speak on the New Testament book of Ephesians at a conference they had planned for the city.[61] His work on Ephesians for the conference in May of that year became the first text of his *Cotton Patch Gospel*. Due to his passion for ending racial animosity in the South and the tensions over racial segregation that had mounted since January, Jordan reimagined the epistle as "The Letter to Birmingham." The implications were unmistakable. At the convention, Jordan declared under no uncertain terms, "Any church that erects a barrier of racial discrimination is guilty of the worst kind of heresy and should no longer consider itself a member of God's family."[62] The Birmingham epistle explained that Jesus's sacrifice nullified the segregation that Black Christians endured and offered, instead, a warm invitation into Christian fellowship.

Jordan imagined Black Birmingham Christians to be the audience for Paul's instructions. Though recast as gentile sinners, they were instructed to remember that they were once outsiders. The implication was that white Southerners who had enslaved Africans, terrorized newly freed people with lynch mobs following Reconstruction, denied African Americans the franchise through the Black Codes, forced Black peonage through insurmountable sharecropping debts and convict leasing, and codified inequality through Jim Crow laws were considered the true heirs of Christian fellowship in Jordan's translation of the Bible. Black people "who were once so segregated" were to receive salvation when they assimilated into white Southern Christianity.[63]

The vast majority of white Christians in Birmingham wanted nothing to do with welcoming Black people into fellowship with them. Despite the reportedly 53 percent of Birmingham pastors who supported the *Brown* decision, laypeople generally advocated for massive resistance to any mandate for racial integration. Moreover, even liberal clergy who supported *Brown* attempted to find a gradualist middle position between staunch segregationists and the few integrationists whom they were prone to dismiss as "extremists." These liberal clergy represented the "white moderate" whom Martin Luther King addressed in his "Letter from Birmingham Jail" later that spring.[64]

White churches hosted teachers of the cultural lesson on segregation that the author Lillian Smith understood "was only a logical extension of the lessons on sex and white superiority and God."[65] The focus on private sins in the sermons, the all-white congregation in the pews, the symbolic lyrics of white purity in the hymns, and the rejection of all things dark in white Christian theology taught white congregations to figuratively wear these moral lessons on "sin, sex, and segregation" as lenses through which to read the signposts of their racially segregated streets, neighborhoods, schools, and towns.[66] As such, there were no true polarities between pulpit and pew. Southerners did not need overt lessons on racial segregation to internalize the ideology of white supremacy that was at the heart of Southern tradition, nor did white Christians need to look far to find the overt lessons. If just over 50 percent of clergy in Alabama supported the *Brown* decision, it is also true that nearly half shamelessly preached their opposition to it.

By January 1963, the tensions between white segregationists, white gradualists, and white integrationists were palpable in Birmingham. The election of George Wallace in the fall of 1962 illuminated the deeply held conviction of a majority of Alabama voters concerning the future of racial segregation, particularly as he expressed their desires in his inaugural address for "segregation now, segregation tomorrow, segregation forever."[67] A liberal opposition of eleven ministers from Jewish, Orthodox, Catholic, and Protestant communities—representing Alabama regions from Montgomery to Birmingham—cautioned Alabamians from persisting with massive resistance to desegregation. They called for prayerful obedience to the law, maintenance of order, and common sense that would lead to respecting the rights that every human deserved. Unfortunately for them, the middle ground was no safer than the integrationist position. The white gradualists were met with vitriolic letters and public denunciations that accused them of rejecting the gospel in favor of a socialist conspiracy, among other things.[68]

If warring words were all that transpired between opponents in the debate over the rights of African Americans, then the devastating events that made Birmingham a historical touchstone for the worst terrors of the 1960s would be shocking. However, for more than a decade, white champions of racial inequality dynamited homes that the city rezoned for Black families and bombed churches where freedom fighters and allies organized about fifty times between 1947 and 1965. The frequency of the bombings earned the city the ominous title "Bombingham." Similar dynamics that sparked racially explosive conflicts in the 1943 Detroit uprising, namely white hostility over expanding housing access to Black residents, motivated the first of the bombings.

In Birmingham, Black churches funded the legal challenge to the city's racially zoned neighborhoods that the US district court ruled unconstitutional in July 1947. For the years that followed, ministers joined Black residents in watching for white vigilantes who used intimidation tactics to scare would-be Black homeowners in neighborhoods like North Smithfield, later known as "Dynamite Hill." That is, well before the 1954 *Brown* decision, Black churches became sites for Black freedom organizing—particularly in the 1940s, when Black residents lobbied for access to public parks. As a result, Black churches became the favorite targets of white terrorists.[69]

Jordan's *Cotton Patch* "Letter to Birmingham" addressed anti-Black violence by introducing Jesus as the abolitionist of "segregation patterns which cause so much hostility." Segregation, according to his translation of Ephesians, was a "silly tradition" that Jesus barred from his fellowship. Jordan's Jesus was an ecclesial integrationist who healed "the hurts." Who exactly needed healing and what they needed to be healed from were not specified in the epistle; from the context, however, it seemed that because Jesus's "sacrifice joined together both sides into one body for God," the division itself was the hurt. According to Jordan, the incarnated Christ came preaching a message of peace to whites, "inside" the church, and Blacks, on the "outside." This, in the reimagined Southern context, was Paul's missionary secret: "Negroes are fellow partners and equal members—co-sharers in the privileges of the Gospel of Jesus Christ." Paul was a prisoner to this missionary secret, "the Lord's cause," and was imprisoned because he held this "conviction on race."[70]

Jordan's conviction was that in the Southern context, everything that applied in the scriptures to the Hebrews needed to be applied to white people. Since Abraham was the first Jew, in the *Cotton Patch* translation he would be "the first white man." In like manner, he replaced Jewish law with white Southern heritage and tradition, neither of which granted white people the inheritances of God. Rather, Jordan explained through his white Paul that

God made a contract not with his "children" but with his one and only child, Jesus. According to this logic, God's contract with Christ could not be superseded by Southern customs that were in place to help white people find discipline until faith in Jesus was an option. With his incarnation, God's son abolished Southern customs. Though the customs were no longer needed—nor were distinctions of white or Negro, slave or free, male or female—assimilation to white anthropology still lay at the heart of Jordan's ecclesial movement. "If you are Christ's men," he translated, "then you are true 'white men,' noble heirs of a spiritual heritage."[71]

In Jordan's predominantly white institutional vision, Black and white people who were initiated into Christian fellowship were supposed to become allies. Jordan limited the historical challenges that Black and white people needed to overcome to nothing more than white ignorance. Yet he placed the responsibility of receiving this invitation on the memories and gratitude of Black outsiders. In the crass language of Southern white tradition, the letter implored Black Birminghamians to "always remember that previously you Negroes, who sometimes are even called 'niggers' by thoughtless white church members, were at one time outside the Christian Fellowship." The former status of Black people, which saw them being denied "rights as fellow believers, and treated as though the gospel didn't apply," left African Americans "hopeless and God-forsaken in the eyes of the world." Now, white Paul explained, "because of Christ's supreme sacrifice, you who once were so segregated are warmly welcomed into the Christian Fellowship."[72] It was a remarkable revision of American religious history in which the ancestors of African converts, who had already made indelible marks on American Christianity during the antebellum period, were somehow newly welcomed into the Christian family in the twentieth century—well after they had established Black Baptist churches in the eighteenth century and national denominations like the African Methodist Episcopal Church in the nineteenth century.

Enslaved Africans in the American South and free Africans in Northern states had converted to Baptist and Methodist Christian denominations in large numbers for about two centuries. In response to revivalist campground meetings in the early nineteenth century, where white and Black experiential Protestant preachers made emotive appeals for all in their hearing to be saved from the fires of hell, African converts transformed the religion of their oppressors into a potentially liberationist spirituality. That liberationist religion inspired faith communities to redefine American democracy to include the most downtrodden of people in the land. African converts like

Richard Allen, founder of the African Methodist Episcopal Church, founded congregations and denominations in the early nineteenth century that became powerful abolitionist outposts in the antebellum period and sites of freedom fighter organizing in the twentieth.

Jordan's Southern Baptist Convention (SBC), however, represented an inimical movement of white Baptists who opposed Black liberationist spirituality and annexed slavery, along with the general social subjugation of Blacks, to their vision of divine order. While the official position of the SBC became its mission to spread the gospel to all people, its original Georgian and South Carolinian founders established it in opposition to a Boston prohibition against slavery in 1845. Their opposition persisted in churches and seminaries like Jordan's Southern Baptist Theological Seminary in Louisville, Kentucky, where, as a New Testament professor, he defiantly held an interracial Bible study.[73]

Jordan humbly submitted his invitation to Black people into white Christian fellowship as one possible translation of the Jewish gospel in the Southern context. "There is no adequate equivalent of 'Jew and Gentile,'" he explained in the *Cotton Patch* notes. To align with his purpose, however, Jordan chose to replace "Jew" with "white" and "Gentile" with "Black." He admitted that his translation was a subjective result of "superimposing my own personal feelings, which" he added, "is the unpardonable sin of a self-respecting translator."[74]

Jordan's *Cotton Patch Gospel* should be understood as a cultural translation for missionary purposes rather than a translation for scholarly purposes. His goal was to convince his audience to transform their culture to match practices that he endorsed. This was why he included a disclaimer concerning imprecision: "Matching present-day people, groups, and settings with their biblical counterparts involves a good bit of guesswork and subjective interpretation, mingled with the best knowledge one has of both the modern and ancient situations." He included examples of choices he made, such as replacing "the Pharisees with church members, and scribes with theologians and seminary professors." He pleaded with the reader to understand his dilemma: "As strained as this may be, this was the best I could do."[75]

Regardless of his ambivalence about finding contemporary equivalents for ancient concepts, Jordan expressed no ambivalence about making "white Southerners" or "white Church members" the protagonists of the biblical narrative. Convinced that this was the only option, he asked rhetorically,

"But in the southern context, is there any other alternative?" An image of a Black Christ displayed in the stained glass of a Black Baptist church in Birmingham suggested that there was, and the white artist who created it seemed to understand the power of a Black Jesus to promote justice in the South in a way that Jordan did not.[76]

On September 15, 1963, white supremacists bombed Sixteenth Street Baptist Church in Birmingham. Black people, no matter their level of participation in the Black freedom movement, faced threats from white segregationists for their symbolic and actual proximity to civil rights activism. As the most conspicuous church for anti–Jim Crow agitators to gather, white militants viewed Sixteenth Street Baptist as the heart of the resistance and made it their central target. This was especially true after Alabama Christian Movement for Human Rights's Reverend Fred Shuttlesworth and the SCLC's Martin Luther King Jr. recruited participants in the Good Friday March in May of that year. The pastor of the church, Reverend John H. Cross, said, "We've been expecting this all along, waiting for it, knowing it would come, wondering when."[77]

That morning, around 200 miles southwest of Koinonia Farm, four girls prepared for Youth Sunday, a tradition Reverend Cross had established by setting aside one Sunday each month for the youth of the congregation to relieve adults from their usual volunteer leadership positions. Carolyn Maull McKinstry, a child survivor of the attack, recalled that the children wore their "Sunday best": the boys wore dark slacks and white shirts, and the girls adorned themselves in white dresses. Without warning, blasts from fifteen sticks of dynamite shook the east side of the church, demolished support structures, and shattered windows. The attack killed three fourteen-year-old girls and one eleven-year-old girl, and injured twelve more people.[78]

Black leaders from local churches and national organizations immediately called for federal intervention. "Unless some steps are taken by the federal government to restore a sense of confidence in the protection of life, limb, and property," Martin Luther King Jr. warned President Kennedy, "we shall see the worst racial holocaust this nation has ever seen after today's tragedy."[79] The president responded quickly by mobilizing the largest FBI action in decades. FBI director J. Edgar Hoover committed to keeping details of the investigation within the bureau. He shared their work with no one, not local officials or even his boss, the US attorney general.

Centuries of experience with deferred justice coupled with Hoover's lack of transparency left African Americans feeling skeptical that anything would be done. James Baldwin spoke for many when, a month later, he called into question the moral resolve of white Christian America and its apparent apathy: "There must have been a day in this country's life when the bombing of the children in Sunday School would have created a public uproar and endangered the life of a Governor Wallace. It happened here and there was no public uproar."[80] To the contrary, many white people blamed King for stirring up trouble back in May and deflected accountability when they suggested that Black communists or freedom fighters had set off explosives that they kept in the basement of the church.

Four thousand miles away, in Wales, white people responded with care and support for Black Birminghamians whom they had never met. Upon learning of the tragic events, people in Cardiff mobilized their town to respond. The sympathies of a Welsh artist named John Petts moved him to create a Black Jesus stained-glass window as a symbol of hope for the Christians of Sixteenth Street Baptist and for the international audience who sympathized with the terrorized community. Petts explained, "Naturally as a father I was horrified by the death of the children. As a craftsman . . . I was horrified at the smashing of all those windows, and I thought to myself: my word, what can we do about this?"[81]

The town organized a fundraising campaign that limited each contribution to no more than half a crown so that everyone in Cardiff could give funds in support of Black freedom in Birmingham. Petts depicted the Black Christ with his right hand pushing away hatred and injustice and the left offering forgiveness and acceptance. In a show of solidarity between the Black people of Birmingham and the world, Petts accompanied the image with the words "You do it to me," based on a verse from Mathew 25:40: "Truly, I say to you, as you did it to one of the least of these my brothers, you did it to me."[82]

Whereas the Black stained-glass Jesus displayed in the Wales window of Sixteenth Street Baptist demonstrated identification with the pain Blacks endured and the campaign for justice, Jordan's white Jesus could only offer sympathy. As the white son of God, he condemned white Birminghamians' hostility toward Black people from within the white community and offered to change only the hearts of Southern segregationists, not the systems that allowed for discrimination and attacks. Through white Jesus's God movement, Jordan questioned the soteriological efficacy of public protests and Supreme Court appeals. Jordan's Paul asked Christians in Atlanta, "If from a purely human standpoint I fought the police dogs at

Birmingham, what good did it do me?"[83] Jordan believed that without the Resurrection, such acts of protest would be pointless. Surely, he agreed in principle with civil rights protesters that racial discrimination was sinful, but he rejected their strategic nonviolent tactics on the grounds that they misrepresented the methods of the God movement.

Jordan was clear that Black and white Americans needed the God movement because it was "a greater and deeper movement than the civil rights movement."[84] A fundamental problem with the civil rights movement, from Jordan's perspective, was that it was overly concerned with outcomes. The God movement was concerned with love, especially for enemies. Certainly Koinonia's charity toward Black neighbors was an important feature of the farm. However, the predominance of white Koinonians on the farm and the centrality of white characters in Jordan's cultural translation suggest that he privileged the needs and perspectives of white people over Black interests. The story of a Black woman from the region of Dalton and Calhoun in the *Cotton Patch* version of Matthew indicates Jordan's comfort with the possibility that the gospel in the South should be interpreted with this privilege. When she approached Jordan's white Jesus for help for her demon-possessed daughter, he said, "I was sent only to needy white people." White Jesus eventually relented to her pleas, but only after she humbled herself by referring to herself and her people as "puppies."[85]

Jordan interpreted the Sermon on the Mount, Matthew 5–7, as teaching a radical reorientation toward enemies of Christian fellowship that required Christians to practice nonresistance to evil. He believed that because the Sermon on the Mount was Jesus's central lesson, no words in the New Testament were more important. Amid the racial conflict, he thought too many Americans cared more about what the state made legal or illegal than what Jesus preached. He complained, "They look to the decisions of the Supreme Court, not to the dictates of the Sermon on the Mount."[86] Those dictates, as he understood them, provided clear guidance on what he interpreted as Christian nonresistance and civil rights nonviolence.

Jordan explained that Jesus did not advocate nonviolence. In his interpretation of "turning the other cheek," which he read as an obvious example of refusing to resist evil, Jordan saw no argument for the claim that Christians should ever resist evil, even if nonviolently. To the contrary, Jordan taught that the Christian response to violence was to give love to the evildoer. Jordan clarified his position on civil rights by offering two critiques. First, public demonstrations had no biblical foundation. Jordan mockingly argued that Jesus never said "if your enemy slaps you on your right cheek, put on a demonstration protesting your rights." Second, Christians had no "rights" except for the right to love. Jesus, according to Jordan, "is not commanding us to demand our rights. . . . That is, you may do nothing to a man who opposes you."[87]

Practically, this meant that while Jordan believed in an interracial Christian fellowship, he opposed the civil rights movement's methods and its appeal to national citizenship rights. As mentioned in chapter 4, Koinonia hosted several civil rights activists in the 1950s. By the 1960s, however, it had become clear that the farm was not an outpost for organizing against Jim Crow, as Black churches had become in Americus and in other cities. When the Americus movement began in 1963, Jordan made his objections to the civil rights movement clear to the Koinonia community.

Divided by Race

As freedom fighters marched on, Jordan's disagreement over methods grew: "I can hardly take it at times when the whole integration struggle is being fought, not in the household of God, but in the bus depots, sitting around Woolworth's counter, arguing over whether you can eat hamburger and drink Cokes together." Koinonians mostly believed that Christian witness was not on streets or lunch counters but rather at the communion table. Jordan complained, "It just burns me up that we Christians with the word of God in our hearts have to be forced to sit around Woolworth's table and that we still segregate Christ's table." His passion for the church to be the city on the hill led him to create Koinonia as a demonstration of what was possible through the Christian gospel, but churches were as segregated as the rest of society. To this he opined, "The sit-ins would never have been necessary if the Christians had been sitting down together in church and at Christ's table these many years."[88]

As resistance increased, Black Christians became less interested in asking for a place to sit in white churches and at interracial gatherings. The spread of Black pride in culture and religion in the late 1960s persuaded many Black Christians that it was enough to celebrate their churches as important spiritual spaces from which to gain strength to face a white society that looked upon them with scorn and pity. In the years that followed, the Black theologies of Cleage, Malcolm X, and James Cone lent spiritual voice to cries for Black Power. Though Cleage's Black Christian National movement never reached the membership of the Nation of Islam or the scholarly reputation of Cone's Black Liberation theology, it aided in fostering the reception of both. Malcolm X, whom many young Black freedom fighters felt was an important mentor, spoke of Cleage as a fellow Black nationalist freedom fighter in his "Bullet or the Ballot" speech. Cone's monumental first book, *Black Theology and Black Power*, recognized Cleage as "one of the few black ministers who has embraced Black Power as a religious concept and has sought to reorient the church-community on the basis of it."[89] In his rejection of the traditional Black Church, Cleage's ideas spread into secular spaces as well. He was received at over forty institutions of higher education, including Morehouse, Princeton Theological Seminary, Howard, Claremont School of Theology, Georgetown, Wayne State, Seattle, Union Theological Seminary, and Yale Divinity.[90]

Black freedom fighters' movements toward Black pride and Black nationalism made the possibilities for collaboration between them and the interracial-fellowship-focused Koinonians less viable. Black Power philosophies rejected forgiving and appeasing white society as legitimate strategies for gaining equal status in the United States. Meanwhile, Jordan's frustrations over methods of the civil rights movement's confrontational forgiveness moved his community further to the other side of the Christian color line, where white allies ignored the ways that race had formed their fellowships. For Jordan and the Koinonians, fellowship at Christ's table represented the unity that Christians shared, where each remembered that they were equally forgiven and individually sinners before God. On this common ground, they believed, rested the greatest possibility for overcoming racial enmity. The disconnect between these two Christologies was that Jordan's white Jesus taught his followers to ignore racial inequalities between Christian allies, and Cleage's Black Jesus used racial identity to encourage Black freedom fighters to demand equality in church and society.

The application of Black racial imaginations to Christian scriptures emboldened Black freedom fighters for generations to come. The imaginations of white interpreters also sustained white allies, who renounced racial prejudice as a problem of the heart, which membership in their Christian communities could heal through reconciling Black and white Christians to one another and to God. Assimilating to these white spaces appealed to very few Black Christians. Those who were attracted to the communities often found that the price for staying was the ongoing subjugation of their right to self-respect, self-governance, and self-improvement. Materially, while these white spaces could offer communal housing, food, and work, they had little to offer Black communities who struggled in cities like Detroit and Birmingham to secure their rights to adequate shelter and nutrition. According to Jordan, Christians had no rights to such things. As a result, he and his followers offered little beyond disappointment to freedom fighters, who came to understand that solidarity with white theologies like Jordan's was a barrier to Black freedom.

Part IV **The Time Is Now**

· ·

6 The White Problem

Our war resistance is justified only if we see that an adequate alternative to violence is developed. Today, as the Gandhian forces in India face their critical test, we can add to world justice by placing in the hands of thirteen million black Americans a workable and Christian technique for the righting of injustice and the solution of conflict.

—Bayard Rustin, "The Negro and Nonviolence"

On March 23, 1940, Pauli Murray sat uncomfortably on a bus in Petersburg, Virginia, talking with Adelene McBean about the possibility of using Gandhi's concept of "satyagraha" to mount a more effective movement for civil rights. "Although inexperienced in Gandhi's method," Murray reflected on the experience, "we sensed the importance of using every opportunity to insist upon humane treatment while we ourselves were courteous in putting forth our demands."[1] Murray had recently read the book *War without Violence: A Study of Gandhi's Method and Its Accomplishments*, by a graduate student who also lived in New York City named Krishnalal Shridharani. Like the title suggests, the book argued that nonviolent direct action was effective "for achieving realistic and needed ends."[2] Equipped with knowledge from that book, the two Black passengers discussed the possibility of using nonviolence to protest segregated seats on the bus.

In her self-titled autobiography, Murray explained, "Ideas about the use of nonviolent resistance to racial injustice, modeled on Gandhi's movement in India, were in the air."[3] For decades—from Harlem to Atlanta, in universities and presses—Black intellectuals had found inspiration in India's liberation movement and thought of Gandhi as a transnational mentor in their struggle for liberation. In Harlem, Black media published articles that noted the promise of India's nationalist movement even before Gandhi moved back to India in 1915. Once the Black media discovered Gandhi's work in the years that followed, Black intellectuals from Howard University in Washington, D.C., and Morehouse College in Atlanta, Georgia, organized trips to meet him in the 1930s. Those who could not travel to India debated the possibility that his methods could work in the US context. Still others attempted to implement nonviolent resistance on segregated buses and in segregated restaurants throughout the 1940s. Gandhi's influence among freedom fighters was expansive.

In the context of the Black freedom movement, Gandhi's nonviolent direct action found a hospitable environment for experimentation in the efforts to wage war on Jim Crow. Thus, when Ralph Templin and Jay Holmes Smith, two white missionaries who had recently returned from India, dreamed of starting an ashram, they found in Harlem a welcome environment to explore the potential of satyagraha to abolish racial segregation. However, the missionaries were ignorant of the history of Black Harlemites' relationship to Gandhi. They had not considered the possibility that Black residents had some practice with applying Gandhi's teachings to freedom initiatives. Therefore, they believed it was their responsibility to save Harlem from its ignorance by delivering the Mahatma's teachings to them in an immersive experience.

Templin and Smith's assumptions of Black ignorance and centering of white members' leadership made the Harlem Ashram inhospitable to freedom fighters. Its founders' implicit tokenism, paternalism, saviorism, and assimilationism demonstrated that white allies' interracial programs paralleled Black freedom movements in such a way that guaranteed their failure to build coalitions with them. That said, programs like these were not only inhospitable to Black freedom fighters but also inhospitable to those rare white people who were willing to prioritize effective action over pure intentions and to favor Black freedom over interracial fellowship.

In this chapter, I will narrate how the inhospitable context of these predominantly white programs created inner conflicts for Templin, since he often cofounded or directed them. I will also show that white ally networks tested Templin when they failed to make common cause with the Black freedom movement. In his roles as missionary, program director, activist, and scholar, he grew frustrated with white allies' failures to adequately address anti-Black oppression. Because of his commitments to resisting evil through the pursuit of justice, he found himself at odds with sponsoring organizations, who through complicity or passivity contributed to what he termed the "white problem." Templin's preference for actions that abolished oppression rather than concepts that merely signaled his good intentions inspired him to confront his peers with the ineffectiveness of their programs. Despite his white Protestant identity, Templin's ideas gained little traction in white ally circles, even though he was vastly networked, widely published, and well respected among the most famous white activists.

One persistent conflict that arose in Templin's experiences with other allies emerged out of his conviction that justice necessitated resisting evil. This conviction compelled him to openly challenge allies, especially when they refused to compromise their nonresistant pacifism. Proponents of nonresistance believed that the purity of their intentions was more important than actively resisting oppression, even if it meant allowing injustice to continue. Templin struggled philosophically in these communities because he shared common religious positions with his Protestant peers, especially in their denunciation of war and desire for interracial community. However, their failures to organize any effective resistance to anti-Black oppression revealed to him the insidiousness of the concept of "white superiority"—that individuals, institutions, religions, nations, and their actions were justified for no other reason than their affiliation with the white race. Templin developed an understanding that the psychology of white superiority was so pervasive that it even influenced the practices that emerged from white anti-segregationists. In Templin's analysis, these anti-segregationists too often failed to recognize justice as a fundamental element that was necessary to end racial segregation. As such, he rendered any notion of freedom in their programs as false. Despite their shared values, Templin concluded that he could not condone their complicity in promoting this "false freedom" and condemned whiteness as an imperialist prison of white Western civilization's own making from which they, too, needed to be free.

Templin's missionary associations and international commitments made it difficult for him to effectively abandon the methods of the predominantly white institutions that had formed him. Over time, he discovered that white progressive institutions were inhospitable spaces for racial justice because their constituencies were more committed to philosophical purity, principled methodologies, token Black representation, white charity, and assimilating the objects of their saviorism than they were to Black liberation. For more than thirty years, Templin wrestled with the "white problem"—a set of institutions, practices, and procedures that promoted this false freedom. He, too, was imprisoned within this problem, because it restricted his ability to join himself to the freedom struggles of colonized people all over the world.

After he was expelled to the United States, Templin found that his commitment to abolitionism, conflicts with pacifists at the Fellowship of

Reconciliation, and entry into the civil rights struggle in Ohio enabled him to name the internalized racial superiority he had inherited from his training in white Christianity. Moreover, he learned that the more closely he worked with Black organizations—like Central State College, the Central Jurisdiction, and the NAACP—the more aware of the problem of whiteness he became. This awareness moved him to lament, and his many affiliations with the most celebrated interracial programs of his generation offered him little comfort. Most importantly, they offered no solution to the influence of white civilization's white prerogative among white radicals, especially as it led them to maintain programs that supported false freedom.

Gandhi in Black Harlem

Fighting for freedom on buses in the South, segregated by white seats in the front and a "colored" section in the back, was not unique to Murray and McBean. Resistance to Jim Crowism on buses was becoming a feature of the freedom struggle for Black people across the Southern states. Over a decade before Rosa Parks famously refused to give up her seat on a bus in Montgomery, Alabama, several Black bus riders had done the same in places like Tennessee and Virginia. Bayard Rustin, who had been convinced of Gandhi's methods, was beaten by four police officers in Nashville, Tennessee, for violating what he saw as an unjust law. Four years later, Carrie Lee Fitzgerald, a Black woman traveling to see her ailing husband near Danville, Virginia, refused to give up her seat when a bus driver demanded that she leave the white section of the bus. A half year after Fitzgerald, the NAACP's defense team took up the case of Irene Morgan, a Black woman recovering from a miscarriage who was arrested for refusing to vacate her bus seat. Black riders were fed up with the unjust bus policies.[4]

Murray and McBean wanted the freedom to go home for Easter dinner, but neither the Greyhound bus nor the American justice system were hospitable to such notions. The two Black passengers waited for the white bus driver, Frank A. Morris, to return and determine whether they could change seats, because moments earlier McBean complained of pain that had arisen from sitting awkwardly due to the wheel well under her seat in the "colored" section. Both passengers noticed that the bus was mostly empty and other seats would suffice, but those empty seats were in the white section. Hoping to avoid a scene, Murray respectfully approached the driver with the hope that if he had the situation explained to him, he might allow them to move. Morris refused with a swift nudge of his elbow and snapped that he would not be bothered with their request until the bus reached Petersburg.[5]

Murray was not one to accept the public humiliation that accompanied segregation customs. On more than one occasion, the activist had responded to public scrutiny from people whose racial and gender identities required conformity with confrontation. In fact, Murray had already challenged the University of North Carolina's anti-Black admission policy, which prohibited Black students from admission to their graduate programs, even if they had white family members who had graduated from the institution, as was the case with Murray. Also, in the three months that led up to the incident in Petersburg, Murray had written letters to newspaper editors describing Black anger over dignity violations. In another letter to First Lady Eleanor Roosevelt, who was becoming a mentor, Murray rebuked her for compromising "on the principle of equality."[6] On this day, however, Murray attempted to acquiesce to the rules of the bus in order to get home until that became untenable, then the travelers considered that a nonviolent course of action might be required.

When the bus driver returned with police officers, McBean announced that she would not be intimidated by their "brass buttons and shiny bullets."[7] The police attempted to de-escalate the situation and left when the New Yorkers finally gained acceptable seats. McBean demanded an apology. Emboldened, Murray requested equal treatment. Morris did not tolerate either, and he left the bus again. This time the police returned and charged the passengers with "disorderly conduct and creating a public disturbance."[8] They were arrested, jailed, convicted in court, and fined five dollars each. They never made it to Easter dinner.

Murray became aware of Gandhi's ideas a year before the Petersburg bus incident, but she had no vision for the part nonviolence would play in confronting racial segregation. As one of the first to participate in such an action, Murray later reflected, "We did not plan our arrest intentionally. The situation developed and, having developed, we applied what we knew of *Satyagraha* on the spot."[9] Their singular goal of freedom allowed them to be open to new strategies. Despite their spontaneity, their unintentional arrest moved others into action. Their satyagraha-inspired protest had more of an effect than the two could have anticipated. News spread of the arrest, leading two local NAACP attorneys to represent them and give notice that they would appeal the ruling. The appeal trial was set for April. In a twist of fate, the bus driver that called the police, Morris, was once again their bus driver on their return trip home. However, this time two Greyhound guards accompanied him. Murray wrote, "It seemed obvious that he was under observation, and we also suspected that this was the beginning of a change of policy toward Negro passengers."[10]

Upon returning to New York City, Murray and McBean needed housing. Between the emotional drain of the arrest, the potential fines and court fees, and the money they paid for the bus ride, the two were exhausted and financially strapped. Thus, their options were limited. Through their activist network, they learned of the Harlem Ashram, an interracial communal experiment that offered an immersive experience in Gandhian inspired Christian living and voluntary poverty. Between their new experience of nonviolent protest in Petersburg and their financial need, the ashram appeared to suit their present situation.[11]

As indicated in Murray's response to anti-Black discrimination on the bus, Black New Yorkers were no strangers to lessons that emerged from the struggle for Indian independence. Harlem was no exception. Indeed, in 1919 Du Bois implored his NAACP readership to join in solidarity with the Indians because "we are all one—we the despised and oppressed, the 'niggers' of England and America."[12] He advocated for a transnational struggle for racial justice "from San Francisco to Calcutta and from Cairo to New York."[13] Three years later, Du Bois wrote a five-page biographical sketch of Gandhi in which he introduced the leader's strategies of noncooperation and nonviolence. In two decades, elementary knowledge of those strategies grew pervasive among Black freedom fighters.[14]

Du Bois's admiration for Gandhi was immediate. His fascination with the possibility of using nonviolence to advance Black freedom motivated him to write to the Indian leader. In 1929, Gandhi responded with a letter, which *The Crisis* printed along with a brief bio. In it, he encouraged Black Americans to carry their history of enslavement with pride and to "realise that the future is with those who would be truthful, pure and loving."[15] Though the two never met, Du Bois did not hide his adoration of Gandhi having named him "the greatest colored man in the world, and perhaps the greatest man in the world."[16]

Word about Gandhi moved through Black colleges and universities as well. Mordecai Johnson, the president of Howard University, shared Gandhian ideas in the 1930s to inspire students with new methods to use in the fight for freedom. His excitement over the possibility that freedom fighters could use the Indian independence movement to further the struggle for Black liberation animated him to urge students to "study and understand Gandhi perfectly."[17] His enthusiasm also led him to encourage Howard

Thurman to lead a delegation to India in the mid-1930s and William Stuart Nelson to visit India in the 1940s.

From November 1935 to March 1936, Thurman led the Pilgrimage of Friendship in India with his partner Sue Bailey Thurman and another couple, Edward and Phenola Carroll. The six-month speaking tour presented opportunities for the group to engage with Indians who questioned the capability of Christianity to overcome racial discrimination in America. The international trip culminated in a meeting with Gandhi. Thurman wrote a letter describing his experiences and sent it to Benjamin Mays, the dean of Howard University's School of Religion, who shared the correspondence with his students and faculty at the burgeoning center of Black higher education.

Mays believed that the possibilities of Gandhi's methods were far-reaching. Upon returning from India, Thurman encouraged Mays to meet Gandhi too, which he did during the Christmas season of 1936. Mays was no stranger to nonviolence, but Gandhi gave him a "broader perspective."[18] First and foremost, Gandhi impressed upon Mays that "nonviolence was not passive resistance but rather it is an active force."[19] He also shared his understanding of caste and the lawfulness of breaking unjust laws. Mays carried these lessons with him for the remainder of his career. After becoming the president of Morehouse College, he became a "spiritual mentor" to many students—including Martin Luther King Jr., who enrolled as a student in 1944. In addition to sharing his experiences with Gandhi at "Tuesday morning Morehouse talks," he frequented the King's family dinner table, where he plausibly shared stories of his encounters with Gandhi. On being admonished by Johnson to study Gandhi at a speech in Washington, D.C., in 1948, King recalled, "Like most people, I had heard of Gandhi, but I had never studied him seriously."[20] Up to that point, it was likely that he experienced Gandhi's methods as being "in the air," like Murray had before the bus incident.

While awareness of Gandhi was ubiquitous in Black intellectual and activist spaces, freedom fighters were not of one mind concerning the practicability of using Gandhi's methods. E. Franklin Frazier, an activist and a professor of sociology at Morehouse, rejected the notion that Christians could win over the hearts of a society that refused to condemn the lynching of thousands of Black people through nonviolence. He found it foolhardy to suggest that Black Americans should dismiss self-defense as an option to fend off their oppressors. And he was not alone. While Du Bois's admiration for Gandhi was undeniable, he wondered whether the American context and the Indian context were similar enough for Gandhi's nonviolence to be transplanted among a Black population that was outnumbered by whites. Perhaps, as Vijay Prashad argues, Frazier mistook Gandhi's methods for the "turn the other cheek" passive resistance of Western Christianity's Jesus; and despite Du Bois's decade of research, maybe he misunderstood the moral ethics of Gandhian nonviolence. Nevertheless, their sincere engagement with Gandhi demonstrates the prevalence of his philosophy in Black freedom discourse.[21]

The Harlem Ashram

With the support of the Fellowship of Reconciliation (FOR), which had met at the Chautauqua Conference in 1940, Templin and Smith founded the Harlem Ashram. The two had been among the E. Stanley Jones–influenced Methodist missionaries to India who challenged Christian missionaries to exclude Western culture from association with Jesus. It was their conviction that Christianity had become so synonymous with imperialism that Indians were being introduced to a Christ encrusted with Western garb. Jones adopted ashrams as spaces of retreat for spiritual refreshment, in-depth Bible study, and reflection in community. As one of his students, Templin understood an ashram to be a "common life of fellowship," an intentional community in which members adhered to a shared discipline.[22] Likewise, Smith taught that an ashram was "a small community of kindred spirits, living together in a deeply sharing and disciplined fellowship, and pursuing common spiritual and social ends."[23]

The former missionaries believed that the social ends that bound them together had granted them mutual responsibility to use the ashram to save Black people from the oppressive forces of racial discrimination in New York. Both men had personally observed the destructive nature of racial discrimination in India under British colonial rule. They had also been stymied in their attempts to communicate effectively with Indians who criticized American Christianity for its anti-Black oppression. For instance, an Indian college student once asked Templin, "If you want to end untouchability, what about Jim Crow?"[24]

With questions like these burning in the souls of the Methodist missionaries, Templin and Smith looked to Harlem because it was "strategically located with respect to America's most pressing and largest problems in reconciliation—anti-Semitism and discrimination against Negroes."[25] Templin was a key theorist in syncretizing Christianity and satyagraha, or love force, into "kristagraha," a Christianized version of Gandhi's term. As a Christian Gandhian, Templin helped plan the ashram, but he did not make his home there. As an eventual Harlem Ashram adviser—along with notables like E. Stanley Jones, A. J. Muste, and A. Philip Randolph—he witnessed the successful propagation of kristagraha through his relationships with two Black freedom fighters who frequented the Harlem commune: Bayard Rustin and James Farmer. There were few better places for kristagraha to take root among Black Americans than Harlem. The sun had set on the years when it was "home to the second-largest Jewish community in the United States."[26] The Manhattan neighborhood gave way to "the New Negro," who, after 1920, created a renaissance where Black "culture came to the forefront of the many-sided debate surrounding African American freedom."[27]

It was Smith who took their detailed plan to address racial discrimination through nonviolent direct action to 125th Street, which he made his home. With the blessing of the FOR, he became the ashram's leader. In an article he published for *Fellowship*, a monthly newsletter published by FOR, Smith explained how he implemented the plan with a small group of activists. He recited the importance of positioning the ashram near Black and Jewish neighborhoods where he could train ashram members—and anyone associated with FOR—in nonviolent direct action. The residents of the ashram were required to commit to voluntary poverty and to hold one another accountable to strict personal disciplines. "Our present group of eleven members," he explained, "includes three negroes and a Hindu."[28] His neglect in naming the white members' race implied that the nucleus of the ashram was composed of white Protestant pacifist allies. In truth, the racially identified members were formidable freedom fighters in their own respect.

Indeed, one of them was none other than Krishnalal Shridharani, the expert in Gandhian nonviolence who wrote *War without Violence*—the book that inspired Murray's bus protest. Others were lifelong nonviolent freedom fighters, who had not yet studied Gandhi in depth: Pauli Murray, Adelene McBean, and James Farmer. Murray and Farmer described the Harlem Ashram as inexpensive, but also far from the New York they longed for.[29] Nevertheless, its low cost persuaded Farmer to make accommodations there anytime he returned to New York. Murray, on the other hand, found the ashram to be entirely inhospitable and left after three months.

Steeped in their own study of Gandhi, New York's Black intellectuals recognized the ideas and spirituality of the ashram.[30] However, some Black participants felt that the white men led the commune in a manner that was reminiscent of the way white missionaries acted in international settings. Templin and Smith had no intention of repeating the missteps they made early in India. Templin wrote that it was common practice for missionary programs in India to appoint unqualified white men, with their "magic skin color and western credentials," to leadership positions, which caused them to "step up over our [kin] who had been long in that work." This was not a self-righteous observation of other missionaries. Templin confessed that he imbibed the spirit of "white superiority" himself when he received his first appointment: "I fear, I was not a little proud of my sudden importance."[31] It was his opinion that this type of pride too often motivated white missionaries to appoint themselves to prestigious positions.

Templin and his partner brought the Bible and a mission to Harlem, a community experiencing a renaissance that the white missionaries did not understand. Equipped with this ignorance as well as concepts they had gained from their experiences with Gandhians, they unwittingly reinstituted white forms of domination in America. They captured the concept of satyagraha, but made it intolerable to the Black Harlemites whom they claimed to serve. Their missionary experience inadequately prepared them for the work they set out to do among their fellow American citizens, whose freedom movements had already found ways to incorporate Gandhi's philosophies.

If Murray's immediate turn to Gandhi's satyagraha for guidance in Petersburg is any indication, then it is no exaggeration to say that the significance of the Indian independence movement in Black freedom activism has been underappreciated. That said, the new disciple of the Mahatma admitted to inexperience in Gandhi's method and was therefore excited to live in the Harlem Ashram, where satyagraha and Christianity were brought together as kristagraha. Shridharani and Haridas Muzumdar, another Gandhian resident whose writing aimed at spreading those ideas in the United States, became conversation partners for Murray. The setting seemed to provide precisely what Murray needed at the time: affordable housing with like-minded people. Murray recalled that "Bayard Rustin and James Farmer, staff members of the pacifist organization Fellowship of Reconciliation (FOR)," participated in the Ashram and "were already experimenting with the technique in small groups."[32]

However, Murray and other freedom fighters felt that the environment was stifling. The commune insisted on prohibiting behaviors that some members deemed as vices, like Murray's cigarette smoking. As a new resident, Murray understood that discipline was important, but she balked at the idea that external prohibitions could cultivate it. "If the ashram is to become a convent or a monastery," Murray commented on the matter, "then I have no place here."[33] Despite departing from the commune, Murray persisted in exploring the potential of Gandhi's methods. Her experience at the ashram was not a waste of time, and she reported at least one positive outcome: "I was a contributing member of FOR and had studied its literature on nonviolent direct action." The young activist had learned enough to begin innovating and creatively applying Gandhi's teachings to the American context. Murray concluded, "The most effective way to use nonviolence in our racial struggle was to combine it with American techniques of showmanship."[34]

James Farmer used those techniques to stage a sit-in while in Chicago a year after Murray left. Farmer's reasons for joining the ashram were like Murray's: "It was nonviolence oriented, and it was the cheapest place to stay."[35] Smith opened the ashram to the staff of the FOR, which included Farmer as race relations secretary. Later, Farmer received the FOR's blessing to leave that role to work as the founder of the Congress on Racial Equality (CORE), which operated separately from the FOR. Beyond the Friday CORE events that he convened at the ashram, Farmer did not have fond memories of the commune. He, like Murray, felt controlled by mandates. He took umbrage with rules that members practice voluntary poverty, show no anger, and tolerate substandard living conditions. "I would not have gone to the ashram had there been a realistic alternative," he explained. He described the decor as "dark and dingy, and the furnishings old, cheap, and tasteless." The meals, he complained, were "an inducement to fasting." He took profound issue with the doctrine of voluntary poverty that permeated the culture of the ashram. Farmer did not believe that "the best way to make common cause with those one seeks to help is to adopt their afflictions and become one with them." In his experience, "poverty was wholly involuntary." The choice to be voluntarily poor was more enticing for the economically affluent than those who never chose poverty. Nevertheless, Farmer made "the best of it," but he confessed that he would have gladly taken a job or financial gift that paid enough to get him out of the ashram's cultural environment, which he found off-putting and out of place in Harlem.[36]

Murray's and Farmer's disappointment in the ashram point to a struggle that Templin first recognized in India: that white men were too often in authority positions over people about whom they knew very little, simply because they were white. Still, he continued to accept leadership roles even after noting that he was appointed to them on account of "white prerogative"—that was, "by no act to our credit, not even by preparation or experience were we thus qualified to step up over our brothers who had long been in that work." He viewed this as a major problem with social justice activism. He had not traveled the world to rule over people. Templin lamented that his white status created barriers between him and the people with whom he hoped to work. The persistent pattern of white men being placed in "superior racial position" convinced him that "color prejudice is indigenous in the white man's psychology." Describing the inescapability of white men's inclination toward the ideology of "white superiority," Templin claimed, "He carries it wherever he goes and for whatever purpose."[37] The pattern continued in Harlem. Templin and Smith—two white men organized for racial justice with no expertise in organizing against anti-Black racial oppression—replicated similar conditions that they loathed in India. Perhaps, Templin pondered, white men could not help themselves to do otherwise. Their Black associates were certainly put off by the culture they had created. Had it not been for the affordable housing accommodations, the ashram may have never even attracted them in the first place.

But Templin's intentions for the ashram had little to do with affordable housing. He had experiences with multiple ashrams during his time in India, through which he conceived of a creative way to "root" Christianity in Indian society: kristagraha. As he explained, "We attempted to distinguish ourselves from the prevailing compromised Christianity."[38] Jones, their missionary mentor, had referred to what they were calling "compromised Christianity" as promoting an "encrusted Christ" that was "bound with the grave clothes of long buried doctrinal controversy."[39] Western civilization and Jim Crow segregation were so regularly associated with Christianity that many of their Indian associates saw no difference. With that obstacle in mind, Jones said, "I dropped out the term 'Christianity' from my announcements (it isn't found in the Scriptures, is it?), for it had connotations that confused." He instructed Methodist missionaries in India: "We are not there to plaster Western civilization upon the East, to make it a pale copy of ourselves."[40] Following Jones's lead, Templin only ever asked one Indian to accept the Christian faith. "To do so," he said, "seems to me unworthy of the spirit of Jesus who, so far as we know, tried only to awaken within all the sense of God's rule of love."[41] According to Templin, "During these years another of our Ashram leaders, a young poet and American-trained theologian, Cyril Modak, conceived and defined Kristagraha as the name, credo and methods of a Christianity vital enough to transplant its roots into the soil of India."[42]

These principles blossomed in the development of the Lucknow Ashram, which provided the inspiration for the commune in Harlem.

Inspired by love and a rejection of Western rule, Templin and his fellow missionaries broadcast an open letter to the British viceroy titled "The Kristagraha Manifesto—with Christ in the Crisis." Templin's analysis of the white race was preeminent in the manifesto. He had already laid out the argument for the manifesto in an article he wrote for a Methodist publication in India called *The Indian Witness* a few months before sending the letter to the viceroy. The article, "A Kristagrahi's Manifesto—a White Man's Appeal to His Race," named the white race as "a race in chains" to three fictions: "the fiction of dominant nationality, the fiction of color inferiority, and the fiction of 'liberty' to maintain industrial injustice." Templin presented these fictions as psychological barriers that were being used to preserve "the lost cause" of white Western rule.[43]

Templin called on the West to abandon state expansion and appeals to white superiority, which were the justifications for exploiting workers of color around the world. In his opinion, "If the building materials of a new order are not gathered and fashioned in readiness for use, there will be nothing to build peace out of except the broken fragments of a dead past, hastily gathered at a late moment when they should have been left lying in ruins." In other words, there was no future in the Western project—no peace and no democracy. Furthermore, if the West did not change directions from the "will to power over others," there would be no future for civilization.[44] As chair of the committee that penned the letter, Templin's was the only missionary name attached to the document. Challenging the viceroy marked him as a problem, which eventually led to his expulsion from his missionary post.

Templin envisioned an end to Western rule in India but did not immediately understand what an end to a racially turbulent American context might look like. Thus, his heart remained in India, not in Harlem. After a short stint at Drew University, the Methodist college in Madison, New Jersey, Ralph Borsodi courted him to lead the School of Living in New York. Because Templin never established Harlem as his home, the ashram became Smith's project, and people like Farmer would remember Templin as an adviser and a man who "chose a life of speaking, writing, and teaching."[45] Had Templin stayed, he would have lived among three of the most consequential freedom fighters of the civil rights era: James Farmer, Pauli Murray, and Bayard Rustin.

Of the three freedom fighters, only Farmer and Rustin continued to associate with the ashram. Farmer, having been disenchanted with the strange environment, reluctantly rented a room when he stayed in New York and used the location to host the New York chapter of CORE. Rustin, who never lived there, often visited the ashram to join the Friday evening CORE meetings. He learned that Smith allowed them to meet because "he looks to the American Negro to assist in developing, along with the people of India, a new dynamic force for the solution of conflict that will not merely free these oppressed people but will set an example that may be the first step in freeing the world."[46] Unfortunately, Smith's invitation for Black people to assist him did not evolve into hospitality to Black leadership in the ashram. If it had, perhaps Murray and Farmer would have remained in closer relationship to the community; instead, they left with very little prospect that the ashram would be beneficial to their freedom work.

The White Problem

Templin spent the next four years of his life with his spouse, Lila, and another couple, Paul and Betty Keene, at the School of Living. Together they directed the school, conducted workshops, and printed its newsletter, the *Decentralist*, which was later renamed *Free America*. Paul Keene, a retired professor of mathematics at Drew University, persuaded Templin to direct the school by comparing it to the culture in India. In a letter to Ralph Borsodi, Templin reported that he was convinced by Keene's appeal when he said, "You will find this program nearest in America to the positive village constructive work under Gandhi's leadership in India."[47] Initially, the Templins stayed at the school as students. It was not long, however, before the board of trustees, which was facing an economic and leadership crisis, noticed their gifts for leadership and asked Ralph to become the director.

Templin was very excited to learn more from Borsodi, the author of what he referred to as "the Great Idea." Borsodi promoted family homesteads as keystones of "decentralization" and "cooperative development." His antistate philosophy proposed that the homestead movement was an essential alternative to nation-state collectivism, and Templin viewed the idea as an avenue to develop kristagraha in the US context. Yet Templin insisted that no one mistake his enthusiasm for a desire to either reimagine the school after his own design or to remain in the United States. His intention was that the School of Living would always be Borsodi's. The clarification was significant because Templin took the position of director at a time of "reorganizing," just as Borsodi stepped down as president. If Templin directed the school, he declared that it would be only for a "temporary" assignment of two years. The Templins desired to return to India, but neither the war nor the imperialist white rule of the British permitted them to do so. Both conditions convinced them to commit themselves to "the propagation of the Great Idea whose hour," they believed, "has come."[48]

The Templins and Keenes shared responsibilities for homesteading and training others in the practice. According to Borsodi, securing a homestead, where the house and the land connected to it were owned free and clear of mortgages, was the beginning of the individual human quest for "the freedom to develop themselves by contributing a share of their time to the labor which furnishes the entire group the essentials of comfort."[49] The main school was located at Bayard Lane in Suffern, New York, and experimental locations were planned for Nyack, New York, as well as New Jersey. The School of Living Foundation provided conventional deeds and mortgages for more than fifty homesteading families. These homeowners participated as active members in the Cooperative Being Club, which was across from the school, and another sixteen families lived in the Bayard Lane Homestead Association. Their homesteads were "held in trust, and for use and inheritance only."[50] Under the influence of Borsodi's philosophy, they became consumer-producers who sought to "control their own destiny" in opposition to the monopolization of land, resources, money, and labor that Templin believed was "characteristic of any collectivistic i.e. centralist society."[51]

It would prove to be a formative time, but for reasons that had less to do with homesteading and more to do with the opportunities it provided for Templin to debate with American pacifists about the underlying causes of world war and the limits of nonresistance. Even while directing the school, Templin wrestled with the problems of war and statism. He debated his views in correspondence with Borsodi, both of them presenting passionate analyses of the underlying problems of the modern West. They laid the problem of war at the feet of industrialization and free market capitalism. They encouraged each other to see that industrialization led to overproduction and the insatiable need for raw materials. The insatiable greed of nation-states motivated them to compete with one another for land, labor, and resources, which resulted in armed conflict. In their minds, these problems needed to be solved through education and active strategies, neither of which were offered by American pacifists.[52]

Most of the white participants in the school during Templin's leadership were pacifists. According to Templin, participants' reasons for visiting the school ranged from religious freedom to pursuing an alternative to doing nothing—which their pacifist communities had yet to offer. Their disillusionment opened a door for Templin to persuade participants to "explore decentralization as a way which provides them with not only something positive which they can do now and always but with the only final alternative to statism, imperialism, and the whole war system."[53] By getting them "to accept decentralization as their way out," Templin thought of the school as a tool for rescuing pacifists from a cycle that could not adequately combat the war system.[54]

Templin viewed decentralization as a resilient practice through which to nonviolently resist the capitalist state. As a student of Gandhi, the distinctions between nonviolence and pacifism were of the utmost importance to him. His nonviolence was guided by two principles: "complete disillusionment about winning any good by war and the belief that the evil must be resisted by an effective method."[55] He came to these positions through his experience of World War I and through an intellectual conversion to abolitionism.

America entered World War I in 1918. At that time, Templin was a young pastor of two churches and a student who could have avoided any participation. Doing nothing, however, was not Templin's style. He left the pulpit and the classroom to volunteer for the army's new Air Service, which was a response to the army pilot failures during the Great War. He graduated from flight school in its first class, just five days after the war ended. But he became disabused of the righteousness of war through the guilt he felt by having had any part in the so-called war to end all wars. In hindsight, it became obvious to him that the Great War did not "make the world safe for democracy."[56] War, he learned, was simply another occasion for exploitation and expansion of capitalist greed, not the extinction of it. Thereafter, he distrusted news that cast nations, like Belgium, as neutral, because it hid the fact that the Belgian government exported a significant number of arms to nations involved in the conflict. He purposed to never be uninformed again.[57]

Templin became a voracious student of the world, reading international politics and history. In 1925, he became a Methodist Episcopal Church missionary to India. There he learned to distinguish nonviolence from American pacifism. Pacifism, as expressed by white American pacifist groups before the 1940s, generally meant nonresistance—the refusal to resist evil. This position often emerged from interpretations of Jesus's command to "not resist evil doers" by Protestant Christian peace churches, like the

Mennonites, Quakers, and Brethren. Templin's Methodist church was not a peace church. In fact, during the American Civil War, the 1864 Methodist General Conference sent a letter to President Lincoln in support of the Union, declaring, "We pledge you our hearty co-operation," to which Lincoln responded, "The Methodist Episcopal Church, not less devoted than the best, is by its greatest numbers the most important of all."[58]

Though he loathed war, Templin adopted the conviction that "evil must be resisted." War, in his view, "was a lesser evil" than nonresistance because it attempted to impede evil from prevailing. Nonviolence won him over as the best response to evil. As Templin learned in India, nonviolence "singled out evil and waged a war against it." Templin saw it as no coincidence that nonresistance had taken root in the West, where the current global imperialism obtained its marching orders. White Christian nonresisters experienced little friction from the West because they presented no real threat, and Templin deemed it worse because they "were allowing that same evil to make a mockery of so-called democracy."[59]

Templin believed that while pacifists in the West allowed violent imperialism to persist, "India was crying out against the aggression and waging a real struggle against it, and an effective one." He found nonviolence convincing because it was effective. Whereas nonresistance represented a principled pacifism that was committed to purity of intention over effectiveness or impact, nonviolence attacked evil systems with strategies to make the world more just. "In fact," he wrote, "I believe that there can be no peace of any kind which lasts, without the justice which involves an end of the white domination of the colored races and all other imperialism, and an end of all such discrimination and exploitation in this country." In other words, violence was implicit in every form of injustice, and the oppressive systems of white imperialism were the primary culprits in its proliferation.[60]

Templin's conviction that he must resist evil took shape during his furlough from India in Ann Arbor, Michigan, between 1931 and 1934, a decade before his time at the School of Living. For one year, while his wife Lila completed a master's degree in elementary education at the University of Michigan, Ralph studied rural education at Columbia University's Teachers College. Thereafter, he spoke at Methodist Episcopal Church congregations on behalf of the Northwest India Conference. Like the founder of Methodism, John Wesley, Templin conceived of holiness, or the freedom to pursue all that is good, as a virtue that necessitated the liberation of the entire world. That struggle crystallized for him in 1933, when, like Wesley, he had a strange warming of the heart while reading a book.

Templin claimed that *The Antislavery Impulse* by Gilbert Barnes catalyzed a religious awakening that enabled him "to cut loose from everything except my allegiance to Christ and His kingdom of love in human hearts, come what may."[61] Barnes's book argued that Christian revivalists combined the emotional impulse to escape the depravity of human existence with a passion for abolishing slavery and, in so doing, "released a mighty impulse toward social reform."[62] Inspired by this impulse, Templin felt that he was liberated to challenge institutions and systems of state oppression that many Americans took for granted. With this newfound sense of freedom, he and Gordon Halstead, another former missionary to India, founded the New Abolition.[63] Through this new group, Templin and Halstead organized "against the evils of our economy such as tenantry, unemployment, [and] exploitation."[64]

The goals of the New Abolition included an American state without prisons or police, which they thought, like war, was only necessary because of imperialism. Though the group resolved to study war no more, it was not pacifist. Ralph Templin's son Lawrence explains, "The New Abolition group felt that pacifism was weak in this country and throughout the West because it overlooked both the violence in the structure of Western society and its own essential resistance with nonviolence."[65] Action marked a major difference between pacifism and nonviolence. Arguing that pacifism could not thwart capitalism, which caused the violence of the 1929 financial collapse in America, Templin clarified, "We believed that active and positive nonviolence should be employed against this vast world system of Western exploitation, of which the depression was only a result; the opposite of this system, universal brotherhood, should be asserted."[66] Capitalism, imperialism, and militarism were part of a white Western system of exploitation that could only be overcome through the solidarity of the masses. Notions of white superiority were sustained by this system. Templin's systemic analysis did not allow his philosophy of freedom to be satisfied with individual solutions. Individuals were oppressed by white Western rule because, in his estimation, "both subtle and frank pretexts of superiority had led to arrogations of advantages of every kind." Moreover, these advantages were made possible when notions of superiority were "hardened into societal structures," which he surmised "had resulted in domination, exploitation, wars, unemployment, poverty, degradation and the like."[67]

Templin's quest for true freedom was as personal as it was political. Through the New Abolition, he made a public declaration that put him on a trajectory to expose how even white allies had normalized white Western imperialism, an insight that eluded the notice of his peers. In the May 24, 1934, edition of the *Michigan Christian Advocate*, he wrote, "I declare my independence, as a Christian, from a materialistic order, ecclesiastic or social." He continued, "I hope to take my Church and my State with me as I move toward a Christian social order, but if that is not possible, I stand ready to repudiate them both, God being my helper. As a Christian I can do no less." Willing to distance himself from Christianity and America set him apart, so much so that as a missionary, he refused to ask anyone to convert to Christianity, and as a white person, he joined his religious impulse with a new passion for race reform. This public declaration set him on a course that combined nonviolence with racial justice. It also welcomed others who desired to join him in this new Christian social order. To him, abolitionism was not an individualist movement; it was "the nonviolent struggle to secure the abolition of all discrimination and oppression inflicted upon my fellows in the name of any of those arrogances, racial, national, class or institutional, by which men debase other men as they promote themselves or their interests."[68]

Templin's abolitionism brought him to the understanding that freedom was the one thing needed in the world, but it was the criticism of Indian audiences responding to his evangelistic invitations that made him aware that his project was marred by the "white problem." Indian critics opened his eyes to the transnational experiences of people oppressed by the white Western political and religious power that legitimized his missionary work. Aware that theirs was not a unique experience, they also cited the hypocrisy of white American Christians for calling on Indians to follow the teachings of Jesus, even as white Americans failed to follow those teachings when they systematically oppressed Black Americans.

A Sikh student from Punjab asked, "Why do you not make your own country Christian?" Expounding upon his question, he said, "I have heard there are places in your country where you do not permit the negro to vote. You will not allow him to sit in the same public places with you." His awareness of Jim Crow segregation demonstrated the capacity of colonized people around the world to understand one another's struggles. He continued, "Negroes are even put to death without trial, so I have been told, by great, frenzied mobs of you white people." His comments, describing the lynching epidemic, were not mere rhetoric. The Indian had a genuine concern for Black Americans, seeing in them an extension of colonized people the world over. "We too are colored people," he pleaded. "Why do you come out here to try to make us Christian when your own country is so black?"

Templin had no answer for the young man's question, but he pondered it for years. "The question could never be answered," Templin lamented, "and it burned its way into my soul." The word "never" was poetic license; he eventually answered it with his analysis of the "white problem."[69]

Templin came to see the white problem as unresolved more than unanswered. It was the true problem of Du Bois's "color line." In contradiction to the idea of "the Negro problem" as white Americans understood it, Templin saw that the true problem was rooted in white Western imperialism. Whether British or American, the white Western state powers established their rule through violent expansionism, intimidating occupation, racial segregation, caste mandates, religious intolerance, and appeals to materialist individualism.

Templin was aware of one manifestation of this individualism in missionary compounds in India, where missionaries were set apart from the people they were sent to evangelize. State leaders assumed that it was from these compounds that missionary families participated in the soft work of colonization. Families, as understood by Westerners, only needed to function well enough to sustain those in their household. The limited responsibilities and limited networks of these families forced individuals to depend on industrialization rather than broader networks for sustenance. This industrial economy was Borsodi's main concern; the isolated family structure that resulted from it was Templin's. Based on his experience in American and Indian Christian communities, Templin believed that family could be defined beyond blood relations.[70]

The relationship of the individual to the family and the family to the community was one significant area of disagreement between Templin and Borsodi. It was not that they disagreed on religion—Borsodi was not religious, and Templin was no doctrinaire. The issue truly boiled down to configurations of communal living. Templin's experiences of religious community influenced his approaches to individualism and tempered his approach to the homesteading movement. Perhaps Templin had no intention of adapting the School of Living to his own designs, but Indian philosophies of family led him to adopt a view that included more people in a family than a genealogy could account for. In contrast, Borsodi could not comprehend a genuine family structure that extended beyond biology. The concept mystified him to the extent that he confessed to sometimes reading Templin's letters multiple times. While Borsodi could understand that the individualist mentality of many homesteaders drew them to his ideas so that they could grow their wealth, Templin's issue with individualist homesteaders was altogether different. He thought that rugged individualists who subscribed to the concept of the nuclear family would fail to comprehend that decentralization was a way to extend the family culture and build new communities that could resist state violence and develop the way ashrams did in India. But that vision was never consummated.[71]

Apolitical Peacemakers

Templin left the School of Living in 1945, when the Suffern homestead closed and was sold to private residents. He moved to Yellow Springs, Ohio, a segregated township in Greene County, where he lived for the next four decades. Templin joined the FOR's executive committee that same year and took with him the foundational concepts he learned as an airman, missionary, abolitionist, and homesteader. These experiences served him well in his work with A. J. Muste's Peacemakers, a national movement that spread FOR's mission to end war and its consequences: "racialism, imperialism, national predation, aggression, fascism, regimentation and the like."[72]

Peacemakers extended FOR's philosophy beyond the fellowship through a newsletter as well as conferences that were held each year, beginning in 1950. Templin saw in this movement, with its commitment to nonviolence and affinity for interracialism, the possibility that it could be of great service in solving the "white problem." Apart from the movement, but in service to it, he announced his personal plans to lead a project he called the School of Community Living in the first issue of *The Peacemaker*, June 1949. The School of Community Living purposed to further his vision that American homesteads could pattern themselves after internationally recognized non-state communities like the Franciscan Order of Friars Minor, Kagawa's Friends of Jesus in Japan, and Kristagraha in India. As a FOR executive committee member and founding member of the Peacemakers, Templin's communal focus and expertise in nonviolence were held in high regard.[73]

Beyond his work with white allies, Yellow Springs provided new opportunities for Templin among Black communities. Instead of the parallel work typical of white allies, who organized movements with interracial visions but interacted with only the few Black people who were the least offended by the assimilationist cultures of most white organizations, Templin entered three Black communities that significantly affected his posture toward his fellow allies. In 1948, he joined the faculty of Central State College as a part-time professor in the Sociology Department. He earned tenure in 1956, the first white professor in Central State's history to do so. In 1954, Templin became the first white clergy to be received into the Central Jurisdiction, an all-Black conference of the Methodist Episcopal Church. He also participated in the local chapter of the NAACP. Of these affiliations, his tenure at Central State College had the most profound effect on his work.[74]

Templin was appointed editor of the *Journal of Human Relations*, which was housed at Central State, and it became the journal through which Templin published most of his essays. After his promotion and tenure, he joined the African Studies Association and used his role as editor to amplify the voices of other association members in the journal. Templin's work at the college continued through the spring semester of 1961, when he formally requested to take leave due to his decreasing eyesight. Templin was a respected and beloved colleague at the school. President Charles H. Wesley voiced as much when he wrote, "We have appreciated your service, professionally and personally, with us and are reluctant to see you go from our midst even for a year." He retired from the university in 1967, stating, "My relations with Central State University have always been most pleasant; and both of the jobs have given scope for developing my own thought and experiences, and thus have contributed much to my own learning and development."[75]

The fruits of Templin's intimate affiliation with these Black institutions became evident in his rebuke of the Peacemakers' refusal to recognize racial discrimination as a violent action that needed their protestations. He had carried the abolitionist mission that "evil must be resisted" for years, but it was not until he relocated to Yellow Springs that the rule caused him to break fellowship with white allies. Yellow Springs provided him opportunities to resist in community that he did not find among the Peacemakers. Templin usually assumed a patient posture of persuasion, leading by example or by voicing difference of opinion with white allies, as he had with Borsodi. But lack of support for mass freedom fighter demonstrations, insufficient opposition to white terrorism, and ally inaction eventually depleted his patience with Peacemakers.

Templin participated in the founding of Peacemakers because of his desire "to start in America the small beginnings of a non-violent revolutionary movement." Despite the group's radical views that refused taxation and conscription, he soon learned that this nonviolent movement was mired in ideological commitments that threatened its efficacy. Historian Marian Mollin explains, "These organizers and grassroots leaders preached the gospel of open-mindedness in their political pursuits; at the same time, they remained profoundly closed to self-criticism and change in their political practice and personal lives."[76] Most in the group were not concerned about the size of their membership, but they were concerned over the "purity" of their philosophies. Over time the resulting ideological disagreements reflected what Templin identified as the "fatal western dichotomy" that divided theory from practice.[77]

Anxieties over purity of pacifist philosophy manifested in the formation of different factions within Peacemakers, which, after an early exodus of polarized parties, chose not to fracture into new organizations. Instead, Peacemakers formed internal sections that, according to Templin, divided "sacred from secular, personal from social, spiritual from material, technology from morals, reform from religion, and the like." In the first conference, their concerns for purity of ideas emerged in groups that some identified as the "godly" and the "ungodly." Many on the polar extremes of these positions abandoned the project; those who stayed claimed a third way that focused on an antiwar position, but they never resolved the polarities in the American pacifist community, floundering to offer anything more than statements. Due to his desire to mount a revolutionary movement, Templin felt compelled to offer direction from Yellow Springs.[78]

The Yellow Springs Peacemaker cell was essential to the FOR offshoot, and no one in the group was more important than the chair of the Toledo FOR, Ralph Templin. When A. J. Muste thought the Peacemakers could publish something like *The Catholic Worker,* he turned to Templin: "Perhaps [the] Yellow Springs group might do it?" In their correspondence, Muste monitored the progress of the newsletter and the organization. Savvy about his relationships with pacifists, Templin used his connection to the Peacemakers to spread the message of nonviolent resistance as the method to end white imperialism. Templin's influence over the newsletter was not total, but with Ralph as the chair and his son, Lawrence, on the publication committee as associate production manager, his influence was significant. As the first person to issue a report of the Yellow Springs group's activities, the elder Templin's mark on the group and the newsletter left lasting impressions. In 1950, when the executive committee considered the possibility of holding a national conference through which they might develop a Peacemakers Center, they asked Templin's cell to take "charge of the organization of it and do the planning."[79]

Templin's correspondence with A. J. Muste followed the pattern he established with Borsodi. He praised Muste's work and wrote of his compatibility with FOR and Peacemakers, often using pacifist jargon but without the nuance he displayed in his later letters to Borsodi. Perhaps the amount of influence he quickly gained as an editor, chair, and executive committee member convinced him that he had too much influence in the organizations to risk compromising his status by arguing over the different meanings of pacifism, especially since the groups seemed open to learning about Gandhi's methods. Over time, however, it became apparent that the allies' commitments to principled pacifism, which refused to resist evil or address politics, were hindrances to freedom. Templin needed to challenge their convictions if he had any hope of using the newsletter or the fellowship to overcome the "white problem."

In a letter to Muste concerning the 1950 Peacemakers Conference, Templin outlined a manifesto to challenge the United Nations' (UN) silence on white imperialism around the world. North Korea had been at war with South Korea for less than a month before the UN issued a resolution "to roll the North Koreans back to the 38th parallel." Templin noticed that the UN had neglected to call for an end to imperialism by other nations. Inspired by a *Christian Century* article that referenced the resolution, Templin proposed that the Peacemakers pressure the UN to condemn all imperialism. If the action had any validity, he argued, "it would have to proceed by a reconsideration of the whole matter of empire in Asia and everywhere and would have to mean that it would end in all the earth." As Templin saw it, the precedent of demanding that North Korea discontinue its imperial expansion should have had implications for the United States in Puerto Rico, Russian-supplied tanks for North Korea, and other nations involved in imperialism "of whatever kind." He believed that a proclamation like this would "appeal to the colored peoples of all the earth" and to his white antiwar fellows.[80]

Muste agreed with Templin that Peacemakers and FOR should confront the UN on its hypocritical condemnation of imperial aggression. Templin was making progress with his articulation of the idea that imperialism had imprisoned white people too. Muste confessed his agreement that it was "very important to appeal morally both to the non-white people and to the whites themselves in order that they may be saved from themselves." Imperialism, as Templin convinced Muste, was not only an act of militaristic expansion or psychological superiority but also a spiritual problem. Muste furthered this point by suggesting that within the FOR Council, "there is a certain amount of 'spiritual' imperialism."[81]

Having been convinced, Muste thought that others might be persuaded too if not for the faction of pacifist purists among them. It was doubtful that a manifesto to the UN calling for a condemnation of imperialism could gain much traction among the faction that identified as apolitical. This was a product of the "fatal western dichotomy" that Templin believed hindered his attempts to rally white allies—be they missionaries, homesteaders, or pacifists—against racial injustices. They were more committed to a philosophical purity that avoided discussing politics than they were committed to resisting evil. Taking cues from Gandhian coalition building, Templin replied to Muste that the Indian movement was not single-minded in its resistance to the British. While nonviolent absolutists were crucial to the Indian movement, they were able to set aside purity of motives and any need for textbook knowledge of the finer points of satyagraha to develop a broad-based movement that embraced people who held a variety of philosophies. Gandhi's ability to respect people's journey and convictions inspired others to do the same. "They were able to avoid being perfectionists in their absolutism," he argued, "because of the stronger element of identification with people in their movement."[82]

Muste told Templin that in addition to avoiding philosophical perfectionism, the greatest "hurdle" would be convincing a significant faction of Peacemakers to jettison "the idea that we ought to keep our nonviolence 'pure' and not go into politics like Gandhi did."[83] They were so concerned with avoiding politics and holding to their absolutist positions that they could not address imperialism. This failure lent their antiwar position to abstraction, which left their movement weak and ineffectual. Black Peacemakers had made similar points before, like when Bayard Rustin said, "I hold that segregation in any part of the body politic is an act of slavery and an act of war."[84] Like Rustin, Templin suggested that condemning imperialism in all its forms must take primacy over identification with an apolitical antiwar philosophy. "If we are going to do such a thing as I have in mind," he wrote to Muste, "those of us who are pacifists, anarchists or otherwise limited to small minorities, have got to keep that in the background of our minds and make concessions." The goal had to be the inclusion of everyone who was "dissatisfied with war and war-motivated national policies." [85] As a member of a pacifist group who had resisted identifying as a pacifist in the past, he knew firsthand the difficulty in doing so.

Templin and Muste had exchanged letters on the issue for over six months without coming to agreements about the order, tone, clarity, or central idea. Templin held no need for credit of the idea, and he suggested that they circulate the document throughout the entire group. Because Muste argued it did not follow the rules of a manifesto, they agreed to publish a working draft of what they called a "statement" in the July issue of *The Peacemaker.*

In the preamble, Templin made certain to get the political issue out of the way. The purpose, he explained to his readers, "is to restore democracy to its original revolutionary function and get it out in popular non-violent struggle, beyond the present national barriers to conventional democratic politics." Knowing that the purists would take issue with the political nature of the statement, Templin attempted to redefine the term "political." He claimed that by making the issue about democracy, it "would mean political struggle so different in both method and purpose as to make the term 'political' as understood in the western world wholly inadequate."[86] In other words, the Western discourse that imagined a sphere for politics whites could opt out of could not contain Templin's vision.

Despite the publication of Templin's statement, Peacemakers continued to bicker over the proper place of politics in pacifism. For five years Templin watched the group's factions restate their philosophical positions. But the post-*Brown* context wore his patience thin. In 1956, as white segregationists resisted the *Brown* decision with violence and the creation of private schools, and Black activists fought for civil rights with boycotts and public demonstrations, Templin called for Peacemakers to give its energies to "the movement to end all segregation and race discrimination."[87]

For the first time since Peacemakers began conferencing, Templin declined to attend their conference that year. "Instead," he decided, "to spend the time fasting." In an angry Christmas Eve letter, he informed the Peacemakers that his fast represented a turning point in his perspective: "It seems to me that our rounds of conferences and Continuation Committee meetings get us nowhere because we circle within our personal convictions, and thus constantly cause to dissipate whatever solidarity and strength of satyagraha we may have been led to feel." As he experienced it, Peacemakers was not a force for truth or love. To the contrary, he experienced the Peacemakers Conference as an exercise in debating "what being a peacemaker means, of where our convictions are leading us personally, of the making of any more 'peacemakers,' of the living in community, or of whether we are qualified to train the nonviolent communities."[88]

Templin lectured his community that an effective nonviolent movement required two components: solidarity and resistance to violence in all forms. His Christmas Eve argument reflected every letter, essay, and speech he had given on the subject for the last eight years. First, he taught them that solidarity required them to "find ways to identify our struggle with those of people ready themselves to struggle, in their particular place and way, with nonviolence." He further implored them to "identify with the needs, aspirations, strivings of the people of our country and of the world." Finally, he admonished them that if they listened to him, then the preconditions that caused war would become clear in the harms produced in the "organization of society for power over people's lives, their earnings, their youth, their time, their labor and products." Templin believed that these were the struggles that were common to people all over the world. He was calling on Peacemakers to start addressing them at home.[89]

A Home for Resistance

At his home in Yellow Springs, Ohio, Templin had the opportunity to demonstrate just how to join in solidarity with the struggles and strivings of his Black neighbors. Yellow Springs was a well-known liberal town that distinguished itself from the surrounding conservative area with its Black population and its businesses that sometimes hired them. Its reputation as a liberal destination, however, did not protect Black residents from racial discrimination in their personal or professional lives.

Coretta Scott King, the future civil rights leader and partner to Martin Luther King Jr., came to realize during her studies at nearby Antioch College, "The North was not some sort of racial utopia." For her first two years at school, it bothered her that other students held an unspoken expectation that she would date the only Black man in her class. She refused to date him because she "did not want to acknowledge that covert assumption." It was not until her junior year that she shared in a romantic relationship with a white Jewish student that lasted for a year until he graduated.[90]

Anti-Black biases were a more significant threat to King's professional life. Given the multicultural and coeducational successes that Antioch represented, King was "terribly disappointed" at the deeply held racial biases she encountered. She was Antioch's first Black elementary education major. The 1950s Yellow Springs Public School would not accommodate her as a student teacher because "the school board and the superintendent refused." The racially segregated school system did not provide any flexibility for the school board to give Black students the same opportunities as their white peers. Known for having a black dog named "Nigger," the president of Antioch was of no help either. She complained that he did nothing to support the professional lives of the college's Black students who paid the same tuition as their white peers.[91]

For her part, King refused to allow these challenges to thwart her "determination to excel." A movement for Black freedom was building among the students at Antioch College, and they soon welcomed students from Wright State College and Central State College as co-conspirators. Student activism provided King with plenty of opportunities to grow her passion to "continue the struggle that Blacks had always fought" through the college chapter of the NAACP, a race relations committee, a civil liberties committee, and a peace movement.[92]

As a professor at Central State College, Templin did not need to go far from his home to join in solidarity with the student freedom fighters. In his twelve years living in Yellow Springs, Templin learned that the Mason-Dixon line was flexible in its ability to move much farther north than the Ohio River. Though he agreed that Yellow Springs was "an island of liberalism," he also noted that it was surrounded by "a somewhat hostile sea of semi-Southern conservatism." It took three years for Yellow Springs to begin desegregating its schools. And despite its liberal reputation, its townspeople, businesses, and local government resisted for years. The students at the local colleges, however, were not willing to stand idly by.[93]

The Antioch NAACP students, led by a white student named Lawrence Rubin, confronted two segregated barbershops in 1960, but only one agreed to serve Black patrons. The owner of the other, Lewis Gegner, told the students, "You know I don't cut Negro hair." The truth was that he had before. During a hearing against Gegner, in which the ACLU accused him of violating Ohio's public accommodation statute, a local Black professor testified that Gegner had cut his hair in the past. The court found Gegner guilty and fined him one dollar, but he stubbornly stayed the segregationist course.[94]

In April 1963, students began a picketing campaign outside Gegner's shop and staged sit-ins inside. To discourage the protesters, Gegner convinced the courts to grant him an injunction limiting them to no more than three picketers, who could not block the entrance to his establishment. Led by the student chapter of the NAACP and the Antioch Committee for Racial Equality, the students would not desist from demonstrating. On March 14, 1964, the conflict erupted into a scene that one historian described as a "southern-style strategy of resistance that would have made Eugene 'Bull' Connor proud."[95] In a confrontation that made national news, police armed with billy clubs, police dogs, fire hoses, and tear gas attempted to halt a mass protest attended by over 250 students, most of them white Antioch students but

also some Black students from nearby Wilberforce College and Central State.
[96] Many involved claimed that officers were "looking for a fight." [97] One student heard officers refer to the demonstrators as "Nigger Commies."[98]

At first the students picketed according to the injunction, but as one white student explained after he was arrested for contempt of court, "When I saw women, girls, and Negro people treated like animals, I felt I should give my support."[99] Another Antioch student, in her first year, said, "I broke the injunction because I believe it is a delaying tactic to keep us from demonstrating." [100] Protesters reported inhumane treatment by the police. Over 100 people were arrested. In keeping with the spirit of the struggle, 500 people from Central State and Wilberforce traveled to the courthouse the next day to march in silence. Because the college threatened future demonstrators with disciplinary action, fewer Antioch students attended.[101]

Templin and two other Central State faculty had supported the students from the very beginning, even promising to violate the injunction themselves if students were too intimidated to violate it themselves. Templin made no reservations about his support to the public. In an August 10 editorial to the *Xenia Daily Gazette*, Templin argued, "The highest citizenship is in resisting immoral law, not in supporting it." He continued, "Students need to get out of classrooms into responsibility for civic affairs." Sounding a lot like the white moderates of Birmingham when they rejected the Southern Christian Leadership Conference as outsiders who used unchristian methods, the *Gazette* editors rebutted, "We insist that court rulings be accepted as obligations and the irresponsible recognize the consequences they may face." The editors maintained their law-and-order position throughout the ordeal, agreeing that Gegner was "morally and legally wrong" but that the protests did not "accord Mr. Gegner the same respect and courtesy that we wish him to extend to others."[102]

The editors of the *Xenia Daily Gazette* were aligned with a sizable portion of people in the region. Editorials in the *Gazette* revealed that the racial battle lines cut deep into religious and political identities. In a flurry of editorials against desegregating the schools and against the barbershop protests, opponents called for Antioch to "discipline" student protesters and labeled them the "Yellow Spring Crusaders." Those were the most moderate of the town voices represented in the newspaper; others accused the students of communism and called them "Masters of Deceit." One insisted that "integration demands ignored geography" because God placed Negroes in Africa and whites in moderate climates.[103]

The freedom struggle in Yellow Springs was taking place on two fronts: at Gegner's barbershop, where students protested segregation, and at the school board, where the NAACP continued its efforts to integrate the high school. Templin was one notable resident who voiced his support for both. As a professor at one of the local colleges and a member of the Greene County NAACP, his letters to the editor addressed his belief that racial integration was essential to a functioning democracy. His regular interactions with the *Gazette* editors earned the attention of many in the community, including the president of Antioch, James P. Dixon, who wrote Templin a letter thanking him for his "identification of the issues" and his "careful definition of the meaning of participation in civic affairs."[104]

What Templin experienced in Yellow Springs, through support from his colleagues and from administrators at neighboring institutions, was a stark contrast from the pacifist organizations that drew his ire in the wake of the *Brown* decision. Instead of making pleas to Peacemakers to join in the fight to end racial discrimination, Templin co-conspired with students, professors, the Greene County NAACP, and concerned citizens to rid their community of anti-Black institutions. He appreciated that his local partners were more concerned with actions that would end segregation than they were with abstractions that might determine the purist methods to demonstrate their moral uprightness.

These coalitions had not solved the "white problem," but they were determined to resist it in ways that Templin had not experienced since his time in India. He was so encouraged by the Yellow Springs resistance movement that he showed little interest in working with his past white networks. For instance, when the president of Templin's alma mater, C. Orville Strohl, offered him a position teaching sociology at Southwestern College, he declined. Templin told Strohl that he had interest in a potential position working in community service with Antioch College and that he would only ever be interested in teaching again if it was at Central State. It was through coalitions between these colleges in Yellow Springs that Templin found a hospitable place for his abolitionism. Moreover, it was in this community that Templin learned the "white problem" was not isolated to Southern conservative states.

The barbershop riots in Yellow Springs signaled that the Mason-Dixon line was no barrier too high for systems of racial segregation to cross. Midwestern city governments were just as willing to resist movements for Black freedom with state violence as were their peers in the South. Black uprisings in response to that violence, however, represented a new attitude that distinguished their expressions of outrage from the nonviolent protests of the civil rights movement. Two years after the barbershop riots, Black citizens in Cleveland proved that the Yellow Springs protests were only one indication of the outrage local governments provoked when they refused to end racial restrictions in their cities. The uprisings that ensued represented a new attitude toward freedom—that if government officials would not grant it, then Black citizens would take it upon themselves to secure it.

7 Black Power

I'm talking now about the role of the Negro, and what seems to me
to be at stake is that somehow the Negro contains a key to something
about America which no one has yet found out about—which no one
has yet faced. Contains maybe the key to life. I don't know; I don't
want to talk about it in such mythical terms. My point is that there
is a tremendous resistance on the part of the entire public to know
whatever it is, to deal with whatever this image means to them.

—James Baldwin, "The Negro's Role in American Culture"

On July 18, 1966, in retaliation for being refused wine and a cup of water at a Jewish bar in the Hough neighborhood of Cleveland, Ohio, a Black patron taped a sign to the door of Seventy-Niner's Café that read, "No Water for Niggers."[1] Word spread throughout Cleveland that Black people were under attack at Seventy-Ninth Street and Hough. One rumor suggested that a Black woman had been shot on a bus; yet another claimed that two white men at a Hough neighborhood bar held Black people at gunpoint and refused to give water to a Black man. In response, uprisers attacked businesses with reputations for anti-Black discrimination and cautiously avoided businesses—Black or white owned—that treated Blacks with respect. An elderly woman voiced her pride in the power the uprisers displayed when she told a reporter, "I think these young folks have proved something to Mr. Charlie tonight. We ain't scared no more!"[2]

The Hough uprising also proved that by neglecting to hear the concerns of oppressed Black communities, politicians and business owners almost assured that in a climate of white resistance to racial equality, Black citizens would express their outrage in some physical manner. On a 1962 radio panel that included guests Langston Hughes and Lorraine Hansberry, James Baldwin explained the abiding state of Black rage, "To be a Negro in this country and to be relatively conscious is to be in a rage, almost all the time." He explained, "Part of this rage is this: it isn't only what is happening to you, but it's what's happening all around you all of the time, in the face of the most extraordinary and criminal indifference, the indifference and ignorance of most white people in this country."[3] The 1964 Harlem uprising proved his words prescient, when he said, "These things happen, in all our Harlems, every single day." The swelling awareness that issues of poverty, hunger, homelessness, and police brutality were pervasive factors in Black urban life, not only in Harlem or Cleveland, was infuriating. He warned, "If we ignore this fact and our common responsibility to change this fact, we are sealing our doom."[4]

Responding to the fury that fueled the increased frequency of rebellions in the United States, the National Committee of Negro Churchmen (NCNC) submitted a statement to *The New York Times* two weeks after the Cleveland uprising. The NCNC, like Baldwin, implored readers to focus on the "sources of these eruptions" rather than the reports of disorder and violence. The clergy blamed "the failure of American leaders to use their power to create equal opportunity in life as well as law." It was their contention that up to that point, federal and state institutions had too often used their power to "manipulate and fracture" the Black freedom movement rather than strengthen it. The NCNC also stated that recent voices denouncing the "anguished cry for Black power" were simply new expressions of the misuse of that institutional authority.[5]

Ralph Templin read the NCNC statement as an answer to the "white problem" that had mystified him for more than three decades. As he heard it, Black power offered liberation to all who faced the evils of white Western imperialism, domestic and abroad. Though Templin believed that his primary mission was to abolish white imperial and colonial rule for people on the other side of the color line, after years of research and activism he concluded that whiteness also bound white people in a prison of their own making. Having imprisoned everyone and freed no one, racial inequality was, in his opinion, the greatest threat to democracy in the West. Templin recognized that economic disparities and nuclear destruction were bound up in this threat to human thriving. He understood that Western powers defined freedom as the liberty to maintain domination and industrial injustice, which meant that maintenance of white freedom required exploiting their supposed "racial inferiors." Black power offered a different definition of freedom—the ability for communities everywhere to determine their own destiny.

This chapter argues that the Black Power movement offered the most convincing program for freedom that Templin had encountered in the United States. Thus, it was the key to solving the white problem and therefore his preferred hope for democracy in the West. Neither the back-to-the-land movement nor his network of Peacemaker pacifists offered him a communal resistance movement that was adequate to face the evil of imperialism or colonial occupation. So he adopted the Black Power movement as articulated by the NCNC, the Student Nonviolent Coordinating Committee (SNCC), the Congress of Racial Equality (CORE), and others. Black Power freed him from the organizational prisons of parallel politics, the tokenizing appeals to diversity, the inequalities necessary for charity, the paternalist philosophies of racial reconciliation, the assimilationist assumptions of interracialist inclusion, and the false freedom propagated by colonial rulers.

Black Power advocates advised their communities against measuring freedom by the standards of "whiteness," which they defined as the policies and procedures that sustained white rule. They taught that to allow white standards to dictate the terms under which Black people lived would internally oppress Black communities. Black Power proponents' analyses of whiteness revealed that the fundamental problem with American society was not simply racial division; rather, the problem was that state-sanctioned racial segregation existed to justify human exploitation and environmental extraction. In other words, Black Power taught that because racial segregationist practices were inherently exploitative and extractive, they needed to be avoided at all costs. With that in mind, voices espousing Black Power called on their communities to nurture the rich resources within those communities. In addition, they demanded that Western empires cease their expansionist ways and make restitution to racially oppressed people. Furthermore, they argued that the material benefits of white imperialist practices of the past should be converted into present-day obligations to everyone and everything that was negatively affected by white rule.[6]

Templin embraced Black Power as good news to Americans of every race and evangelistically spread its message so that he might convert anyone who would listen. He claimed to find true freedom in the obligations that Black Power made of him. For decades he had wrestled with the white problem, analyzing it, critiquing it, organizing to overcome it, to no avail. It was not that he viewed white people as a problem; rather, he distinguished the literal color and biology of people from the white political identity that Western nations proclaimed as superior to all other racial groups. Templin referred to this proclamation of superiority as "aspiring whiteness," a concept he defined as a false narrative of racial superiority that Western states used to justify their predatory policies.[7] He found the West's assertions of white superiority weak, and the predatory actions of whiteness repugnant.

In contrast, he thought Black Power represented strength, justice, equal opportunity, beauty, and solidarity with humanity because it aimed to abolish imperialism through instilling pride in Black culture and promoting political resistance for downtrodden peoples. Templin appreciated Black Power's call for Black Americans to "recognize their resources" in themselves and to "gain power sufficient to change this nation's sense of what is now important and what must be done now."[8] Just as the Indian independence movement had freed India from British rule, he believed that Black pride might lay the foundation for finding true democracy in America. Interpreting Black Power this way, Templin believed that it offered freedom for the entire nation.[9]

Through analyzing Templin's adoption of Black Power, we see that the philosophies enabled him to articulate a material analysis of whiteness that avoided vague appeals to psychological maladies or spiritual deficiencies. As a Christian, Templin believed that racial divisions created psychological and spiritual problems, but he maintained that those problems emerged from the material exploits of the West, which Western nations gained through imperial expansion and colonial rule. In studying the Black Power philosophies, particularly as expressed in SNCC and the NCNC, Templin hoped that Black Power could free not only Black Americans but white Americans as well—and potentially all people who lived under the oppressive rule of Western powers.

The rise of the Black Power movement is essential to understanding both Templin's reception of the concept and its contributions to the Black freedom movement. In what follows, I narrate the challenges that the call for Black Power presented to the nonviolent movement for civil rights. Black Power encouraged those who longed for freedom to replace the fear that their voices would go unheard, or that their quest for freedom was futile, with pride in their capability to transform the world around them. Black Power turned the tide. It was no longer Black communities that needed to fear; it was political leaders who refused to represent the needs of all Americans who needed to fear reprisals from Black people who were empowered by racial pride. The fears that white elected officials and their middle-class constituents communicated about Black Power spoke to the real threat that it presented to the status quo.

This was, in part, what Templin found so attractive. Civil rights demonstrations that had once disrupted Jim Crow segregation and intimidated political officials who feared that mass demonstrations would destabilize their authority seemed to have lost their effectiveness. For a time, nonviolent resistance caused the state to acquiesce to Black demands and pass legislation to protect their civil rights. However, skilled state resistance to civil rights activism had improved. Local governments learned that ignored demonstrations did not garner as much attention. In the passion to make demonstrations relevant, leaders raised the intensity of protests by seeking contexts where resistance was most virulent. The pictures of children attacked by police dogs, college students dragged by police from downtown streets, and middle-aged church folk beaten on bridges captured the attention of the American public. However, Black Power advocates held the value and dignity of demonstrators too high to deliver more beloved Black bodies into harm's way. They were done with asking for their rights to be granted. Instead, they demanded that the state give them the freedoms they were owed as human beings and American citizens. It was the next step in resisting the evil of racial segregation—a step that Templin was ready to take.

Black Uprisings

The Hough uprising was among the first in a series of uprisings in the summer of 1966, marking an emerging trend away from belief in the efficacy of nonviolent resistance toward belief in the philosophies and methods of Black Power. Malcontents in Cleveland, Omaha, Amityville, and Baltimore were fed up with the second-class treatment they received in their homeland. What appeared to be irrational destruction of their own neighborhoods from the uninformed perspectives of outsiders represented responses to years of repeatedly aggravated indignities. The Hough uprisings were set in motion by the racially discriminatory practices of the cashiers at white businesses who were pleased to take the hard-earned money of Black workers but refused to treat them with basic human decency. According to those close to the unrest in Cleveland, the outrage in Hough needed to be understood in the context of similar uprisings in other Midwestern cities like Detroit, Rochester, Dayton, and Chicago, where in addition to dealing with daily indignities, Black people suffered from high unemployment, housing insecurity, white terrorism, and police harassment. It was a daunting task in the aftermath of an uprising, however, to convince a white middle class, which had habitually criticized nonviolent civil rights marchers for years, that the communal rage that arose from years of deferred dreams justified the willful destruction of private property.[10]

Unlike civil rights spokespeople who blamed overzealous officials and aggressive policing for the conspicuously ruinous conditions in the wake of a nonviolent protest, street fighters boasted of willfully unleashing years of justified rage on their cities. Yet no matter how artfully they articulated the underlying conditions that sparked their rebellions, the fact that they could not deny the destructive character of their uprising made messaging very difficult. A community organizer in Hough named this reality even as he enjoyed the greater sense of freedom he felt as a result of the uprisings that began the day before: "It is easy to predict what would happen after the shock had worn off." Having paid attention to the Detroit and Watts uprisings a year earlier, he discerned a pattern: "The demonstration would not be explained as the predicted revolt of people who had nothing to lose but their rat-infested streets, their high-rent hovels, but as the result of the hoodlum elements stirred by outside subversive elements—a few radicals and communist agitators."[11]

Blaming outside agitators was a successful tactic employed time and again by city officials from Birmingham, Alabama, to Yellow Springs, Ohio. Speculation that Robert F. Williams's Revolutionary Action Movement was somehow involved in Cleveland conjured notions that clandestine communist sympathizers had incited crowds to violent outbursts. The fact that Williams was living in exile in Cuba made such an assertion unlikely, but the idea that something was in the air that had not been before that summer was not far-fetched. Even though uprisings were not new in 1966, white politicians mistakenly assumed that Black locals were neither angry enough nor strategically skilled enough to organize uprisings that could cost the city millions of dollars. As wrong as they were on that front, it was true that a new spirit empowered these uprisings. It had been stirred up on a remote dusty road in Mississippi—breathed from the mouth of an unknown young firebrand intent on setting the nation ablaze with Black rage.

From Civil Rights to Black Power

A month before the Hough uprising, Stokely Carmichael, the president of SNCC, introduced the phrase "Black Power" to freedom fighters as a point of departure from experiments with Gandhian nonviolent resistance. Precisely what Carmichael meant by the phrase was not entirely clear, but he insinuated that Black people should be ready to take by force that which white society was slow to give to them by choice. Carmichael's Black Power was a direct affront to mass nonviolent demonstrations that emerged out of decades of transnational intellectual exchanges between Indian independence and Black American freedom movements. He was no longer willing to accept a method that did not quell the most racially violent impulses of government officials who authorized police to brutalize defenseless activists. Nor was he satisfied with ineffectual coalitions between white pacifists and Black civil rights workers, in which white leaders dictated that finding philosophical purity was the first step in addressing injustices in any community, institution, or system.

Carmichael's experience with white allies in predominantly white institutions led him to conclude that the dictates of white philosophical purity were hindrances to the freedom movement. He was an ambitious student activist, whose journey from Trinidad to the Bronx and then to Lowndes County, Mississippi, had helped him fashion a mercurial public persona through which he charismatically electrified crowds and earned the respect of elders in the Black freedom movement. After seizing the helm of the Student Nonviolent Coordinating Committee from its former chair, future congressperson John Lewis, he helped organize mass demonstrations to combat Jim Crow segregation with the Southern Christian Leadership Conference (SCLC) throughout Alabama and Mississippi. An organizer involved in the pinnacle of civil rights protests and the chief popularizer of the Black Power movement, Carmichael's 1960s leadership in SNCC and the Black Panther Party made him the transitional figure of the Black freedom movement as it morphed from organizing for civil rights to becoming a movement energized by demands for Black Power. Inspired by his confrontational and sometimes impulsive personality, freedom fighters lost their enchantment with passive resistance and caught the spirit of self-determination. Peniel Joseph captured the importance of Carmichael's place in Black freedom history when he described the pupil of Martin and the protégé of Malcolm as "a revolutionary who passionately believed in self-defense and armed rebellion even as he revered the nation's greatest practitioner of nonviolence; a gifted intellectual who dealt in emotions as well as words and ideas; and an activist whose radical political vision remained anchored by a deep sense of history."[12]

Carmichael's historic stature was forged in the sweltering heat of a Mississippi march that was conceived by James Meredith, who became the first Black student to attend the University of Mississippi in 1962. Meredith was warned not to undertake the March against Fear, as he called it, because as noble as such a trip through the South may have sounded, his colleagues feared for his safety. Since opposing fear was the point of the march, Meredith commenced to walk alone from Memphis, Tennessee, to Jackson, Mississippi, on Sunday, June 5, 1966, in a defiant display of his

American civil rights. Unfortunately, his supporters' fears were fulfilled the next day when Aubrey James Norvell—a white man described by his neighbors as a kind Christian veteran, who had no known ties to any white supremacist organizations—shot him three times with a shotgun.[13]

Despite their belief that Meredith's march was absurd, Cleveland Sellers—a member of SNCC—said his friends were "enraged" when they received news that "he had been killed." Two hours later, when they found out that Meredith was alive but had been knocked unconscious by bird shot, they rushed from Little Rock, Arkansas, to see him. The next day, King, Carmichael, Sellers, Floyd McKissick, and Stanley Wise met Meredith at the hospital where they agreed to continue his march. With the leadership of the SCLC's King, CORE's McKissick, and SNCC's Carmichael, Meredith's March against Fear blazed a new path in America's racial journey. The freedom fighters set out to complete a march, but they stumbled into a new movement.[14]

Tensions were high as they set out on June 7 to continue the march from Hernando, the location where Norvell shot Meredith. Carmichael was hot with anger. As they marched with locked arms, they sang, "We Shall Overcome." A white state trooper heckled the marchers, who had already had a long night and were now walking in sweltering ninety-degree Mississippi summer heat. King shouted back, reminding the trooper that they had every right to be there. Not taking kindly to King's defiance, the trooper pushed the group off the highway. Because they were walking arm in arm, the officer's assault caused King to stumble into Sellers, knocking him to the mud and Carmichael to one knee. Incensed by the trooper's action, Carmichael released his left arm from the group with a compulsion to strike back, only to be restrained by King's unrelenting hold on his other arm. The group continued to sing, but this time the young SNCC participants skipped the verse that heralded "black and white together."[15]

Criticisms of white allies, both moderates and liberals, were plentiful as the civil rights leaders marched, but the senior freedom fighters had resigned themselves to the idea that they needed white people's participation. They were skeptical that it was possible to advocate for a future beloved community if they sacrificed ally participation to satisfy momentary frustrations. At a meeting concerning the goals of the march, Whitney Young, executive director of the National Urban League (NUL), and Roy Wilkins from the National Association for the Advancement of Colored People (NAACP)—the last two to arrive at the twenty-day march—attempted to assert their authority over Carmichael and his colleagues. Undeterred and emboldened by his return to Lowndes County, where SNCC had tremendous support and influence, Carmichael proposed that the organizers prioritize Black participation and welcome the Deacons of Defense as escorts. Cleveland Sellers, Carmichael's SNCC colleague, recalled, "He argued that the march should deemphasize white participation, that it should be used to highlight the need for independent, black political units."[16] Including the Deacons of Defense, an armed group from Louisiana, signaled to Carmichael's seniors that their nonviolent consensus was no longer intact. McKissick threw the support of CORE behind Carmichael's plan, but Wilkins and Young would not agree to limiting participation to local Blacks or using armed escorts. After King voted with CORE and SNCC, the NAACP and NUL leaders packed up and returned to New York.[17]

With the addition of the Deacons of Defense, the marchers continued toward Jackson. Black locals watched admiringly as they caught their first in-person glimpses of King. At night they gathered to hear King's and Carmichael's extemporaneous speeches, which enlivened the audiences. The Deacons secured the group by interrogating white people who approached their camp, which helped the marchers abate danger for the first ten days.[18]

On the morning of June 16, the police in Greenwood, where Carmichael was well-known for his organizing efforts in previous years, thwarted a team of marchers from erecting their tents on the grounds of a Black high school that the city had previously granted them permission to use as their campsite. Later that evening, as they prepared an alternative camp at a Black elementary school, the demonstrators learned that the city had not only barred them from the high school but also banned them from camping at any public school. [19] Accompanied by two city commissioners and nine police officers, the chief of police, B. A. "Buff" Hammond, told the police to arrest anyone who touched the tent. Carmichael and two of his colleagues, one from SNCC and the other from CORE, defiantly grabbed the tent. The officers charged them with trespassing and held them at the Greenwood police station.[20]

News of Carmichael's arrest traveled quickly. Willie Ricks, Carmichael's aide, used the arrest to the demonstrators' advantage. Just as aggressive policing had fueled support for the Birmingham movement against Bull Connor, jailing Carmichael in a town where his Black support rivaled King's ratcheted up the people's support for the sojourners. Within a few hours of Carmichael's release, hundreds of people gathered in Greenwood's Broad Street Park, where the city permitted the demonstrators to set up a campsite.[21]

Ricks rigged a stage using a tractor trailer, upon which a newly freed Carmichael could speak to the crowd. McKissick, King, and Ricks were the first to make use of the makeshift stage to share their indignation over Carmichael's arrest with the crowd. When Carmichael climbed up on the tractor, Sellers recalled, "The crowd greeted him with a huge roar," to which he responded with the gesture that would stand as the symbol of Black Power—a raised arm and clenched fist.[22] "This is the twenty-seventh time I have been arrested," he informed them, "and I ain't going to jail no more." Unfettered by the confines of jail and emancipated to speak to an impassioned crowd, Carmichael spoke his mind freely: "The only way we gonna stop them white men from whuppin' us is to take over." All eyes were on him, and the crowd hung on his every word. "We been saying freedom for six years and we ain't got nothin.' What we gonna start saying now is Black Power!"[23] Knowing that he had the crowd's full attention and desire to follow his lead, Carmichael shouted the question, "What do we want?"—to which they chanted in unison, "Black Power!" In call-and-response fashion, the crowd and their new preacher continued to chant, inserting a new spirit of power into the Black freedom movement.[24]

It is not an overstatement to say that Carmichael's Black Power canticle, debuted during the Meredith march, transformed the Black freedom movement. As Peniel Joseph writes, "Carmichael, through the act of naming this unacknowledged force in American politics, turned the Meredith March into a watershed historical event."[25] As the summer unfolded, Black organizations postured themselves relative to their embrace or repudiation of the slogan, even though it was not entirely clear what this call for Black Power meant. Members of the SCLC shared with King a concern that the slogan connoted organized violence. SCLC staff accused CORE of being more enthusiastic for this power than SNCC. McKissick announced Black Power as the official philosophy of CORE at the organization's summer gathering. The NAACP cut ties with groups associated with the phrase and distanced themselves from former partners at its conference.

Outside of fracturing Black coalitions, Black Power gave white politicians and white media a new Black freedom ethic around which to unify and to lambaste as a call for violence. More responsible journalists clarified that Carmichael's Black Power validated self-defense as a legitimate response to white aggression, but the headlines failed to communicate any nuance. Whether or not the headlines shaped white public opinion, a CBS poll at the end of the summer made it clear that 73 percent of white liberals did not support the civil rights movement—up from 58 percent in June. White politicians like Daniel Patrick Moynihan voiced sympathy with the desire for Black Power but warned that the uprisings of 1966 had whittled away white support.

Nuance could be found by anyone looking for it. King and others chimed in with definitions of their own that added texture to utterances of Black Power. King repeatedly defined it as "a cry of disappointment," which allowed him to sympathize with Carmichael but still preach his wholehearted commitment to nonviolence.[26] King feared that the cries of Black Power would lead to organized violence, but he understood that if America denied racial justice, the cries would increase.

Adam Clayton Powell, the Harlem preacher and politician, suggested that King misunderstood Black Power and offered his own definition. "It means dignity; it doesn't mean violence," he explained. Powell also felt it necessary to clarify what he saw as a misconception, that Black Power was opposed to white people: "It means integrity. It doesn't mean anti-white. It means pride in being black." In response to CBS's Mike Wallace, who pressed his guests to explain what Black Power meant for white people, Powell said, "It means you're willing to cooperate with your white brother and sister if they're going to cooperate with you, in terms of giving you the same things that they have." The right to refuse cooperation implied at least the veiled possibility of violence. Daniel Watts, the editor of the Black radical magazine *Liberator*, clarified that there was no veil; Black Power was a threat. For Watts, it meant "finally forcing a direct confrontation with the white power structure" through uprisings, like the nation witnessed in the "hot summers" of 1964, 1965, and 1966.[27]

The summer of 1966 provided Carmichael with ample opportunities to explain what Black Power meant when applied to discontented Black Americans in the nation's cities. In Chicago, he delivered his "What We Want" speech just days after the Hough eruption. His remarks reshaped the terms of debate by urging his audience to no longer acquiesce to laws and ideas that they had no part in making. Carmichael went on to address two essential elements of Black Power: self-determination and Black pride. He noted that the power to define reality with words and ideas that dignified Black experiences was a significant source of self-determination.

Likewise, Carmichael proposed redefining words that had traditionally been used to justify anti-Black discrimination and transforming them to encourage racial pride. He suggested that ideas like "success" needed to be defined more by how much food was made available to the community than by how much an individual's status was elevated. Of course the press homed in on his perspective on urban unrest. Aware that the language of a riot signified disorder—irrational frenzy, chaos, and indiscriminate violence—Carmichael offered "rebellion" as a term that signified a response to oppression. He persuaded those in his hearing to see that "what's happening is rebellions not riots." He also dismissed terms that mischaracterized Black Power. "In the first place don't get confused with the words they use like 'anti-white,' 'hate,' 'militant' and all that nonsense like 'radical' and 'riots,'" he implored. [28] A reporter returned to the subject of riots after the speech ended and asked Carmichael what he thought about the looting and Molotov cocktails in Cleveland. He quipped, "I'm not opposed to violence."[29]

Widely recognized as the architect of the Black Power movement, Carmichael's comments carried more weight than those of other freedom fighters, even if the white press and politicians hoped that the words of nonviolent leaders won the day. Wherever Carmichael visited, the eyes of the US Congress, the FBI, the media, and concerned white citizens—liberal and conservative alike—were upon the man who *Time* magazine made the face of "the New Racism." The negative press he received raised expectations that Carmichael would make incendiary remarks against the United States whenever he spoke on the subject, and he rarely disappointed. Over the next year, he received invitations to speak to journalists, appear on radio shows, and participate in television panels, where he shaped the Black Power conversation.[30]

A Solution

In Yellow Springs, Ohio, Templin watched closely as Midwestern cities faced the anger of aggrieved residents, reactively aggressive police, and politicians who attacked Black Power by characterizing it as anti-white and treasonous. He listened as reverse racism charges against Black Power resounded from former Black and white allies alike. Wilkins and Young suggested that Carmichael's slogan was hardly distinguishable from the policies of South African apartheid. Vice President Hubert Humphrey affirmed this notion as he denounced racism of any kind at that year's NAACP convention. Attendees at the convention welcomed not only his antipoverty programs and civil rights commitments but also his rejection of SNCC- and CORE-style activism. Alluding to the emergence of Black Power, Humphrey cautioned, "And we must reject calls for racism, whether they come from a throat that is white or one that is black."[31]

From Humphrey's national security perspective, it was in his interest to reject antiwar messages, but from Templin's antiwar perspective, Carmichael's Black Power encouraged more people to defy the draft. Ohio congressman John Sweeney accused Carmichael of being a "subversive whose long-range intentions are to inflict great harm upon the United States of America."[32] A chorus of politicians agreed. Some recommended that the Department of Justice try him for treason. Others publicly urged the military to draft him as punishment during a time when it was well known that the war effort lacked enough draftees. One more Black soldier would do nothing to win the war, but the idea spoke to white America's willingness to force Black bodies to fight for a nation that was not fighting for them. In October, Robert McNamara, the US secretary of defense, created a program to enlist people who had failed basic requirements to be soldiers—due to low test scores or physical ailments—in previous rounds of the draft. When CBS reporter Mike Wallace directly asked if he planned to continue encouraging Black men to dodge the draft in the future, Carmichael said, "I most certainly do. I look at the recent statement by racist McNamara who says that thirty percent of the people that are going to be drafted now under his new system are going to be Black people. And that's nothing more than Black urban removal."[33]

Templin, another Ohioan, welcomed Carmichael's analysis. As a career anti-imperialist, Templin received Carmichael's unrelenting criticism of the draft as an example of issues absent from white Christian pacifists' discourse. Through his Black Power analysis, Carmichael connected anti-Black oppression to the imperialist spread of capitalism. As Templin understood it, the racial enmity created by anti-Black systems, the inequality inherent to capitalism, and the extractive nature of imperialism constituted the preconditions for war that his pacifist peers routinely refused to address. Unlike other white allies, whose attitudes toward civil rights demonstrations cooled as freedom fighters' call for Black Power heated up, Templin began consuming Black Power messages with a hermeneutic of trust he had likely developed through his associations at Central State, the local NAACP, and CORE. In addition to Carmichael, Templin sought out evangelists who offered a wide range from which to interpret Black Power: Floyd McKissick, Frantz Fanon, Nathan Wright, Kenneth Clark, Eldridge Cleaver, Vincent Harding, and hosts of others. Their proclamations represented the good news that Templin believed could finally save white America from its bondage to whiteness—white prerogative, Western imperialism, and capitalism.

Templin created a Black Power file on other white intellectuals who demonstrated sympathies for the struggle. He filled the collection with newspaper clippings, book chapters, and notes on white professors, pastors, and politicians who spanned the American Midwest, South, and East Coast. Some, like fellow Ohio professor Wilson McWilliams at Oberlin College, announced in triumphal terms that "Black power is not the assassin of the Civil Rights Movement; it is its undertaker."[34] Others, like psychologists Robert Coles and Thomas Pettigrew, offered their insights into the effects that inequality had on Black America. Harry Fleischman suggested that white liberals had done too little, and that Black Power had convinced him that it was the duty of white people to convert "fellow whites to support equality."[35]

Templin agreed. He took special note of white intellectuals who explained Black Power to white Christian audiences. The smallest events gained his attention, like a seminar in Kansas City, Missouri, hosted by Saint Paul School of Theology professors, who interpreted Black Power to an audience of 100 students during a three-day seminar.[36] At Metropolitan Duane Methodist Church in Manhattan in 1966, Claude Williams, a presbyterian minister whose ordination credentials had recently been restored after enduring decades of accusations of heresy on account of his pro-union and pro-Black activism, argued, "Black power offers an approach to both Black and white in the South." Though speaking in the North, Williams, a lifelong Southerner, had a special message for his homeland: "Today, every white youngster who grows up in the South must deliberately choose whether he will become a decent person or remain a willfully blinded bigot. In this choice," he concluded, "is the first hope for the decent instinct that makes for an ally in the struggle." For Templin, that choice was imperative for white Americans—Northern or Southern, liberal, conservative, and radical alike—to make. The problem, as Templin was aware, was that most allies did not believe, as Williams did, that "Black power is one of the most positive developments in the American people's movement."[37]

Templin's own experiences, as discussed in chapter 6, had convinced him that white people suffered from an imperialist psychology in which they believed "white made right." With few challenges to that notion, white citizens took imperialism for granted and Christians accepted foreign missionary endeavors as rightful extensions of US expansion around the globe. On the expansion of American Christian ideals, white Christians across the nation had little disagreement, especially as they related to fighting communism at home and abroad. The perspectives of white people in the North and the South were shaped by different regional contexts, but the major influences in those contexts were white presses, white pastors, and white politicians. Segregation isolated white people from Black perspectives, but news of Black unrest—civil rights demonstrations and urban uprisings—on radio and television forced white people to hear and see the positions that Black people were taking in the politics of the 1960s—positions that suggested that Black people were taking the Black Power position.

Christianity and Black Power

Christian responses to the Black Power movement were mixed. Black church leaders were not of one voice concerning the Black Power shift. Members of the SCLC voiced their fears that Black Power implied violence and separatism. Clergy like Rev. Albert Cleage, on the other hand, embraced the student-led Black Power movement as the true representation of the Christian church on earth. Rev. Adam Clayton Powell, pastor of Abyssinian Baptist Church in Harlem and the congressman who chaired the Education and Labor Committee, had communicated the need for Black power at Howard University's baccalaureate, four weeks before Carmichael led his Black Power chant. As he explained the ongoing struggle for civil rights, he combined his Christian faith with the pursuit of political power: "To demand these God-given rights is to seek *black power*—the power to build black institutions of splendid achievement."[38] He was not territorial about his proclamation to students; as soon as Carmichael championed the cause, Powell quickly became a supporter of Carmichael's new position.

If Templin's white Christian pacifist colleagues—who, unlike freedom fighters, had largely refrained from direct participation in civil rights demonstrations—commented on Black Power at all, they did so from their position as white allies who felt pushed out. Their analysis lacked the nuance of the nonviolent wing of Black clergy, who lauded Black pride but disliked the violence implied in Carmichael's use of slogans like "by any means necessary." Dorothy Day, who saw Carmichael on a taped interview, joined others who decried the new policies of SNCC "as black nationalist."[39] In her June 1966 *Catholic Worker* column "On Pilgrimage," Day reported that the new leadership recommended "a purge of the white workers in the organization."[40] For Day, who was a board member of the Catholic Interracial Council, which had rejected Black leadership in an interracial organization, Carmichael's instruction for white workers to go into white communities to "develop moderate bases" conflicted with the interracialism that she adopted from its Catholic champion, John LaFarge. On behalf of *The Catholic Worker*, Day especially disagreed with Carmichael's stated desire to "intensify the program in terms of the political arena."[41] A Black political party that was built for Black people and by Black people captured a central principle of Black Power organizing. Day noted Carmichael's defense of this desire, that these strategies were not anti-white, but her only commentary on the topic signaled that she carried suspicions about the direction Black Power policies would take organizations like SNCC, CORE, and the Poor People's Corporation.[42]

The NCNC had no misgivings about the direction Black Power could take their congregations, communities, and the nation. Templin believed that their statement best captured the essence of Black Power. The religious leaders, forty-seven men and one woman, put their full support behind the need for Black Power. Unlike their white counterparts, their experience within Black communities provided them with context through which they could interpret Black rage and rebellions sympathetically. In this spirit, they appealed to Americans to understand that uprisings were a reaction to white American leaders, whom they accused of tying a proverbial "white noose of suburbia" around the necks of Black Americans. From their vantage point, inattention to Black unemployment during a period of economic growth, and segregated education systems in one of the world's most technologically advanced nations, reflected a great failure of white leaders to govern in a way that created equal opportunity for all the nation's people. Had their white suburban constituents spoken out against segregationist policies, elected officials would have needed to address racial inequality. Because they did not, politicians interpreted their silence as an endorsement of the discriminatory racial policies that had governed their cities from the beginning. Therefore, unlike pacifist purists, who were reluctant to label political actions as setting the stage for physical conflict, the NCNC statement condemned white suburban support for segregation as "silent and covert violence."[43]

The attention the NCNC statement drew to the complicity of white suburbanites in racial oppression represented a Black tradition that was at least as old as Frederick Douglass's post–Civil War proclamation: "The thing worse than rebellion is the thing that causes rebellion."[44] It was a tradition that did not celebrate violence but understood that violent conflict was the predictable outcome of uninterrupted injustices. King, too, reflected this tradition in his own response to white disapproval of riots that raged in the mid-1960s, saying that "riots do not develop out of thin air." King called attention to the fact that "little was done about the conditions that create riots," and he defined "riots" during the Black freedom era as "the language of the unheard."[45] If white Americans wanted to prevent them, then they needed to understand that social justice and progress were the only guarantors. "So in a real sense," King lectured to students at Stanford University, "our nation's summer riots are caused by our nation's winters of delay. And as long as America postpones justice, we stand in the position of having these recurrences of violence and riots over and over again."[46]

Black freedom fighters like Douglass and King lived at different times and advocated different methods of protest, but they interpreted uprisings as responses to an anti-Black state. The NCNC statement drew on this tradition. "It is of critical importance," they preached, "that the leaders of this nation listen also to a voice which says that the principal source of the threat to our nation comes neither from the riots erupting in our big cities, nor from the disagreements among the leaders of the civil rights movement, nor even from the raising of the cry for 'black power.'" They refused to condemn riots, activist agitation, or Black Power, because they understood that these uprisings were the people's attempts to voice generations of frustration at local and national officials who chose not to listen to them.[47]

The NCNC asserted that there were consequences to ignoring the people: "The judgment of God [is] upon our nation for its failure to use its abundant resources to serve the real well-being of a people, at home and abroad."[48] With their sermonic statement, Black church affiliates inserted their voice into the Black freedom cause to support and offer leadership to a grassroots movement. Lending their Christian support to militant students confounded opponents of the Black Power movement. Clergy became apologists for Black militancy, penned a treatise on uprisings, and condemned neglectful politicians. Their show of solidarity with Black students demonstrated their comprehension of the importance of the Black Church's public endorsement of revolutionaries, especially as their methods were contrasted with the nonviolent methods of their elders.

Templin appreciated not only the support the NCNC gave to students but also the statement's recognition that Black Power met "conscienceless power" with "powerless conscience."[49] Black Power promoted an ethic of siding with economically and politically oppressed people and therefore had moral authority that the state, guided by capitalism, did not. From Templin's anti-capitalist perspective, the military and the police were brutal enforcers of Western greed. In his experience, despite the noble declarations behind militaristic missions of Western states, the buying and selling of weapons that nations used to capture lands and exploit racially minoritized people—people who, whether a numerical majority or not, lost power to shape the future of their communities—were land grabs in service of increasing the wealth of the most militaristically powerful nations. Once those nations established colonies, their police controlled the land and prioritized protecting the interests of white property owners. Powerless conscience was a position from which Black people could assert moral strength that Templin believed was sufficient to achieve "honest interracial interaction."[50] Through honest interactions, they could move beyond the politics of philanthropy to the politics of economic development. Economic development could be used to empower Black residents to transform their communities.

Black Power Conventions

Templin did not reside in a Black community, but he had grown comfortable in spaces where he was one of few, if not the only, white person. His tenure at a Black college introduced him to long traditions of Black scholarship, culture, and institution building. By the time he joined the Methodist Church's Central Jurisdiction as the first white ordained elder, he had already gained the acceptance of Black colleagues and students after six years of teaching. Assured that his teaching, scholarship, and ministry were in harmony with fellow clergy from Black church traditions and colleagues from Black intellectual traditions, Templin also joined the African Studies Association. Thus, his public life—as an ordained Methodist elder and a tenured professor of sociology at Central State—was transformed by Black spaces.

Perhaps this explains why he felt comfortable attending the Black Power conference in Philadelphia. The 1968 National Conference on Black Power that met August 29–September 1 at Benjamin Franklin High School was the third assembly of conferences that were organized as "intimate family gatherings."[51] Since the white press gave unflattering accounts of the first gathering in Washington, D.C., organizers specified that the conferences would be exclusively for Black attendees in the future. Templin's presence, then, not only spoke to the level of his comfort but, more importantly, spoke to the level of trust that he had earned from Black leaders who had ample reasons to be wary of white allies. The impression that the conference left on him was immeasurable. He quoted a Black Methodist clergy who exclaimed that there was something noticeably different between his experiences at

Methodist Central Jurisdiction meetings, hosted by clergy who referred to themselves as "Negroes," and the Philadelphia Black Power conference, where African culture decorated the event and participants celebrated Black pride.[52]

Those who gathered in the first of the Black Power conferences would have been proud to know that their labor was still producing fruit two years later. The 1966 Planning Conference in Washington, D.C., was convened by Adam Clayton Powell for one day on September 3 and was attended by "169 delegates from 37 cities, 18 states, and 64 organizations."[53] The entire purpose of the gathering was to plan for a major Black Power conference with an entire program composed of speakers and workshops. In the District of Columbia, they appointed Dr. Nathan Wright—a Black Episcopal priest and author of three books on civil disorder—as chair of the continuations committee. Wright believed that Black Power was "the most creative social concept of this present century," but he believed it was more than an important social concept solely for this moment. "Potentially," he said in an interview, "[Black Power] is the most productive theological and philosophical concept of all time."[54]

With Wright's leadership, the second Black Power conference, but perhaps the first one of major importance, met in Newark, New Jersey, just four days after a rebellion erupted there. Outraged residents of Newark responded to the police beating of a Black cab driver. The conflict between police and residents left 26 people dead and more than 200 injured—which included children, men, women, and police.[55] The purpose of the conference, as stated in the registration form, was "to explore the issue of power as it relates to specific problem areas in the life of black Americans." The invitation to explore power, however, was not for everyone. One paragraph, subtitled "Who May Attend," explicitly stated that the conference welcomed "representative leadership from *all segments of the Black community*."[56] According to Chuck Stone, a journalist and workshop leader at the Newark conference, the gathering of around 1,000 attendees was monumental. "If the National Conference on Black Power did nothing else, it buried once and for all the traditional civil rights movement," he boasted in his glowing report, because the Black Power emphasis "raised serious questions about the ultimate values of integration." Stone said that it also "shoved the myth of the so-called 'Big Five' of 'Negro Leadership' into the dungeon of obscurity and forged a new weapon of mass black leadership ready to take charge of the black man's destiny."[57]

Stone noted the absence of Martin Luther King Jr., Roy Wilkins, Whitney Young, and Bayard Rustin as a good thing, because it implied that Black Power empowered the people, not just the leaders. NAACP representatives joined the gathering, even though its leadership had made known their opposition to Black Power just a year prior. CORE's Floyd McKissick, who had eagerly spoke in support of the Black Power movement since it emerged after the Meredith march, was the only director of the five established civil rights organizations in attendance. CORE, with the attendance of McKissick and James Farmer, who hosted a workshop on Cooperation and Alliances, was well represented. Unlike other gatherings that made special invitations to elite dignitaries, this was "not a leaders' conference." Organizers purposed it to represent the aims of the Black Power movement itself—it was for the people.[58]

The first conference planned no space for criticism of Black Power. According to Cedric Johnson, "Dissent was often tabled or suppressed for the sake of symbolic unity." Stone's conference report minimized the seriousness of ideological conflicts in a manner reflective of the spirit of the organizing committee's hopes for the conference—that they were working for "the unity of Black people and the greatest good for all." He described the delegates as a "single-purposed group." At some point during the four-day conference, he suggested that the institutional affiliations that they brought with them ceased to matter. "One fact alone bound them together," he wrote, "white oppression because of their black skins." Perhaps the greatest accomplishment of the conference was that nationwide Black representatives from media, religious organizations, businesses, nongovernmental organizations, political interest groups, local government offices, police departments, universities, student groups, and international associations gathered to discuss important issues related to Black Power. That they were all unified in their Black identity was not plausible. Interpretations of Black identity varied, and what Black Power meant for those identities was negotiated in relation to their unique regional, institutional, and community affiliations.[59]

Thus, delegates debated from their particular Black experiences, which presented obstacles for working together to address the economic, political, and social issues they assumed to have in common. Disagreements emerged between radical and middle-class participants over the role of Marxism or capitalism in securing a future for Black life. The youth work group led by Cleveland Sellers engaged in a heated argument between a young woman who suggested replacing capitalism with cooperatives and a bourgeois dressed man who rebutted that capitalism was the best system. In other sections, militants and moderates quarreled over the use of violent or nonviolent means in the revolution. And Black nationalists feuded with integrationists over the legitimacy of appointing exclusively Black leaders to empower Black communities or allowing white allies help. One disagreement on how to engage the white press inspired a group of "young Black militants" to interrupt a press conference, break television cameras, and drive the white reporters from the room. Stone's celebratory reporting aside, disagreements were to be expected. The concept of Black Power, as a new term replacing nonviolent direct action, engendered questions regarding the efficacy of movement politics, institutional politics, electoral politics, party politics, and racial politics.[60]

The 1968 Philadelphia conference mirrored many of the debates that delegates witnessed in Newark. The most radical edges of those debates were dulled by appeals to work within existing systems and build Black electoral power. The emphasis built on the Newark Black Manifesto, which attendees agreed upon at the end of the 1967 conference. The manifesto called for addressing the economic needs for "buy back policies," establishing "a National Black Education Board," and appointing "a Black Power Lobby in Washington, DC." Those debates persisted, but passions for political representation turned those concerns toward Black political leadership. In Jim Thomas's economic work group, a hospital union representative from New York City who worked under Jewish leadership drew the ire of skeptical attendees who asked if Black Power could exist in an environment where Black leaders were not in control. In other words, instead of discussing whether racial inequality was inherent to capitalist systems and should be solved by a socialist system, participants focused on the racial identity of the persons leading the cause. These questions regarding the role of white people in the movement were a product of one interpretation of the Black leadership ethic of Black Power—questions that Cedric Johnson suggests "illuminates the fashion in which the rhetoric of black control might obscure the necessarily issue-based nature of political organizing."[61]

Templin's presence at the third conference embodied the tensions involved in welcoming white participation to the movement. His attendance was unusual and was likely justified by his intimate affiliations with Black religious groups and Black higher education. Given that around 4,000 people attended the conference, Templin may not have been the only white person there. His reflections on the conference implied that there were very few other white people, if any at all. The official policy excluded them. "I don't get the feeling they hate white people. That is not the reason they have excluded them from the conference," he wrote in an unpublished essay. "Rather," he continued, "it is because they bring extraneous issues." In his experience, white allies too often asked questions and forced discussions about issues that centered white interests and were hardly pertinent to Black concerns. Excluding white people, then, was necessary for the intra-racial goals of the conference. He understood it as a simple fact that "white people can't help them." His insights into the need for Black pride, Black control, and Black caucusing deepened his resolve to defend whatever philosophy of Black Power surfaced from the City of Brotherly Love.[62]

Besides attendance being four times greater than the last gathering, the Philadelphia conference was different from the Newark event in ways that Templin could not have been sensitive to, being that it was his first Black Power conference. For one, a greater number of prominent leaders attended, including Michigan congressman John Conyers, SCLC representative Jesse Jackson, and Whitney Young of the Urban League. Young, who had walked out of deliberations with King and Carmichael when they arranged to continue Meredith's march and routinely made public criticisms of Black Power afterward, presented a more establishment-friendly tone to the assembly. Perhaps this change was the first sign of a transition taking place in the spirit of these meetings. It was transitioning from the revolutionary spirit that energized the Newark conference following the city's uprisings to a reformist spirit that was willing to work with government systems and strategize for greater Black representation in electoral politics. Whereas the 1967 conference celebrated the "Black Manifesto from the National Conference on Black Power" in the tradition of protest, the 1968 conference resolved to build political power by establishing a Black party "in every Black community for the development of radical social change and for the liberation and survival of Black people."[63]

This shift aligned with the vision that Templin had laid out in *Democracy and Nonviolence* in 1966. For true freedom to prevail in the United States, he argued, white rule—constituted by the ideologies of white supremacy, capitalism, and Western imperialism—had to end. Black pride, as the antithesis of so-called white superiority, was necessary to empower Black communities to see that they had within them the leadership skills, intellectual creativity, and collective power to meet white rule with political demands that could make the United States a true democracy. For Templin, democracy belonged to the people, not the state. It was the best form of government to foster true freedom, which, despite disagreements that persisted throughout the conferences, everyone agreed they were seeking. Resolutions proposed by conference delegates that called for Black self-determination and political independence coalesced well with Templin's vision of "the continuous peaceful shaping and reshaping of governments and society by the people."[64]

The Promise of Black Power

Templin returned from Philadelphia in full agreement with the NCNC statement that "the concept of 'black power' reminds us of the need for and the possibility of authentic democracy in America." Democracy, as it existed under the regime of racial segregation, called on Black America to integrate into a proverbial "burning house." The representations of Black Power that Templin experienced at the conference presented opportunities to build what King called a "world house" or the beloved community. In contrast to King's plan, which called on the federal government to include Black people in building that community, Templin, a white man, worked to be included in the Black Power movement. He believed that initiatives "by and for" Black Americans would usher in "a community of people overcoming all differences and uniting people for the welfare of all—in God's way."[65]

Having been convinced himself, Templin carried this message to any church gathering or media outlet interested in hearing about his new hope. A month after attending the Black Power conference, he made headlines in Dayton newspapers as a "white 'Black Power' advocate." He began evangelistically spreading his beliefs like never before. This was a significant shift for Templin from his early career as a missionary. He had attempted to convert people in India to Protestant Christianity, but he quickly soured on religious conversions upon learning that Indian culture, in its religious diversity, had a lot to teach Western Christians. "I was never able to bring myself to ask another person of some other faith to accept my faith," he said. Instead, he "tried only to awaken within all the sense of God's rule of love." Templin believed that spreading the message of Black Power was different. Black Power was worthy of the spirit of Jesus, because it taught Black people to love themselves and it confronted white Americans with their complicity in anti-Black exploitation and imperialist extraction of other nations. If Black people truly loved themselves and white people repented from the false freedoms and democracies that prohibited them from loving oppressed people, then Templin believed that America could be born anew. Instead of persuading people to abandon their culture, the message of Black Power might awaken Americans to "God's rule of love." Unlike the civil rights movement, which emphasized loving anti-Black enemies through nonviolent direct confrontation, Black Power began with love for Black life. That fact, instead of making the movement anti-white, enabled Black people to decide the terms by which they would interact with white society.[66]

It had become commonplace for the white press to demand that proponents of Black Power define the term, often for the sake of determining whether they opposed white people. On August 21, 1966, members of the white press led a discussion of Black Power that framed the concept as violent and anti-white on a ninety-minute special edition of *Meet the Press*. The news show, created by Lawrence Spivak, invited a panel that included Martin Luther King Jr., Whitney Young, Roy Wilkins, Floyd McKissick, James Meredith, and Stokely Carmichael. After Spivak noted that Carmichael had accused the white press of distorting the Black Power slogan, he asked, "Will you tell us here and now exactly what you mean by 'Black power' so that all of us can understand your meaning without misquoting or distorting you?" Carmichael replied, "I am sorry that you asked that question now because two days ago the Student Nonviolent Coordinating Committee decided that we are not going to define the term 'Black Power' anymore."[67]

Spivak followed up by asking if *The New York Times* misquoted SNCC when it published the words of a position paper that stated: "When we view the masses of white people, we view in reality 180 million racists." Spivak seemed far less interested in a definition of Black Power than he was in its potential significance for white people. He pressed once more, "Will you yourself answer, do you believe that there are 180 million racists in this country?" This time, Carmichael obliged, not by defining Black Power but by offering a definition of systemic racism that "has nothing to do with the white person himself." He explained, "He or she may be a good guy or a bad guy, but . . . the system just allows [white people] to see black people as inferior, and . . . the few black people that are allowed to escape [the system] are seen . . . as exceptions to the rule."[68]

The other panelists also avoided defining the term. Whitney Young did not allow his thoughts about Black Power to be misconstrued as speaking against other Black organizations. "Well, I can only speak for the Urban League," he began. "We took a position that we should be very cautious about trying to interpret the slogans of other organizations." Similarly, when Rowland Evans of the *Chicago Sun-Times* asked Roy Wilkins if Black Power is what has white people concerned, the director of the NAACP pivoted to the possibility that white people resent competing with Black candidates for jobs. Floyd McKissick was the only leader to offer a definition. He said that Black Power was "the self-determination to determine the direction and the pace at which [Black people] will become total citizens in this society." Putting it more simply, he clarified, "That means putting power in black people's hands."[69]

If there was no uniform agreement among civil rights leaders or Black Power innovators to define Black Power, then what role did Templin, a white man struggling to free himself from whiteness, have in defining the term? Moreover, if he did not define it, then how could he speak to white audiences about the importance of supporting the Black Power movement? With these concerns in mind, Templin defined Black Power in the true spirit of the movement, recognizing what was at stake for his Black colleagues and his white audience. He told audiences that Black Power meant "change by and for blacks." It was a conscientious way for him, as a white sociologist, to refrain from appearing to colonize Black Power with his own definitions. He was aware that King, Carmichael, McKissick, Young, Wilkins, and others defined the concept differently. Templin's explanation grasped Carmichael's belief that Black communities "shall have to struggle for the right to create our own terms through which to define ourselves and our relationship to society and to have these terms recognized." It also made room for multiple definitions to exist at once.[70]

Centering white concerns in a discussion of Black Power was likely what Templin tried to avoid when he restrained himself from synthesizing definitions that, in his view, could only be adjudicated by members of the Black community. He was, however, willing to offer a synthesis of history. Templin taught his audiences that European imperialism had presented the world with the destructive thesis that "the white man is and should be 'separate and superior.'" He blamed this thesis for "spreading conditions that subjugated Blacks and other non-whites." He taught that Black Power was a necessary historical intervention because it was the antithesis to white power, "the rising opposition to the domination by whites," and the means by which humans could achieve "harmony and equality." In his historical interpretation, Black Power confronted the world with the proposition "that separatism and white supremacy must come to an end." The conflicts that arose when these powers met were necessary if America hoped to achieve "true democracy, non-violence, harmony, and understanding."[71]

Democracy, as Templin advocated for it, required everyone's voice and contribution. Black Power, then, did not erase white people; it rearranged their relationship to American society. Templin taught that white people had a role in the Black Power movement, but it was not a leading role. Instead, it required a desire among white people to share an equal role with Black people. He took his cues concerning the role of white involvement from Kenneth Clark's book *Dark Ghetto*. Therein, Clark identified that strong tensions between Black Power and white resistance might make mutuality untenable. He wondered if relationships between white liberals and Black freedom fighters, "who have needed each other in the past, will survive the test of transformation of roles from dependence of the advantaged and disadvantaged upon each other." If they could not, there was little hope that they could reach "a common commitment to mutually desired goals of justice and social good."[72]

It was not only Clark who had advice for white supporters of Black Power. Carmichael, too, had opinions on the matter. He recommended, "There's no reason why they should stop supporting the movement now." SNCC's decision to exclude white allies from decision-making did not mean that they had no role in the movement. He saw no contradiction in the new policy. The Black Power architect felt that white people who were genuinely interested in the well-being of Black people would support a course that Black people chartered and a program that Black people believed in, such that they would continue to give to it. This was precisely what Templin did through reading, writing, speaking, and attending conferences.[73]

Giving to the Black Power movement was not only about making financial contributions but also about making time. Templin adopted Carmichael's belief that the Black Power movement needed "more white people to civilize whites." As a student demonstrator, Carmichael had seen firsthand the savagery of everyday middle-class white Americans, young and old, terrorize peace-loving protesters. And he fumed over the events in Cicero, Illinois, in which a group of 250 CORE demonstrators were met with bricks and bottles as they attempted to march through a mob of angry white residents who held tightly to a history of violently excluding Black people from taking residence there. Carmichael repeatedly implored white audiences to focus less on whether Black people were growing more violent or anti-white and more on the violence that emanated from their own communities. "One of the most disturbing things about white supporters of the movement," he opined, "has been that they are afraid to go into their own communities—which is where the racism exists—and work to get rid of it." Templin's Black Power tour through Ohio and Missouri, teaching white people to embrace nonviolence and racial equality, was his way of answering Carmichael's call.[74]

Templin's message demonstrated deep understanding of Carmichael's problem with white people, especially liberals. In the "white problem" section of Carmichael's treatise, *What We Want*, he identified that white people's first concern was "of themselves" and "of their feelings of rejection." Those feelings compelled white liberals to insist on a supposed right to allyship in the form of interracialism or racial reconciliation. Interracialism and racial reconciliation philosophies assumed that without coalitions with white groups, Black people would never overcome racial oppression in America. In his experience, the problem with this line of thinking was that white groups usually betrayed the freedom movement by undermining Black initiatives to gain power or absorbed Black leadership in the name of friendship. Choosing between freedom and friendship was not a choice Carmichael was willing to make—he chose freedom every time. Carmichael welcomed help and white friends, but he insisted on "the right to decide whether anyone is, in fact, our friend." It was not for white liberals to dictate the terms under which Black Power organizations would build coalitions with predominantly white organizations, as had happened in the past. Those coalitions too often resulted in white allies undermining Black leadership or dictating the terms by which they would lend their aid. Thus, his solution to the white problem was to take the power of deciding the terms of their relationship with Black people away from white people. "We will not be told whom we should choose as allies," he declared.[75]

Based on the lessons he learned from the NCNC statement, the Black Power conference, Clark, and Carmichael, Templin seemed to understand that solidarity with the Black freedom movement as it moved in the direction of Black Power meant that white people would not be centered. These were lessons that many allies did not learn. Instead, they rejected Black leadership, like when Dorothy Day undermined Arthur Falls's economic education program, or when Clarence Jordan rejected King's civil rights demonstrations. By choosing solidarity over allyship, Templin positioned himself to learn from Black leaders as they determined the future of their movement and their role in American democracy. In so doing, Templin deepened his Black colleagues' trust in his relationship to them and the cause for freedom.

Templin's legacy has largely been lost to history. Dorothy Day, Clarence Jordan, and nearly any white proponent of interracialism or racial reconciliation hold greater stature among white people who consider themselves allies. Perhaps Templin's choice to abandon the pacifist movement determined the fate of his renown. Nevertheless, he was content to occupy a supporting role in the work he did. As the director of the School of Living, he championed the program as Ralph Borsodi's "big idea." As a board member of Peacemakers and editor of its newsletter, he communicated his vision for a pacifism that paid greater attention to racial segregation as a primary issue in the conflicts of America and the world, but he never made his disagreements with the Fellowship of Reconciliation or Peacemakers public. His personality inclined him toward working outside the headlines—until he was confronted with the Black Power movement.

Templin's lost legacy might also be explained by his willingness to headline newspaper articles as a Black Power advocate. Templin's humility did not keep him from the spotlight. He wrote a book and numerous articles, challenging an imperial government with only the power of his pen. While his articles were few, he publicly showed his solidarity with the Black Power movement at a time when his white peers smeared Black Power as an ideology that was anti-white and too violent to be a force for good. He supported the Black Power movement at a time when it was not popular to do so. His white peers' nostalgia for the golden age of civil rights and ignorance of Black community made Templin an outlier. Perhaps, then, he did not lose a legacy as much as he lost "the curse of whiteness," which had bound him to predominantly white networks that failed to confront imperialism, capitalism, and anti-Black oppression with the same passion with which they opposed war. Templin joined in solidarity with Black Power to free himself from this bondage. Thus, he laid down his white associations and leaned into supportive roles in predominantly Black organizations.

In so doing, he gained the trust of Black university presidents, Black clergy, and Black Power leaders, who viewed him as worthy of invitations to familial gatherings. Few of his white contemporaries, even those with great reputations for their countercultural interracial communities, found a place in the Black Power movement. Templin did because he saw in the "white problem" the globally destructive power that it inspired. As a result, he accepted that an anti-imperial movement based in Black organizing was the best solution. Accepting an evangelistic role that advocated for white people to join in solidarity with Black Power all but ensured that he would not be celebrated by a white America that largely stood in opposition to even the notion that Black people should have equal rights as citizens in the United States, let alone that they had a right to demand that it be so. At the same time, Templin understood that the future of Black people in America was not his to determine. He also understood that the future of white America depended on agreeing that Black Power held the key to initiating the true freedom that would come when democracy was shared by all Americans. Templin's commitment to freedom, then, meant that it was not up to him to decide whether he was an ally to Black people, and it certainly was not up to his white networks. Rather, it was his responsibility to choose that which would bring about the liberation of all who suffered from the white problem. He chose Black Power.

Epilogue

The End of Allyship?

• •

Allyship has come under increased scrutiny in recent years with the emergence of the Black Lives Matter (BLM) movement. Black freedom fighters, inspired by their Black Power predecessors, have thrown off the shackles of respectability politics in favor of unapologetically Black public protests, which demonstrate less patience for white critiques. Instead of relying on electoral politics or institution building in the mold of nineteenth-century race leaders, twenty-first-century freedom fighters have embraced rage-filled public disruptions of white spaces: streets lined with riot police, private property, and political rallies. These new Black protests were taking place as progressives quickly announced that electoral politics had once and for all proven that race was no longer a factor in American life after the election of Barack Obama, America's first Black president. However, increased awareness of the school-to-prison pipeline, disproportionate representation of Black citizens in mass incarceration, the persistence of the racial wage gap, and inescapable images of police brutality proved that announcement premature. In truth, the resilience of racial inequality in virtually every sector of American life required a new racial analysis that called for something beyond racial diversity and inclusion initiatives. Lacking more than ethics of racial deference and symbolic identity, white progressives' self-proclaimed ally identity proved insufficient to satisfy freedom fighters who rebelled against racially color-blind politics and demanded structural revolution, particularly related to what they identified as white progressives' self-congratulatory antiracism.[1]

The disruptive actions of two Black women at a campaign rally for US senator Bernie Sanders in 2015 exemplified the new posture of twenty-first-century Black protests. "My name is Marissa Janae Johnson, cofounder of BLM Seattle," a young Black woman wearing long braids and large gold cross earrings introduced herself calmly into the microphone she had just commandeered from democratic socialist presidential candidate Bernie Sanders. "I was gonna tell Bernie how racist this city was, filled with progressives," she continued over a cacophony of boos, "but you already did it for me. Thank you. Now that you've covered yourself in your white supremacist liberalism I will formally welcome Bernie Sanders to Seattle."[2] The white crowd there to support the democratic socialist responded with a mixture of jeers, applause, and demands to remove Johnson and her Black Lives Matter partner Mara Willaford, who protested by her side in a raised fist Black Power pose. Once again white allies and Black freedom fighters were at odds. This time allies boasted of supporting the civil rights era and electing America's first Black president. Their candidate had marched in the former and supported the latter.

Moments before the Black Lives Matter activists had taken the stage, Sanders lauded the excited crowd: "Thank you, Seattle, for being one of the most progressive cities in the United States of America!" Sanders's words incensed Johnson, who had made her way to the stage shouting, "BLACK. LIVES. MATTER!"[3] Johnson said that they had planned their disruptive action earlier that summer, after Black Lives Matter protesters interrupted the progressive-leaning Netroots Nation political conference that hosted Sanders, among others, and promised every democratic candidate that they should expect to be confronted until they address BLM concerns. Johnson and Willaford confronted Sanders to expose white progressives' class reductionist politics because they lacked substantive racial analysis. Johnson proceeded to formally welcome Sanders by educating him, and the crowd, on Seattle's long list of failures to address racial injustice. With Sanders's presence, the failures represented something larger than a critique of Seattle. Black freedom fighters across the country were amassing an analysis of white allies' failures to advocate explicitly for Black liberation. In their view, allyship never truly threatened the benefits white people received from the system that disenfranchised, denigrated, and discriminated against Black communities. In this way, Seattle was the perfect representative of white ally politics, in which allies boasted of supporting Black people while benefiting from policies that kept Black citizens from economic and social liberation.[4]

"Bernie Sanders," Johnson began, "I would like to welcome you to this place called Seattle." Opening with a land-back liturgy that would have been familiar to the Pacific Northwest progressives, she stated that Seattle "is actually occupied Duwamish land, stolen and hypocritically named after Chief Si'ahl." The main point of Johnson's address was to identify the anti-Black structural realities that contradicted the naming of Seattle as America's most progressive city. Like other places across the United States, Johnson noted that the city venerated civil rights history, but it also participated in the school-to-prison pipeline. "We are located in King County where the silhouette of Martin Luther King reigns high while we spend $210 million dollars [*sic*] building a new jail to imprison black children," she explained. This was a county "where the Seattle school department suspend black students at a rate six times higher than their counterparts." Johnson continued with a critique of the city's criminal justice system, "where the Seattle police department have been under federal consent decree for the past three years and yet has been riddled by use of force, racial profiling and scandals throughout the year." Finally, she called out Westlake, the neighborhood in which they stood "where we've said Black Lives Matter on Black Friday," but "we have undergone intense gentrification in the Central District which used to be the only place where we Black people could live legally in Seattle." Johnson offered one final exasperated "Welcome." Then she concluded, "This is what we have to deal with here."[5]

In her first interview after the rally, Johnson clarified that her protest was not primarily about Bernie Sanders. She believed that confronting Sanders was essential to the BLM strategy because he symbolized the Democratic Party's most radical wing. "Sanders is supposed to be as far left and progressive as you can possibly get and in Seattle's political context?" she asked rhetorically.[6] Her question evoked the dissonance felt in a city where white progressives celebrated with chants of "Black lives matter!" while seemingly ignoring stories of police brutality, carceral education, new prisons, and gentrification. Johnson pointed out that white allies had done very little to change these realities. "We have hordes and hordes of white liberals and white progressives and yet we still have all the same racial problems," she complained.[7] Like Seattle's white allies, Sanders claimed to stand in the tradition of King, but one month after BLM confronted him in Arizona, he still had no discernible strategy to combat white supremacy.

The resilience of the structures that exploit Black people in progressive white communities is not unique to Seattle or to Sanders. The most popular white progressive visions for ending racism use the legacy of King to imagine an identity politics in which white ally proximity to Black freedom fighters is the totality of an antiracist strategy. Rather than promoting solidarity with Black freedom movements, this form of antiracism promotes diversity as the antidote for the problems of racial inequality and anti-Black animosity. It was this form of allyship that moved an audience of Black and Latinx women to audibly groan when Sanders answered a question about how he planned to handle the rise of white supremacist organizing. Sanders reminded the She the People group, "I was actually at the March on

Washington with Dr. King back in 1963."[8] He went on to list his support of Jesse Jackson in 1988 and his career-long dedication to fighting racism and sexism. The problem was that he did not answer the question, and his appeal to proximity to King and Jackson offered no strategy for changing policies; he offered only his participation in historic movements and electoral politics. In contrast, BLM activists like Willaford and Johnson carried demands for structural changes to racially discriminatory policies, along with the traditions of King's disruptive, confrontational nonviolence. The progressive antiracism of Sanders and Seattle is built upon the symbols of diversity in the form of statue building and state-permitted marching of white allies. These symbols, while demonstrating attitudes that oppose anti-Black oppression in theory, allow anti-Black policies to persist.

Martin Luther King Jr.'s disappointment with white allies is now well known. He reserved the title of "the great stumbling block" for what he called "the white moderate." These moderates were people he described as a group "who constantly says: 'I agree with you in the goal you seek, but I cannot agree with your methods of direct action.'" In King's "Letter from Birmingham Jail," he explained that the white moderate "is more devoted to 'order' than to justice; . . . prefers a negative peace which is the absence of tension to a positive peace which is the presence of justice."[9] At a time when marches and statements that suggested racial equality were illegal, the actions of Sanders and other allies were in solidarity with freedom fighters who sought systemic changes to property laws, voting rights, equal employment, economic sustainability, and the right to self-determination.

Bernie Sanders's progressivism continues to draw crowds of thousands. His democratic socialism, like the socialism of his hero, Eugene Debs, addresses the structure of capitalism, but it inadequately recognizes capitalism's dependency on racial hierarchies in America.[10] Thus, his supporters tend to lack a substantive racial analysis. White allies' failure to strategize with people most directly affected by the racial exploitation they claim to oppose echoes King's criticism of the 1960s white moderate. The progressive strategies that follow—marches, social media posts, workshops, and teach-ins—proclaim opposition to structural injustices but result in little more than personal opinions about electoral politics. These strategies allow white allies to oppose racial prejudice through diversity, equity, and inclusion (DEI) initiatives, but only until corporations and higher education give up on them. The activism of today's white allies are authorized by city forms that permit peaceful protestors to gather in opposition that does little to challenge the structures that guarantee that anti-Black oppression will persist.

Freedom fighters who call for an end to white allyship do so largely on the grounds of its ineffectiveness. Feminista Jones, a Black community activist and author, joined in the attack on allyship when she shouted through a bullhorn at a 2015 rally in Harlem, "I am not interested in white allies. What we need are co-conspirators."[11] In 2017, activist Alicia Garza, cofounder of BLM, expressed her hatred for the term "allies" because she finds no meaning in it. Instead, Garza prefers the term "co-conspirators" because "co-conspirators are people who are *actively fighting* against the system of white supremacy and in particular the benefits they receive from it."[12] Recent concerns about the validity of white allyship, like Jones's and Garza's, have led freedom fighters to reject the role of allies in the Black freedom movement.

From Jones's perspective, allies are not trustworthy because their participation is not based in mutuality. "The people who tend to call themselves allies are usually the people with privilege, who will not have a mutual benefit from whatever they're trying to help with," she explained during an interview. That the outcome of a particular movement would not directly affect their communities meant that allies could choose the terms of their participation. Even more, after they marched and protested in support of Black lives, they returned to their white communities. "What I need," she explains, "is for people to come and work with us in the trenches and be there alongside us."[13]

Relocating to Black spaces from where they could work alongside Black freedom movements has not been a hallmark of white ally traditions. This was likely one of the reasons why Jones aimed her reproof at allies who had joined the Black Lives Matter protests in Harlem. For as committed as allies have been in words and public protests, the frustrations of freedom fighters like Jones and Garza demonstrate a deep distrust.

This distrust may appear unwarranted to a protest-era generation in which best-selling books describe *How to Be an Antiracist,* institutions have established DEI offices, and demonstrations are commonplace on college campuses. If so, it is because they fail to see that popular antiracism education teaches participants to concern themselves with personal identity rather than collective actions. Moreover, they fail to connect institutional abandonment of DEI with the impotence of diversity programs to mount a formidable threat to institutional anti-Blackness. Neither antiracist identity nor DEI have persuaded liberal university administrators nor progressive politicians to join in solidarity with student activists who demand that the violence in Gaza be identified as a genocide. Even these radical students, raised on antiracism education and in inclusive-minded communities do not often view whiteness as the Western imperial logic behind both settler colonialism in Palestine and anti-Blackness in the United States. This is likely because antiracist identity and inclusive community does not require allies to build multi-racial coalitions based in solidarity. This lack of solidarity with Black freedom organizations was indicative of another problem Jones found in allies: "An ally can be adjacent, an ally can be parallel, an ally can exist outside of a struggle and they can easily extract themselves from the struggle."[14] Yet even if they extract themselves from the struggle, they stand out among their white peers, some of whom deplore them as race traitors, while others celebrate their activities as courageous, heroic, exemplary, or even saintly.

If allies are adjacent, parallel, or outside the struggle, then on what basis might we assess their courage, heroism, or saintliness? Perhaps, such judgments are based on our sense of the good intentions of the allies? For Jones and Garza, whose communities will be directly affected by the outcome of racial justice activism, intent is far less important than impact. From the perspectives of Black communities, parallel movements that appear to be moving in line with Black freedom goals eventually fail to be trustworthy partners in achieving the prize of freedom because their goals are often related to maintaining their own sense of goodness and self-proclaimed "antiracism."

Even elite allies, who have bestselling antiracism books and social media accounts with thousands of followers, are not above reproach. Over the last decade, Robin D'Angelo and Tim Wise, two of the most well-known white allies, have faced criticisms over the profits they earn as antiracism educators. Some Black educators and activists argue that such high-profile allies are taking up space and financial resources. They believe that these resources should benefit Black activists, educators, and their communities, who have championed these ideas for centuries. From their incredible profits to their appropriation of ideas—and even appropriation of identities— the role of white people in movements to secure equality for Black Americans reveals the legacy of parallel racial projects and competing racial radicalisms.[15]

Today's white progressives carry the legacy of yesterday's white allies. They build institutions and organize politics that invite interracial participation, but they fail to create structural policies. By focusing on diversity instead of policies and procedures that exploit people and extract resources, predominantly white institutions can add visible racial diversity—when people representing that diversity are available—without ever exploring the mission or vision of their projects. In these projects, white allies often celebrate charity, or service, in predominantly white organizations, especially in higher education and religious institutions, which reinforces a racial hierarchy that requires white wealth and the extraction of resources from Black communities to validate them as progressive and antiracist. White allies' emphasis on relationships over analyses of power and structural revolution encourages individual exploration of healing and cross-racial friendships rather than coalition building and solidarity across racially segregated communities who face similar threats of food deserts, carceral violence, and toxic habitats.

My desire is that *Damned Whiteness* will help focus the energies of Black freedom fighters on strategies for communal self-determination, especially when they find themselves struggling for liberation in predominantly white settings. In addition, I want this project to reveal to white allies the all-too-common impediments that allies bring to efforts that purpose to build effective antiracist coalitions. By recognizing white allies' physical distance from the centers of Black life, they may consider how the creation of white spaces impairs their ability to clearly see the structural issues that enable Black exploitation. Allies' refusal to take seriously the syncretistic religious and political philosophies of Black radicals and opt instead for absolutist ideals has made it nearly impossible for large groups of white people to join in solidarity with Black freedom initiatives in ways that further their efforts. White Christian theologies that imagine white divinity as the locus for ethical behavior and communal action deny the creativity of a Black spirituality that transformed the religion of their oppressors into sometimes revolutionary community, which in turn fueled movements to abolish racially discriminatory laws.

White liberal replacement of Black Power's attack on racial capital with diversity and inclusion, even when individual Black professionals benefit from such programs, does nothing to transform anti-Black economic structures that make those diversity programs necessary. Such practices leave charity as the only option to temporarily alleviate the pain of living impoverished. But receiving this criticism requires white Christians to listen to Black conversations as multilayered and contested discourses, and to mature as people who understand that their future is bound up with those who suffer the most under the weight of Western imperialism. This is a reality, because the problems that modern imperialism has caused with its industrial pollution, climate crisis, human-made famines, global inequality, resource extraction, and exploitation of labor cannot be solved without an empow-ered majority of citizens on this planet. To put it frankly, there are too few white people to address these issues on their own, and the rest of the world has enough people to eventually solve these problems without them.

For now, if we learn these historical lessons well, we might avoid mistakes that waste political time and material resources that could help us all—co-conspirators and freedom fighters in solidarity—to abolish the white West-ern imperialist machine that today shows no sign of slowing down. The work and voices of freedom fighters like Johnson, Willaford, Jones, Garza, and others provide clear strategies for enabling us to do so. Unfortunately, our collective ignorance of the history of allies in freedom movements along with the superficial understandings of our complex racial history, racially discriminatory policies, and shortsighted efforts to build interracial friend-ships hinders us. This ignorance can, in part, be traced to the history I nar-rate in these pages—that white allies have favored fellowship with Black people on white terms, in white spaces, without seeking to comprehend Black analyses of white supremacist projects in the United States. There is a better way. It will, no doubt, require a collective movement of diverse political actions—electoral, economic, organizational, institutional, and cul-tural—to get there. Freedom demands more than dreams and friendship; it requires a politics of solidarity with oppressed peoples that will empower them to free themselves. Without it, we may all be damned.

Acknowledgments

Writing *Damned Whiteness* was a labor that took six years to complete. That work was made possible by the support of colleagues, archivists, friends, and family, who generously gave their time to read, listen to, or offer suggestions along the way. The editors at UNC Press, Mark Simpson-Vos and Thomas Bedenbaugh, provided me with essential encouragement throughout the publication process. It is no exaggeration to say that the work that went into writing this book was a collective effort. I would not have been able to complete it alone.

I am grateful to Eastern Mennonite University's Roselawn Writing Collective, who read and offered feedback on early drafts of chapters. Long conversations with colleagues helped me clarify concepts and absolved me of ideas that could have led me astray. Students in the Racial Healing and the Blue Eyed Soul course helped me clarify my thoughts on the figures in this book. Indeed, the entire EMU community's support for my sabbatical and public presentations helped me understand how my work might be received by larger audiences. For that, I am grateful.

Much of what I have written was made possible by the United Methodist Archives and History at Drew University. As a student at Drew, I worked in the archives and learned that an archive is not only a place where materials are held but a place where people dedicate themselves to the craft of curating and maintaining primary sources that allow for historians like me to interpret those sources so that wider audiences may discuss, debate, and learn from them. I would also like to acknowledge the Swarthmore College Peace Collection staff for their help in locating materials on the Harlem Ashram. Similarly, the University of Georgia Special Collections Libraries provided me with access to materials related to Koinonia. Tracy K'Meyer, who offered notes from interviews she conducted in Americus, deserves my gratitude as well.

Many of my colleagues double as dear friends who asked me tough questions or encouraged me that this work was important. A few of those people became writing partners who met me at awfully early hours of the morning to struggle together as we wrote our own unrelated projects. Catherine Osborne, I appreciate your open invitation to write with you and the conversations that we had about the Catholic Worker movement and Dorothy Day along the way. Sarah Bixler, it was incredibly helpful to carve out Fridays to write together. Christy Cobb, my colleague, friend, and fellow Drewid, I am incredibly grateful for your consistency and dedication to scholarly writing that is deeply connected to relationships and justice. You have encouraged me from the beginning of this journey and have been a witness to how many versions of this book were necessary to reach publication.

My sincerest appreciation goes out to others who were willing to discuss concepts that led to the book as it is presented here: Morrey Davis, Peter Dula, Dennis Edwards, Felipe Hinojosa, Katie Mansfield, Tobin Miller-Shearer, Xavier Picket, Geoff Pollick, Kevin Seidel, Tim Seidel, Doug Strong, and many others.

I would like to thank my family members for supporting me by forgiving long absences, both physical and cognitive. You all have been generous and very present to my process. I think first of Isaac, Solomon, and Sarah. All along, your encouragement and presence has been essential to completing this book. I appreciate the insights my uncle and grandmother provided concerning the geography and culture of Detroit in the 1960s. Joseph Harris, thanks for believing that whatever I was up to was worthy of sharing with your networks.

And to my mom, Cheryl Evans, I hope you recognize some of our conversations in this book. Most importantly, I hope that you can be proud of what you see in the pages that follow.

Finally, having acknowledged the tremendous community of people who have contributed in myriad ways to this manuscript, I take responsibility for any mistakes contained herein, but I invite us all to share any praise that this book receives.

Notes

Abbreviations

GCAH   General Commission on Archives and History, Drew University, Madison, NJ

SCPC   Swarthmore College Peace Collection, Swarthmore College, Swarthmore, PA

UGSC   University of Georgia Special Collections Libraries, Athens, GA

UTL   Union Theological Seminary, New York, NY

Prologue

1. McClaren, *New Kind of Christianity.*
2. hooks, "Oppositional Gaze," 462–70.

Introduction

1. McKissick, *Meet the Press*, 18.
2. McKissick, *Meet the Press*, 11.
3. McKissick, *Meet the Press*, 11.
4. Smith, "Telegram to Floyd McKissick," July 1966, in *How Am I to Be Heard?*, 351.
5. Smith, "Are We Still Buying a New World with Old Confederate Bills?," 481.
6. Smith, "Right Way Is Not a Moderate Way," 335.
7. Smith, "Telegram to Floyd McKissick," 351.
8. McKissick, *Meet the Press*, 18.
9. McKissick, *Meet the Press*, 18.
10. Farmer, *Lay Bare the Heart*, 255.
11. Farmer, *Lay Bare the Heart*, 256.
12. Farmer, *Lay Bare the Heart*, 255.
13. Farmer, *Lay Bare the Heart*, 140.
14. Farmer, *Lay Bare the Heart*, 140.
15. Smith, "The Day It Happens," 295.
16. Smith, "The Day It Happens," 298.
17. Bell, "*Brown v. Board of Education.*" Derrick Bell's "interest convergence" theory provides important explanatory power for substantive changes in US law and white favorability toward Black civil rights. Bell's theory explains that "the interest of blacks in achieving racial equality will be accommodated only when it converges

with the interests of whites" (523). There is ample historical evidence that this is indeed the case. It explains, for instance, why seventy years after *Brown*, whites have largely chosen to abandon racially balanced school enrollment. But a question that remains for whites who dedicate their lives to racial justice, racial equality, and interracialism is, Why are they often out of step with strategies that are developed and led by Black communities? Such questions require careful attention to primary sources.

18. M. L. King, "I Have a Dream," 85.

19. M. L. King, "Birth of a Nation."

20. M. L. King, "I Have a Dream," 85.

21. Douglass, *Two Speeches*, 22.

22. Midwest Catholic Workers, "Lament. Repent. Repair."

23. Peters, "Is the Catholic Worker Racist?"

24. Roden, "Evidence."

25. Roberts, *Dorothy Day*, 5; Loughery and Randolph, *Dorothy Day*; Cep, "Dorothy Day's Radical Faith."

26. Kragen, "Lamb's Players' *Cotton Patch Gospel*."

27. Hambright et al., *Dorothy Day*.

28. Southern, *John LaFarge*, 149.

29. Downing, *Clarence Jordan*, 14.

30. Worth, "'Black Power' Is Needed," *Journal Herald*, October 11, 1968, GCAH.

31. "The Harlem Ashram," SCPC.

32. Ralph Templin, "Interracial Brotherhood and American World Leadership," *Human Frontiers, Journal of Human Relations* 9, no. 4 (1961): 462, GCAH.

33. Templin used this term to describe the power of white elites to determine which programs, policies, and people would be used to rule over nonwhite populations. "White prerogative" was like the concept of white privilege in this way, but it spoke more to the authority white people assumed to enforce their economic and political plans in intercultural settings.

34. Tatum, "Teaching White Students."

35. Harvey, *Raising White Kids*, 227.

36. C. Brown, *Refusing Racism*, 1.

37. C. Brown, *Refusing Racism*, 1.

38. Butler, *White Evangelical Racism*.

39. K. Johnson, *One in Christ*.

40. Quiros, *God with Us*.

41. Du Bois, *Souls of Black Folk*; Du Bois, *Black Reconstruction*; Ellison, *Invisible Man*; Baldwin, *The Devil Finds Work*; Morrison, *Playing in the Dark*; hooks, "Oppositional Gaze," 462–70.

42. Joseph, *Stokely: A Life*; Joseph, *Waiting 'Til the Midnight Hour*.

43. Hall, "Long Civil Rights Movement."

44. Dorrien, "New Abolition," 89–102; Azaransky, *This Worldwide Struggle*; K. J. Johnson, "Another Long Civil Rights Movement"; Quiros, *God with Us*.

45. Ignatiev, "Treason to Whiteness," 24.

46. Gilmore, "Worrying State."

47. Gilmore, *Abolition Geography*, 438.

48. Walker, *Walker's Appeal*; Apess, *Son of the Forest*.

49. Morrison, *Playing in the Dark*.

50. Morrison, *Playing in the Dark*, 38.

51. Morrison, *Playing in the Dark*, 6.

52. Morrison, *Playing in the Dark*, 17.

53. Kidd, *The Forging of Races*.

54. Baldwin, "On Being White," 90.

55. Carby, "The Multicultural Wars," 13.

56. D. Day, *Duty of Delight*; D. Day, *All the Way to Heaven*; D. Day, *Loaves and Fishes*; D. Day, *Long Loneliness*.

57. Jordan, *Cotton Patch Gospel*; Jordan, *Essential Writings*.

58. K'Meyer, interviews; K'Meyer, *Interracialism and Christian Community*.

59. Templin, *Democracy and Nonviolence*.

Chapter 1

1. Schwerin, *Got to Tell It*, 142; Marovich, *City Called Heaven*, 299.

2. Southern Negro Leaders Conference, "Statement"; Tye, *Rising from the Rails*, 132; NAACP, "The Civil Rights."

3. Sernett, *Bound for the Promised Land*, 2.

4. D. Brown, *Back to the Land*, 7.

5. Gould, *At Home in Nature*.

6. M. L. Davis, *Methodist Unification*, 127. People like Robert Jones, bishop of the Methodist Episcopal Church, advocated a separate but equal understanding.

7. "Dr. Benjamin Mays," *Carolina Times*, November 2, 1968.

8. J. M. Lawson, "From a Lunch Counter Stool."

9. Du Bois, *Souls of Black Folk*, 183.

10. M. L. King, "Give Us the Ballot," 208–13.

11. Randolph, "Statement at Prayer Pilgrimage for Freedom," 243–47.

12. Lawson, *Running for Freedom*, 39.

13. Ransby, *Ella Baker*, 155.

14. Marshall, *Thurgood Marshall*, 42.

15. Tushnet, *Making Civil Rights Law*, 232.

16. Marshall, *Thurgood Marshall*, 42.

17. Brown v. Board of Education of Topeka, 347 U.S. 483 (1954).

18. Marshall, *Speeches*, 42.

19. Kruse, *White Flight*, 170–71.

20. J. K. Day, *Southern Manifesto*, 82.

21. "U.S. Passes Year without Lynching; but Study by Tuskegee Finds 'Rather Similar Forms of Violence' Still Prevail," *New York Times*, December 31, 1952.

22. J. K. Day, *Southern Manifesto*, 9.

23. Pérez-Peña, "Woman Linked to 1955 Emmett Till Murder"; Associated Press, "A Grand Jury Declined to Indict a Woman Whose Accusations Set Off Emmett Till Killing," NPR, August 9, 2022, www.npr.org/2022/08/09/1116562931/grand-jury

-emmett-till-woman-carolyn-bryant-donham; Guidry, "Carolyn Bryant Donham." The actual events are disputed, but Carolyn Bryant Bonham, the woman who made the accusation, has died, leaving no one alive who can clarify what happened that day.

24. Woods, *Black Struggle*, 5.

25. Randolph et al., "Call to a Prayer Pilgrimage for Freedom," 152.

26. M. L. King, "Give Us the Ballot."

27. Randolph, "Statement at Prayer Pilgrimage for Freedom," 247.

28. Randolph, "Statement at Prayer Pilgrimage for Freedom," 247.

29. Randolph et al., "Call to a Prayer Pilgrimage for Freedom," 152.

30. Ralph Templin, "Total Pacifism and Farm Communities," Ralph T. Templin Collection, United Methodist Church Archives, GCAH. "The pacifist farm community became a 'grass roots' commitment to the way of cooperative Labor in meeting the needs of all of God's children." Roberts, *Dorothy Day*, 14.

31. Appelbaum, *Kingdom to Commune*, 38.

32. D. Day, *Loaves and Fishes*, 45.

33. D. Day, *Loaves and Fishes*, 45.

34. D. Day, *Loaves and Fishes*, 48.

35. D. Day, *Loaves and Fishes*, 51.

36. Ralph Templin, "Total Pacifism and Farm Communities," in "Report of Conference on Pacifist Farming Communities, 1942," 5–6, GCAH.

37. Ralph Templin, "The National School of Living," Ralph T. Templin Collection, 1, GCAH.

38. Borsodi, *Flight from the City*, 6–7.

39. Borsodi, *This Ugly Civilization*.

40. Borsodi, *Flight from the City*, 5.

41. Borsodi, *Flight from the City*, 25.

42. Borsodi, "Green Revolution," 867.

43. Addams, *Peace and Bread in a Time of War*, viii.

44. Appelbaum, *Kingdom to Commune*, 137.

45. Ralph Templin, "Total Pacifism and Farm Communities," unpublished notes, 1941–45, GCAH.

46. "Declaration of Principles for Decentralists," 1–3, GCAH; Templin, "Total Pacifism and Farm Communities," unpublished notes, 1941–45, GCAH.

47. Ralph Templin, *The Decentralist Way*, 1–3, GCAH.

48. See Childress and Kennedy, *Will Campbell*. Will Campbell was another well-known white anti-segregationist Southern Baptist preacher.

49. Clarence Jordan, "Koinonia Farm, Americus, Georgia, Newsletter #12," March 9, 1957, GCAH.

50. Day, "On Pilgrimage—May 1957," 3, 6.

51. Campbell, "Remembering Clarence," *Cotton Patch Gospel*, ix.

52. Day, "On Pilgrimage—May 1957," 3, 6.

53. Day, "On Pilgrimage—May 1957," 3, 6.

54. Clarence Jordan to Ralph Templin, September 29, 1956, GCAH.

55. Wally Nelson to Ralph Templin, March 27, 1957, GCAH. Juanita Morrow was a founding member of the Cleveland, Ohio, chapter of CORE in 1944.

56. Wally Nelson to Ralph Templin, March 27, 1957, GCAH.

57. Danielson, *American Gandhi*, 71.

58. US Congress, "Fellowship of Reconciliation," *Reports and Documents*, 1954, 307.

59. Du Bois, *Souls of Black Folk*, 13.

60. Roberts, *Christ and Ourselves*, 34.

61. Farmer, *Lay Bare the Heart*, 101.

62. Farmer, *Lay Bare the Heart*, 98–99.

63. Farmer, *Lay Bare the Heart*, 103.

64. *Peacemakers Newsletters*, GCAH; see Danielson et al., *Religious Left in Modern America*, 112.

65. Logan, *The Betrayal of the Negro*, 171–73, 183, 272–75.

66. I agree with Gary Dorrien and Ralph Luker that Black social gospel Christians like Reverdy Ransom and, later, Martin Luther King offered social gospel solutions to Jim Crow contexts that were distinct from those of their white counterparts.

Chapter 2

1. Barry, *Rising Tide*, 32–46, 143–56. Arguments over the best way to tame the Mississippi river included cut-offs, outlets, and levees. Some argued for some combination of the three, but the Army Corps of Engineers believed that levees were the best and only way.

2. "Negro Labor on Levees Exploited by U.S. War Dept.," *Catholic Worker* May 1, 1933, 1–2.

3. Rice, "Catholic Worker Movement," 56.

4. Du Bois, *Souls of Black Folk*, 13.

5. Kelley, *Hammer and Hoe*, xiv; see also Peters, "Is the Catholic Worker Racist?" Rice's claim that "anti-racism was not essential to [Day and Maurin's white liberal] praxis[,] and neither constructed a theology of racial justice steeped in black sources" accurately describes Day's thin analysis of race relations. Benjamin Peters charges that Rice's criticism assumes that Day understands race and class as co-constituting political categories, which I cannot substantiate by her words or actions.

6. Wilkins, "Mississippi Slavery in 1933," 82.

7. Wilkins, "Mississippi Slavery in 1933," 82.

8. Mizelle, *Backwater Blues*, 12.

9. McMurchy, "'Red Cross Is Not All Right!,'" 87.

10. Spencer, "Contested Terrain," 175.

11. Pearcy, "After the Flood."

12. McMurchy, "'Red Cross Is Not All Right!,'" 88.

13. Daniel, *Shadow of Slavery*, 50.

14. Wilkins, "Mississippi Slavery in 1933."

15. Du Bois, *"The Crisis,"* 10.

16. Du Bois, "Negro and Radical Thought."

17. New York State Joint Legislative Committee, *Revolutionary Radicalism,* 1318–19. The committee investigated Black radical groups in the state of New York in 1920 and estimated that *The Crisis* had a circulation of 104,000.

18. Owen, "DuBois on Revolution," 88–92.

19. DuBois, "NAACP and the Class Struggle," 86–87.

20. J. W. Johnson, *Black Manhattan,* 237.

21. Bridges, "Six Demands."

22. Mair, "Hypocrisy of White Liberalism," 153.

23. Mair, "Hypocrisy of White Liberalism," 151–55.

24. D. Day, *Long Loneliness,* 204.

25. D. Day, *Long Loneliness,* 236.

26. Cornell, "Catholic Worker," 87–101.

27. D. Day, *All the Way,* 69.

28. Roberts, *Dorothy Day,* 64–65.

29. Roberts, *Dorothy Day,* 6.

30. D. Day, *Loaves and Fishes,* 17.

31. Roberts, *Dorothy Day,* 107–8.

32. D. Day, *Long Loneliness,* 27.

33. Roberts, *Dorothy Day,* 179.

34. Wilkins, "Mississippi Slavery in 1933."

35. McCoyer, "Levee Camps"; McMurchy, "'Red Cross Is Not All Right!,'" 87.

36. Wilkins, "Mississippi Slavery in 1933."

37. Mizelle, *Backwater Blues,* 124–25.

38. Wilkins, "Mississippi Slavery in 1933."

39. "Negro Labor on Levees Exploited by U.S. War Dept.," *Catholic Worker,* May 1, 1933, 1–2.

40. Trotter, *From a Raw Deal,* 113.

41. Rossi, "First Scottsboro Trials," 1.

42. D. Day, "Communists, Despite Noise," 2.

43. Kelley, *Hammer and Hoe,* xiii.

44. Kelley, *Hammer and Hoe,* xv.

45. Debs, "Negro in the Class Struggle."

46. Zumoff, "American Communist Party."

47. Du Bois, "Postscript: Communism."

48. Du Bois, "Marxism and the Negro Problem."

49. Kelley, *Hammer and Hoe,* xi.

50. Kelley, *Hammer and Hoe,* 38.

51. Kelley, *Hammer and Hoe,* 38. See also Kelley's description of the 1930 "Draft Program for Negro Farmers in the Southern States" in *Hammer and Hoe.* He argues that the document "expressed the Central Committee's doubt as to the ability of black sharecroppers and tenants to create an autonomous radical movement, and a few months later James Allen, editor of the *Southern Worker,* argued that only in-

dustrial workers were capable of leading tenants and sharecroppers because the latter lacked the collective experience of industrial labor" (38).

52. "Communists Seek Entry to Negro Churches," *Catholic Worker*, September 1933, 9.

53. The ILD first represented Black defendants in the 1930 Atlanta Six trial in which defendants were accused of violating Georgia's anti-insurrection law. In 1932, the ILD represented Angelo Herndon, who was indicted for attempting to overthrow the government. See J. Moore, "Angelo Herndon Case," 60–71; Martin, "Communists and Blacks," 131–41.

54. Du Bois, "Marxism and the Negro Problem."

55. Du Bois, "Die Negerfrage in den Vereinigten Staaten."

56. See Major, "Race, Labor," 383–93. In this essay, Major argues that there is a consistent Marxist logic through which Du Bois analyzes the place of the Black laborer in relation to "the Northern worker, the Southern worker, the Negro and the employer." He offers Du Bois's projects, mentioned above, as evidence.

57. Gary, "Beyond the Color Line," 171.

58. Du Bois, "Conservation of Races (1897)," 20–27.

59. Richard, "The Scourge of Christ," 414.

60. Du Bois, "Why I Won't Vote."

61. Du Bois, "Marxism and the Negro Problem."

62. Pickens, Letter to the editor.

63. Du Bois, *Black Reconstruction*, 110.

64. Du Bois, *Black Reconstruction*, 26.

65. D. Day, "Radical but Not Communist."

66. D. Day, "Radical but Not Communist."

67. B. Moore, *Kindred Spirits*.

68. Deshmukh, "Claude McKay's Road to Catholicism," 148–68.

Chapter 3

1. Du Bois, "Postscript: The Negro and the Catholic Church."

2. Quoted in Ochs, *Desegregating the Altar*, 222.

3. C. Davis, *History of Black Catholics*, 171–73.

4. Nickels, "Thomas Wyatt Turner," 222.

5. Ochs, *Desegregating the Altar*, 293.

6. Southern, *John LaFarge*, 211.

7. Cressler, *Authentically Black*, 9. I join with Cressler in refusing to use the term "Black Catholic" in a way that flattens the varieties of Black Catholic experiences.

8. Landers, *Black Society*; Landers, "Black Frontier Settlements," 28–29; S. D. Williams, *Subversive Habits*, 3. Uncles was ordained in 1891, Dorsey in 1902, and Plantevigne in 1907. Agee, *Cry for Justice*; Mosely, Daniel A. Rudd, 105–12.

9. Agee, *Cry for Justice*; C. Davis, *History of Black Catholics*; C. Davis, "Future African-American Catholic Studies," 1–9; Lackner, "The American," 1–24.

10. C. Davis, *History of Black Catholics*, 193.

11. C. Davis, *History*, 171.

12. Carlen, *The Papal Encyclicals*, 287.

13. C. Davis, *History*, 192.

14. C. Davis, *History*, 193.

15. C. Davis, *History*, 171–72. The first Black lay congress met January 1–4, 1889. The first lay congress met November 11–12, 1889, to commemorate the centennial of American Catholic hierarchy.

16. McGreevy, *Parish Boundaries*, 7–11. Clergy like Bishop Michael Curley, for example, endorsed Jim Crow in churches because there existed a "keen race distinction" in America that the Catholic Church in America "could not solve." McGreevy explains that white ethnic priests encouraged their members to move into church neighborhoods. By doing so, those communities were less welcoming and less attractive to Black people, Catholic or otherwise.

17. Raboteau, "Relating Race," 20–21.

18. Du Bois, *Souls of Black Folk*, 3; Raboteau, "Relating Race," 22.

19. Nickels, "Thomas Wyatt Turner," 215–32.

20. Thomas Wyatt Turner to Attorney Gustave B. Aldrich, March 18, 1931, American Catholic History Classroom, Catholic University Libraries, https://guides.lib .cua.edu/c.php?g=1403556&p=10388178.

21. Gillard, *Catholic Church*, 47; McGreevy, *Parish Boundaries*, 7. The number of Black Catholics increased from 200,000 in 1930 to 300,000 in 1940. That number represented a slight increase in the percentage of Blacks who were Catholic in America from 2 percent to 2.5 percent over the decade.

22. McGreevy, *Parish Boundaries*, 8.

23. Dolan, *American Catholic Experience*, 355.

24. John LaFarge, "FCC: Underlying Principles," ca. 1930, Georgetown University Library Special Collections.

25. LaFarge, "What Is Interracial?," 55.

26. Southern, *John LaFarge*, 362.

27. Southern, *John LaFarge*, 211.

28. LaFarge, "What Is Interracial?"

29. LaFarge, *Catholic Viewpoint on Race Relations*, 31, 64.

30. Southern, *John LaFarge*, 358.

31. Rice, "Confronting the Heresy."

32. Maurin, *Green Revolution*, 4.

33. Day, *Loaves and Fishes*, 29.

34. Colossians 3:14.

35. Catholic Church, *Catechism of the Council of Trent*, 425.

36. Fitzgerald, *The Great Gatsby*; Carnegie, *Autobiography*; Bok, *Americanization of Edward Bok*; Riis, *Making of an American*.

37. Maurin, "Easy Essays," *Catholic Worker*, February 1934, 1.

38. D. Day, *Loaves and Fishes*, 29, 30, 31.

39. D. Day, *Loaves and Fishes*, 34.

40. D. Day, *Loaves and Fishes*, 34.

41. D. Day, *Loaves and Fishes*, 38.

42. Parker, "Saint for Difficult People."

43. Dorothy Day to Edward Breen, October 1938(?), in *All the Way*, ed. Robert Ellsberg (Milwaukee: Marquette University Press, 2008), 124.

44. Day to Breen, October 1938(?), 125.

45. Day to Breen, October 1938(?), 125.

46. D. Day, "Fear in Our Time," 5, 7.

47. D. Day, *Loaves and Fishes*, 39.

48. D. Day, *Loaves and Fishes*, 38.

49. D. Day, *Loaves and Fishes*, 38.

50. D. Day, *Loaves and Fishes*, 39; D. Day, *Duty of Delight*, 44. Breen died on May 20, 1936.

51. D. Day, *Loaves and Fishes*, 42, 43.

52. Falls, "Interview with Arthur Falls and Francis Sicius."

53. Unsworth, "A Lonely Prophet Falls."

54. Arthur G. Falls,The Chicago Letter, *Catholic Worker*, June 1936, 1, 3.

55. K. J. Johnson, *One in Christ*, 46.

56. Arthur G. Falls, The Chicago Letter, *Catholic Worker*, December 1935, 8.

57. Arthur G. Falls, The Chicago Letter, *Catholic Worker*, November 1936, 1, 5; Sicius, "The Chicago Catholic Worker," 85.

58. Arthur G. Falls, The Chicago Letter, *Catholic Worker*, December 1935, 8.

59. Arthur G. Falls, The Chicago Letter, *Catholic Worker*, December 1935, 8; for more on milk strikes, see A. F. White, *Plowed Under*, 65–110.

60. D. Day, *Loaves and Fishes*, 39, 41.

61. Sicius, "Chicago Catholic Worker," 62.

62. Falls, The Chicago Letter, *Catholic Worker*, November 1936.

63. Seligman, *Block by Block*, 23; Seligman, "Block by Block," 8.

64. Cogley, *Canterbury Tale*, 8.

65. Cogley, *Canterbury Tale*, 8.

66. Sicius, "Chicago Catholic Worker," 67.

67. Falls reimbursed every member of the credit union.

68. Falls, The Chicago Letter," *Catholic Worker*, June 1, 1936, 3.

69. Sicius, "Chicago Catholic Worker," 71.

70. Ward, *Social Creed*.

71. "Catholic Worker Prevents United Front, Says Ward," *Catholic Worker*, June 1, 1937.

72. See Evans, "To Rid the Italian Soul"; Dorrien, *New Abolition*; Luker. *Social Gospel in Black and White*.

73. Duke, *In the Trenches*, 209.

74. Harry F. Ward, "The Call of the Wild," sermon, October 27, 1907, Henry Frederick Ward Papers, UTS, quoted in Duke, *In the Trenches*, 70.

75. Sicius, "Chicago Catholic Worker," 80.

76. D. Day, "More Houses of Hospitality Are Needed."

77. Sicius, "Chicago Catholic Worker," 79, 80.

78. Sicius, "Chicago Catholic Worker," 82.

79. Rice, "Confronting the Heresy," 73, 75–76.

Chapter 4

1. Martin, "Race, Gender," 256.
2. Martin, "Race, Gender," 251–68.
3. Martin, "Race, Gender," 251–68.
4. Koinonia Farm Inc. pamphlet, 1940, GCAH.
5. Koinonia Farm Inc. pamphlet, Kentucky, 1939, GCAH.
6. Koinonia Farm Inc. pamphlet, Kentucky, 1939, GCAH.
7. Koinonia Farm Inc. pamphlet, Kentucky, 1939, GCAH.
8. Koinonia Farm Inc. pamphlet, Kentucky, 1939, GCAH.
9. Martin, "Race, Gender," 251–68.
10. Hope, *From Whence*, 15–29, 125–27; Quiros, *God with Us*, 59; Alston, "Bethesda Baptist Marks 150 Years"; T. K. Hall, "The Bells Are Coming!"
11. Martin, "Race, Gender," 259.
12. Koinonia Farm Inc. pamphlet, Kentucky, 1939, GCAH.
13. Jordan to Friends of Koinonia, January 12, 1951, GCAH.
14. King to Jordan, 1958, GCAH.
15. Lee, *The Cotton Patch Evidence*, 19–21.
16. Koinonia Farm pamphlet (emphasis added), Templin Collection, GCAH.
17. Lee, *The Cotton Patch Evidence*, 32–33; Quiros, *God with Us*, 23.
18. Jordan, "Clarence Jordan Tells the Koinonia Story."
19. Jordan, "Clarence Jordan Tells the Koinonia Story."
20. Patricia Appelbaum, *From Kingdom to Commune*, 151–52.
21. Florence Jordan, interview.
22. Blackmon, *Slavery by Another Name*, 157.
23. Frederick Douglass, "Address to the People of the United States at a Convention of Colored Men Held in Louisville, Ky., September 24, 1883," in Douglass, *Three Addresses*, 3–23.
24. O'Brien, *Special History*, 23.
25. Du Bois, "Postscript: The Board of Directors on Segregation."
26. Washington, "Farming Problem in the Black Belt."
27. K. J. Ferguson, "Caught in 'No Man's Land,'" 33–54; White, *Freedom Farmers*, 34.
28. A. Jones, "Improving Rural Life," 105–14.
29. K. J. Ferguson, "Caught in 'No Man's Land.'"
30. K. J. Ferguson, "Caught in 'No Man's Land.'"
31. Carver, *How to Build Up Worn Out Soils*.
32. M. M. White, *Freedom Farmers*, 60.
33. Du Bois, "Where Do We Go from Here?," 146–63.
34. Marable, *How Capitalism Underdeveloped Black America*, 79. "In 1879, Sojourner joined the wave of "Exodusters" who fled the post–Reconstruction era South and settled in Kansas City. Unlike most Black male leaders, she urged her people to buy land and to develop a sufficient economic basis from which to wage their various struggles for social and political justice."

35. "'We Must Continue to Witness' Koinonia's Reply to Racist Attacks," *Peacemaker*, March 25, 1957, GCAH.

36. Collum, "From John M. Collum, Americus, GA, July 25, 1913," 243–44.

37. "Koinonia Community's Market Stand after an Explosion Directly Attacking the Interracial Community, 1957," *Atlanta Journal-Constitution*, April 15, 1957, UGSC.

38. K'Meyer, *Interracialism and Christian Community*, 154. Mabel Barnum remembered that during Koinonia's crisis years, "When people saw that little group wasn't going to let the Klan run them off, they knew from that time on that you don't have to be scared of the Klan." Lena Turner added, "Koinonia had demonstrated to young Negroes of Americus something everything else in their world has denied: that white and black can live and work and build together."

39. Martin Luther King Jr. to Clarence L. Jordan, February 8, 1957, MLKP-MBU, Martin Luther King Jr., Papers, 1954–1968, Boston University, Boston, MA, https://kinginstitute.stanford.edu/king-papers/documents/clarence-l-jordan.

40. King to Jordan, February 8, 1957, MLKP-MBU, Martin Luther King Jr., Papers, 1954–1968, Boston University.

41. Quiros, *God with Us*, 97–98.

42. K'Meyer, *Interracialism and Christian Community*, 20.

43. Tuck, *Beyond Atlanta*, 161; Quiros, *God with Us*, 86–97.

44. Quiros, *God with Us*, 93.

45. Quiros, *God with Us*, 141–47.

46. Salahu-Din, "Hidden Herstory."

47. Salahu-Din, "Hidden Herstory."

48. Coble, *Cotton Patch*, 161–62.

49. Coble, *Cotton Patch*, 162.

50. Coble, *Cotton Patch*, 162.

51. Coble, *Cotton Patch*, 162.

52. Kingto Clarence Jordan, March 24, 1958, UGSC.

53. Harding and Pierce, "Loving Respect," 103.

54. Marsh, *Beloved Community*, 51–86.

55. K'Meyer, *Interracialism and Christian Community*, 72. The document read, "We desire to make known our total, unconditional commitment to seek, express, and expand the Kingdom of God as revealed in Jesus the Christ. Being convinced that the community of believers who make a like commitment is the continuing body of Christ on earth, I joyfully enter into a love union with the Koinonia and gladly submit myself to it, looking to it to guide me in the knowledge of God's will and to strengthen me in the pursuit of it."

56. Sue Angry, interview by Tracy K'Meyer, part of interviews with Koinonia members and Americus residents; K'Meyer, *Interracialism and Christian Community*, 58, 72.

57. K'Meyer, *Interracialism and Christian Community*, 129.

58. Willis, *Audacious Agitation*, 102–3.

59. K'Meyer, *Interracialism and Christian Community*, 50, 58, 87. K'Meyer explains on page 58 that "Con Browne remembered that the older people used to sit

separately at lunch, out under a tree, instead of at the table. In addition, many whites, including the sheriff, and even some older blacks steered people away from Koinonia."

60. D. Day, "On Pilgrimage—May 1957," 5.

61. D. Day, "On Pilgrimage—May 1957," 5.

62. D. Day, "On Pilgrimage—May 1957," 5.

63. Lee, *The Cotton Patch Evidence*, 38.

64. Lee, *The Cotton Patch Evidence*, 38.

65. Lee, *The Cotton Patch Evidence*, 39.

66. K'Meyer, *Interracialism and Christian Community*, 86–87.

67. Wood, "Wally and Juanita Nelson."

68. Wood, "Wally and Juanita Nelson," 192.

69. Wood, "Wally and Juanita Nelson," 193.

70. "A Letter of Clarification and Justification on the Status of Edward Johnson's Noviceship," May 27, 1956, UGSC.

71. "Letter of Clarification and Justification on the Status of Edward Johnson's Noviceship," May 27, 1956, UGSC.

72. K'Meyer, *Interracialism and Christian Community*, 43.

73. K'Meyer, *Interracialism and Christian Community*, 73.

74. Angry, interview by Tracy K'Meyer.

75. Clarence Jordan, Koinonia Partners pamphlet, 1968, GCAH.

Chapter 5

1. Cleage, *Black Christian Nationalism*, dedication.

2. Blum and Harvey, *Color of Christ*, 12.

3. X, *Autobiography*, 253.

4. Cleage believed that self-hate, what some refer to as internalized racial oppression, was the great sin from which Black people needed to repent. He created a liturgy that renounced integration, individualism, and ignorance. It went on to ask the Black Nation for forgiveness, with the belief that it would support the necessary changes that the Black Messiah called for.

5. Cleage, *The Black Messiah*, 44, 37; Thurman, *Footprints of a Dream*. Interestingly, Cleage shared with Howard Thurman the view that Jesus had an ethic to be followed. But how they understood and applied that ethic differed greatly. The two served as leaders in the same interracial community, the Fellowship of All Peoples in San Francisco, but they did not overlap there. Cleage soured on ministering to white people because of his time ministering in that church.

6. Cleage, *The Black Messiah*, 45.

7. Cleage, *The Black Messiah*, 45.

8. W. R. Jones, *Is God a White Racist?*

9. Quiros, *God with Us*, 54–55.

10. By replacing the Jewishness of Jesus with American racial identities, both men made supersessionist moves. My goal is not to assess the moral goodness or depravity of these decisions—theologians, biblical scholars, and ethicists can weigh

in on their validity. Rather, I am interested in understanding what these racial hermeneutics—Black hermeneutics and white radical hermeneutics—produce in the Christian communities that adhere to them.

11. Cleage, *The Black Messiah*, 57–58.

12. Cleage, *The Black Messiah*, 57–58.

13. Cleage, *The Black Messiah*, 20.

14. Cleage, *The Black Messiah*, 8.

15. "Note on *The Cotton Patch Gospel*—Paul's Epistles," 216, 217.

16. "Letter to the Churches of the Georgia Convention (Galations)," 97.

17. Jordan, "The Distinct Identity," 118.

18. Quiros, *God with Us*, 10.

19. Cleage, *The Black Messiah*, 80.

20. Walker, *Walker's Appeal*.

21. Turner, "God Is a Negro," 185, 186.

22. Turner, "God Is a Negro," 186.

23. Garvey, "The Image of God," 75. For an extended discussion on the Black Jesus tradition from a theological perspective, see Wiley, "God," 75–93.

24. Baldwin, *The Fire Next Time*, 58.

25. Baldwin, *The Fire Next Time*, 71.

26. Baldwin, *The Fire Next Time*, 61.

27. Dillard, *Faith in the City*, 240.

28. "The Great Migration, 1910 to 1970," US Census Bureau, September 13, 2012, www.census.gov/dataviz/visualizations/020/508.php; Dillard, *Faith in the City*, 136.

29. "Great Migration, 1910 to 1970"; Dillard, *Faith in the City*, 136.

30. Dillard, *Faith in the City*, 139.

31. R. M.-C. Williams, *Run Home*, 42–65.

32. R. M.-C. Williams, *Run Home*, 42–65.

33. Dillard, *Faith in the City*, 9.

34. Martin Luther King Jr., "The Great March to Freedom," Detroit, June 23, 1963, in King, *Speeches by Martin Luther King*, 31:47, https://music.apple.com/tr/album /speeches-by-martin-luther-king-the-ultimate-collection/445492123.

35. Dillard, *Faith in the City*, 268–70.

36. Cleage, *The Black Messiah*, 3.

37. P. A. Turner, *Ceramic Uncles*, 72–73.

38. Cleage, *The Black Messiah*, 76, 94.

39. Cleage, *Black Nationalism*, 16. The liturgy says: "I have been an Uncle Tom and I repent. I have served the interests of my white oppressor all of my life because in ignorance I identified with him and wanted to be like him, to be accepted by him, and to integrate with him. I loved my oppressor more than I loved myself. I have betrayed my Black brothers and sisters to serve the interests of my oppressor. Because of self-hate I did not recognize my enemy. I have been individualistic in everything that I have done. I have done nothing to hasten the liberation of Black people. I have misunderstood the will of God in failing to realize that nothing is more sacred in his sight than the liberation of Black people. I ask forgiveness of God and of my Black brothers and sisters in the Black Nation. With the help and support

of the Black Nation I believe that I can change and bury my individualism in the life of the Black Nation. With Jesus, the Black Messiah, as my guide and helper I will try, so help me God. In all honesty and sincerity I can say that I feel that I have been born again."

40. Cleage, *The Black Messiah*, 68, 15.

41. Cleage, *The Black Messiah*, 62.

42. Cleage, *The Black Messiah*, 77.

43. Ryan, *Roy Wilkins*, 58.

44. Thurman, *Footprints of a Dream*. Church leaders like Benjamin Mays dedicated their lives to church integration. And Howard Thurman, the Christian mystic, reflected his experiences in interracial ministry in his book.

45. Dillard, *Faith in the City*, 253.

46. Cleage, *The Black Messiah*, 79.

47. Dillard, *Faith in the City*, 259.

48. Cleage, *The Black Messiah*, 79.

49. Cleage, *The Black Messiah*, 92.

50. King, "Great March to Freedom," Detroit, June 23, 1963.

51. Malcolm X, "Message to the Grassroots," November 10, 1963, Detroit, MI, in *Voices of a People's History of the United States*, edited by Zinn, Howard, and Anthony Arnove, 400–403. New York: Seven Stories Press, 2004.

52. Lassiter, *Detroit under Fire*. The first witness was arrested for carrying a concealed knife, but because it was legal to do so, they later dropped the charges. This was the only knife that the police had in their possession from the encounter. Only one witness, who did not see the actual shooting but claimed to see only Scott's body face-down with a knife in her hand, provided an account that could have aligned with the police's version of the story. Six others testified that they saw the police shoot Scott in the back as she either walked or ran away.

53. Locke, *Detroit Riot*, 26–27; Farley, "Detroit Fifty Years," 206–41.

54. Darden, "Historical Causes," 1–28.

55. Cleage, *The Black Messiah*, 151.

56. Cleage, *The Black Messiah*, 54.

57. Cleage, *The Black Messiah*, 91.

58. Cleage, *The Black Messiah*, 4.

59. Cleage, *The Black Messiah*, 126.

60. Cleage, *The Black Messiah*, 11.

61. K'Meyer, *Interracialism and Christian Community*, 131.

62. Jordan, "Biased Churches Guilty of Heresy," 44; Snider, *"Cotton Patch" Gospel*, 53.

63. "Letter to the Christians in Birmingham (Ephesians)," 307.

64. Bass, *Blessed Are the Peacemakers*, 16.

65. Smith, *Killers of the Dream*, 90.

66. Smith, *Killers of the Dream*, 90.

67. D. T. Carter, *Politics of Rage*, 109.

68. Bass, *Blessed Are the Peacemakers*, 18.

69. Eskew, "'Bombingham,'" 371.

70. "Letter to the Christians in Birmingham (Ephesians)," 308–9.

71. "Letter to the Churches of the Georgia Convention (Galatians)," 300.

72. Jordan, *Cotton Patch Gospel*, 307.

73. Jones and Williams, *Removing the Stain of Racism*.

74. "Note on *The Cotton Patch Gospel*—Paul's Epistles," 217.

75. "Note on *The Cotton Patch Gospel*—Matthew and John," 4.

76. "Note on *The Cotton Patch Gospel*—Paul's Epistles," 217.

77. May, *Informant*, 88.

78. McKinstry, *While the World Watched*, 2. Two other teenagers were killed in related incidents. Two suburban white boy scouts killed a Black child miles away, and the police shot a Black teen in the back after they alleged that he threw a rock at them and ran away.

79. Martin Luther King Jr., "King to Kennedy," September 15, 1963, John F. Kennedy Presidential Library and Museum https://civilrights.jfklibrary.org/media-assets/the-bombing-of-the-16th-street-baptist-church.html#Shock-Waves.

80. "A Talk to Teachers," 331.

81. John Petts, "1987 Interview," quoted in "The Wales Window of Alabama" by Cerith Mathias, Wales Arts Review, May 6, 2020, www.walesartsreview.org/against-the-evil-of-violence-the-wales-window-of-alabama/.

82. Blum and Harvey, *Color of Christ*, 23–24.

83. "Letter to the Atlanta Christians (I Corinthians)," 272.

84. K'Meyer, *Interracialism and Christian Community*, 162.

85. "Matthew," *Cotton Patch Gospel*, 33.

86. Jordan, *Substance of Faith*, 105.

87. Jordan, *Substance of Faith*, 72.

88. Jordan, *Substance of Faith*, 108.

89. Cone, *Black Theology*, 116.

90. "Albert Cleage Is Dead at 88; Led Black Nationalist Church," *New York Times*, February 27, 2000, www.nytimes.com/2000/02/27/us/albert-cleage-is-dead-at-88-led-black-nationalist-church.html.

Chapter 6

1. Murray, *Autobiography*, 145.

2. Murray, *Autobiography*, 138.

3. Murray, *Autobiography*, 201.

4. Rustin, *Time on Two Crosses*; D'Emilio, *Lost Prophet*, 1; Holt, *Movement*; Rosenberg, *Jane Crow*.

5. Murray, *Autobiography*, 132–37.

6. Bell-Scott, *Firebrand and the First Lady*, 64.

7. Murray, *Autobiography*, 140.

8. Murray, *Autobiography*, 142.

9. Murray, *Autobiography*, 144.

10. Murray, *Autobiography*, 146.

11. Rosenberg, *Jane Crow*, 100–101.

12. Du Bois, "Egypt and India," 4.

13. Du Bois, "Egypt and India," 4.

14. Du Bois, "Gandhi and India," 203–7.

15. Gandhi, "To the American Negro," 225.

16. Gandhi, "To the American Negro," 225.

17. Kapur, *Raising Up a Prophet*, 86.

18. L. E. Carter, *Walking Integrity*, 54.

19. L. E. Carter, *Walking Integrity*, 54.

20. M. L. King, *Autobiography*, 23.

21. Prashad, "Black Gandhi," 3, 13.

22. Ralph T. Templin, *Between Two Worlds: The Story of a Missionary's Experiences in International Fellowship* (New York: Fellowship, 1948), 8, GCAH.

23. "A Memorandum concerning a New York Ashram," SCPC.

24. R. T. Templin, *Between Two Worlds*, 8, GCAH. See also E. S. Jones, *Christ of the Indian Road*, 107. Questions like those asked of Templin were common enough that Jones also wrote of Indians who challenged him with questions about racial injustice in America. He wrote of one who asked, "Don't you lynch Negroes in America?"

25. "Tentative 1941–42 Program of the Bronx-Harlem Ashram," August 14, 1941, SCPC.

26. Gurock, *Jews of Harlem*, 12.

27. J. B. Ferguson, *Harlem Renaissance*, 1.

28. J. Holmes Smith, "Our New York Ashram," *Fellowship*, January 1941, SCPC.

29. Farmer, *Lay Bare the Heart*, 149.

30. Du Bois, "Egypt and India," 4.

31. R. T. Templin, *Between Two Worlds*, 2, GCAH.

32. Murray, *Autobiography*, 201.

33. Rosenberg, *Jane Crow*, 101.

34. Murray, *Autobiography*, 201.

35. Farmer, *Lay Bare the Heart*, 149.

36. Farmer, *Lay Bare the Heart*, 150.

37. R. T. Templin, *Between Two Worlds*, 2, GCAH.

38. R. T. Templin, *Between Two Worlds*, 29, GCAH.

39. E. S. Jones, *Christ of the Indian Road*, 15.

40. E. S. Jones, *Christ of the Indian Road*, 15.

41. R. T. Templin, *Between Two Worlds*, 2, GCAH.

42. R. T. Templin, *Between Two Worlds*, 4, GCAH.

43. R. T. Templin, *Between Two Worlds*, 28, GCAH.

44. R. T. Templin, *Between Two Worlds*, 28, GCAH.

45. Farmer, *Lay Bare the Heart*, 149.

46. Rustin, *Time on Two Crosses*, 84–91.

47. Templin to Ralph Borsodi, October 29, 1970, GCAH.

48. Templin to Borsodi, March 7, 1941, GCAH.

49. Borsodi, *This Ugly Civilization*, 234.

50. "Reorganization of Independence Foundation, Inc.," 1941, GCAH.

51. Templin to Borsodi, October 29, 1970, GCAH.

52. Borsodi to Templin, April 28, 1941, GCAH; Ralph Borsodi, *This Ugly Civilization*, 234; Templin to Borsodi, March 7, 1941, GCAH.

53. Templin to Borsodi, June 26, 1941, GCAH.

54. Templin to Borsodi, June 26, 1941, GCAH.

55. Templin to Borsodi, June 26, 1941, GCAH.

56. Templin to Borsodi, June 26, 1941, GCAH.

57. Johnson, *Wingless Eagle*. On Belgian "neutrality," see Anckaer, "Dangerous Opportunities"; Hull, *Scrap of Paper*.

58. Richey et al., *Methodist Experience in America*, 304–5.

59. Templin to Borsodi, June 26, 1941, GCAH.

60. Templin to Borsodi, June 26, 1941, GCAH.

61. L. Templin, "Excellent Piece of Work," 233.

62. Barnes, *Antislavery Impulse, 1830–1844*, 11.

63. R. T. Templin, *Democracy and Nonviolence*, 325–26.

64. L. Templin, "Excellent Piece of Work," 233.

65. L. Templin, "Excellent Piece of Work," 233.

66. R. T. Templin, *Democracy and Nonviolence*, 325–26.

67. R. T. Templin, *Democracy and Nonviolence*, 325–26.

68. R. T. Templin, "Declaration of Independence."

69. R. T. Templin, *Between Two Worlds*, 4, GCAH.

70. Templin to Borsodi, February 15, 1941, GCAH; Ralph Templin, "Interracial Brotherhood and American World Leadership," *Human Frontiers* 9, no. 4 (1961), GCAH. See also Copland, "Christianity as an Arm of Empire."

71. Templin to Borsodi, February 7, 1941, GCAH; Borsodi to Templin, February 11, 1941, GCAH.

72. *Peacemaker*, June 5, 1949, GCAH.

73. Loomis, "The Life"; *Peacemaker*, June 5, 1949, GCAH; Templin to Borsodi, February 7, 1941, GCAH; A. J. Muste, "Peacemakers," December 14, 1948, GCAH.

74. Templin to President Wesley, April 27, 1948, GCAH; Charles H. Wesley to Templin, May 7, 1948, GCAH; Charles H. Wesley to Templin, June 26, 1948, GCAH. The Central Jurisdiction stood apart from the other governing episcopal bodies of the Methodist Episcopal Church because it was singled out as a racial conference, while the other conferences represented regional interests. That meant that all Black pastors and bishops, no matter their location, were members of the Central Jurisdiction. As a white clergy, Templin's action was inconceivable to most.

75. Templin to President Wesley, July 18, 1960, GCAH; Templin to President Wesley, May 19, 1961, GCAH.

76. Mollin, *Radical Pacifism*, 1.

77. Templin to Muste, August 2, 1955, GCAH.

78. Templin to Muste, August 2, 1955, GCAH.

79. A. J. Muste, "Peacemakers," December 14, 1948, GCAH; Winifred R. to Templin, October 26, 1950, GCAH.

80. Templin to Muste, July 15, 1950, GCAH; "Out of Darkness, Hope!" editorial, *Christian Century*, July 12, 1950, 837–39.

81. Muste to Templin, August 25, 1950, GCAH.

82. Muste to Templin, August 28, 1950, GCAH.
83. Muste to Templin, August 28, 1950, GCAH.
84. Rustin, *Time on Two Crosses*, 28.
85. Templin to Muste, January 19, 1951, GCAH.
86. Templin to Peacemakers, December 24, 1956, GCAH.
87. Templin to Peacemakers, December 24, 1956, GCAH.
88. Templin to Peacemakers," December 24, 1956, GCAH.
89. Templin to Peacemakers," December 24, 1956, GCAH.
90. C. King, *My Life with Martin*, 40.
91. C. King and Reynolds, *My Life*, 27.
92. C. King and Reynolds, *My Life*, 27.
93. Ralph Templin, "How Could This Happen in Yellow Springs?," GCAH.
94. Mills, *Cutting along the Color Line*, 192–94.
95. Mills, *Cutting along the Color Line*, 194.
96. Bob Burns and Al Pikora, "Demonstrators Explain Defiance of Court Order Limiting Pickets," March 14, 1964, *Dayton Daily News*, GCAH.
97. "Some Things That Weren't Reported," *Antioch College: Record* 19, no. 33 (March 20, 1964), GCAH.
98. Doug Carpenter and Dan Droog, "Today–March 14, 1964"; *We Stand Together Equal*, GCAH.
99. Burns and Pikora, "Demonstrators Explain Defiance of Court Order Limiting Pickets," March 14, 1964, *Dayton Daily News*, GCAH.
100. Burns and Pikora, "Demonstrators Explain Defiance of Court Order Limiting Pickets," March 14, 1964, *Dayton Daily News*, GCAH.
101. Mills, *Cutting along the Color Line*, 192–94; "Barber to Close Shop in Ohio Racial Dispute," *Washington Post*, March 16, 1964, GCAH.
102. Ralph Templin, "As Others See It: Takes Issues with Views," August 10, 1963, *Xenia Daily Gazette*, 11, GCAH.
103. "Integration Demands," *Xenia Daily Gazette*, GCAH.
104. James Dixon to Templin, September 3, 1963, GCAH.

Chapter 7

1. Lapeyrolerie, "'No Water,'" 5.
2. Robenalt, *Ballots and Bullets*, 116.
3. James Baldwin et al., "Negro's Role in American Culture," 80–98, 81.
4. "Report from Occupied Territory," 423.
5. "'Black Power' Statement by National Committee of Negro Churchmen," *New York Times*, July 31, 1966.
6. Joseph, *Waiting 'Til the Midnight Hour*; R. T. Templin, *Democracy and Nonviolence*, 150–51.
7. Ralph Templin, "Interracial Brotherhood and American World Leadership," *Human Frontiers, Journal of Human Relations* 9, no. 4 (1961), GCAH.
8. "'Black Power' Statement by National Committee of Negro Churchmen."

9. Ralph Templin, "Black Power: A Concept of Identity and Presentation of Self for the Black American's Self-Preservation," *Journal of Human Relations*, 3, GCAH.

10. Robenalt, *Ballots and Bullets*, 111–22; Perry, *Black Mayors*, 75–106.

11. Robenalt, *Ballots and Bullets*, 116–17.

12. Joseph, *Stokely: A Life*, xi.

13. Joseph, *Waiting 'Til the Midnight Hour*, 132–33; Goudsouzian, *Down to the Crossroads*, 46–47.

14. Sellers, *River of No Return*, 160–61.

15. Joseph, *Wait 'Til the Midnight Hour*, 131–35; Goudsouzian, *Down to the Crossroads*, 33. King said, "I restrained Stokely—nonviolently."

16. Sellers, *River of No Return*, 162.

17. Joseph, *Waiting 'Til the Midnight Hour*, 133.

18. Sellers, *River of No Return*, 162–66.

19. Sellers, *River of No Return*, 165–66.

20. Goudsouzian, *Down to the Crossroads*, 133–34.

21. Joseph, *Waiting 'Til the Midnight Hour*, 141–42.

22. Sellers, *River of No Return*, 166.

23. Sellers, *River of No Return*, 166–67.

24. Joseph, *Waiting 'Til the Midnight Hour*, 141–42.

25. Joseph, *Stokely: A Life*, 103.

26. M. L. King, "Black Power (1967)."

27. "Black Power, White Backlash," *CBS Reports*, September 27, 1966.

28. Carmichael, *Black Power*, 4.

29. "A 'Black Power' Speech That Has Congress Aroused," *US News and World Report*, August 22, 1966, 6.

30. "Civil Rights," *Time*, July 1, 1966.

31. Joseph, *Waiting 'Til the Midnight Hour*, 149.

32. Mary McGrory, "McNamara's New Front in Anti-Poverty War," *Washington Star*, August 23, 1966, 29.

33. "Black Power, White Backlash," *CBS Reports*, September 27, 1966.

34. Wilson C. McWilliams, "On Black Power," *Activist*, Fall 1966, 13–15, GCAH.

35. Harry Fleischman, "Black Rage and White Guilt," *New American Socialist*, September 30, 1968, GCAH.

36. Helen T. Gott, "Theologists Interpret Black Power Seminary," *Kansas City Star*, Templin Collection, GCAH.

37. Claude Williams, "A White Man's View of Black Power," *National Guardian*, December 3, 1966, 6–7, GCAH.

38. Stone, "National Conference on Black Power," 189. See Powell, "My Black Position Paper," 257–60. Powell outlines seventeen points: (1) Black pride, (2) Black leadership, (3) Black communal stakeholders, (4) proportionate share of vote and positions of power, (5) Black people support Black politicians, (6) Black people must seek audacious power, (7) economic self-sufficiency and political power, (8) white-collar jobs, (9) local leadership, (10) leaders should have national clout, (11) nonviolence, (12) defy immoral laws, (13) intra-racial uplift/support, (14) war on poverty

must produce jobs, (15) federal end to segregation in schools, (16) education must focus on STEM, (17) voter registration.

39. D. Day, "On Pilgrimage—June 1966," 2.

40. D. Day, "On Pilgrimage—June 1966," 6.

41. D. Day, "On Pilgrimage—June 1966," 8.

42. D. Day, "On Pilgrimage—June 1966," 8.

43. "'Black Power' Statement by National Committee of Negro Churchmen."

44. Douglass, "Reconstruction," 763.

45. "Dr. King Deplores 'Long Cold Winter' on the Rights Front," *New York Times*, June 20, 1967, www.nytimes.com/1967/06/20/archives/dr-king-deplores-long-cold-winter-on-the-rights-front.html.

46. "Martin Luther King Jr., "The Other America," Stanford University, April 14, 1967, https://diva.sfsu.edu/collections/sfbatv/bundles/191473.

47. "'Black Power' Statement by National Committee of Negro Churchmen."

48. "'Black Power' Statement by National Committee of Negro Churchmen."

49. "'Black Power' Statement by National Committee of Negro Churchmen."

50. R. Templin, "Black Power: A Concept of Identity and Presentation-of-Self for the Black American's Self-Preservation," 3, GCAH.

51. C. Johnson, *Revolutionaries to Race Leaders*.

52. R. Templin, "Black Power," 3, GCAH.

53. Stone, "National Conference on Black Power," 191.

54. The Rev. Nathan Wright Jr., interview, April 18, 1968, *The Church Awakens: African Americans and the Struggle for Justice*, www.episcopalarchives.org/church-awakens/items/show/331.

55. Curvin, *Inside Newark*.

56. See the registration for the National Conference on Black Power, Newark, July 20–23, 1967, https://archive.org/details/NwkAfAm006.

57. Stone, "National Conference on Black Power," 195.

58. Stone, "National Conference on Black Power," 195.

59. C. Johnson, *Revolutionaries to Race Leaders*, 69; Stone, "National Conference on Black Power," 191–92, 194. Stone identified representatives from more than sixty organizations.

60. C. Johnson, *Revolutionaries to Race Leaders*, 68–69; Stone, "National Conference on Black Power," 196.

61. One should not confuse the Newark Black Manifesto of 1967 with James Forman's Black Manifesto of 1969. Stone, "National Conference on Black Power," 196; C. Johnson, *Revolutionaries to Race Leaders*, 68.

62. R. Templin, "Black Power," 14, GCAH.

63. C. Johnson, *Revolutionaries to Race Leaders*, 66–67.

64. "'Black Power' Statement by National Committee of Negro Churchmen"; R. T. Templin, *Democracy and Nonviolence*, 29.

65. "White 'Black Power' Advocate Spreads Belief," *Dayton Express*, October 24, 1968, GCAH.

66. Ralph Templin, *Between Two Worlds: The Story of a Missionary's Experiences in International Fellowship*, 4, GCAH.

67. Martin Luther King Jr., Roy Wilkins, Whitney Young, Stokely Carmichael, Floyd McKissick, and James Meredith, "Negro Leaders on *Meet the Press*," 89 Cong. Rec. S21095–21102 (1966).

68. King et al., "Negro Leaders on *Meet the Press*."

69. King et al., "Negro Leaders on *Meet the Press*."

70. R. Templin, "Black Power," GCAH; Carmichael and Hamilton, *Black Power*.

71. "White 'Black Power' Advocate Spreads Belief," 23, GCAH; William Worth, "Black Power Is Needed Says White Ex-Prof," *Journal Herald*, October 11, 1968, GCAH.

72. R. Templin, "Black Power," 17, GCAH.

73. "Black Power, White Backlash."

74. Carmichael, "What We Want," 35.

75. Carmichael, "What We Want."

Epilogue

1. Black Lives Matter emerged in 2013, when, according to its website, "three radical Black organizers—Alicia Garza, Patrisse Cullors, and Opal Tometi—created a Black-centered political-movement-building project called #BlackLivesMatter in response to the acquittal of Trayvon Martin's murderer, George Zimmerman." It became the most important national organizing entity protesting racial injustice, especially related to American law enforcement protecting "stand your ground" laws and police killing of unarmed Black people. One of its hallmarks became its decentralized leadership, which enabled BLM chapters to emerge at any time in any place people had the will to assert that Black lives matter. I personally experienced the openness of the organization to input when I offered to post my online article "Precious Blackness and the Politics of Distraction" to the BLM Facebook page. Evans, "Precious Blackness"; Francis, *Ferguson and Faith*; C. Johnson, *After Black Lives Matter*.

2. Jackson, "Marissa Johnson Was Right."

3. Jackson, "Marissa Johnson Was Right."

4. Johnson, "1 Year Later."

5. Jackson, "Marissa Johnson Was Right."

6. Ferguson, "Marissa Janae Johnson Doesn't 'Give a F*ck.'"

7. Ferguson, "Marissa Janae Johnson Doesn't 'Give a F*ck.'"

8. "At a Minority Women's Event, Bernie Sanders Faced a Tough Reception, Pointing to Challenges Ahead," *Washington Post*, April 26, 2019, www.washingtonpost.com/gender-identity/at-a-minority-womens-event-bernie-sanders-faced-a-tough-reception-pointing-to-challenges-ahead.

9. Bass, *Blessed Are the Peacemakers*, 246.

10. See B. Sanders, *Our Revolution*. He writes, "In 1979, after discovering that most of the college students I spoke to had never heard of Eugene Victor Debs, I produced a thirty-minute video on his life and ideas. . . . The life of Eugene V. Debs, his vision of world peace, justice, democracy, and brotherhood, has always been an inspiration to me. I have a plaque of Debs on a wall in my Washington Senate office." See also Tensley, "Racism."

11. Hackman, "'We Need Co-Conspirators, Not Allies.'"

12. Garza, "What Did We Learn?"

13. Hackman, "'We Need Co-Conspirators, Not Allies.'"

14. Chattopadhyay, "Feminista Jones Doesn't Think You're an Ally."

15. Viren, "Native Scholar Who Wasn't"; Flaherty, "White Lies"; Flaherty, "Passing in the Classroom." Danzy Senna's book review is a good example of this; see Senna, "Robin DiAngelo and the Problem with Anti-Racist Self-Help." See also Bergner, "'White Fragility' Is Everywhere."

Bibliography

Primary Sources

Archives

Athens, GA
    University of Georgia Special Collections Libraries
        Clarence L. Jordan Papers
Madison, NJ
    United Methodist Archives and History Center
        General Commission on Archives and History
            Ralph T. Templin Collection
New York, NY
    Burke Library Archives
        Henry Frederick Ward Papers
    Union Theological Seminary
Swarthmore, PA
    Swarthmore College
        Swarthmore College Peace Collection
            Harlem Ashram Collected Papers
Washington, DC
    Georgetown University Archival Resources
        John LaFarge, SJ Papers

Periodicals

Black World/Negro Digest	*Human Frontiers*
Carolina Times	*Interracial Review*
Catholic Worker	*Journal Herald*
Chicago Defender	*Messenger*
Christian Century	*Nation*
Congressional Record: Proceedings	*New York Times*
and Debates of the Congress	*Root*
Crisis	*Time*
Essence	*Tuskegee Experiment Station Bulletins*

Books, Chapters, and Articles

Addams, Jane. *Peace and Bread in a Time of War.* New York: Macmillan, 1922.
Apess, William. *A Son of the Forest and Other Writings.* Edited by Barry O'Connell.
    Amherst: University of Massachusetts Press, 1997.

Atlanta Journal-Constitution. "Koinonia Community's Market Stand after an Explosion Directly Attacking the Interracial Community, 1957." AJCP221–024g, Atlanta Journal-Constitution Photographic Archives. Special Collections and Archives, Georgia State University Library. https://dlg.usg.edu/record/gsu_ajc_12335.

Baldwin, James. "On Being White." *Essence* 14, no. 12 (April 1984): 90–92.

——. *The Devil Finds Work*. New York: Vintage International, 2011.

——. *The Fire Next Time*. New York: Vintage International, 1993.

——. *The Price of the Ticket: Collected Nonfiction, 1948–1985*. New York: St. Martin's Press, 1985.

——. "A Report from Occupied Territory." In *The Price of the Ticket: Collected Nonfiction, 1948–1985*. New York: St. Martin's Press, 1985.

——. "A Talk to Teachers." In *The Price of the Ticket: Collected Nonfiction, 1948–1985*. New York: St. Martin's Press, 1985.

Baldwin, James, Nat Hentoff, Lorraine Hansberry, and Langston Hughes. "The Negro's Role in American Culture." *Black World/Negro Digest* (March 1962): 80–98.

Barbour, Floyd B., ed. *The Black Power Revolt: A Collection of Essays*. Boston: Porter Sargent, 1968.

"Black Power: White Backlash." *CBS Reports*, September 27, 1966.

Bok, Edward William. *The Americanization of Edward Bok: The Autobiography of a Dutch Boy Fifty Years After*. New York: C. Scribner's Sons, 1920.

Borsodi, Ralph. *Flight from the City: An Experiment in Creative Living on the Land—Moving to the Country; Fresh Food, a Large Rural Home, and a Relaxed, Happier Life*. New York: Harper & Bros., 1933.

——. "The Green Revolution: Back to the Land!" *Christian Century* (July 1943).

——. *This Ugly Civilization*. New York: Harper & Bros., 1933.

Bridges, William. "Six Demands." *Challenge* (August 1919): 82–83.

Campbell, Will. "Remembering Clarence." In Clarence Jordan, *Cotton Patch Gospel: The Complete Collection*. Macon, GA: Smyth & Helwys, 2012, ix.

Carmichael, Stokely. *Black Power: Notes and Comment*. Chicago: Student Nonviolent Coordinating Committee, 1966.

——. "What We Want." *New York Review of Books*, September 22, 1966, 5–8.

Carmichael, Stokely, and Charles V. Hamilton. *Black Power: The Politics of Liberation in America*. New York: Vintage Books, 1967.

Carver, George Washington. *How to Build Up Worn Out Soils*. Bulletin no. 6, Experiment Station, Tuskegee Normal and Industrial Institute, 1905.

Catholic Church. *Catechism of the Council of Trent for Parish Priests, Issued by Order of Pope Pius V*. Translated by John A. McHugh and Charles J. Callan. New York: Joseph F. Wagner, 1934.

Clarke, Benjamin. "Speech in Americus," July 5, 1965. *Willie Bolden and the Americus Movement*, 2023. https://www.youtube.com/watch?v=3_GN7-omJUw.

Cleage, Albert B., Jr. *Black Christian Nationalism: New Directions for the Black Church; Including Papers Presented to the First Black Christian Nationalist Convention.* Edited by George Bell. New York: W. Morrow, 1972.

———. *The Black Messiah.* New York: Sheed and Ward, 1968.

Cogley, John. *A Canterbury Tale: Experiences and Reflections, 1916–1976.* New York: Seabury Press, 1976.

Cone, James H. *Black Theology and Black Power.* New York: Seabury Press, 1969.

Day, Dorothy. *All the Way to Heaven: The Selected Letters of Dorothy Day.* Edited by Robert Ellsberg. Milwaukee, WI: Marquette University Press, 2010.

———. "Communists, Despite Noise, Are Not Only Defenders of Scottsboro Case." *Catholic Worker,* May 1, 1933.

———. *The Duty of Delight: The Diaries of Dorothy Day.* Edited by Robert Ellsberg. Milwaukee, WI: Marquette University Press, 2008.

———. "Fear in Our Time." *Catholic Worker,* April 1967.

———. *Loaves and Fishes.* Maryknoll, NY: Orbis Books, 1997.

———. *The Long Loneliness: The Autobiography of Dorothy Day.* San Francisco: Harper & Row, 1981.

———. "More Houses of Hospitality Are Needed." *Catholic Worker,* March 1, 1938.

———. "On Pilgrimage—May 1957." *Catholic Worker,* May 1957.

———. "On Pilgrimage—June 1966." *Catholic Worker,* June 1966.

———. "Radical but Not Communist." *Catholic Worker,* July–August 1933.

Day, John Kyle. *The Southern Manifesto: Massive Resistance and the Fight to Preserve Segregation.* Jackson: University Press of Mississippi, 2014.

Douglass, Frederick. "Reconstruction." *Atlantic Monthly,* December 1866, 761–65.

———. *Three Addresses on the Relations Subsisting between the White and Colored People of the United States.* Washington, DC: Gibson Bros., 1886.

———. *Two Speeches by Frederick Douglass, One on West India Emancipation, Delivered at Canandaigua, Aug. 4th, and the Other on the Dred Scott Decision, Delivered in New York, on the Occasion of the Anniversary of the American Abolition Society, May, 1857.* Rochester, NY: C. P. Dewey, 1857.

"Dr. Benjamin Mays Honoree at N.C. Mutual." *Carolina Times,* November 2, 1968, 1–2. https://newspapers.digitalnc.org/lccn/sn83045120/1968-11-02/ed-1/seq-1/.

Du Bois, W. E. B. *Black Reconstruction in America: Toward a History of the Part Which Black Folk Played in the Attempt to Reconstruct Democracy in America, 1860–1880.* New Brunswick, NJ: Transaction, 2013.

———. "The Conservation of Races (1897)." In *A W. E. B. Du Bois Reader,* edited by Andrew G. Paschal. New York: Macmillan, 1971.

———. "*The Crisis.*" Editorial. *Crisis,* November 1910, 10–11.

———. "Die Negerfrage in den Vereinigten Staaten (The Negro Question in the United States)." Translated by Joseph Fracchia. *CR: The New Centennial Review* 6, no. 3 (2006): 241–90. www.jstor.org/stable/41949542.

———. "Egypt and India." *Crisis,* June 1919.

———. "Gandhi and India." *Crisis,* March 1922, 203–7.

———. "Marxism and the Negro Problem." *Crisis,* May 1933, 103–4, 118.

——. "The NAACP and the Class Struggle." In *Voices of a Black Nation*, edited by Theodore G. Vincent. San Francisco: Ramparts Press, 1973. http://archive.org /details/voicesofblacknatoooovinc. Originally published in *The Crisis*, August 1921.

——. "The Negro and Radical Thought." Opinion. *Crisis*, July 1921, 102–4.

——. "Postscript: The Board of Directors on Segregation." *Crisis*, May 1934, 147–49.

——. "Postscript: Communism." *Crisis*, September 1928, 320–21.

——. "Postscript: The Negro and the Catholic Church." *Crisis*, March 1933, 68–69.

——. *The Souls of Black Folk*. New York: Bantam Books, 1989.

——. *A W. E. B. Du Bois Reader*. Edited by Andrew G. Paschal. New York: Macmillan, 1971.

——. *W. E. B. Du Bois: A Reader*. New York: Macmillan, 1995.

——. "Where Do We Go from Here? (A Lecture on Negroes' Economic Plight)." In *A W. E. B. Du Bois Reader*, edited by Andrew G. Paschal. New York: Macmillan, 1971.

——. "Why I Won't Vote." *Nation*, October 20, 1956.

Falls, Arthur G. Interview by Francis Sicius, Western Springs, IL, June 19, 1976. In "The Chicago Catholic Worker Movement, 1936 to the Present," by Francis Joseph Sicius. PhD diss., Loyola University Chicago, 1979.

Falls, Arthur G. "The Chicago Letter." *Catholic Worker*, November 1936.

——. Interview by Francis Sicius, Western Springs, IL, June 19, 1976. In "The Chicago Catholic Worker Movement, 1936 to the Present," by Francis Joseph Sicius. PhD diss., Loyola University Chicago, 1979.

Farmer, James L. *Lay Bare the Heart: An Autobiography of the Civil Rights Movement*. Sixties—Primary Documents and Personal Narratives, 1960–1974. Fort Worth: Texas Christian University Press, 1998.

Federated Colored Catholics. "Mission Statement, 1927." *Moorland-Springarn Research Center, Howard University*, 1927. https://cuomeka.wrlc.org/items /show/398.

Friends and the War: Addresses Delivered at a Conference of Members of the Society of Friends and Others, Held at Llandudno, September 25th 30th, 1914. 2nd ed. London: Headley, 1914.

Gandhi, Mahatma. "To the American Negro: A Message from Mahatma Gandhi, May 1, 1929." *Crisis*, July 1929, 225.

Gary, Dorothy P. "Beyond the Color Line." *Crisis*, May 1929, 153–71.

Gillard, John Thomas. *The Catholic Church and the American Negro: Being an Investigation of the Past and Present Activities of the Catholic Church in Behalf of the 12,000,000 Negroes in the United States, with an Examination of the Difficulties Which Affect the Work of the Colored Missions*. Baltimore, MD: St. Joseph's Society Press, 1930.

Harlow, Poppy. *CNN Newsroom with Poppy Harlow*, August 9, 2015, 3:00 P.M.–4:01 P.M. PDT. http://archive.org/details/CNNW_20150809_220000_CNN_Newsroom _With_Poppy_Harlow.

Johnson, Marissa Jenae. "1 Year Later: BLM Protester Who Interrupted Bernie Sanders' Rally Discusses the Moment and the Movement." *Root*, August 9, 2016. www.theroot.com/1-year-later-blm-protester-who-interrupted-bernie-sand-1790856353.

Jordan, Clarence. "Biased Churches Guilty of Heresy—Ga. Cleric." *Jet*, June 27, 1963.

———. "Clarence Jordan Tells the Koinonia Story." Cotton Patch Productions. Speech given November 10, 1956, at Fellowship House, Cincinnati, Ohio. www.youtube.com/watch?v=2g1Z-v-TpI0.

———. *Cotton Patch Gospel: The Complete Collection*. Macon, GA: Smyth & Helwys, 2012.

———. *Essential Writings*. Edited by Joyce Hollyday. Maryknoll, NY: Orbis Books, 2003.

———. "A Letter to the Atlanta Christians (I Corinthians)." In Jordan, *Cotton Patch Gospel: The Complete Collection*. Macon, GA: Smyth & Helwys, 2012.

———. "The Letter to the Christians in Birmingham (Ephesians)." In Jordan, *Cotton Patch Gospel: The Complete Collection*. Macon, GA: Smyth & Helwys, 2012.

———. "The Letter to the Churches of the Georgia Convention (Galatians)." In Jordan, *Cotton Patch Gospel: The Complete Collection*. Macon, GA: Smyth & Helwys, 2012.

———. "A Note on *The Cotton Patch Gospel*—Matthew and John." In Jordan, *Cotton Patch Gospel: The Complete Collection*. Macon, GA: Smyth & Helwys, 2012.

———. "A Note on *The Cotton Patch Gospel*—Paul's Epistles." In Jordan, *Cotton Patch Gospel: The Complete Collection*. Macon, GA: Smyth & Helwys, 2012.

Jordan, Florence. Interview by Vicki Ragsdell. Recorded in the studio of the Southern Baptist Theological Seminary, March 18, 1986. http://hdl.handle.net/10392/4087.

King, Coretta Scott. *My Life with Martin Luther King, Jr.* First revised edition. New York: Henry Holt and Company, 1993.

King, Coretta Scott, and Rev. Dr. Barbara Reynolds. *My Life, My Love, My Legacy*. New York: Henry Holt, 2017.

King, Martin Luther, Jr. *The Autobiography of Martin Luther King, Jr.* Edited by Clayborne Carson. New York: Intellectual Properties Management, 1998. Published in association with Warner Books.

———. "The Birth of a Nation." Sermon delivered at Dexter Avenue Baptist Church, Montgomery, AL, April 17, 1957.

———. "'The Birth of a New Age,' Address Delivered on 11 August 1956 at the Fiftieth Anniversary of Alpha Phi Alpha in Buffalo." *The Martin Luther King, Jr. Research and Education Institute*. https://kinginstitute.stanford.edu/king-papers/documents/birth-new-age-address-delivered-11-august-1956-fiftieth-anniversary-alpha-phi.

———. "Black Power (1967)." In *I Am Because We Are: Readings in Africana Philosophy*, edited by Fred Lee Hord (Mzee Lasana Okpara) and Jonathan Scott Lee. Rev. ed. Amherst: University of Massachusetts Press, 2016.

———. *A Call to Conscience: The Landmark Speeches of Dr. Martin Luther King, Jr.* Edited by Clayborne Carson and Kris Shepard. New York: Hachette, 2001.

———. "'Give Us the Ballot': Address Delivered at the Prayer Pilgrimage for Freedom, May 17, 1957, Washington, DC." In *A Call to Conscience: The Landmark Speeches of Dr. Martin Luther King, Jr.*, edited by Clayborne Carson and Kris Shepard. New York: IPM (Intellectual Properties Management), in association with Warner Books., 2001.

———. "The Great March to Freedom." Detroit, June 23, 1963. In *Speeches by Martin Luther King: The Ultimate Collection*, by Martin Luther King Jr., 31:47, https://music.apple.com/us/album/speeches-by-martin-luther-king-the -ultimate-collection/445492123.

———. "I Have a Dream." In *A Call to Conscience: The Landmark Speeches of Dr. Martin Luther King, Jr.*, edited by Clayborne Carson and Kris Shepard. New York: IPM (Intellectual Properties Management), in association with Warner Books, 2001.

———. *The Papers of Martin Luther King, Jr.* Vol. 4, *Symbol of the Movement, January 1957–December 1958*. Edited by Clayborne Carson, Susan Carson, Adrienne Clay, Virginia Shadron, and Kieran Taylor. Berkeley: University of California Press, 2000.

———. "Rev. Dr. Martin Luther King, Jr. at Stanford." *Bay Area Television Archive.* https://diva.sfsu.edu/collections/sfbatv/bundles/191473.

———. *Speeches by Martin Luther King: The Ultimate Collection.* 2011. https://music .apple.com/us/album/speeches-by-martin-luther-king-the-ultimate-collection /445492123.

———. "A Statement to the South and Nation." Southern Negro Leaders Conference on Transportation and Nonviolent Integration, January 10, 1957, to January 11, 1957. Martin Luther King, Jr. Research and Education Institute. https:// kinginstitute.stanford.edu/king-papers/documents/statement-south-and -nation-issued-southern-negro-leaders-conference.

Marshall, Thurgood. *Thurgood Marshall: His Speeches, Writings, Arguments, Opinions, and Reminiscences.* Edited by Mark V. Tushnet. Chicago: Lawrence Hill Books, 2001.

Midwest Catholic Workers. "Lament. Repent. Repair: An Open Letter on Racism to the Catholic Worker Movement." Midwest Catholic Worker Faith and Resistance Gathering, December 9, 2017. https://docs.google.com/document/u /1/d/1SVVOhTn4Zm1Q5UL1kqElB1eW8djePBgu3cQEgVc57Ok/edit?usp=embed _facebook.

New York State Joint Legislative Committee Investigating Seditious Activities. *Revolutionary Radicalism: Its History, Purpose and Tactics; with an Exposition and Discussion of the Steps Being Taken and Required to Curb It.* 4 vols. Albany, NY: J. B. Lyon, 1920.

Powell, Adam Clayton. "My Black Position Paper." In *The Black Power Revolt: A Collection of Essays,* edited by Floyd B. Barbour. Boston: Porter Sargent, 1968.

Randolph, A. Philip. "Statement at Prayer Pilgrimage for Freedom at the Lincoln Memorial (1957)." In *For Jobs and Freedom: The Selected Speeches and Writings of A. Philip Randolph,* edited by Andrew E. Kersten and David Lucander. Amherst: University of Massachusetts Press, 2014.

Randolph, A. Philip, Martin Luther King Jr., and Roy Wilkins. "Call to a Prayer Pilgrimage for Freedom." In *The Papers of Martin Luther King, Jr.*, vol. 4, *Symbol of the Movement: January 1957–December 1958*, edited by Clayborne Carson, Susan Carson, Adrienne Clay, Virginia Shadron, and Kieran Taylor. Berkeley: University of California Press, 1992.

Roberts, Richard. *Christ and Ourselves*. London: Student Christian Movement, 1916.

Smith, Lillian. "The Day It Happens." In *A Lillian Smith Reader*, edited by Margaret Rose Gladney and Lisa Hodgens. Athens: University of Georgia Press, 2016.

——. *How Am I to Be Heard? Letters of Lillian Smith*. Edited by Margaret Rose Gladney. Chapel Hill: University of North Carolina Press, 1993.

——. *A Lillian Smith Reader*. Edited by Margaret Rose Gladney and Lisa Hodgens. Athens: University of Georgia Press, 2016.

——. "The Right Way Is Not a Moderate Way." *Phylon* 17, no. 4 (1956): 335–41.

Stone, Chuck. "The National Conference on Black Power." In *The Black Power Revolt: A Collection of Essays*, edited by Floyd B. Barbour. Boston: Porter Sargent, 1968.

Templin, Ralph T. *The Decentralist Way for Post-War Reconstruction*, vol. 7, part 2. Suffern, UK: Town & Country Church, 1944.

——. "Declaration of Independence: Is the Servant Greater Than His Lord?" *Michigan Christian Advocate* 61, no 21 (May 24, 1934): 3.

——. *Democracy and Nonviolence: The Role of the Individual in World Crisis*. Boston: Porter Sargent, 1965.

Turner, Thomas W. "President's Annual Address." September 2, 1932. https://cuomeka.wrlc.org/items/show/399.

Tushnet, Mark V. *Making Civil Rights Law: Thurgood Marshall and the Supreme Court, 1936–1961*. New York: Oxford University Press, 1994.

Walker, David. *Walker's Appeal, in Four Articles; Together with a Preamble, to the Coloured Citizens of the World, but in Particular, and Very Expressly, to Those of the United States of America*. Baltimore, MD: Black Classic Press, 1993.

Wilkins, Roy. "Mississippi Slavery in 1933." *Crisis* (April 1933): 81–82.

Secondary Sources

"Abolish the White Race: An Interview with Noel Ignatiev of *Race Traitor*." ¡The Blast!, Number 2, June/July 1994: 14–15, 24.

"African-American Catholics." American Catholic History Classroom. Last updated September 16, 2024. https://cuomeka.wrlc.org/exhibits/show/fcc.

Agee, Gary B. *A Cry for Justice: Daniel Rudd and His Life in Black Catholicism, Journalism, and Activism, 1854–1933*. Fayetteville: University of Arkansas Press, 2011.

Alston, Beth. "Bethesda Baptist Marks 150 Years." *Americus Times-Recorder*, January 4, 2016. www.americustimesrecorder.com/2016/01/04/bethesda-baptist-marks-150-years.

Anckaer, Jan. "Dangerous Opportunities? Reassessing Belgian Neutrality during the Crimean War (1853–1856)." *Journal of Belgian History* 44, no. 4 (2014):

68–111. www.journalbelgianhistory.be/en/journal/journal-belgian-history-xliv
-2014-4/dangerous-opportunities-reassessing-belgian-neutrality.

Appelbaum, Patricia. *Kingdom to Commune: Protestant Pacifist Culture between World War I and the Vietnam Era*. Chapel Hill: University of North Carolina Press, 2009.

Azaransky, Sarah. *This Worldwide Struggle: Religion and the International Roots of the Civil Rights Movement*. New York: Oxford University Press, 2017. https://doi .org/10.1093/acprof:oso/9780190262204.001.0001.

Barnes, Gilbert Hobbs. *The Antislavery Impulse, 1830–1844*. New York: Harcourt, Brace & World, 1964.

Barry, John M. *Rising Tide: The Great Mississippi Flood of 1927 and How It Changed America*. New York: Simon & Schuster, 1998. http://catdir.loc.gov/catdir /enhancements/fy0641/96040077-s.html.

Bass, S. Jonathan. *Blessed Are the Peacemakers: Martin Luther King Jr., Eight White Religious Leaders, and the "Letter from Birmingham Jail."* Baton Rouge: Louisiana State University Press, 2001.

Bell, Derrick A., Jr. *"Brown v. Board of Education* and the Interest-Convergence Dilemma." *Harvard Law Review* 93, no. 3 (1980): 518–33. https://doi.org/10 .2307/1340546.

Bell-Scott, Patricia. *The Firebrand and the First Lady: Portrait of a Friendship; Pauli Murray, Eleanor Roosevelt, and the Struggle for Social Justice*. New York: Alfred A. Knopf, 2016.

Bergner, Daniel. "'White Fragility' Is Everywhere. But Does Antiracism Training Work?" *New York Times Magazine*, July 15, 2020. www.nytimes.com/2020/07 /15/magazine/white-fragility-robin-diangelo.html.

Blackmon, Douglas A. *Slavery by Another Name: The Re-Enslavement of Black Americans from the Civil War to World War II*. London: Icon, 2012.

Blum, Edward J., and Paul Harvey. *The Color of Christ: The Son of God and the Saga of Race in America*. Chapel Hill: University of North Carolina Press, 2012.

"The Bombing of the 16th Street Baptist Church," December 18, 1962, John F. Kennedy Presidential Library and Museum. https://civilrights.jfklibrary.org /media-assets/the-bombing-of-the-16th-street-baptist-church.html#Shock -Waves.

Boyd, Drick. *White Allies in the Struggle for Racial Justice*. Maryknoll, NY: Orbis Books, 2015.

Brown, Cynthia Stokes. *Refusing Racism: White Allies and the Struggle for Civil Rights*. New York: Teachers College Press, 2002.

Brown, Dona. *Back to the Land: The Enduring Dream of Self-Sufficiency in Modern America*. Madison: University of Wisconsin Press, 2011.

Brown, Lonnie. "A Tale of Prosecutorial Indiscretion: Ramsey Clark and the Selective Non-Prosecution of Stokely Carmichael." *Scholarly Works* 62 (October 2010): 1.

"The Brutal Murder of Cynthia Scott: Detroit under Fire: Police Violence, Crime Politics, and the Struggle for Racial Justice in the Civil Rights Era." *HistoryLabs*. https://policing.umhistorylabs.lsa.umich.edu/s/detroitunderfire /page/the-brutal-murder-of-cynthia-scott.

Butler, Anthea. *White Evangelical Racism: The Politics of Morality in America.* Chapel Hill: University of North Carolina Press, 2021.

Carby, Hazel V. "The Multicultural Wars." *Radical History Review* 1992, no. 54 (Fall 1992): 7–18. https://doi.org/10.1215/01636545-1992-54-7.

Carlen, Claudia, ed. *The Papal Encyclicals.* Vol. 3, *1903–1939.* Raleigh, NC: Pierian Press, 1990.

Carnegie, Andrew. *Autobiography of Andrew Carnegie.* Edited by John Charles Van Dyke. Boston: Houghton Mifflin, 1920.

Carter, Dan T. *The Politics of Rage: George Wallace, the Origins of the New Conservatism, and the Transformation of American Politics.* Baton Rouge: Louisiana State University Press, 2000.

Carter, Lawrence Edward, ed. *Walking Integrity: Benjamin Elijah Mays, Mentor to Martin Luther King Jr.* Macon, GA: Mercer University Press, 1998.

Cep, Casey. "Dorothy Day's Radical Faith: The Life and Legacy of the Catholic Writer and Activist, Who Some Hope Will Be Made a Saint." *New Yorker,* April 6, 2020.

Chattopadhyay, Piya. "Feminista Jones Doesn't Think You're an Ally." Out in the Open. Podcast audio. October 26, 2018. https://www.cbc.ca/radio/outintheopen /allies-1.4850186/feminista-jones-doesn-t-think-you-re-an-ally-1.4850215.

Childress, Kyle, and Rodney Wallace Kennedy. *Will Campbell, Preacher Man: Essays in the Spirit of a Divine Provocateur.* Eugene, OR: Wipf and Stock, 2016.

"Civil Rights: The New Racism." *Time,* July 1, 1966. https://content.time.com/time /subscriber/article/0,33009,835847,00.html.

Coble, Ann Louise. *Cotton Patch for the Kingdom: Clarence Jordan's Demonstration Plot at Koinonia Farm.* Scottdale, PA: Herald Press, 2002. http://archive.org /details/cottonpatchforkioo00cobl.

Collum, John M. "From John M. Collum, Americus, GA, July 25, 1913." In *The Booker T. Washington Papers.* Vol. 12, *1912–14,* edited by Louis R. Harlan and Raymond W. Smock. Urbana: University of Illinois Press, 1982.

Copland, Ian. "Christianity as an Arm of Empire: The Ambiguous Case of India under the Company, c. 1813–1858." *Historical Journal* 49, no. 4 (December 2006): 1025–54.

Copeland, Mary Shawn, LaReine-Marie Mosely, and Albert J. Raboteau. *Uncommon Faithfulness: The Black Catholic Experience.* Maryknoll, NY: Orbis Books, 2009.

Cornell, Tom. "The Catholic Worker, Communism and the Communist Party." *American Catholic Studies* 125, no. 1 (March 2014): 87–101.

Cressler, Matthew J. *Authentically Black and Truly Catholic: The Rise of Black Catholicism in the Great Migration.* New York: New York University Press, 2017.

Curvin, Robert. *Inside Newark: Decline, Rebellion, and the Search for Transformation.* New Brunswick, NJ: Rutgers University Press, 2014.

Daniel, Pete. *The Shadow of Slavery: Peonage in the South, 1901–1969.* Urbana: University of Illinois Press, 1972.

Danielson, Leilah. *American Gandhi: A. J. Muste and the History of Radicalism in the Twentieth Century.* Philadelphia: University of Pennsylvania Press, 2014.

Danielson, Leilah, Marian Mollin, and Doug Rossinow, eds. *The Religious Left in Modern America: Doorkeepers of a Radical Faith*. Cham, Switzerland: Palgrave Macmillan.

Darden, Joe T., and Richard W. Thomas. "Historical Causes and Consequences of the 1967 Civil Disorder: White Racism, Black Rebellion, and Changing Race Relations in the Post–Civil Disorder Era." In *Detroit: Race Riots, Racial Conflicts, and Efforts to Bridge the Racial Divide*, 1–28. East Lansing: Michigan State University Press, 2013.

Davis, Cyprian. "The Future of African-American Catholic Studies." *US Catholic Historian* 12, no. 1 (1994): 1–9.

——. *The History of Black Catholics in the United States*. New York: Crossroad, 1990.

Davis, Morris L. *The Methodist Unification: Christianity and the Politics of the Jim Crow Era*. New York: New York University Press, 2008.

Debs, Eugene. "The Negro in the Class Struggle." *International Socialist Review* 4, no. 5 (November 1903).

D'Emilio, John. *Lost Prophet: The Life and Times of Bayard Rustin*. New York: Free Press, 2003.

Deshmukh, Madhuri H. "Claude McKay's Road to Catholicism." *Callaloo* 37, no. 1 (2014): 148–68. www.jstor.org/stable/24264876.

Dillard, Angela D. *Faith in the City: Preaching Radical Social Change in Detroit*. Ann Arbor: University of Michigan Press, 2007.

Dolan, Jay P. *The American Catholic Experience: A History from Colonial Times to the Present*. Notre Dame, IN: University of Notre Dame Press, 1992.

Dorrien, Gary. *The New Abolition: W. E. B. Du Bois and the Black Social Gospel*. New Haven, CT: Yale University Press, 2015.

Downing, Frederick L. *Clarence Jordan: A Radical Pilgrimage in Scorn of the Consequences*. Macon, GA: Mercer University Press, 2017.

"Dr. King Deplores 'Long Cold Winter' on the Rights Front." *New York Times*, June 20, 1967. www.nytimes.com/1967/06/20/archives/dr-king-deplores-long -cold-winter-on-the-rights-front.html.

Duke, David Nelson. *In the Trenches with Jesus and Marx: Harry F. Ward and the Struggle for Social Justice*. Tuscaloosa: University of Alabama Press, 2003.

Editor. "Marissa Johnson Was Right: The Politics of Silence at the Bernie Sanders Rally." *South Seattle Emerald*, August 12, 2015. https://southseattleemerald.org /commentary/2015/08/12/marissa-johnson-was-right-the-politics-of-silence-at -the-bernie-sanders-rally.

Ellison, Ralph. *Invisible Man*. New York: Vintage International, 1995.

Eskew, Glenn T. "'Bombingham': Black Protest in Postwar Birmingham, Alabama." *Historian* 59, no. 2 (Winter 1997): 371–90. www-jstor-org.emu.idm .oclc.org/stable/24449974.

Evans, David F. "Precious Blackness and the Politics of Distraction." *Bearings Online*, August 28, 2014. collegevilleinstitute.org/blog/precious-blackness -politics-distraction.

——. "To Rid the Italian Soul of One Dark Blot: Recognising Race in White Christian Religion." *Journal of Religious History* 39, no. 3 (2015): 370–85. https://doi.org/10.1111/1467-9809.12161.

Farley, Reynolds. "Detroit Fifty Years After the Kerner Report: What Has Changed, What Has Not, and Why?" *RSF: The Russell Sage Foundation Journal of the Social Sciences* 4, no. 6 (September 1, 2018): 206–41. https://doi.org/10.7758/RSF.2018.4.6.10.

Ferguson, David. "Marissa Janae Johnson Doesn't 'Give a F*ck' If Protest at Seattle Bernie Sanders Rally Drives People Away." *Raw Story*, August 11, 2015. www.rawstory.com/2015/08/marissa-janae-johnson-doesnt-give-a-fck-if-protest-at-seattle-bernie-sanders-rally-drives-people-away.

Ferguson, Jeffrey Brown. *The Harlem Renaissance: A Brief History with Documents.* Boston: Bedford/St. Martin's, 2007.

Ferguson, Karen J. "Caught in 'No Man's Land': The Negro Cooperative Demonstration Service and the Ideology of Booker T. Washington, 1900–1918." *Agricultural History* 72, no. 1 (1998): 33–54.

Fitzgerald, F. Scott. *The Great Gatsby.* New York: Scribner, 1925.

Flaherty, Colleen. "Passing in the Classroom." *Inside Higher Ed*, June 14, 2015. www.insidehighered.com/news/2015/06/15/academics-weigh-curious-case-rachel-dolezal.

——. "White Lies." *Inside Higher Ed*, September 3, 2020. www.insidehighered.com/news/2020/09/04/prominent-scholar-outs-herself-white-just-she-faced-exposure-claiming-be-black.

Francis, Leah Gunning. *Ferguson and Faith: Sparking Leadership and Awakening Community.* St. Louis, MO: Chalice Press, 2015.

Garvey, Marcus. "The Image of God." In *The Philosophy and Opinions of Marcus Garvey: Or, Africa for the Africans*, edited by Amy Jacques Garvey. Dover, MA: Majority Press, 1967.

Garza, Alicia, "What Did We Learn?" Interview by W. Kamau Bell and Hari Kondabolu. *Politically Reactive*, podcast, season 2, ep. 27, October 5, 2017, https://podcasts.apple.com/us/podcast/politically-re-active-with-w-kamau-bell-hari-kondabolu/id1125018164?i=1000393102269.

Gilmore, Ruth Wilson. *Abolition Geography: Essays towards Liberation.* London: Verso, 2022.

——. "The Worrying State of the Anti-Prison Movement." *Social Justice*, February 23, 2015. https://socialjusticejournal.org/the-worrying-state-of-the-anti-prison-movement/.

Goudsouzian, Aram. *Down to the Crossroads: Civil Rights, Black Power, and the Meredith March against Fear.* New York: Farrar, Straus and Giroux, 2014.

Gould, Rebecca Kneale. *At Home in Nature: Modern Homesteading and Spiritual Practice in America.* Berkeley: University of California Press, 2005.

Guidry, Michael. "Carolyn Bryant Donham, Whose Accusations Led to the Killing of Emmett Till, Has Died." *All Things Considered*, April 27, 2023. www.npr.org/2023/04/27/1172584418/carolyn-bryant-donham-whose-accusations-lead-to-the-killing-of-emmett-till-has-d.

Gurock, Jeffrey S. *The Jews of Harlem: The Rise, Decline, and Revival of a Jewish Community*. New York: New York University Press, 2019.

Hackman, Rose. "'We Need Co-Conspirators, Not Allies': How White Americans Can Fight Racism." *Guardian*, June 26, 2015. www.theguardian.com/world/2015/jun/26/how-white-americans-can-fight-racism.

Hall, Jacquelyn Dowd. "The Long Civil Rights Movement and the Political Uses of the Past." *Journal of American History* 91, no. 4 (March 2005): 1233–63.

Hall, Tracy K. "The Bells Are Coming! The Bells Are Coming!" *Americus Times-Recorder*, March 2, 2023. www.americustimesrecorder.com/2023/03/02/the-bells-are-coming-the-bells-are-coming.

Harding, Vincent, and John Pierce. "Loving Respect, Clear Disagreement." In *Roots in the Cotton Patch: The Clarence Jordan Symposium 2012*, edited by Kirk Lyman-Barner and Cori Lyman-Barner. Eugene, OR: Cascade Books, 2014.

Harvey, Jennifer. *Raising White Kids: Bringing Up Children in a Racially Unjust America*. Nashville: Abingdon Press, 2017.

Hines, Linda O. "George W. Carver and the Tuskegee Agricultural Experiment Station." *Agricultural History* 53, no. 1 (1979): 71–83.

Holt, Thomas C. *The Movement: The African American Struggle for Civil Rights*. New York: Oxford University Press, 2021.

hooks, Bell. "The Oppositional Gaze: Black Female Spectators." In *Media Studies: A Reader*, 3rd ed., edited by Sue Thornham, Caroline Bassett, and Paul Marris, 462–70. Edinburgh: Edinburgh University Press, 2009.

Hope, Warren C. *From Whence They Came: Origins of the Missionary Baptists in Southwest Georgia, 1865–1900*. Bloomington, IN: AuthorHouse, 2012.

Hull, Isabel V. *A Scrap of Paper: Breaking and Making International Law during the Great War*. Ithaca, NY: Cornell University Press, 2014.

Jackson, Reagan. "Marissa Johnson Was Right: The Politics of Silence at the Bernie Sanders Rally." *South Seattle Emerald*, August 12, 2015. https://southseattleemerald.org/commentary/2015/08/12/marissa-johnson-was-right-the-politics-of-silence-at-the-bernie-sanders-rally.

Johnson, Cedric. *After Black Lives Matter*. London: Verso Books, 2023.

———. *Revolutionaries to Race Leaders: Black Power and the Making of African American Politics*. Minneapolis: University of Minnesota Press, n.d.

Johnson, Herbert A. *Wingless Eagle: U.S. Army Aviation through World War I*. Chapel Hill: University of North Carolina Press, 2003.

Johnson, James Weldon. *Black Manhattan*. New York: A. A. Knopf, 1930. http://archive.org/details/blackmanhattan00john_1.

Johnson, Karen J. "Another Long Civil Rights Movement: How Catholic Interracialists Used the Resources of Their Faith to Tear Down Racial Hierarchies on JSTOR." *American Catholic Studies* 126, no. 4 (Winter 2015): 1–27. www.jstor.org/stable/44195804.

———. *One in Christ: Chicago Catholics and the Quest for Interracial Justice*. New York: Oxford University Press, 2018.

Jones, Allen. "Improving Rural Life for Blacks: The Tuskegee Negro Farmers' Conference, 1892–1915." *Agricultural History* 65, no. 2 (1991): 105–14.

Jones, E. Stanley. *The Christ of the Indian Road.* New York: Abingdon Press, 1925.

Jones, Kevin, and Jarvis J. Williams. *Removing the Stain of Racism from the Southern Baptist Convention: Diverse African American and White Perspectives.* Nashville, TN: B&H, 2017.

Jones, William R. *Is God a White Racist? A Preamble to Black Theology.* Garden City, NY: Anchor Press, 1973.

Jordan, Clarence. "The Distinct Identity." In *The Substance of Faith, and Other Cotton Patch Sermons,* edited by Dallas Lee. New York: Association Press, 1972.

———. *The Substance of Faith, and Other Cotton Patch Sermons.* Edited by Dallas Lee. New York: Association Press, 1972.

Joseph, Peniel E. *Stokely: A Life.* New York: Basic Civitas Books, 2014.

———. *Waiting 'Til the Midnight Hour: A Narrative History of Black Power in America.* New York: Macmillan, 2007.

Kapur, Sudarshan. *Raising Up a Prophet: The African-American Encounter with Gandhi.* Boston: Beacon Press, 1992. www.gbv.de/dms/bowker/toc /9780807009147.pdf.

Kelley, Robin D. G. *Hammer and Hoe: Alabama Communists during the Great Depression.* Chapel Hill: University of North Carolina Press, 2015.

Kidd, Colin. *The Forging of Races: Race and Scripture in the Protestant Atlantic World, 1600–2000.* Cambridge, UK: Cambridge University Press, 2006.

K'Meyer, Tracy Elaine. *Interracialism and Christian Community in the Postwar South: The Story of Koinonia Farm.* Charlottesville: University Press of Virginia, 1997.

Kragen, Pam. "Lamb's Players' *Cotton Patch Gospel* Adds Some Twang and Laughs to the Jesus Story." Review, dir. Deborah Gilmour Smyth, Moonlight Amphitheatre, Vista, CA. *San Diego-Union Tribune,* July 4, 2023. www .sandiegouniontribune.com/2023/07/03/lambs-players-cotton-patch-gospel -adds-some-twang-and-laughs-to-the-jesus-story/.

Kruse, Kevin M. *White Flight: Atlanta and the Making of Modern Conservatism.* Princeton, NJ: Princeton University Press, 2013.

Kumanyika, Chenjerai, Naomi Klein, Astra Taylor, and Keeanga-Yamahtta Taylor. "The Corporate Coup in Global Context: An Emergency Town Hall," February 17, 2025. https://www.youtube.com/watch?v=iyLiNN_NMO4.

Lackner, Joseph H. "The American Catholic Tribune: No Other like It." *US Catholic Historian* 25, no. 3 (Summer 2007): 1–24.

LaFarge, John. *The Catholic Viewpoint on Race Relations.* Garden City, NY: Hanover House, 1960.

———. "What Is Interracial?" *Interracial Review,* March 1933, 54–55. https://guides .lib.cua.edu/c.php?g=1403556&p=10388999.

Landers, Jane. "Black Frontier Settlements in Spanish Colonial Florida." *OAH Magazine of History* 3, no. 2 (1988): 28–29.

———. *Black Society in Spanish Florida.* Urbana: University of Illinois Press, 1999.

Lapeyrolerie, Olivia. "'No Water for Niggers': The Hough Riots and the Historiography of the Civil Rights Movement." *Cleveland Memory,* October 1, 2015. https://engagedscholarship.csuohio.edu/clevmembks/28.

Larson, Claudia, dir. *Dorothy Day: Don't Call Me a Saint*. Edited by Alejandro Valdes-Rochin. Los Angeles: One Lucky Dog Productions, 2007.

Lassiter, Matthew D., and the Policing and Social Justice HistoryLab. *Detroit Under Fire: Police Violence, Crime Politics, and the Struggle for Racial Justice in the Civil Rights Era*. Ann Arbor: University of Michigan Carceral State Project, 2021. https://policing.umhistorylabs.lsa.umich.edu/s/detroitunderfire/page/home.

Lawson, James M., Jr. "From a Lunch Counter Stool." *Motive*, February 1966, 17–18.

Lawson, Steven F. *Running for Freedom: Civil Rights and Black Politics in America since 1941*. Hoboken, NJ: John Wiley & Sons, 2011.

Lee, Dallas. *The Cotton Patch Evidence*. New York: Harper & Row, 1971.

Lehman, Christopher Paul. "Civil Rights in Twilight: The End of the Civil Rights Movement Era in 1973." *Journal of Black Studies* 36, no. 3 (January 2006). www.jstor.org/stable/40035018.

Locke, Hubert G. *The Detroit Riot of 1967*. Detroit, MI: Wayne State University Press, 1969.

Logan, Rayford Whittingham. *The Betrayal of the Negro, from Rutherford B. Hayes to Woodrow Wilson*. New York: Collier Books, 1965.

Loomis, Mildred. "The Life and Work of Ralph Borsodi." *Green Revolution* 34, no. 10 (December 1977): 10–11.

Loughery, John, and Blythe Randolph. *Dorothy Day: Dissenting Voice of the American Century*. New York: Simon & Schuster, 2021.

Luker, Ralph E. *The Social Gospel in Black and White: American Racial Reform, 1885–1912*. Chapel Hill: University of North Carolina Press, 1998.

Lyman-Barner, Kirk, and Cori Lyman-Barner, eds. *Roots in the Cotton Patch: The Clarence Jordan Symposium 2012*. Vol. 1. Eugene, OR: Cascade Books, 2014. http://search.ebscohost.com/login.aspx?direct=true&scope=site&db=nlebk&db=nlabk&AN=834179.

Mair, Ernest E. "The Hypocrisy of White Liberalism." In *Voices of a Black Nation: Political Journalism in the Harlem Renaissance*, edited by Theodore G. Vincent. San Francisco, CA: Ramparts Press, 1973.

Major, Aaron. "Race, Labor and Postbellum Capitalism in Du Bois's 'The Negro Worker in America.'" *Critical Sociology* 49, no. 3 (March 2022): 383–93. https://journals.sagepub.com/doi/10.1177/08969205221135194?icid=int.sj-abstract.similar-articles.8.

Marable, Manning. *How Capitalism Underdeveloped Black America: Problems in Race, Political Economy, and Society*. Boston: South End Press, 1983.

Markoe, John. "John Markoe, 'Letter to Thomas W. Turner,' September 23, 1932." Howard University, September 23, 1932. https://cuomeka.wrlc.org/items/show/397.

Marovich, Robert M. *A City Called Heaven: Chicago and the Birth of Gospel Music*. Urbana: University of Illinois Press, 2015.

Marsh, Charles. *The Beloved Community: How Faith Shapes Social Justice from the Civil Rights Movement to Today*. New York: Basic Books, 2008.

Martin, Charles H. "Communists and Blacks: The ILD and The Angelo Herndon Case." *Journal of Negro History* 64, no. 2 (1979): 131–41. https://doi.org/10.2307/2717204.

——. "Race, Gender, and Southern Justice: The Rosa Lee Ingram Case." *American Journal of Legal History* 29, no. 3 (July 1985): 251–68. https://doi.org/10.2307/844758.

Mathias, Cerith. "Against the Evil of Violence—The Wales Window of Alabama," *The Very Best of Wales Art Review,* vol. 1. March 13, 2015, 43–45. www.pdf-archive.com/2015/03/13/very-best-of-war/very-best-of-war.pdf.

Maurin, Peter. *The Green Revolution: Easy Essays on Catholic Radicalism.* 2nd revised edition. Fresno, CA: Academy Guild Press, 1961.

May, Gary. *The Informant: The FBI, the Klu Klux Klan, and the Murder of Viola Luzzo.* New Haven, CT: Yale University Press, 2005.

McClaren, Brian D. *A New Kind of Christianity: Ten Questions That Are Transforming the Faith.* New York: HarperOne, 2010.

McCoyer, Michael. "Levee Camps." *Mississippi Encyclopedia.* Center for Study of Southern Culture, July 11, 2017. https://mississippiencyclopedia.org/entries/levee-camps/.

McGreevy, John T. *Parish Boundaries: The Catholic Encounter with Race in the Twentieth-Century Urban North.* Chicago: University of Chicago Press, 2016.

McGrory, Mary. "McNamara's New Front in Anti-Poverty War." *Washington Star,* August 23, 1966.

McKinstry, Carolyn. *While the World Watched: A Birmingham Bombing Survivor Comes of Age during the Civil Rights Movement.* Cambridge, UK: Tyndale House, 2011.

McKissick, Floyd B. *Three-Fifths of a Man.* New York: Macmillan, 1969.

——. "Negro Leaders on Meet the Press, August 21, 1966." In *Congressional Record: Proceedings and Debates of the 89th Congress,* 21095–102. Washington, DC: Government Printing Office, 1966.

McMurchy, Myles. "'The Red Cross Is Not All Right!' Herbert Hoover's Concentration Camp Cover-Up in the 1927 Mississippi Flood." *Yale Historical Review* 5, no. 1 (2015): 87–113.

Mills, Quincy T. *Cutting along the Color Line: Black Barbers and Barber Shops in America.* Philadelphia: University of Pennsylvania Press, 2013.

Mizelle, Richard M., Jr. *Backwater Blues: The Mississippi Flood of 1927 in the African American Imagination.* Minneapolis: University of Minnesota Press, 2014.

Mollin, Marian. *Radical Pacifism in Modern American: Egalitarianism and Protest.* Philadelphia: University of Pennsylvania Press, 2006.

Moore, Brenna. *Kindred Spirits: Friendship and Resistance at the Edges of Modern Catholicism.* Chicago: University of Chicago Press, 2021.

Moore, John Hammond. "The Angelo Herndon Case, 1932–1937." *Phylon* 32, no. 1 (1971): 60–71. https://doi.org/10.2307/273598.

Morrison, Toni. *Playing in the Dark: Whiteness and the Literary Imagination.* Cambridge, MA: Harvard University Press, 1992.

Mosely, LaReine-Marie. "Daniel A. Rudd: Civil Rights Leader and Black Catholic Lay Animator." *American Catholic Studies* 122, no. 4 (Winter 2011): 105–12.

Murray, Pauli. *Pauli Murray: The Autobiography of a Black Activist, Feminist, Lawyer, Priest, and Poet.* Knoxville: University of Tennessee Press, 1989.

National Association for the Advancement of Colored People. "The Civil Rights Era—NAACP: A Century in the Fight for Freedom." *Exhibitions—Library of Congress.* Webpage, February 21, 2009. www.loc.gov/exhibits/naacp/the-civil -rights-era.html.

Nickels, Marilyn W. "Thomas Wyatt Turner and the Federated Colored Catholics." *US Catholic Historian* 7, no. 2/3 (1988): 215–32.

O'Brien, William Patrick. *Special History Study: Jimmy Carter National Historic Site and Preservation District, Georgia.* Washington, DC: US Department of the Interior, National Park Service, 1991.

Ochs, Stephen J. *Desegregating the Altar: The Josephites and the Struggle for Black Priests, 1871–1960.* Baton Rouge: Louisiana State University Press, 1993.

Owen, Chandler. "DuBois on Revolution: A Reply." In *Voices of a Black Nation: Political Journalism in the Harlem Renaissance.* San Francisco, CA: Ramparts Press, 1973.

Parker, James. "A Saint for Difficult People." *Atlantic,* March 2017. www.the atlantic.com/magazine/archive/2017/03/a-saint-for-difficult-people/513821/.

Pearcy, Matthew T. "After the Flood: A History of the 1928 Flood Control Act." *Journal of the Illinois State Historical Society (1998-)* 95, no. 2 (2002): 172–201.

Pérez-Peña, Richard. "Woman Linked to 1955 Emmett Till Murder Tells Historian Her Claims Were False." *New York Times,* January 28, 2017. www.nytimes.com /2017/01/27/us/emmett-till-lynching-carolyn-bryant-donham.html.

Perry, Ravi K. *Black Mayors, White Majorities: The Balancing Act of Racial Politics.* Lincoln: University of Nebraska Press, 2013. https://doi.org/10.2307/j.ctt1 ddr82j.

Peters, Benjamin. "Is the Catholic Worker Racist?" *Church Life Journal,* July 17, 2023. https://churchlifejournal.nd.edu/articles/is-the-catholic-worker-racist/.

Pickens, William. Letter to the editor. *Daily Worker,* April 24, 1931.

Pope, Catholic Church, and Claudia Carlen. *The Papal Encyclicals: 1958–1981.* Ann Arbor, MI: Pierian Press, 1990.

Prashad, Vijay. "Black Gandhi." *Social Scientist* 37, no. 1/2 (2009): 3–20.

Quiros, Ansley Lillian. *God with Us: Lived Theology and the Freedom Struggle in Americus, Georgia, 1942–1976.* Chapel Hill: University of North Carolina Press, 2018. https://search.ebscohost.com/login.aspx?direct=true&scope=site&db =nlebk&db=nlabk&AN=1904959.

Raboteau, Albert J. "Relating Race and Religion: Four Historical Models." In *Uncommon Faithfulness: The Black Catholic Experience,* edited by Copeland M. Shawn, LaReine-Marie Mosely, Albert J Raboteau, and Timothy Matovina. Maryknoll, NY: Orbis Books, 2009.

Randolph, Asa Philip. *For Jobs and Freedom: The Selected Speeches and Writings of A. Philip Randolph.* Edited by Andrew E. Kersten and David Lucander. Amherst: University of Massachusetts Press, 2014.

Ransby, Barbara. *Ella Baker and the Black Freedom Movement: A Radical Democratic Vision.* Chapel Hill: University of North Carolina Press, 2003.

Rice, Lincoln R. "The Catholic Worker Movement and Racial Justice: A Precarious Relationship." *Horizons* 46, no. 1 (June 2019): 53–78. https://doi.org/10.1017/hor.2019.9.

——. "Confronting the Heresy of 'The Mythical Body of Christ': The Life of Dr. Arthur Falls." *American Catholic Studies* 123, no. 2 (2012): 59–77.

Richard, Paul. "The Scourge of Christ." *Crisis*, December 1929.

Richey, Russell E., Kenneth E. Rowe, and Jean Miller Schmidt. *The Methodist Experience in America.* Vol. 2, *Sourcebook.* Nashville, TN: Abingdon Press, 2000.

Riis, Jacob August. *The Making of an American.* New York: Grosset & Dunlap, 1901.

Robenalt, James. *Ballots and Bullets: Black Power Politics and Urban Guerrilla Warfare in 1968 Cleveland.* Chicago: Chicago Review Press, 2018.

Roberts, Nancy L. *Dorothy Day and the "Catholic Worker."* New York: State University of New York Press, 1985.

Robinson, Cedric J. *Black Marxism: The Making of the Black Radical Tradition.* 3rd ed. Chapel Hill: University of North Carolina Press, 2020.

Roden, Renée. "Evidence of Dorothy Day's Radical Sainthood Heads to Rome." *AP News*, December 10, 2021. https://apnews.com/article/religion-new-york-sainthood-timothy-dolan-06cb53148fb7644fce4ba8a99dd341e5.

Rosenberg, Rosalind. *Jane Crow: The Life of Pauli Murray.* New York: Oxford University Press, 2017. https://search.ebscohost.com/login.aspx?direct=true&scope=site&db=nlebk&db=nlabk&AN=1472859.

Rossi, Faust. "The First Scottsboro Trials: A Legal Lynching." *Cornell Law Faculty Publications* 29, no. 2 (January 2002): 1–6.

Rustin, Bayard. *Down the Line: The Collected Writings of Bayard Rustin.* Chicago: Quadrangle Books, 1971.

——. *Time on Two Crosses: The Collected Writings of Bayard Rustin.* Edited by Devon W. Carbado and Donald Weise. New York: Cleis Press, 2015.

Ryan, Yvonne. *Roy Wilkins: The Quiet Revolutionary and the NAACP.* Lexington: University Press of Kentucky, 2013.

Salahu-Din, Tulani. "Hidden Herstory: The Leesburg Stockade Girls." National Museum of African American History and Culture. Accessed April 24, 2025. https://nmaahc.si.edu/explore/stories/hidden-herstory-leesburg-stockade-girls.

Sanders, Bernard. *Our Revolution: A Future to Believe In.* London: Profile Books, 2016.

Sanders, Katrina. "The Federated Colored Catholics' Chronicle, 1929–1932: A Monitor and Barometer of American Race Relations." *Journal of the Black Catholic Theological Symposium* 11, no. 1 (December 1, 2018): 61–78. https://ecommons.udayton.edu/jbcts/vol11/iss1/7.

Schwerin, Jules Victor. *Got to Tell It: Mahalia Jackson, Queen of Gospel.* New York: Oxford University Press, 1994.

Seligman, Amanda I. *Block by Block: Neighborhoods and Public Policy on Chicago's West Side.* Chicago: University of Chicago Press, 2005.

———. "Block by Block: Racing Decay on Chicago's West Side, 1948–1968." PhD diss., Northwestern University, 1999. Accessed May 28, 2024. www.proquest .com/pqdtglobal/docview/304514224/abstract/B24DD3A8BE4B488APQ/1.

Sellers, Cleveland. *The River of No Return: The Autobiography of a Black Militant and the Life and Death of SNCC.* Jackson: University Press of Mississippi, 1990.

Senna, Danzy. "Robin DiAngelo and the Problem with Anti-Racist Self-Help: What Two New Books Reveal about the White Progressive Pursuit of Racial Virtue." *Atlantic,* September 2021. https://theatlantic.com/magazine/archive/2021/09 /martin-learning-in-public-diangelo-nice-racism/619497.

Sernett, Milton C. *Bound for the Promised Land: African American Religion and the Great Migration.* Durham, NC: Duke University Press, 1997.

Shapiro, Nina. "Marissa Johnson Part of a New, Disruptive Generation of Activists." *Seattle Times,* August 15, 2015. www.seattletimes.com/seattle -news/marissa-johnson-a-generation-of-activists-who-believe-in-disruption.

Sicius, Francis Joseph. "The Chicago Catholic Worker Movement, 1936 to the Present." PhD diss., Loyola University Chicago, 1979. www.proquest.com /pqdtglobal/docview/302936003/9F07C248147445B8PQ/1?sourcetype =Dissertations%20&%20Theses.

Smith, Lillian. "Are We Still Buying a New World with Old Confederate Bills?" *Georgia Review* 66, no. 3 (2012): 480–87.

———. *Killers of the Dream.* New York: W. W. Norton, 1994.

Snider, P. Joel. *The "Cotton Patch" Gospel: The Proclamation of Clarence Jordan.* Lanham, MD: University Press of America, 1985.

Southern, David W. *John LaFarge and the Limits of Catholic Interracialism, 1911–1963.* Baton Rouge: Louisiana State University Press, 1996.

Spencer, Robyn. "Contested Terrain: The Mississippi Flood of 1927 and the Struggle to Control Black Labor." *Journal of Negro History* 79, no. 2 (Spring 1994): 170–81.

Sullivan, John F. *The Fundamentals of Catholic Belief.* New York: P. J. Kenedy & Sons, 1925.

Tatum, Beverly. "Teaching White Students about Racism: The Search for White Allies and the Restoration of Hope." *Teachers College Record* 95, no. 4 (1994): 462–76.

Templin, Lawrence H. "'An Excellent Piece of Work': Education as Evangelism; The Missionary Careers of Ralph and Lila Templin at Mathura, India, 1925–1940." *Methodist History* 33, no. 4 (July 1995): 226–37.

Tensley, Brandon. "Racism, Bernie Sanders and the Limits of 'Respect.'" CNN, October 29, 2019. www.cnn.com/2019/10/29/politics/bernie-sanders-race -police-respect-2020/index.html.

Thurman, Howard. *Footprints of a Dream: The Story of the Church for the Fellowship of All Peoples.* New York: Harper, 1959.

Trotter, Joe William, Jr. *From a Raw Deal to a New Deal: African Americans 1929–1945.* New York: Oxford University Press, 1996.

Tuck, Stephen G. N. *Beyond Atlanta: The Struggle for Racial Equality in Georgia, 1940–1980.* Athens: University of Georgia Press, 2001.

Turner, Henry McNeal. "God Is a Negro." In *The Speeches of Bishop Henry McNeal Turner: The Press, the Platform, and the Pulpit*, edited by Andre E. Johnson. Jackson: University Press of Mississippi, 2023.

——. *The Speeches of Bishop Henry McNeal Turner: The Press, the Platform, and the Pulpit*. Edited by Andre E. Johnson. Jackson: University Press of Mississippi, 2023.

Turner, Patricia A. *Ceramic Uncles and Celluloid Mammies: Black Images and Their Influence on Culture*. New York: Anchor Books, 1994.

Turner, Thomas W. "President's Annual Address: New York, September 2, 1932." *American Catholic History Classroom*. New York: Catholic University of America. https://guides.lib.cua.edu/ld.php?content_id=76803674.

Tye, Larry. *Rising from the Rails: Pullman Porters and the Making of the Black Middle Class*. New York: Henry Holt, 2005.

Unsworth, Tim. "A Lonely Prophet Falls." *National Catholic Reporter*, March 3, 2000. http://natcath.org/NCR_Online/archives2/2000a/030300/030300k.htm.

Vincent, Theodore G. *Voices of a Black Nation: Political Journalism in the Harlem Renaissance*. San Francisco, CA: Ramparts Press, 1973. http://archive.org /details/voicesofblacknatoooovinc.

Viren, Sarah. "The Native Scholar Who Wasn't." *New York Times Magazine*, May 25, 2021. www.nytimes.com/2021/05/25/magazine/cherokee-native -american-andrea-smith.html.

Ward, Harry Frederick. *The Social Creed of the Churches*. New York: Abingdon Press, 1912.

Washington, Booker T. *The Booker T. Washington Papers*. Vol. 12, *1912–14*. Edited by Louis R. Harlan and Raymond W. Smock. Urbana: University of Illinois Press, 1982.

——. "The Farming Problem in the Black Belt." *Southern Workman*, April 1, 1901, 189.

White, Ann Folino. *Plowed Under: Food Policy Protests and Performance in New Deal America*. Bloomington: Indiana University Press, 2014.

White, Monica M. *Freedom Farmers: Agricultural Resistance and the Black Freedom Movement*. Chapel Hill: University of North Carolina Press, 2018.

Wiley, Dennis W. "God." In *The Cambridge Companion to Black Theology*, edited by Dwight N. Hopkins and Edward P. Antonio. Cambridge, UK: Cambridge University Press, 2012.

Williams, Rachel Marie-Crane. *Run Home If You Don't Want to Be Killed: The Detroit Uprising of 1943*. Chapel Hill: University of North Carolina Press, in association with the Center for Documentary Studies at Duke University, 2021.

Williams, Shannen Dee. *Subversive Habits: Black Catholic Nuns in the Long African American Freedom Struggle*. Durham, NC: Duke University Press, 2022.

Willis, Vincent D. *Audacious Agitation: The Uncompromising Commitment of Black Youth to Equal Education after Brown*. Athens: University of Georgia Press, 2021.

Wood, John W. "Wally and Juanita Nelson and the Struggle for Peace, Racial Equality and Social Justice: 1935–1975." PhD diss., Morgan State University, 2008.

Woods, Jeff R. *Black Struggle, Red Scare: Segregation and Anti-Communism in the South, 1948–1968*. Baton Rouge: Louisiana State University Press, 2003.

X, Malcolm. *The Autobiography of Malcolm X*. New York: Random House, 2015.

Zumoff, J. A. "The American Communist Party and the 'Negro Question' from the Founding of the Party to the Fourth Congress of the Communist International." *Journal for the Study of Radicalism* 6, no. 2 (2012): 53–89.

Index

abolitionism, 34, 17, 20; New Abolition, 192–93
Abyssinian Baptist Church, 75–76, 220
Addams, Jane, 54; Hull House, 51, 112
agronomics, 21, 26, 73; agronomic universities, 48
Allen Chapel, 132
American Catholic Tribune, 91–92
American Federation of Labor (AFL), 68, 76, 79
Americus movement, 33, 131–36, 170, 288
Angry, Sue, 135–36, 141
anti-capitalism, 10
Antioch College, 201–4
Army Corps of Engineers, 63

back-to-the-land movement, 30, 39, 47, 49–51, 56
Baker, Ella, 24–25, 29, 32, 42, 44
Baldwin, James, 23, 28, 151, 168, 206, 207
Barber, William, 16
beloved community, 11–12
Bethesda Baptist, 132
Birmingham, AL, 5, 33, 81, 162–65, 169, 172, 203, 211, 214
Black churches: in Americus, 121–22; Black Catholicism, 21, 88–89; Catholic Worker teaching, 98–99, 103, 106–8; charity, 10, 24, 29, 31, 47–49; charity model of ministry, 89–90; and resistance to racism, 90–93
Black freedom, 12, 19, 21–22, 25, 37–40, 42–47, 84, 104, 199–221, 128, 131, 133, 136, 156–59, 172, 177–82, 215; from capitalism, 73, 79; from church and

state, 52, 59; hindrances to, 198; Roosevelt's four freedoms, 155–56; vs. white freedom, 207–11; in Yellow Springs, 202–5
Black Lives Matter movement, 235–37, 239
Black nationalism, 6, 9, 44, 144–45, 156, 220
Black Power, 4–8, 18, 24–25, 34, 159, 170–71, 206–12, 216–36; white advocates for, 219
Black press, 64–70
Black radicalism, 29, 64, 65, 69, 85; newspapers, 29, 64
Borsodi, Ralph, 49–53, 187–89, 194, 196–97, 233
Bridges, William, 70
Brotherhood of Sleeping Car Porters (BSCP), 29, 32, 37, 42, 50
Browne, Conrad, 135
Brown v. Board of Education, 25, 37; integration efforts, 129, 131, 156, 162–64, 204; resistance to, 43–45, 148, 200
bus protests, 175, 178
Byrd, Harry Flood, 45

Campbell, Gene, 66
Campbell, Joseph R., 132
Campbell, Will, 54
Campbell Chapel AME, 122
capitalism, 15, 26, 30, 32, 34; anti-Black, 64–65, 79–80, 84–86, 127–28, 218, 222, 225–27; 238; and Christianity, 72–73, 104–105, 111; a condition for war, 189, 192; resistance to, 47–48, 52, 59. *See also* Ward, Harry F.